# Here's what people are saying about
# DREAM OF THE WATER CHILDREN…

"Like a swimmer who has made it through the break, Fredrick Cloyd looks back at the far shore of his war-touched past with fresh eyes. Eloquent, passionate and continually surprising, his meditation on history and the individual provokes and tantalizes the reader through a shared process of remembering. This is an ocean of a book."

—Walter Hamilton
Author of *Children of the Occupation: Japan's Untold Story* (2013)

"About simultaneously remembering and forgetting, Frederick D. Kakinami Cloyd's *Dream of the Water Children* wrestles with his "occupied" subjectivity as a post-WWII Afro-Asian 'Amerasian' child of a Japanese national mother and an African American father who met while his father was stationed in Japan in the 1950s. Weaving together ghostly dream-scapes and poetic fragments that chart 'collective memory in story,' Cloyd reflects on childhood narratives of growing up in Japan with his single mother. It is through these recollections that Cloyd reveals the stark realities of prejudice his brown body engenders in his present-day home of San Francisco, raising larger questions about the geopolitical forces that produced his very existence."

—Laura Kina
Artist and Associate Professor at DePaul University
co-author of *War Baby/Love Child: Mixed-race Asian American Art* (2013)

"At the nexus between memoir and social history, Fredrick D. Kakinami Cloyd's work crosses boundaries of race, nation, discipline, and genre to give us a glimpse into little known territory—the Black Pacific collective memory. *Dream of the Water Children* is a meditation on the condition of a Black Japanese diaspora born of war and u.s. imperialism as much as it is a personal story of love, loss and spiritual redemption. Written in multiple voices, Cloyd lets his ghosts speak. This book is a beautiful tribute to his mother and sister, and to all the water children that have been swept under the rug of history."

—Grace M. Cho
Author of *Haunting the Korean Diaspora:*
*Shame, Secrecy and the Forgotten War* (2008)

"Can be read as a ghost story, a meditation on how to disassemble the heartbreak machines; a catalog of copious tears and small comforts. *Dream of the Water Children* is a challenging example of personal bravery and filial love. It puts the 'more' in memory."

—Leonard Rifas, Ph.D
Communications, University of Washington

"Fredrick Cloyd reaches deep into violent pasts, encounters and experiences, and digs up memories of the American Occupation of Japan, even when doing so hurts. These memories have shaping power beyond the era of Occupation; they are intergenerational and transnational. *Dream of the Water Children* is an enactment of such irresolution — multilayered, jarring, shattering, and often elegiac. Its narrative lets loose an aesthetic authority punctuated by vivid remembrances and dream-like sequences, dialogues with himself and with his Japanese mother that appear at once near and far. The narrator is a mixed-race Black Japanese, an Amerasian fathered by an African American serviceman and raised in Japan and the United States. One would not find solace where it is expected. A chronicler of his own and mother's life and times, Cloyd sets in motion the pulsating pursuit of "unbelonging"; to take this Afro-Amerasian journey demands the refusal of normative thinking and historicity. The reader must be prepared to unlearn."

— Yuichiro Onishi, Ph.D
Professor of Asian-American Studies and
African American Studies at University of Minnesota

"In *Dream of the Water Children,* Fredrick Kakinami Cloyd delineates the ways imperialism and war are experienced across and between generations and leave lasting and often excruciating legacies in the mind, body, and relationships. The book is particularly good in detailing these costs as experienced by women and children, most vividly in cataloguing the life and emotions of Cloyd's mother, and of Cloyd himself as a child and young man. In incident after incident of military violence, sexual violence, social ostracism, intrafamilial cruelty, self-harm, and bullying, Cloyd shows how the social conditions created by war reverberate in our most intimate relationships. At the same time, Cloyd and his mother are never just victims: Cloyd's spirited mother in particular defies stereotypes of Asian women and war brides as passive and silent. Throughout, Cloyd also traces moments of friendship and communal support among women and children of other mixed-race military families, as they navigated the conditions of multiple societies and cultural norms. *Dream of the Water Children* is not an easy read, as Cloyd illuminates not only the devastating effects of war between nations but also the pain of internal violence perpetrated within communities, societies, racial groups, and families. However, the persistent reader will be rewarded with a multifaceted, thought-provoking, and deeply introspective exploration of how large-scale historical forces shape our conditions of being and inevitably make us who we are."

— Wendy Cheng
Associate Professor of American Studies, Scripps College

"'This is a mature book that moves fluidly, as the mind moves, untroubled by traditional distinctions between writing considered to be academic vs. creative, memoir vs. personal essay, sure-footed in unexpected ways. This genre-bending book is not 'experimental writing.' The author knows what he wants to say and he knows how he wants to say it, seeking, in his own words, "restoration and reclamation" for silenced voices and histories never erased because they have not yet been written. *Dream of the Water Children* demands that its reader rigorously consider the constructed nature of memory, identities, and historical narrative. And it is also an enormously kind and passionate chronicle of a son's long journey with his mother. To read it is to marvel, to learn, and to discover anew what surrealist poet Paul Éluard said: 'There is another world, but it is in this one.'"

—Patricia Mushim Ikeda, Buddhist teacher/activist

"Fredrick Douglas Kakinami Cloyd has written a profoundly moving and thought-provoking book. He courageously challenges our neat categories of identity, going beyond broadening our understanding of mixed-race to touch what is human in all of us. This book will shift readers" perceptions and assumptions and may change many lives. Above all, Cloyd is a master story-teller who honors and respects memory."

— Roxanne Dunbar-Ortiz, Indigenous Rights activist, historian and writer

# Dream of the Water Children

# Dream of the Water Children

Memory and Mourning in the Black Pacific

水子の夢
太平洋の陰影に見る記憶と悲嘆

by Fredrick D. Kakinami Cloyd

Edited by Karen Chau

Introduction by Gerald Horne
Foreword by Velina Hasu Houston

2LEAF PRESS

FLORIDA ■ NEW YORK
www.2leafpress.org

2LEAF PRESS INC.
New York Offices
P.O. Box 4378
Grand Central Station
New York, New York 10163-4378
editor@2leafpress.org

2LEAF PRESS INC. is a
nonprofit 501(c)(3) organization that promotes
multicultural literature and literacy.
Stephanie Ann Agosto, Executive Director
www.2lpinc.org

FOR MORE INFORMATION
VISIT FREDRICK D. KAKINAMI CLOYD'S WEBSITES
https://dreamwaterchildren.net/
https://www.dreamwaterchild.com/

*Editor:* Karen Chau
*Book cover:* Kenji C. Liu
*Book design and layout:* Gabrielle David

Special thanks to Carolina Fung Feng and
Cathy J. Schlund-Vials for additional copy editing.

Library of Congress Control Number: 2014930046

ISBN-13: 978-1-940939-28-5 (Paperback)
ISBN-13: 978-1-940939-29-2 (eBook)

10   9   8   7   6   5   4   3   2   1

Published in the United States of America

First Edition | First Printing

2Leaf Press trade distribution is handled by University of Chicago Press / Chicago Distribution Center (www.press.uchicago.edu) 773.702.7010. Titles are also available for corporate, premium, and special sales. Please direct inquiries to the UCP Sales Department, 773.702.7248.

I dedicate this book to persons and communities whose histories remain invisible,
in the Pacific Rim and beyond, where multiple oppressions continue to fuel liberatory practices for all.

This book is especially dedicated to my mother, Kiyoko Kakinami Cloyd.

# Contents

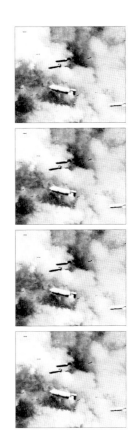

# Acknowledgements

THIS PROJECT TOOK OVER two decades to accomplish, with starts, stops, do-overs, makeovers, re-thinking, study, and reflections. Through all this time, and after countless ups and downs, many people have helped sustain me as person, thinker, student, teacher, and writer. I will try to do justice and remember as many people as possible who helped with the formation of this book. I deeply thank:

Gabrielle David at 2Leaf Press, for being a force for writers-of-color in the United States and to dedicate herself to publishing my book, and doing it with attention, care, and tough-minded tenacity.

Karen Chau at 2Leaf Press, for painstakingly and mindfully editing my book.

Velina Hasu Houston, for her generosity and support in writing the forward for my book.

Gerald Horne, for taking the time to write the wonderful introduction and even before this, creating the first question in my mind about a Black Pacific.

Kenji Chienshu Liu, for creating the fantastic cover for my book. As a guest editor of *Kartika Review,* he worked with me to write and publish my poem dedicated to my mother, which is also in this book. He also invited me to readings and gave me invaluable assistance in finding contacts as well as.

Although I had already begun putting together my journal notes from when I was a teenager, both a collection of notes from everyday life as well as dream journals, I didn't take my writings and thinking seriously until I met Rick Leonard and Karen Maeda Allman in Seattle. Because of them, I began to form a book out of all of my memories. Thank you Rick and Karen.

The late Dan Soloff, one of my teachers at Antioch University Seattle, who became a trusted colleague and friend, and pushed me to go to graduate school to further my thinking and writings. I want to thank Therese Saliba of Evergreen College, my academic coach at Antioch University Seattle, who pushed me to read more multicultural activist writers and who, along with Dan, urged me to go to graduate school.

Leonard Rifas, Alejandro Urruzmendi, and Richard Clark for their support, valuable comments, advice, and editing of my first final draft. Richard has also been my go-to person for video projects linked to my book.

Leon Sun and Peter Yamamoto, from Japantown Arts in San Francisco, for great discussions, support, and ideas regarding my projects.

My friend Ryan Whitney who painstakingly went through every nook and cranny of my first and second drafts of this book and offered much-needed emotional and living support, friendship, and encouragement during this whole process.

Julie Thi Underhill and Robert Ricardo Reese have been phenomenal allies in working on different aspects of the Black Pacific, which have informed my later edits on this book.

Duncan Ryuken Williams, first at University of California Berkeley, then at University of Southern California, for his generosity and support in marketing my work and inviting me to cultural academic events related to the Asia-Pacific, Japan, and mixed-race histories; and for contributing to my knowledge.

Lily Anne Welty for generously sharing her knowledge, important contacts, and wonderful encouragement toward my project.

Vicky Murakami-Tsuda at Japanese American National Museum and Discover Nikkei Online Journal for publishing excerpts of my book.

Rosalyn Tonai and Betty Kano at the National Japanese American Historical Society for their generous time and energy in publishing articles related to the earlier versions of my book and for inviting me to read my poetry at their grand opening event, Generation Nexus: Peace in the Postwar Era, for the National Japanese American Learning Center.

Akane Nobusa at Japan Pacific Resource Network in Oakland, California for her support, encouragement and providing opportunities for me to work with Japanese college students traveling to the United States, to learn of the Japanese Amerasian histories and to question identity.

The wonderful kick-ass thinker-writer-activist folks at As(I)Am for continued spaces for interrogating and challenging the boundaries of Asian-Americanness, race, class/caste, gender, sexualities, and nationalisms.

KB Tuffy and Celeste Chan at Queer Rebels who have continued to provide a forum for readings of my work at the annual Queer Rebels shows and festivals.

Shirley Gindler-Price for being an ally from an Afro-German perspective, and her openness in sharing links between Amerasians and Afro-Asian identities with Afro-German postwar identities and issues, and her generosity in sharing information and images for my book.

Black Okinawan colleagues Eriko Ikehara and Mitzi Uehara Carter for intellectual and cultural inspiration along the lines of Japaneseness, blackness, and third-space identities, and for creating a much needed, heartful Blasian connectedness.

Erica Padilla-Morales, for connecting me to local San Francisco area Black Japanese and Black Okinawan thinkers.

Sabrena Taylor and Ramon Calhoun for being invaluable allies, as Black Japanese writer/artists, who have helped with critically reading my manuscript and offering suggestions.

Writer/photographer Heidi Restrepo Rhodes for her keen and warm support of my work and helpful comments and suggestions on my work, as well as support in creating marketing and publishing ideas.

Stephen Shigematsu Murphy at Stanford University, who has provided invaluable support and who has been one of the original activist-scholars who have opened doors for thinking about Japanese/American mixed-race identity.

Linda Austin, for being a solid ally and generous with her information and labor and in providing contacts and encouragement for my projects.

Edward Sumoto, a representative of the Mixed Roots Japan group, who created the subtitle for this book in Japanese, after my own struggles at translating the concept of the Black Pacific into legible Japanese concepts. I also thank him for being a great ally for my work.

Mushim Ikeda Nash, for her generous and incredible time, support and assistance with my first final draft, both as a Buddhist nun and teacher-activist.

Walter Hamilton, Grace Cho, Eric Robinson, Laura Kina, Roxanne Ortiz, Yuichiro Onishi, and Wendy Cheng for their encouragement and wonderful commentaries of my original manuscript.

Bernard Scott Lucious for his article about Afro-Vietnamese Amerasians which, for me, was an invaluable impetus for writing and thinking a Pan-Amerasian, Black Pacific conceptual framework.

I would like to offer a special thank you to Angana Chatterji and Richard Shapiro, who worked as hard as they could to train an aging student like myself, in thinking differently and broadening my intellectual with great care, with an eye towards transformative social change.

The late Philip Kapleau, my first Zen teacher, who returned my life to me in no small fashion with rigorous care, beyond imagination.

Pei Hsuan-Wu and Amanda McBride, who have stuck with me through thick and thin, up and down, so that I may continue to live with friendship and finish my book. 目

# The Making of an Anti-Memoir

Velina Hasu Houston

FREDRICK D. KAKINAMI CLOYD'S *Dream of the Water Children* is a global nonfiction peregrination of multi-ethnic, multinational lives that span continents, eras, and generations. In the author's musings and reflections, time, as the reader may think of it and construct it, is undone. The reader is encouraged to follow the author's instinctual callings to events and stories that shaped and shape the actuality of his uncompartmentalized being in a world that thrives on being able to categorize everything. Kakinami Cloyd is an absolute example that multiethnicity cannot be pigeonholed, which has been an irritation, or sometimes even a curse, for those who think of themselves as belonging to a pure mono-race. This book cannot even be classified. I try, unsuccessfully in my view, to call it global nonfiction, but it is not nonfiction in the way that most readers and critics consider nonfiction. What is it most like? Nothing. But the reader may decide that it is memoir, as in a straightforward account of a person's life. Kakinami Cloyd calls the book an anti-memoir. This may be the most suitable description of his creation. It does not chronicle a life, but rather presents us with fragments, ideologies, pictures, dreams, and unsortable memories that cannot be placed into recognizable equations to be solved. Life is not that black and white. It never is. Even when one thinks it is. Especially when one thinks it is.

Kakinami Cloyd knows that and so do I. I live a multiethnic life that includes the blood of Africa; my ethnicity, as I understand it, includes Japanese, African, Cuban, and Native American Indian. My DNA also revealed France, Armenia, India, the Philippines, China, North America, Central America, the Caribbean, and South America. As a literary artist, I have trekked the circuitous pathways from which these racial and cultural amalgamations spring from, in the form of written plays, essays, poetry, and opera. I grew up in a small Kansas town where people liked to believe that everything was black and white, so as I navigate Kakinami Cloyd's anti-memoir, I identify with a great deal of his challenges. In this anti-memoir, I also recognize the courage of being a global and multiethnic human being in a world that speaks of the global village, but which is in practice, as microscopic as a nanoparticle. Humanity may aspire to a global village, but the reality is that human beings live in tribes, and multiethnic citizens do not fit into any of those tribes, despite the perpetual attempts to shoehorn them in. That lack of fit is not painful but, rather, freeing and enlightening. The multiethnic citizen sees the lines and everything between them. He or she must be aware, beyond a surface level, not in order to be intellectually astute, but in order to stay alive, truly alive.

Kakinami Cloyd's life is not a programmed one. Many lives are not conditioned, by nature, but become so through sociopolitical forces. We are told what a good and right life is, and we are told what constitutes a bad life. Formulae are created and passed on with fervor. This is, in fact, as Kakinami Cloyd points out, the way that Japan became a democratized nation with deeper Western ties than any other Asian nation. The U.S.' social engineering of Japan during its occupation purposefully set out to shape new values for the defeated nation, including the notion of the nuclear family and U.S. concepts of race and racism. These Western values were placed upon the Japanese consciousness like an ill-fitting shirt. The Japanese, psychologically debilitated—and, yes, angered—by defeat, let it be put on them, perhaps thinking that one day they would take it off. But inside the shirt, the Japanese nation transformed so that, if there was a moment when they wanted to remove it, they no longer could.

"I was then too young to realize how the Japanese price-guessing show was one of the ways in which intense American consumer culture began to take shape in the post-World War period." In Japan, before coming to the U.S., the author watched *Zubari Atemashou*, a television show in which people guess the prices of household appliances being made in Japan, courtesy of U.S. influence. Kakinami Cloyd's insight about how the West invaded Japan with commercial goods and services, replacing ancient ways of industrial operation with Western methodology, is a history lesson one will not learn in school. This book allows the reader to view how the author's own life paralleled this sociopolitical intercourse with the intentional advancements of Western ideology. A big part of him held on to his own sociocultural roots and refused, in the most organic manner, to give way. The author aptly notes that: "Complex intersections of democracy and domination are what forge nations." He speaks to the rebuilding of Japan after the end of World War II as the U.S. set to conquer Japan in newer, more insidious ways with movies, documentaries, songs, and shows created in a Western framework, filling the Japanese consciousness.

Coming in second was not new to Japan.

> "Colonialism and the racist ideology that accompanied it, were too entrenched in Western countries to allow an "upstart" non-white nation [Japan] to enter the race for natural resources and markets as an equal. Many of the misunderstandings between the West and Japan stemmed from Japan's sense of alienation from the West, which seemed to use a different standard in dealing with European nations than it did with a rising Asian power like Japan." [1]

And so, history repeats itself (again). During the occupation of Japan, the U.S. engineered cities and roads, and changed the way that government and business operated; however, it could not re-engineer the core of Japanese be-

---

1    "The Meiji Restoration and Modernization," Asia for Educators, Columbia University, Downloaded January 4, 2014, at http://afe.easia.columbia.edu/special/japan_1750_meiji.htm, © 2009 Asia for Educators, Columbia University | http://afe.easia.columbia.edu.

ing. Despite westernization—which is strong in Japan—the core of the Japanese being remains intrinsically different than that of the U.S. The U.S. may have taken Japan out of the gutter of defeat at the end of World War II and transformed the nation into a democratized ally, but the imprint of the seven virtues of Bushido consciousness—rectitude, courage, benevolence, respect, honesty, honor, and loyalty—remain. My mother tirelessly evoked these notions in my upbringing, including the notion of living in the present moment, a reflection contained in my play *Asa Ga Kimashita (Morning Has Broken)* and that also emanates from Bushido philosophy: the character of Fusae (drawn from my maternal grandmother) says to her daughter Haruko, "There is never anything but the present moment, the one we can grasp in our fists and feel." During the U.S. occupation, the dual impact of the loss of land and residence, coupled with the devastation of defeat in war and the supremacy of U.S. occupational edicts, humbled the Japanese. In the play, Kiheida, a character drawn from my maternal grandfather, reveals this sense of dispiritedness:

> "What a nightmare I had: fire bombs everywhere again…my wife falling like she did last year, during the air raids… Setsuko cringing by the river, waiting for death. Sometimes I never want to sleep. Sometimes I never want to wake up. You look like you have not slept at all."

—The character of Kiheida Shimada in
*Asa Ga Kimashita (Morning Has Broken)*

The character's disheartened nature is amplified by other Western intrusions including his youngest daughter and niece's interest in U.S. American men. These relationships re-engineered Japan as much as the social engineering strategies of the occupational machine.

Kakinami Cloyd is Japanese and American. His American ethnicity is fascinatingly complicated with Native American Indian and African American heritage. His Japaneseness is equally complicated with Chinese and Austro-Hungarian bloodlines. He has been called "Jap" by U.S. Americans, and "nigger" by both Japanese and U.S. Americans. As Kakinami Cloyd notes in the book, "Without ever knowing us, people speak and hear us through their programming." The prejudged idea of what it must mean to be of Asian and African American derivation is the myth of the beholder. As are many people who are raised to live rather than to merely exist, the author is inextricably tied to his mother's womb in a figurative sense as she defines cultural identity and markers: spiritualism, customs, cuisine, sociocultural views, and all the rest. Recalling the fortitude of maternal gifts is a return, seeking reaffirmation and re-remembrance before the body must navigate and tussle with the Real World.

Some may confront the author's interesting background and see confusion, tragedy, and ludicrousness. But that is because such people believe in the notion of racial purity. *There is no racial purity. There is no race.* Race is a construct of Western modernity made to categorize and classify people in the belief that such sorting will bring greater understanding, but, of course, as with most matters, it is in point of fact about power and control. Understanding humanity has never been easy; it cannot and does not depend on whether something is A or B. If there ever was an ethnic purity, it dissolved tens of thousands of years ago as DNA migrated across multiple terrains and mutated to fit the needs of new environments. If anything, Kakinami Cloyd is a return to the beginnings of humanity, to the finely blended DNA of old, and not inbred by marrying repeatedly into the same "race." When I first saw Kakinami Cloyd, I thought of how admirably out of the ordinary he must be because of his multiple ethnicities. He is organically connected to a global experience that most Americans avoid as "foreign/alien/Other." I feel privileged to have read this book and contemplated his journey. His background makes me wondrously reflect upon my own. I am overwhelmed at these rich veins of organic knowing that merge in the being of this author.

And it is not just this multiethnic perspective, but also his understanding of the United States. Life on the east coast, west coast, and Chicago are their own realities, but the U.S. also includes the Midwest, South, Northwest, and Southwest. Until one has experienced at least some of those facets of life in the United States, one cannot truly have a grasp of what "America" is. Like Kakinami Cloyd, I have seen a great deal of this country and a small town in Kansas is not Cleveland, is not New York is not North Carolina is not Texas, and so on. Even within each state, rural areas and small towns and cities differ culturally in a multitude of ways. Perhaps if we begin to understand these multiplicities we too easily call "America," as if they were uniform, we can understand the beautiful complexity of an individual such as Kakinami Cloyd.

The history of how multiethnic Japanese and African-descent children were treated during the U.S. occupation is also absent in formal education. Our understanding of that history comes through people like Kakinami Cloyd and other authors such as Dr. Christine Iijima Hall, Dr. Michael Thornton, Dr. Teresa Williams-Léon, Dr. Curtiss Takada Rooks, Dr. H. Rika Houston, and attorney Philip Tajitsu Nash. There is something sad and inhuman about the postwar savagery of both Japan and the U.S. against such children; neither nation wanted to claim the children as their own. These children were niggers, water children, love children—any unkind and marginalizing term that could be conjured up by U.S. Americans and Japanese to pigeonhole them as "other." Moreover, many African Americans wanted nothing to do with these multiethnic children; they were too Japanese, not as relatable as partial whiteness. It is a shameful history for both nations, but it is a history still in the making. Today, the loathing continues, sometimes veiled and therefore harder to identify, but palpable nonetheless. It comes from those who perceive themselves as being Japanese, Asian, Asian American, African American, Latino, Hawai'ian with more white blood than not, Native American Indian with more white blood than not, Caucasian, and even from multiethnic individuals who believe they have no African ancestry.

Kakinami Cloyd tells a story about being in a PX (the U.S. military base equivalent to a department store) with his mother in 1962. Three white women called her a "nigger bitch," marginalizing and disassociating from her because they saw her son and categorized him, despite his multiethnic phenotype. They were taught to only see black and white; what was not white was black. This was the mindset of early U.S. history too when Benjamin Franklin disparagingly called Germans, Eastern Europeans, and Jews "black," desiring to separate what was white (Anglo) from what was not. The PX memory reminded me of being at a JCPenney in Junction City, Kansas, with my mom. A white man flirted with her until he saw my five-year-old self and her gripping my hand and saying, "This is my daughter." The man was astonished, and astonishment quickly drifted into shock. "But why? Not you. You didn't have to do that!" he exclaimed. I understood and understand that he only had two crayons in his war chest: a white one and a black one. Like many others, he could only see difference as foreign/alien/Other.

When I was living in Kyōto, I visited Takashima-ya, a popular department store. A Japanese man was exiting an elevator and looked at me, startled to see my cinnamon-colored skin. He expressed shock in Japanese, too myopically narrow-minded to consider that I might understand him. When I was shopping in the kimono section of the same store, two Japanese saleswomen whispered about the color of my skin, again too myopic to consider that I might comprehend. I've had a white maître d' in Los Angeles seat me by the kitchen. I have had African Americans call me names because they saw me as Latina, and Latinos call me names because they saw me as black. A Japanese female clerk in the Shiseido store in Little Tōkyō, Los Angeles, looked dismayed when I entered and nodded to her store clerk to tail me. In a boutique in Santa Monica, California, a white female clerk did the same thing, but with less subtlety. In Trader Joe's in West Los Angeles, a white female clerk asked me to step out of the "cash only" line because, for some reason, one glance at me made her decide that I could not possibly have cash (I was the only person of color in line and the only one not wearing jeans and a T-shirt). The day that the death of O.J. Simpson's wife was announced on the news, I was getting physical therapy at a West Los Angeles site. Behind a curtain, my ethnicity was not apparent to the two white men watching the news in the room's center. When the news broke, one responded with, "Dear God, I hope it's the black one," (O.J. Simpson's first wife was African American) and the other replied, "Me, too." I opened the curtains and exchanged a long gaze with them. These are the adventures of not looking white in U.S. or Japanese society. Perhaps in any society. But I believe there is still hope and goodness. I have many friends in Japan who embrace me as a multiethnic Nikkei; I have many friends in the U.S., Asia, and Europe who embrace me for being me. I understand from Kakinami Cloyd's writing and from conversations with him that he, too, has experienced this hope. And so we take a step forward. In so doing, we move beyond caring about what is acceptable to people with nanoparticle minds.

Kakinami Cloyd writes of a slogan developed in Japan to help the military and the society to endure hardships during the war: "Let us contribute with our labor." The slogan, Kakinami Cloyd notes, "applies to working hard to contribute to something bigger." This book is also a contribution to something bigger—something about the dignity of the human spirit that may be fully recognized and respected in the future. Perhaps, again, hope is required. Kakinami Cloyd contributes this labor of love in the midst of constant demands from a self-proclaimed monoracial society that insists he choose a known and recognizable category and, gosh darn it, stay put. A casting director at the Mark Taper Forum theatre in Los Angeles once told me with regard to a multiethnic character in one of my plays, "Velina, there are not people like this. Where do you expect me to find people like this?"

In the mirror? I see them all the time, even when they cannot see themselves.

Kakinami Cloyd sees himself—and, it seems, every reader as well. I celebrate his multiethnicity and multinational view of the world, and especially his attentive humanity. How refreshing. How needed.

*Please listen.* ⍤

Velina Hasu Houston is an American playwright, essayist, poet, author, editor, and screenwriter. Dr. Houston is Professor of Theatre, Resident Playwright at the University of Southern California School of Dramatic Arts. She serves as Director of the Master of Fine Arts in Dramatic Writing, and Associate Dean of Faculty Recognition & Development. She holds a PhD from USC's School of Cinematic Arts, and an MFA from the University of California at Los Angeles' School of Theater, Film, and Television.

# A Personal Exploration of a Transnational Migration

Gerald Horne

THIS IS A BOOK THAT SIMPLY MUST BE READ. It sheds light on the pressing global question of this century: how the U.S. will adapt to the rise of Asia, given this North American nation's origin as a white supremacist redoubt. It also sheds light on the pressing domestic question of past centuries and today: How will this North American nation adapt to the legacy of slavery and Jim Crow and how this might warp or compromise the pressing global question of adapting to Asia's—and China's and India's—rise? That is, will the restiveness induced by the rise of Asia—a so-called "non-white" continent, so unnerve the rulers of the U.S. that it will make them less prone to adapt in a meaningful way to the just demands and aspirations of the so-called "non-white" population on these shores, African Americans not least?

In a recent book of mine,[1] I pointed out that in November 1942 African Americans in East St. Louis, Illinois, fed up with racism, were engaged in military drills in uniform awaiting a Japanese military invasion of the U.S. that they planned to join on the side of Tōkyō's forces. This was a direct outgrowth of the fact that a quarter of a century earlier, there had been a bloody pogrom ignited against the population of African ancestry in this town, leading to mass executions, immolations and random lynchings. And this group of African Americans decided that the better part of wisdom was to take up arms in order to prevent and forestall more bloodletting.

These events in 1942 were a byproduct of the reality that in the prelude to the bombing of Pearl Harbor in December 1941, Japan had cultivated assiduously what had been called the U.S. Negro population. Booker T. Washington, Marcus Garvey and W. E. B. Du Bois had contradictions between and among themselves but all were united in their pro-Tōkyō sympathies, not least because the very existence of Japan tended to invalidate the essential predicate

---

1    Gerald Horne, *Facing the Rising Sun: African Americans, Japan and the Rise of Afro-Asian Solidarity,* New York: New York University Press, 2018.

of white supremacy, i.e. only those of "pure European descent"—to use the now musty British term—could build an advanced society.

Japanese who migrated to the U.S. were more prone to avoid Jim Crow praxis in the restaurants and boarding-houses they controlled, while Tōkyō's ships were more prone to avoid Jim Crow praxis on the vessels headed across the Pacific. There were protests against lynchings of African Americans in Japan, while an earthquake that leveled Tōkyō in 1923 led to an outpouring of grief—and donations to victims—on the part of African Americans. The music we now know as "jazz" found an early and mass audience in Japan, a trend that continues to this very day in what has become one of the more sturdy expressions of solidarity between and among Japanese and African Americans.

In the prelude to December 1941 there had been a proliferation of pro-Tōkyō organizations among African Americans that encompassed those who were involved in military drills by November 1942, including the Pacific Movement of the Eastern World; the Moorish Science Temple; the Peace Movement of Ethiopia; and the Allah Temple of Islam, which formed the precursor of what is today's Nation of Islam. Many who read the wonderful book in your hands may be familiar with the term "Asiatic Black Man" still used by certain rappers and lyricists who consider themselves to be "conscious" but even they may not know that this term stems from an era of strict solidarity between and among African Americans and Asians, principally Japanese.

As the Pacific War was unfolding, these militants were arrested, indicted, convicted and imprisoned. However, the more sober elements in the U.S. ruling elite realized that it was contrary to national security to harbor a population so maltreated that they would join invaders and this was a harbinger of the agonized retreat of the more egregious aspects of U.S. apartheid that was initiated in the 1950s.

The Pacific War was concluded and punctuated with the atomic bombing of Hiroshima and Nagasaki, a gross example of mass murder and an indicator of how seriously Japan's putative violation of racial norms was taken. This was followed by an occupation force—a Jim Crow occupation in the beginning—that brought the father of F. D. K. Cloyd to Japan. The author speaks at length of Tachikawa Air Base in Japan. Tellingly enough, sited simultaneously at this facility was James Meredith, who became the first student of African ancestry to desegregate the University of Mississippi in the early 1960s and—as I note in the aforementioned book—asserted that his experience in Japan steeled him for the dauntingly enervating experience of knocking down the walls of apartheid in Dixie.

I hope and I trust that readers of this riveting and insightful book are aware of its potency. It touches on some of the more critically important issues of the day in prose that is both graceful and illuminating. This is a book that should not only be read—but savored. ≋

Gerald Horne holds the Moores Professorship of History and African American Studies at University of Houston. His research has addressed issues of racism in a variety of relations involving labor, politics, civil rights, international relations and war. He has also written extensively about the film industry. Dr. Horne received his Ph.D. in history from Columbia University and his J.D. from the University of California, Berkeley and his B.A. from Princeton University.

# CHAPTER 1

# Unending Dream きりがない夢

I write:

> 水 *("mizu" — water in Chinese/Japanese) What the hell is this?*

I write:

> 子 *("ko" — child, baby, infant in Chinese/Japanese) What the hell is going on?*

Then, I write:

> 水子 the two characters together.
> *Mizuko* is a common name for girls and women.
> It can be read as, and literally means, *water child* or *water children.*

> *It's the middle of the damn night! It's 2 in the morning! Ugh! Tossing and turning. Turning and tossing.*

> I hardly ever write in Japanese. Something is going on.

> *Mizuko* is also the Japanese euphemism for:
> *Aborted fetus.*

"To say that a life is precarious requires not only that a life be apprehended as a life, but also that precariousness be an aspect of what is apprehended in what is living."

—Judith Butler, *Frames of War: When is Life Grievable?* [1]

IT WAS MY LIFE, ACCUMULATING. A focused and delayed response to the thirty years it took me to finish writing this book that you, the reader, are reading. In the last two years, I put everything together. It was resurrection and re-living certain events, and deciding what to insert and what to cut out. The gathering of life, in pain and heartache, is not easy to articulate, nor to reflect that life accurately, especially when I, or someone like myself, an anonymous figure in American and Japanese society (or any society), decides the pain is beyond "personal." Of course, it's not just about pain. The pain only foregrounds what is important. What do we see? What do we create? What do we oppress?

> *War child, occupation child, abandoned child.*
> *Unwanted child. Troubled child. Violent child. Sad child.*
> *Mistake.*
> *Black, White, Yellow, Red, Brown.*
> *Obedient, Inscrutable, Untrustworthy, Primitive, Uncivilized, Undemo-*
> *cratic. Colored.*
> *slant-eye, ching-chong, faggot, Dragon-lady, Whore, Seducer,*
> *savage, insect, monkey, Jap, Nigger, jigaboo, coolie,*
> *charcoal, left by the ship, curly, child of the dust, con lai, buidoi, hyonhyol,*
> *monkey, kurombo, nognog, bye bye daddy,*
> *Fu-Man Chu, Mama-san, Sex-Toy, slave . . . .*
> *Just plain weird.*

I was born in Japan in 1955. A watershed year for many things. To say that I was born as one of a second-wave Amerasian population in Japan to an African American father and Japanese mother is not enough. These labels are not enough. I was born in the period during the Korean War, during the tail end—the falsely labeled "after"—of the U.S. Occupation of Japan. My mother lived through the terror of U.S. bombings; my father joined the U.S. military during Jim Crow America. This reality is not apart. It revives and continues the desires of European colonizers who entered the Asian and Pacific region before the Americans, and left legacies of abandoned women and babies. I did not make these legacies and histories, yet they twine through my life and cannot be shaken. The same is true for anyone else in the world, tangled in amnesia and the refusal of histories except for those they choose. As these histories are made invisible, so am I. So are my loved ones and fellow strangers alike. I refuse this process. *I refuse this history. I write.*

This refusal confronts national writings and national memories that have crafted (our) selves and lives through textbooks, through cultures, through hierarchies imposed. These writings put forward certain things and hide others. It obscures and lies. People, and everything else in the world, are not labels, and myself-as-label (the Amerasians) is not the truth. It is peculiar and painful, and begs to be written against. But this is how we approach life. *I refuse.*

Mama-as-label is one of *those* women. Yes, those women—who got together with U.S. Occupation soldiers after World War II, following in the footsteps of millions of women who linked themselves sexually and culturally, in the most direct ways, to the colonizers and occupiers from Europe and America: women from Korea, China, the Philippines Archipelago, the Marshall and Cook Islands, Papua New Guinea, Tonga, Tuvalu, Vietnam, Thailand, Laos, Cambodia, Samoa, Micronesia, Guam, Fiji, Australia, Hawai'i, and more—those places where Europeans and Americans penetrated the Asia-Pacific. *Annexed, governed, occupied, controlled, raped, displaced and "civilized." Named.*

Tall buildings and shiny modernization cannot hide devastation, displacements, the smiles of domination, or bombs.

*We live in a civilized society.*
*We are citizens in civilization.*
*First, we had to become "civilization-alized."*
*We have been civilized.*
*Beautiful, exotic, normal, perfect, handsome, hard-working.*

In most writings in mainstream literature and textbooks, people like me are written and depicted and desired within the same types of narratives, over and over:

anomaly
tragic, obscure, abandoned
dark, evil
confused
problem, scorned, hated
unnecessary, mistake
result of unacceptable/illegal sex
child of whores
military misgivings and shame
exotic beauty
the United Nations "the wonderful future mixed-race human"
War babies and War Brides. Named: *Illegitimates, traitors, whores*

Amerasians and the mixed-race children of European colonizers who entered the Asia-Pacific before the Americans are linked in close sociological and psychological kinship. *Named.*

In all these cases, we Amerasian Black Japanese and Blasians (Black Asians) especially are not represented except to serve as objects for stories feeding into dominant narratives of hierarchy, amusement, and sentimentality—a discourse that dominates, that affirms the hegemonic "goodness" in recognizing pain and empathy. These terms formed through a certain construction of the past and persist among the boundaries and crevices where blood and dreams thrive.

So…この夢、 this Dream.

Writing family history not as a "history" or confessions. Writing from that breaking and being broken, from that breaking-free. We break our selves as we need to, even as we break our prisons, shaped by cultural and national rules that erase so that other priorities—priorities of those dominant cultures and sub-cultures—may write anew. We return to a place that cannot be returned to. This is no autobiography. This is not linear Western memory. This does not seek redemption. There is nothing to redeem.

> In Breakdowns—
> > Ghosts
> > > Come Alive.

*Freedom is un-free.*

*The interstices carry that which the dominant and obvious choose to disregard, ignore, refuse, crush.*

I refuse you. I *REFUSE* YOU.

In writing this—in writing memory—there are those who are no longer here, who speak, but are no longer (cannot be) heard. We live in worlds that create us as we create these worlds. My words and body are a finger pointing at memory, assimilating memory as it creates and resists assimilation.[2]

*I name this work: Anti-Memoir.*

Memoir, from the French mémoire, from a linear and "understood" memory. Memory is active. It is beyond reflection.

I share the struggle. I chart the inter-generational and transcontinental memory — the collective, traversing diverse families, disconnected in blood but related in politics and sociology.

Or more bluntly, connected through legacies of *killing and being killed — legacies* linked by common roots, spiritual and physical. Linked within regimes the entire world now lives under, linked beneath the threat of constant genocidal impulse.

But also present within resistance. Within practices to defuse unnecessary suffering. Within possibilities for certain kinds of understanding — across power, resentment, love, forgetting, and remembering.

≋ ≋ ≋

Mama and I in Albuquerque, circa 1963. *Fredrick Cloyd Family Archive.*

THIS WAS NOT REMEMBERING. This represents encounters with the struggle of ancestors, and the struggle to read existences linked in the right-now.

Dreams aren't real, yet are very real.

*The Dream* is memory and waking-world action. *The Dream* is understanding, grasping for possibilities of new paths, of questioning who and what we are accountable to, and how this relates to cultural histories.

It is each of us and our perceptions in the biopolitical.[3]

*What kinds of ghosts walk in our bodies and among others?*
*What and who walks between us? Who hears them speaking?*

I listen.

They whisper:

> *We visit you.*
> *We visit because you cannot forget.*
> *We are not here without purpose, for fear or amusement.*
> *Who are you, as person and ancestor,*
> *As time,*
> *As other,*
> *As violent,*
> *As loving,*
> *if we do not show you, speak to you,*
> *Become you?* 㣇

# CHAPTER NOTES

1. Judith Butler, *Frames of War: When Is Life Grievable?* (NY: Verso, 2010).

2. This is a direct reference to Zen Buddhism's oft-quoted dialogue of a Zen teacher, when asked what Zen practice is, what Nirvana is, what "Truth" is, what enlightenment is. The teacher responds: It is like the finger pointing at the moon. Whatever I say about it, it is not the moon itself. People mistake the finger for the moon.

3. "Biopolitics," or "biopower," are terms used in social scientific thought, developed by French philosopher, historian, and literary critic Michel Foucault (1926-1984), which points to forms of power and control exerted through mass populations. I use it here, as an underpinning of this entire project. For example, ideas of a national or cultural "being," and what is best or not, are examples of how this is enforced through governmental institutions and laws, then spread and maintained by individuals internalizing these dynamics. Studies of population statistics, birthrate, and hygiene, are just a few examples of control mechanisms used in biopolitics.

# CHAPTER 2

# Dream of the Water Children

*Mizuko.* 水子
*The Born-dead The Unborn*
*Waters    Women    Children*
*Men    People who aren't these "things"*
*Ecologies    Desire    Ashes    Hope*
*Dreams.*

IN THE PROCESS OF WRITING, I prepared for it by recalling my grieving, and trying to realize those moments that were beyond words. With the hands of ghosts, I remembered and conjured things unconscious. *Grieving for, and with, history* is not only sentimental and simplistic remembrance of the dead. For what, and how, did people die? Can we be empowered to make different lives besides those prescribed to us by our dominant cultural hierarchies? In doing nothing beyond the ascribed jobs and families and civilizational things, we uphold certain kinds of death. Each of us creates and maintains a culture fashioned through how the elites govern and control lives—a culture of death and dying. As systems of hierarchy and domination live, so they must be resisted and changed. In writing this dream, these boundaries are traversed and returned to, tested and crossed as Mama and I had crossed the waters of the Pacific, or as Dad had crossed it and other seas many more times.

What is common in this story is the demotion and enslavement of the darker bodies. The islanders, the indigenous tribes, the Aboriginal, the mixed-African, the mixed-black, the mixed-Aboriginal, the black.

So many military occupations. So many colonial expansions. Uniformed men and women crossing and intersecting with local

Aboriginal farmers in Victoria, Australia in 1858. Aborigines from the South Seas and the Pacific Islands were kidnapped or forcibly taken by Australian, American and European businessmen to toil on plantations and coal mines, a practice that continued well into the 1970s. *Photo courtesy of State Victoria Library / AU.*

women, creating babies. The British and the French, the Dutch, the Spanish, Germans, and the Portuguese, who penetrated before the Americans.

≋ ≋ ≋

My particular way of presenting a trajectory of a *Black Pacific* in all of its forms and subversions posits questions that point to breakdowns and reconstructions within things already present. This refers to a general amnesia plaguing our global postcolonial life in the 2000s[1] and simultaneously offers spaces and thoughts to consider and resist forms of oppression. Gerald Horne posed the question: "What of the Black Pacific?"[2]

What of it? It is not one "thing." It is not merely a geocultural time or location. The Black Pacific I speak of is a struggle for understanding, justice, and diversity, an ethics and fullness in a world that increasingly valorizes an emptiness the elite can then fill, birthing new spaces where hegemony can play.[3]

*I resist.*

What questions can the dream of the Black Pacific answer? What vision of a Black Pacific am I dreaming?

*First, it wrestles with both a global hierarchy and establishing subaltern populations reflective of relations of domination and submission.* The theater of global hierarchy positions these locales and psychologies within a dialogue of equality and victimhood or villainy, which it frames as opposing stances. The fragmentation and obliteration of egalitarian systems through colonialism and globalization (not only in the past but continuing into the present) begs for different strategies and considerations of subaltern peoples—those people outside the "mainstream," in whatever identity category—as well as new models of "success," "leadership," and "power" as much as the "normal" and "natural." These are not, as the dominant thinking imagines, singular roles, but shifting layers. The subaltern flickers and hides, as identities always do. What complex positioning and relations are at play? Certainly not *equality.* For Blasians (Black Asians) and Blackanese (Black Japanese) people like myself, often considered only through predetermined categories and within pre-determined hierarchies in any given society, or flattened within *forced equalities,* what possibilities are there to live or to die?

*Second, it involves an active re-memorying of the Pacific slave trade in order to map a Black Pacific concept in a world hell-bent on remembering slavery within the strict contexts of the Trans-Atlantic slave trade.* So often referencing a concept such as a "Black Pacific" is met with refusal, rendering it mute yet threatening to identities invested in foregrounding the Trans-Atlantic slave trade as most important in the history of blackness and its relation to whiteness. Vying for access to the dominant narrative in order to gain legitimacy pits people of color against each other and invites nationalisms to further divide and conquer, revitalizing the strength of (various forms of) white supremacy.

*What is legitimate? Who determines?*

In rethinking globalization, I write a history of Pacific relations to America and Europe. Australian and New Zealander nation-building, Philippine resistance to Spain, Portugal, Great Britain; the Asia-Pacific War, with European colonial military acquisition and use of Black Asian slaves from the Pacific islands alongside conscripted African soldiers and forced African labor. It is a history of bodies.

O.S. Captain Geary commanding California heavy artillery in Cavite, Philippines, showing American pride with locals just after the Spanish-American War and just before the start of the Philippines-American War, circa 1898. *Photo courtesy of Naval History and Heritage Command.*

Following World War II, African American servicemen and women moved into Asia via various American military base installations forced upon Asian and Pacific locals. How white servicemen treated these local communities paralleled how they treated African American soldier-brothers and sisters, producing the existing incarnations of white supremacy and U.S. military presence in the Pacific today. The treatment and behaviors of white elites, as well as the contradictory treatment and view of black bodies, represented the offerings of a civilized and victorious nation, and of civilization and nation-building itself.

These patterns of mimicry and entitlements that make it easier for nation-elites to do business kills the extant diversities that once thrived. Practices of domination by non-American and non-Western Europeans, join with their individual pre-colonial cultural practices, linking and intensifying patriarchal and heterosexist hierarchies and forms of nationalism. Through time, concepts of power in leadership, (so-called) "freedom," which the American, especially, transformed into jingoistic ideals, and legitimacy were instilled across the globe. This elevated and solidified structures of male chauvinism and contours of violence.[4] In many cases, resistance to domination joined with domination itself to form, for example, the realities of Japanese imperialism, of which my family has history on both sides. Do I civilize? Am I resisting civilizing itself as an act of civilizing?

Another aspect of this "Black Pacific map" is the often-ignored and invisibilized indigenous peoples of Australia and Asia and the Pacific Islands, such as the Negrito peoples. Even as white supremacy is challenged on a global scale, many

American commanders and the soldiers of the Tagal army round-up members of Igorrot and Gadennes black aboriginal tribes in the Philippines in 1899. *Photo by Neely F. Tennyson.*

African American scholars and activists would assimilate *all black peoples* into the *"All humans are from Africa"* origin story, using an unproven scientific theory to foreclose on diversity in assimilating all black people into a single reductive narrative of geography and psychology. Furthermore, many African Americans represent blackness not as diverse and historical, but increasingly as its own urban American forms. In resistance to global white supremacy, seen as a single unity, black single-origin stories repeat the sameness-as-unity colonial practice, trivializing and threatening Aboriginal stories that refute these claims. Yet the black tribes of Asia and various Pacific and South Seas Island peoples were often treated the same as African slaves during the push for nation-building by American and European forces. A naturalization and hierarchy of killing ensues, an ordering that is constantly constructed and maintained, against nature.

This ordering of nation-states and cultures along the lines of primitive versus modern, rural versus urban, dark versus light elaborates upon the metaphysics of death by introducing a political-militaristic notion of color and history. It paved the way for the expansion politics of Manifest Destiny and the might and right of Western militaries to dominate lands and peoples outside their own boundaries. It also intensified hypodescent,[5] pitting coalitions of "people of color" against or apart from those of "indigenous peoples." This ideology rationalizes and naturalizes Western colonial ideas of progress, modernity, and identity while dividing and conquering indigenous and people of color at once, as well as poor white communities. Hypodescent and its techniques link with the idea of primitives, indigenous, farmers, people of color, etc., along with "the poor," which will become extinct by some "natural" law of evolution. Those lower (darker, poorer) stand to be modernized, civilized, "upgraded." To upgrade, in this system, signals destruction.

≋ ≋ ≋

*These points reveal the space from where I write.*

*Resisting dominant mind-maps and geography maps. Redrawing mine.*

MY DREAM IS NOT ONLY my own. It is collective, spanning many space-times. It did not originate with or within me. It is an act of remembering in the present and an act of re-navigating the past in the present to change the present-future. I am restless. I turn over. I resist. Through telling my mother's and my own, I reveal spaces for those who want change to consider. I open.

**Revolution**

Since the images you demand
cling to me
I cannot form my own image. I am forced to live
by your images,
I am always living like that,
[and] so
I understand
revolution is really body aching.

–Junko Nishi
From *Women Poets of Japan*[6] 目

# CHAPTER NOTES

1. The idea of the Black Pacific has become a new language of reference, interpretation, and study since Paul Gilroy's studies of the Black-Atlantic as a reference point for the legacies of the Atlantic Slave trade and its terrains in the Black-Atlantic diaspora, including its cultural forms, which, by its very nature, would include identity, continuities, ruptures, and cross-space legacies. See books by Paul Gilroy, *The Black Atlantic: Modernity and Double Consciousness,* (Brooklyn, NY: Verso 1993); *There Ain't No Black In the Union Jack: The Cultural Politics of Race and Nation,* (London, U.K.: Hutchinson, 1987); and *After Empire: Melancholia or Convivial Culture?* (New York: Routledge, 2004).

2. Gerald Horne, *The White Pacific: U.S. Imperialism and Black Slavery in the South Seas after the Civil War* (Hawaii: University of Hawaii Press, 2007), as one of the first books that brings to light the existence of a Black Pacific.

3. Merriam-Webster defines hegemony as: (1) Preponderant influence or authority over others: domination, and (2) the social, cultural, ideological, or economic influence exerted by a dominant group. However, I stress the notion of cultural imperialism as a tool for cultural hegemony, a concept outlined by the great Italian thinker Antonio Gramsci. Cultural imperialism lurks within the everyday, maintaining the status quo of difference. The hierarchy of socio-cultural classes within any society may practice cultural dominance as a means to encourage lower classes to adopt (internalize) and therefore enact and police the status quo. This includes structural forms of language-concepts and language use, as explored by Judith Butler, Homi Bhaba, Jacques Derrida, and Michel Foucault, among others.

4. In modern nations, a criminal justice system, military and police forces, and the educational system are probably the most obvious systems that governs and practices violence. In the past, these "givens" were not concepts of living as societies and perhaps unnecessary. In this way, the "contours" of what kinds of violence occurs and how it is confronted (or not), are normalized and regulated, yet constantly changing according to how the dominant will conceive of violence, and what it refuses or not, and ultimately the recognition of what is violent or not.

5. This term was coined in 1963 by the late University of Florida anthropologist Marvin Harris. In anthropology, it is used to note how nations enact a hierarchy of color, with lighter as higher and darker as lower, in gradations. Mixed-race people were often placed in the "darker" category even if their ancestry was mostly white European, which pointed to the contradictions of identity-as-blood, one-drop rules, etc. In the way I use it here, it links with Patrick Brantlinger's idea of progress defining the legitimized and naturalized notion of primitivity equaling extinction, therefore giving genocide a way to naturalize the killing of darker peoples. As well, in *The Nation and Its Fragments,* (Princeton University Press, 1993), author Partha Chatterjee states that the modern idea of nations-states and nation-building would undeniably include within its idea the extinction of the peasant.

6. Kenneth Rexroth and Ikuko Atsumi, eds. *Women Poets of Japan* (New Directions 1977), 132. Junko Nishi's life is unknown. Two mimeographed collections, 物語 *Monogatari (Story)* and 長い手紙 *NagaiTegami (Long Letter)* were published in 1970 in Amagasaki in Hyōgo Prefecture. Junko Nishi could never be located (disappeared).

# CHAPTER 3

# The Waters 水

"What am I doing here in this endless winter?"

— Franz Kafka, *The Metamorphosis and Other Stories*[1]

MY BROWN BODY BEGAN WRITING the Sino-Japanese character 水 *(water)* when I was four years old. Growing up in Japan, I began writing Chinese characters before I knew any of the simpler phonetic kana characters of Japanese. I hadn't even heard of English then. And what I knew of China were my Mama's Chinese friends in Japan, and the Chinese waiters and waitresses we encountered at Chinese restaurants.

At nine, my interest grew to include Sino-Japanese brush calligraphy. I began visiting the school library at Tachikawa Air Base to browse books about China, a tradition I continued even after we moved to Albuquerque. I particularly liked *The Good Earth* by Pearl S. Buck.[2] I had been introduced to that book on an assignment and, once I read it, I was addicted. I grew obsessed with the drawings of Chungking City and Chinese *coolies*,[3] and began drawing replicas myself. I felt I could smell the fragrance of their coolie pants, the dirt, and the large straw hats. I didn't know it then, but Buck had been working to draw attention to children of particular parentage—that of Western men, particularly U.S. American military fathers, and women of the Asia-Pacific. She was credited for coining the term "Amerasian" in international politics and championing the cause of children of American servicemen abandoned in Asia until her death in the 1970s.

Mama would smile when she saw me drawing and coloring Chungking town scenes at the table, devoting sometimes the entire day. But when she asked where I learned these things and why I liked it so much, all I could say was *"Shiranai"* (I don't know).

21

American writer, novelist, and Nobel Prize winner Pearl S. Buck (center), who is credited with coining the term "Amerasian" in international political and charity circles, with Amerasian orphans in Japan. *Photo courtesy of Pearl S. Buck International, www. pearlsbuck.org.*

Once, in Albuquerque, when Dad was home for a few days from Vietnam, he asked what I wanted him to bring back from Southeast Asia. I said a straw coolie hat, like the ones I had seen the Chinese wearing in those drawings and photos.

*I think now about ghosts.*

Nowadays, when answering the question, "What are you?" I prefer to respond with "I'm Black Japanese Amerasian." Usually about eight out of ten people then start talking to me about *Vietnam*. This has led me to consider who I'm responding to and to what effect, and which "label"could, or should, apply. Labels are controlled fictions. Hapa, mixed-race, Blasian, Asian-American, Black-American, etc. And while it's true that commonalities may exist among Amerasians, it is also important to say I am not Vietnamese. "Black Japanese" situates me as postwar Japanese and within the United States, linking my histories with a war (though not of Southeast Asia) and an occupation—the u.s. Allied Occupation of Japan. Vietnam is the most recent place-memory that created "Amerasians," but people need to understand the long history.

The history precedes the Vietnam War. Vietnam is a continuation of European encroachment in the Asia-Pacific, yet the encroachment is not yet over. These issues persist as people and communities continue to struggle today. The "American" identity as white-position, occupier, and victor, joins with traditions of French, Dutch, British, German, Portuguese, Spanish, Australian, Canadian, New Zealander and other histories that have survived in the region and within political strategies of culture, laws, and institutions. There are disjunctures and continuities. It is not a question of one or two nations or cultures, enmeshed in conflict. There are reinforcements.

ON A WARM Albuquerque night.

> *Mama dōyatte Dēri ni atta no?*
> (Mama, how did you and Dad meet?)

> *Hora, Dēri wa amerika senryō guntai no ato, Nihon ni kite. . . .*
> (Well, after the war, after the American occupation, Daddy had come to Japan)

Then she stopped. She wouldn't—or couldn't—tell me how they exactly met.

I never thought about Mama's life and how she met Dad, or what her life was like before my Dad arrived. Or even about what Japan was, what role it played in (my) family, longing, desire, hatred, life, having or lacking patience, crying, endurance, remembering, forgetting, repelling, attracting, or coexisting.

I was fifteen when I began to *consciously* unravel the threads of my family history.

≋ ≋ ≋

I WAS IN SEARCH.

It was a little grocery store near Sacramento Street in Chinatown where I recalled seeing those blue cans of mock duck meat that I like to fry up with onions and soy sauce and garlic with my rice. I had just remembered to pick some up but was so far from my usual market...so yes—I found a small Chinese grocery store. I entered, stopped by a Chinese man, looking about forty-ish, thin and stern, with khaki pants and a cream-colored button-down shirt. "You no come in," he says.

I wrinkled my brow.

"We close now!"

It didn't compute. I saw people going in and out of the store, mostly Chinese or Vietnamese people, I thought, and some white people. Then I understood. He was one of the owners, or, at least, the caretaker. I asked, "What time are you closing? Other people are going in now, so why can't I go in?"

I took a step to try to pass him to go inside.

"No!"

He blocked my way. And then I knew.

"My mother's Chinese and Japanese," I said.

He stared at my face. "We close. You go."

"You know this is illegal," I said, attempting to resist him without calling him names. I gave up. Too tired. My insides were boiling. I left without the mock duck meat.

> If we understand the whole world to have gone through ideological, economical, and cultural changes through nation-making and colonization—which it has been—then all humans are occupied.

Another time: On a city bus going downtown from the Mission District, I overheard a conversation between three young women in their mid-twenties, visiting San Francisco.

慰安婦か。　悲しい時代だったね、戦争の後の日本って。

ねー。

でもあの時代の人たちはもう年とってもうすぐみんな死んじ
ゃうんだから、ほとんどん日本人はあんな悲しい歴史を聞か
ない時がくるのを待っているんじゃない？

*Comfort women! Seems like those were sad times in Japan.*

*But people living in those days are old now, and are going to die. Most
Japanese people are waiting for the day we won't have to talk like this or
hear sad histories any more.*

I was irritated, but could not stop reliving that conversation throughout the
day. To think that this is what my life and histories amounted to...
I felt my own body-mind linking with Mama's.
On September 20, 2001, then-U.S. President George W. Bush, used the
"Day of Infamy" phrase in response to the attacks on the World Trade Center in
New York. He spoke of this as a day of infamy to connect those same emotions
and memories with President Franklin D. Roosevelt's words following the Japanese attack on Pearl Harbor. Japan and the U.S. and a 1940s World War, alive
again in the 2000s. Who connects what and for what reasons? What positions
do people play in this? What do the Iraqis and all those who remember being
occupied think of Occupation, as they both hate or love their occupiers? What
relations form? What laws? What norms? What my life and histories represent
is built within the space-time I occupy in relation to war, race, nation, culture
and memory. Aren't you still living with occupation and war—those things that
define your identity and relationships, just like I am? And how do death, water
and children connect to this?

水子　水子　水子

In July 2011, the Japanese women's national soccer team won the World Cup.
On Twitter and Facebook, the congratulations for the Japanese women and praise
for the U.S. team were also met with hundreds of responses evoking Hiroshima
and Pearl Harbor as proof of the need for Japan to learn its "place."
In August 2012, the U.S. defeated Japan for the title. This time, thousands of
tweets and Facebook comments noted how the U.S. victory was revenge for Pearl

Harbor. Victory and defeat were evoked through time. *We're dominant, so you are not.* Where are the lines between self and institution, military and self, military and institution, freedom and imprisonment, death and life? In becoming, what techniques do we adopt to inflict pain. How much of our everyday lives arises from violence and dominance?

*And what does this have to do with my family?*

I read:

*Shintō and Buddhist institutions were outlawed by SCAP,[4] the U.S. Occupation administration, at the beginning of the formal occupation period in Japan in 1945, in order to purge spiritually-motivated Japanese nationalisms that had fueled its war against the U.S. This contributed to the deformation of Japanese history and the disjuncture of its imperialist ideologies from Japanese chauvinism.[5] Before World War II, Japanese people faced their own compulsory system of nationalistic jingoes and militarized economic and educational systems. With the desperate postwar confusion and devastation, the people, psychologically defeated, socially exhausted, and despairing, were made ripe for a takeover.*

Who steps into that crevice to corral the nation and its people into another homogenized mentality? The Americans. And never completely.

Everything encounters complex assimilations and resistances.

Grieving mothers, who could neither forget nor remember their dead or stillborn, or aborted children, were bewildered as they reckoned with their grief and loss. Grief went underground, into the so-called "private" realm, with women often carrying that burden alone. In a devastated, starving Japan, many women didn't want to consider raising their babies without husbands or their clan. Some women hated their babies because it reminded them of the American, Australian, or European soldier who abandoned or betrayed them. In other cases, the family pressured the woman to get rid of the baby—the enemy baby, the occupier baby.

In some towns, large numbers of children and adults were now without family. Without familiar communal spaces for grieving, many women grieved alone. They also faced the added magnitude of unimaginable shame. Women without men were scorned.

*Mizuko Kuyō* 水子供養 were religious rites and rituals for grieving parents of aborted children, originally created by Buddhist leaders in Japan a decade after

Jizo statues, protectors of unborn babies, usually mark the Mizuko kuyo ceremonial temples. This one is at the Hasadera Temple in Kamakura Japan, circa. 1970. *Fredrick Cloyd Family Archive.*

the end of World War II when the SCAP ban on religious rituals had lifted. In the 1970s, they became much more well-known (and necessary). After a decade of repressed grief, mothers could now visit a shrine-site to pray to the memory of their aborted babies. The mothers of dead children also came to these places as well, to close their eyes with hands palm-to-palm to pray in smoky 白檀 *byakudan* (sandalwood) incense-filled spaces within lost time. Yet religious organizations charged high prices to provide these services. Mizuko Kuyō was criticized for exploiting women for wealth.[6]

*I was beginning to understand.*

The occupation of Japan was not altogether some horrible thing. That is not an assumption I wish to make. Like most things in life, there are contradictions and struggles. There is no question that there was a takeover, an undoing. Occupation was a regime-change that brought Japan under the control of global powers. I say "under" because it is a foregone conclusion about who was, and remains, at the top—at least, for the moment. It is not Japan. Or any other Asian or black nation, but Asian and black nations must be accountable for their own violences. Colonial systems helped strengthen and organize these violences through transnational ties, resource-gathering, and the solidification of boundaries. It did not, however, create them. Erasure and mis-remembering ensues alongside the construction of identity; and memory is disfigured, layered, political, emotional and physical. Occupation, imperialism, killing, death, remembering, forgetting—these "normal" and therefore forgettable operations of life—must be forgotten if we are to begin to assimilate. To refuse assimilation means death, means being killed. To assimilate is also death. To kill a part of ourselves so we can become the other.

By asking Mama what music she loved, I invited Occupation to thread through the now. She said Japanese war songs reminded her of her soldier-friends, all boys who went to war and never returned. She said some songs reminded her of her first American soldier-boyfriends. She doesn't remember the names of some of the Japanese songs but...

"'Diana,' toka... 'Putto Yo-ah Heddo on Mai Shorudaaah' toka . . .
hontoni Pōru Anka no uta daisuki!"
(Songs like "Diana" and "Put Your Head on My Shoulder"... I really love Paul Anka songs!)

*"... 'Hon de Tenesheewarutsu'... suteki."*
(... And 'Tennessee Waltz'... wonderful)

Then I ask — *"Nihon no utasukijanai no?"*
(Don't you like Japanese songs?)

She responds — *"Betsuni"*
(Not particularly)

Why American songs? Why not Japanese?

Some people refuse to refuse *History* (capital "H"): that mainstream, repeated story, that "object" controlled by dominant culture that makes us subjects.

This refusal to refuse yields certain consequences for a world that creates reality. Who writes and claims History? What are the consequences of refusal? Do we accept them?

Mama watched her friends die. She saw Japanese children die. Her relations died. *Friends died. Loved ones died.* Her dreams died, just as new ones were being born. Birth and death intertwine. And all the while during the bombings by the U.S., they knew that they were being killed because they were hated, and intentionally exploded and burned into ashes. What grows and disappears inside hearts and minds after bombs stop falling? What does a person become when death is unnatural?

*I am not the only water child.*
*So many water children. There are so many water children.*

It comes from war. Even if the nations are peaceful. Even if our nation is not "actively" invading. Even if we are living just fine while the government is doing terrible things. What are we taught to ignore? What dreams are made while others are deemed unworthy or in need of elimination? What do we suppress? What creates this world we live in?

Our ghosts will tell.
*Whispering* "忘れないで" Don't forget me. 目

Mama in 1948, Ōme, Japan. *Fredrick Cloyd Family Archive.*

# CHAPTER NOTES

1.  Franz Kafka, *The Metamorphosis: And Other Stories* (The Schocken Kafka Library, 1995).

2.  Pearl S. Buck (1892-1973) was an American writer who was the first American woman to win the Pulitzer Prize for literature (1932). *The Good Earth* was the best-selling fiction book in the U.S. in 1931 and 1932. She was immensely popular in China, as she wrote often of the peasant life in China. She was famous for her work with Asia-Pacific orphans whose fathers were born of American servicemen. Through her work, the term "Amerasian" became known in popular culture in the United States. Her Chinese name is Sai Zhenzhu 賽珍珠.

3.  Coolie has an etymology whose origins begin as far back as the Ottoman Empire and indentured laborers in China, South Asia and Southeast Asia. In some places, it is considered a pejorative word. Generally, laborers began being looked upon with increasing condescension globally in the nineteenth century.

4.  Supreme Command Allied Powers (SCAP), the official administrative body of the U.S. Occupation of Japan (1945-1952) with General Douglas MacArthur as the "supreme commander."

5.  Any book about the Occupation of Japan would state this fact as part of the administration's plan.

6.  For more information on Mizuko Kuyō, see Elizabeth G. Harrison, "Strands of Complexity: The Emergence of Mizuko Kuyō in Postwar Japan," *Journal of the American Academy of Religion* 67/4 (1999): 769-796; and "Buddhism and Abortion in Contemporary Japan: Muzuko Kuyō and the Confrontation with Death," *Japanese Journal of Religious Studies* 15, no. 1 (1988). See also, Anne Page Brooks "Muzuko Kuyō and Japanese Buddhism," *Japanese Journal of Religious Studies* 8, no. 3-4 (1981).

# CHAPTER 4

# Denver, Colorado 1982

"Upon the death of the other we are given to memory, and thus to interiorization, since the other, outside U.S., is now nothing. And with the dark light of this nothing, we learn that the other resists the closure of our interiorizing memory...death constitutes and makes manifest the limits of a *me* or an us who are obliged to harbor something that is greater and other than them; something *outside of them within them.*"

— Jacques Derrida, *The Work of Mourning*[1]

Hey, Boy!........Yeah. You. I'm talking to you, Boy![2]

*Yes, officer,*

I said to the policeman calling out to me at 11:00 at night as I walked home from volleyball practice at the YMCA. He shined the flashlight onto my face as I turned to face him. There are two of them. They violently pushed me onto the police car and told me to put my hands up as they laugh.

What are you doing out here?

*I'm coming home from volleyball practice.*

Don't you have a car? Let's see your ID.

They searched me with their hands. They turned me around violently to face them again.

You got drugs?

*No, I don't do drugs.*

Yeah, that's what you all say.

They both laughed.

One was white, the other appeared Latino. Both about my height. They told me to open my mouth so they can look inside. They also touched between my thighs to feel for packages.

Can't you see you just jay-walked?

*Jay-walked? It's almost midnight and there aren't any cars anywhere. Not one.*

Don't smart-mouth us Boy!

They ticketed me for jay-walking.

I swore at them.

They threatened me with arrest.

You better shut up, Boy!

When I told my friend, he told me I should've kept my mouth shut. Even when I brought up that this happened the previous week, and the week before, and all the other times.

*Why? Do you know how many times I've been humiliated by them?*

Just forget it, Fred.

*Shut the fuck up. I wish you could go through it just once, then multiply it five thousand times. Then let's hear what you have to say.*

I REALLY ONLY UNDERSTOOD MY BLACKNESS through Japanese eyes during the 1950s and 1960s. My body represented Japan's intense relationship with its former-enemy-now-recent-occupier. Mine was a westernized, self-displaced body that grappled feelings of inferiority, that was coming to terms with all of the normalized ways in which nation-states structured and elevated white supremacy.

Mama with me in my military regalia as a three-year-old. My blackness and military heritage on display. *Fredrick Cloyd Family Archive.*

I knew nothing of American black history or civil rights then, unknowledgeable about what "Amerika" was all about, except for seeing huge demonstrations on American television and listening to Mama's explanations. My experiences of anti-black racism after moving to the U.S. were a continuation of my experiences in Japan, which I had not yet explored or understood. But I didn't understand the historical context of African American culture in the U.S. It was painful, struggling with these subjugating and violent forces, but in the process, it also brought brave and kind friends to my defense. Others, of course, were oblivious, or chose to ignore it. I often do not consider myself as "black" in a cultural sense, but this is what often happens when skin color supersedes one's culture and heritage. But in all of the white nations, this happens often—anyone that is not-white becomes black.

By the time I was in my twenties, police talking down to me became normal. I had been told by teachers and others that I should learn to "swallow my dignity," be "good and quiet," and avoid getting into trouble. There was, of course, a gentlemanly, non-violent way to possess dignity, and I learned it from watching my Dad. But to those police officers and others like them, they tried to crush whatever dignity I possessed. It is this continuing sadism that enlivens subjugation. And it was *my* problem.

Others watched as if it were a sideshow attraction. There is tacit agreement in neutrality. Those more privileged and protected people understood that it was my own battle to fight, and none of their business. Between their admonishments to "stop crying and complaining" and "quit being a baby," I questioned. I thought. What to do? What to do?

*Time goes on.*
*Assimilating us.*

**March 2010**

MAMA AND I SPOKE on the telephone. She wondered:

*Mama no jinsei nan no riyū ga arundarou?*
(I wonder what reason my life has?)

I responded:

*Mmm......Furetto mo tokidoki onaji koto o kangaeru no yo, jibun no koto.*
(I don't know......I sometimes think the same question about myself.)

Now, in 2011, so removed from yet so intimate with Mama's words, I lie in the dark, staring. Thinking. Returning.

≋ ≋ ≋

I HAVE ALWAYS LOVED WATER. I feel comfortable in it. I love being around it.

When I took my first swimming lessons at the pool on Tachikawa Air Base, the instructor marveled to my parents how quickly I learned, and how natural it was, that I almost needed no instruction.

I love oceans. And hot baths—especially the Japanese kind, *ofuro*. Turkish baths. And long hot showers in the U.S. and Europe. Waterfalls hypnotize and soothe me. And whenever I get the chance to go camping, I insist on setting up tent near a lake or pond or stream. Whenever my friends and I would go camping in Colorado in the 1980s, I loved to sit by waterfalls as long as I could, just watching and listening.

In my hometown in Japan in the 1950s, the sewage canals were everywhere, just out in the open. The American military kids called them "benjo ditches." *Benjo* is the old and crude Japanese word for *toilet*. Water, no matter how nice or stinky, was always heard, since the sewage system were canals that circled the towns where I grew up. Sometimes I remember the stench was *wow! really bad.* Water, brown and dark, ran dirty all through the town.

And then there was the stream where Mama and I used to go wash our clothes. There were no washers and dryers back then. We used to carry baskets of our clothes for a half-hour walk to the stream just outside our cluster of wooden houses, with Mama carrying one handle and me carrying the other.

We'd pull out the wooden washboard and the bars of soap, singing and laughing as we scrubbed the clothes on the washboard. Back and forth, back and forth. *Rhythm.* I loved those moments with Mama. The water was all around and soaked us. Mama rolled up her slacks or her Western-style skirt so they wouldn't get wet. The sound of the water running over the rocks and down to somewhere we couldn't see was a joyful noise. Everything was just perfect.

Even so, I've almost drowned three times during my life.

When I was four years old, I loved playing with my toy truck, a Tonka truck shipped to me by a Dad I didn't yet know, who lived in some faraway place called "Amerika." One day, while playing near the creek Mama told me not to go near, I ran my truck over this tiny swinging wooden bridge that ran across the canal by our house. I concentrated so hard on making the truck noises that I tripped on the side of the bridge's edge and fell thirty or forty feet into the canal. I screamed, *"Tasukete! Tasukete!"*

No one could hear me. I realized that the water level that was, at first, waist-level was now just below my lower lip. I didn't panic. I thought, *how am I supposed to die now? Should I just let myself drink the water? Should I hold my breath until I can't? What's going to happen?*

*I was a strange child. I was going to die that day in complete calm.*

*Perhaps I was calm because I knew it was water.*

*Water.*

Mama was so angry with me later when some Japanese field workers on the U.S. base rescued me and brought me home. When she opened the door and the men told her what had happened, she yelled at me, chastising me for how stupid and disobedient I was. She threw a bucket of cold water over me and locked me out of the house. I shivered and cried, but I knew it was all my fault.

The second time was when I was almost washed away by the ocean at Camp Erdman in Hawai'i, a summer camp that Dad enrolled me in when I was eleven. I loved those two summers I went. The camp was awesome. My friends had wanted me to join them while they body-surfed the big waves. I struggled as the waves caught me and kept me under. I had to hold my breath, searching for something to grab. My breath was running out. I saw sand amid the foam under the water. I held on. The wave washed away. I clung to it and realized I was on the sandy beach. I had to muster all my strength to crawl away. I washed up on another part of the beach where no one else was. I remember, later that day, when the beach had closed, the waves were twenty feet high.

≋ ≋ ≋

THE YEAR 1955 HAD A SERIES OF WATERSHED MOMENTS. In April, there was an international conference — the Bandung Conference in Indonesia — which gathered the world's African and Asian nations' leaders to discuss their roles in response to global white supremacy and the Cold War. Richard Wright famously wrote of his response to this event. This, and subsequent meetings of the Afro-Asian nations, led to the now defunct non-aligned movement, which left lasting legacies for continued resistance and alliance. Japan, South Korea, and Taiwan, along with India at the time, had undergone tremendous changes in order to rise up into the new global order, which also included maintaining strong ties to the U.S.[3]

During this time, Japan openly acknowledged the beginning of the "new" Japan. The political system was called "The 1955 System" *(55年体制 Gojūgonen Taisei).* It was a one-and-a-half political party system that unified all diverse parties into a semi-conservative power. Consumer products began intensifying their intrusion and expansion into Japanese life. It was really a mandate from the U.S. Occupation administration and, most likely, required to rebuild Japan.[4]

I grew up loving television. I still enjoy it. It came as the new thing, the modern thing, the must-have, for the Japanese. We were not living on Tachikawa Air Base yet. We were then living outside the fences of the base.

I often watched television and listened to music to block-out......

*war-baby, yellow-baby, red-baby, tar-baby.*
*war-baby, yellow-baby, red-baby, tar-baby.*

*war-bride* 戦争花嫁, *dragon lady, whore* 夜の女, *bitch, yellow, communist, negro,*

*nigger, half-breed, mutt, confused, Oriental, Jap, slant-eye, sneaky, insect, monster,*

*ching-chong, gook, chink, sissy, fag, faggot, mama's boy, traitor, boy, ainoko* 愛の子, *kurombo* 黒んぼ, *konketsuji* 混血児, *un-american,*

*non-japanese* 日本人じゃない.

*Boy.*

We visit you.

How can anyone tell these memory-stories without betraying the past?[5] 目

# CHAPTER NOTES

1.     Jacques Derrida, *The Work of Mourning* (IL: University of Chicago Press, 2003).

2.     The term "boy" was used as a condescending term for black men during the days of slavery and post-slavery (Jim Crow) in the U.S. that is still used today. When my father was angry at me and he used the term "boy" to call me out, even at that young age, I understood the deeper significance of its meaning.

3.     See Richard Wright, *The Color Curtain* (Jackson: University Press of Mississippi, 1995). First published in 1956, *The Color Curtain* arose from Wright's participation in a global African and Asian nations conference held in Bandung, Indonesia, in April 1955.

4.     Tim Weiner, *Legacy of Ashes: The History of the CIA* (NY: Anchor, 2008). Weiner's book covers some of this history, along with his article, "C.I.A. Spent Millions to Support Japanese Right in 50's and 60's." *New York Times,* October 9, 1994. Accessed September 19, 2015. http://www.nytimes.com/1994/10/09/world/cia-spent-millions-to-support-japanese-right-in-50-s-and-60-s.html

5.     Cathy Caruth, *Unclaimed Experience: Trauma, Narrative, and History* (Baltimore: Johns Hopkins University Press, 1996), 27. These are questions posed by many writers, but I believe this dilemma is an immediate consequence of Caruth's work.

# CHAPTER 5

# Watermelon Seeds, 1964 Shōwa Year 39
# スイカの種 1964年 昭和39年

"One of the remarkable features of this group is that it seems that all the war children receives[sic] a stigma, whether the father was an enemy soldier or an allied.... We have to understand that this stigma often is associated with the status of the mother."

— from *The War Children of the World*[1]

Lovers—a Japanese man and French woman:

He:  *You saw nothing in Hiroshima. Nothing.*

She:  *The reconstructions have been made as authentically as possible.*

*The illusion, it's quite simple, the illusion is so perfect that the tourists cry....*

*I've always wept over the fate of Hiroshima. Always.*

He:  *No. What would you have cried about?*

She:  *I saw the newsreels...*

He:  *You saw nothing. Nothing.*

(*Hiroshima mon amour* 18-19)[2]

IT's A SUMMER DAY IN ALBUQUERQUE. Hot with the noise of cicadas buzzing, the sky bright and blue as it moves across the world. Two of Mama's friends and their families are talking loudly as they walk through our door for a rare visit. They bring their sons. One of them, Kevin, is about sixteen or seventeen, a junior or senior in high school. His dad is a white Air Force man I've never met. Mama had a kind of friendship with their mother, which sometimes involved visiting each others' homes. I always found it strange. I was fifteen when this happened.

"So what part of Japan is your Mom from?" I asked Kevin.

"I don't know. It's probably Tōkyō."

"Do you speak any Japanese?"

"No, we speak English at home. Mom tried to teach us some words and sometimes we can say *arigato* and some simple stuff."

"Have you been to Japan?"

I was trying to find some kind of connection with Kevin. So far a failure.

"No."

A familiar loneliness returned for an instant. To him, *miso shiru* was something strange, but tasty, that he ate at home, that his Mom cooked. It was a certain connection between him and his mother. And nothing else.

For me, being born in Japan has a whole history that underpins eating and drinking *miso shiru* and other Japanese foods. Food is not just food. Those who don't understand may laugh at this. This is the problem.

*You saw nothing. Nothing.*

People have different kinds of memories of World War II and Japan. So many people have different opinions about the war, the U.S. Occupation, and the postwar without ever having been alive then, or ever having been to Japan. Movies about Hiroshima (and only Hiroshima, not Nagasaki or the other places where daily bombings took place in Japan) are one of the many ways in which people learn "history" and internalize, create, and structure opinions and positions in relation to it. Books, music, television and all forms of media; corporations, schools, and the government; our parents, relatives and friends—all of them help define the choices we make, the parameters we live in, and the identities we create. In most cases, the memories of our experiences (realized or not) become "reality," whether we were there to witness it or not. We are all guilty with how we (re)interpret memory.

That the bombing of Hiroshima and Nagasaki was a devastating first is a fact. That it has, so far, not been repeated in history is also a fact. But the memories of my (and my mother's) country, the atomic bomb, and subsequent economic recovery are for so many, the only memories they have of Japan. What is the purpose of our memories? What is it exactly that we know or presume to know? And why? How do we use what we know? Who benefits, and what benefits? What is silent and therefore remains unchanged?

*I call them ghosts, accumulating. Ghosts upon ghosts.*

The French woman in *Hiroshima mon amour* may obliterate the horror of Hiroshima by knowing it as something that exists in the intimacy between her and her Japanese male lover, as if this was all Hiroshima ever was—a site of America's bomb. What is Hiroshima?[3] Certainly the protests of the *hibakusha*—the "Hiroshima Bomb survivors"—are important conversations about war that should be worth mentioning. But Mama is made invisible in this struggle. Mama—and her town—were bombed daily. She wasn't in Hiroshima. But there was more destruction and fatality in the daily bomb raids in other towns, but Mama considers her story trivial and boring.

Internalized oppressions.[4] It makes for perfect silent citizens, who go to work and marry and have children and raise families. After all, everyone knows war is horrible. When it's finished, it's not worth speaking about. It's an event. A video game. A blip in an otherwise peaceful existence. Hiroshima, as meme, has been displaced from its cultural, historical and political contexts, is a space through which both Japan and the u.s. play their political games.

One way that Mama survived in America was to internalize the process of assimilation into immigrant identity. Mama's process began in the American military schools and moved into the direct occupation outside of the u.s.

*Oh, the reach. The reach.*

Mama became an outsider (immigrant, Oriental, Asian, Japanese, wife of a military man, "war bride," wife of a Negro American), in the u.s. Singing "The Star-Spangled Banner" after taking the citizenship test, and being reminded of just how much she was "other" in the process of becoming a citizen. Becoming a civilized something, civilizationalized.

Mama knew this "outside" very well. In Japan, she was an outsider as well.

Born in China, migrating to Japan, marrying an American serviceman who happened to be a black man—the ways in which people viewed Mama (viewed me, viewed Dad)—were prefigured by others (and ourselves as we internalized these processes). Without ever knowing us, people speak and hear us through their programming.

Survival is complex. Surviving barrages of preconfigured notions and opinions and concepts everyday is not typically viewed as an act of survival. But it is. It goes unrecognized. People attribute it to "personality" or dismiss it as a bygone (and unimportant) past because the present stands alone. When explaining this, people trivialize it, making it an even more violent survival that withstands assaults on its experiential meaning.

Postwar Japan lives on. For most of the Western world, that August Day in 1945 when the atomic bomb was dropped on Nagasaki and Hiroshima was a happy ending. War no more! Joy! A celebration of kisses! For the Japanese, and the entire Pacific region, it is a continuing struggle, perhaps changed by circumstances but persisting in new forms. Seeds planted. "New" Japan. A different u.s.

*New Mama, new America.*

## Seeds

THROUGH MANY OF MY OWN CHILDHOOD SUMMERS, Mama used to mention スイカの種 *suika no tane* (watermelon seeds). She couldn't be bothered to spit the seeds out whenever she ate them. I copied her and didn't spit out the seeds either.

She said they had to take the seeds out of her stomach through surgery. I was about six or seven years old when I first saw the five-inch vertical scar that ran below her bellybutton. I asked what it was. *Suika no tane.*

When I was little, Mama and I used to eat the Japanese watermelons to cool us during the summer. Sometimes we'd eat with some of Mama's friends, or my only other close friend, Ritchie, and his sister and mother. Those days, I wondered when my surgery to remove the watermelon seeds would be. I continued to wonder even after our family moved and moved—Ōme, Tachikawa, Murayama Heights, Tachikawa Air Base, Albuquerque, Kirtland Air Force Base, Halawa, Aiea, Tachikawa Air Base again, Murayama, Shōwa, then back to Albuquerque—all before I was sixteen years old. It was when we were living in Albuquerque that I ran to ask the mother of one of my Mexican American friends from school if I would need surgery from swallowing watermelon seeds.

She laughed and said, *"Pobrecito, no."*

The truth was difficult to process.

Just after my ninth birthday during a conversation over *genmai-cha* and *o-sembe* with Mama, she blurted:

*Futsū no umarekata ja nakatto no yo Furetto. Furetto ga umarerareru you ni koko shizutsu sareta no yo.*

(You weren't born in the regular way Fred. I was operated on here so you could be born. )

So I found out it wasn't watermelon seeds as I suspected, but a Caesarean birth. Then on this day, Mama lifted her loose-fitting shirt and I glanced once again at the vertical scar. When I stared, she turned to me, and leaned toward me as if sharing a secret:

*Ne-eh Fretto. Fretto wa mou ōkiku nattakara yuukedo, Fretto wa futago no ko datta no yo. Fretto ni toshi-ue no onē-san ga ita no yo. Shinjatta kedo....*

She turned her head to look away into the distance.

I swallowed.

Now that I was older, she says it's time to tell me that I was one of a pair of twins and that I had *a twin sister. And she died. Died.*

*Not only was I born through Caesarean, but there is now a dead twin sister in the room.*

*I am still an only child. But now my only child identity was not the same as just a moment before. I was only born alone because a sister had died.*

Fragments of the unknown become apparent. I felt relieved. Some things fell into a certain reasoning; perhaps it was a certain logic that offered comfort. I was an only child, but now I reasoned that a protector-twin had been watching over me, saving me from the few near-death experiences I've had. It could also explain the intense waves of loneliness and longing that coursed through me sporadically. Sometimes, in those moments, I thought I was going insane. Oh, *so it's my sister's presence and her absence.*

Mama rolled the extra-large T-shirt down from above her head to cover herself again. A big drawing of Betty Boop decorated the front. She had that shirt since before I was born. Now faded and worn-out, it still served her. *What was Betty Boop doing in Japan?*

The T-shirt's size allowed it to cover the polyester lime-green pants that fit loosely on her, the bottom cuffs stopping just above her ankles. Perhaps it was my old-fashioned Japaneseness or the way my mother raised me to read others and moments. I didn't press her to explain anything about my twin sister right then. I felt that it would be too painful for her.

On television was an episode of *Gilligan's Island.* It was the one where some white guy wore thick, oversized black-rimmed glasses with slits drawn as eyes onto the lenses. He had a long drooping Fu Manchu mustache, too, signifying that he was playing "Japanese." They found him in a tiny submarine lurking below the

African-American soldiers transferring to Guam for the Pacific War on August 4, 1945. *Photo courtesy of U.S. National Archives.*

water. He spoke like some kind of strange creature with some supposedly Japanese accent, yelling *"Banzai!"* in completely nonsensical contexts.

I seethed with anger while Mama scowled at the screen. Although she didn't understand the words (I barely did), she saw the Japanese soldier uniform and the strange cartoonish look of this guy. I changed the channel to *The Mickey Mouse Club*. Mama's pains in life were accumulations. Her brothers and friends that died in the war were not like the cartoon. But this was ten years later. Why were we seeing this now? At the time, I wasn't asking those kind of questions.

I half-watched Frankie Avalon and Annette Funicello on the screen with their big smiles and huge mouse ears. I asked Mama about Betty Boop. I had grown up with these characters, Betty and Bugs Bunny and Popeye both in Japan and in my early years in the U.S., and they were as natural as *onigiri* (rice balls), beef stew, *ochazuke* (green tea poured over rice and vegetables) and apple pie. American kids on the military bases in Japan enjoyed watching these cartoons but I was always disturbed. They often had episodes where Japanese pilots with buckteeth flew in puttering zero fighter-planes while Bugs Bunny or Popeye tried to kill them. And this was alongside the blackface shows and black mammies on screen, which minimized me and drove me to watch other television shows.

*My Dad is African American. Mama is from Japan.*

The laughter of my friends watching these non-white faces on television for the first two decades I lived in the U.S. confirmed and prolonged my inward feeling of being battered. Television. Slant-eyed Fu Manchus, black-faced white people, white kids (and their parents) laughing. The norm. I think that for most of these friends of mine, it was not just raucous enjoyment, but a confirmation of their superiority. Even as they ate Mama's juicy and crunchy *gyoza* (potstickers) or fried rice, which she often labored to make at the white boys' request.

Mama pulled out a scratch pad from one of the dresser drawers and drew a beautiful and perfect Betty Boop.

> *Ano toki minna Amerika no manga ya ironna mono o gakkō de narawasareta no yo. Kurisumasu purezento to ka...*
> (In those times we were required to learn American things like cartoons and Christmas presents...)

Mama and I smiled at each other, enjoying the drawing. *Jōzu janai, Mama!*

I was struck that year with the question of her silent suffering. They had to draw Betty Boop and learn what December 25 meant, and who Santa Claus was in the context of a new Japanese holiday. It wasn't as though Mama cringed. She loved it. But there were things she needed to negate about herself in order to enjoy it.

Many American viewpoints in textbooks and fiction have described the Japanese only as willing and wanting. Yes, after a war where everything was decimated and people were left impoverished, we want the new, the alive, and to be empowered. At the same time, Mama didn't totally love her own imperial army and the life they lived. Self-hatred and progress are often related. There is also the matter of organizing, strategizing, and implementing policy (which becomes "culture") in order to create something that benefits the overlords (internalized colonization). The leaders of Japan sought to benefit themselves and the U.S. The U.S., after all, didn't want to continue with its Japanese-as-enemy structure. After defeating them in war, the U.S. wanted Japan to be a pawn in their quest for global dominance. The business of the Cold War was just over the horizon. The Korean War would benefit Japan in more ways than one.

To master the Pacific, Japan was vital. America sought to educate the Japanese with American ways and structures; American but not completely. Liberalism requires that people maintain their own cultural identities. America, of course, decided what that would mean for the Japanese.

Education was most important in making a "new" civilized people.[5] Japaneseness became more intertwined with American values and systems. After all, what else is occupation for but to discipline and construct? What did Dad think of all this as a young black soldier? Did he know about my twin sister and her death? He never mentioned to me that I had a sister. Ever. What other things did I not know about life? My sister? Did *he* even know?

My sister died in the 1950s.
Postwar babies died.
But did they just "die?"
Or does that only take the sting off of the fact that many babies were killed?

I don't think mothers should be blamed for the death of their babies, although they have been in most countries. I think it comes from ghosts, histories, and the conditions of living that emerge through our institutions which shape us, and it is our choice to either adopt or resist them. In many cases, these conditions only appear in statistical manuals, case studies and historical books as anomalies and

Tōkyō in 1945, after nights of American firebombing. On the first night of bombing, over 100,000 people died and fires from the bombs continued for days, as was planned by the Americans. *Photo courtesy of U.S. National Archives.*

sorrows. But in life, in front of our eyes, in our rooms, these things are made to happen and they do. How do we participate?

The killing of the young has a history in all parts of the world. In Japanese history, most scholars note that this began intensely during the Tokugawa period (1603-1868). The ghosts of that system moved into the Meiji period, and into the imperial war-time period, which continues through the present. At times of poverty and societal breakdown, parental entitlement connects to a child's life in a way that questions and links survival and death.

*Death and the afterlife also have different meanings in different societies.*

In Japan, the mother's bond with the child remains intact after death. Death-inducing poisons and certain kinds of *shiatsu* pressures would drop the babies[6] from the mother's body, practices administered by their mothers or grandmothers or midwives. While it was sometimes desired by the mothers, it was also a form of child oppression in many cases, as these children are under the complete dominion of the parent and family who wish them dead. And sometimes, even after these babies were born, some mothers could not care for them, and would abuse them. Other mothers, even as they wanted to keep and raise their children, lost their babies to disease and malnutrition. Death wishes and killing are integral aspects of nations. America and Europe's socioeconomic rise in the world came at the expense of Native American children during its campaigns of genocide and assimilation, as well as through the ownership of African slave-babies and their parents, along with other forms of labor, genocide, and societal exclusion. Japan reproduced these forms in different ways, and for different motives.

Throughout history, many babies have been killed by all kinds of communities and peoples for various reasons. Japan had its particular systems like any nation. As part of a country, a cultural milieu, we determine how to survive. We all create an increasingly recognizable world where equality and inequality become much more clearly defined by the markers of global success.[7] The child, the mother, and the community play particular roles as objects to control. *Who lives? Who dies? Who decides?* And how are these decisions made, overtly or covertly? After the war, many women endured complications from ill-health during their months of pregnancy, from searching for food during and after the bombings. Some of them lived with trace chemicals in their bodies. And being alone with child was not something a mother announced.

In Mama's case, she was carrying two *ainoko* (love child). Black bred. Japanese bred. Enemy bred, American bred. Incomplete. Too complete. Mutt. Impure. All reminders of war and defeat that inevitably was not Japanese. While not all Japanese or Americans thought these things, its actions speak for themselves: aligning with Jim Crow laws that American soldiers carried into Occupation and practiced on Japanese soil for all to see (and learn). Women who carried Jim Crow-in-the-flesh children of the enemy-now-occupier represented an ugly contamination which threatened a "pure" culture that the Japanese now envisioned.

The way we see pregnant women or the unborn child represents a dominant norm. Both in Japan and throughout the world, the anti-black racism of Jim Crow U.S.A. that became transnationalized after the war made Mama's resulting pride and fears about being pregnant with American Black Japanese babies,was immense. Mama gave birth to me and sister here, into this space and time. What did this silence, before she told me, mean? What would knowing my dead twin's existence mean? Was it only to forget that she existed, or that Mama gave birth to us, or that Dad's existence made this? For Mama, it was not only a sense of being a victim of these societal norms, it was a practice of defiance.

Did Mama pray for my sister at a Mizuko Kuyō? Was sister alive for a while and I just don't remember? Was she dead at birth? Was she aborted and dead before she was born? In the hospital? Questions upon questions. I asked her. Mama was defiant.

> *Mizuko Kuyō? Doushite sonna tokoro ni iku hitsuyou ga aru no? Sonna tokoro ni iku mon ka!*
> (Why would I have a reason to go to such a place? I wouldn't dare go to such a place!)

What did her insistent and strong response mean? I believed I had only asked a simple question about her attending a ceremony for my sister. Why did she respond with how she wouldn't dare go to such a place? How and when did my twin sister die? Why? What was Mama defying? What did honoring my dead sister at a Japanese ceremony for dead children mean? Was it something else?

*You saw nothing. Nothing.* 冒

# CHAPTER NOTES

1. Kai Grieg, *The War Children of the World,* is a report of the War and Children Identity Project (Bergen, 2001). Accessed September 19, 2015. http://www.academia.edu/2189623/The_war_children_of_the_world

2. *Hiroshima mon amour (Hiroshima My Love)* (二十四時間の情事 *Nijūyojikan'nojōji, Twenty-four-hour affair*) is a 1959 drama film directed by French film director Alain Resnais, with a screenplay by Marguerite Duras. It is the documentation of an intensely personal conversation between a French-Japanese couple about memory and forgetfulness. It was a major catalyst for the Left Bank Cinema, making innovative use of miniature flashbacks to create a nonlinear story line.

3. The word, city, and place "Hiroshima" written in English uses this spelling. In the Japanese language, there are three ways to write "Hiroshima" using three different scripts. I have chosen the katakana script (ヒロシマ)which is used for non-Japanese words, often by anti-nuclear and anti-war activists in Japan to denote a "foreignness" and alienation from a non-local perspective. This notion challenges historical and popular imaginations of Hiroshima, rejecting the memorializing of war-criminals and imperial Japan as part of a glorious and desired past. This is expressed quite eloquently in the book by Lisa Yoneyama, *Hiroshima Traces: Time, Space, and the Dialectics of Memory* (Berkeley: University of California Press, 1999), 48-49.

4. For more on internalized oppression, see Ann E. Cudd, *Analyzing Oppression* (London, UK: Oxford University Press, 2006); or Mary Elizabeth Hobgood, *Dismantling Privilege: An Ethics of Accountability* (Cleveland, OH: Pilgrim Press, 2009).

5. Naoko Kato, *War Guilt and Postwar Japanese Education,* Master's dissertation (University of British Columbia, 2002), is a good example on Japanese education and Americanization.

6. In traditional Japanese, orosu (堕ろす) is a popular term for aborting a fetus. It can also sound out the verb "to lower," or "to drop, let go."

7. My perception and definition of globalization and occupation comes from various subaltern studies, and feminist, post-structural and, postcolonial thinkers and workers. My insistence and take on this came from Arjun Appadurai, *Fear of Small Numbers: An Essay on the Geography of Anger* (Durham, NC: Duke University Press, 2006), and Dirk A. Moses, *Empire, Colony, Genocide: Conquest, Occupation, and Subaltern Resistance in World History* (NY: Berghahn, 2008).

# CHAPTER 6

# Ghosts

"To get to the ghost and the ghost's story, it is necessary to understand how the past, even if it is just the past that flickered by a moment before, can be seized in an instant, or how it might seize you first."

— Avery Gordon, *Ghostly Matters: Haunting and the Sociological Imagination*[1]

### 1970

*"Oi! Hiroshima wa omae ga yattanda yo!"*
(You're the one that fucked Hiroshima!)

A Japanese man said this to me at a Shinjuku bookstore that Mama and I frequented.

Mama screamed at him, *"Damare koitsu me!" (Shut the fuck up!)*

We hurried out.[2]

### 1980

"You motherfuckers attacked us in Pearl Harbor," a white guy blurts out at me.

I turned and said: "My Dad's American. You saying we attacked ourselves?"

The guy sneered and walked away.

THESE ARE NOT RANDOM DIALOGUES. They are part of a process meant to dictate a kind of dominance as "fact." Because this self-propelling dominant positioning must be constantly established, it

51

wounds, invisibilizes, and sequesters the "other" outside of their existing self-definitions to claim their countries, nations, groups, colors, and ways of living. Whatever actions, thoughts, legislations, policies, weapons or cultural forms are used, they are intended for a particular effect. Certain resistances and forms may arise in relation to those tactics that maneuver towards dominance in different contexts. *Blowback.*[3]

> *American authorities also insisted on a legal system that accorded special status to* u.s. *nationals, both during and after the formal Occupation, much as colonial codes discriminated between citizens and subjects.*[4]

Citizens and subjects are not just bodies. The *local* represents a relationship between what has been displaced and demoted, and subsequently subjected to terror and violence, and the beautification and prioritizing of things named, elevated, and enforced as "good" and desirable. The engines of war that reorganize, recreate or maintain, and intensify wealth and status have created new cultural struggles in their attempts to reorder the world into predetermined homogeneity. My body carries this memory-as-reminder-of-pasts in others' eyes, but it also represents an intimate aspect of what has carried over as heritage, love, and strength. Carried over as awkward, hurtful moments, which need to be ignored, acknowledged, believed (or not) with sheer grit and determination. Silence and loathing. *Surviving.*

There are some moments that linger in our lives. People, thoughts, ideas, feelings, and compulsions tumble into and through our lives, and we cannot forget—much less cut—them from our bodies. Sometimes we don't even recognize them. We begin calling them our identity or labeling it in others. Loss becomes something else by name and look and smell, but nevertheless remains a *loss.* Those losses are the mountains and rivers that shape us.[5] Pearl Harbor, as a place and idea, and Hiroshima, as a place and idea, run through me in a way that makes me a *target.* This is not something I created.

Should we learn from history? From Hiroshima? From Pearl Harbor? The happy link between learning and suffering is not always clean, if ever. Ghosts linger to tell us, to teach us, so that we will never forget; to discover and learn about things that have felt mysterious or unrecognizably normal. We may discover things that are still silent. We are pre-occupied with happiness and trauma.

### San Francisco, January 2011

I walk in the mission district in San Francisco on a drizzly day and turn into my favorite café, the Café La Boheme. Former Central American revolution-aries and Asian American, white, and Latin American leftists argue in Spanglish over the fate of Cuba and the global economic crisis. Writing groups and chess games dot and flourish between the different tables. I order a *cafe americano*, and they hand me the porcelain white cup / *Made in China* / full to the brim. It's perfect in this chilly winter weather. In front of me, a slender Korean woman in her twenties with a thick accent orders a mocha latte while the barista behind the counter begins preparing her order. I chat with a customer about his upbringing in Mexico, and his decision to migrate here for better money, which his family relies upon each month. He tells me his family had many troubles. *I quickly, and wrongfully, imagined ICE raids on the border. How did Mama and I get here?* What is entailed in this "getting here?" *What is the history?*

On my laptop, I open an article from the *Japan Times Online* about a Black Japanese man, Demian Akhan, who was raised in the Elizabeth Saunders Home for Mixed-Race Children in Kanagawa Prefecture during late 1940s Japan before being adopted into an American family, and now lives in New York.[6]

> *In some ways, aren't most of us, as Mama and I are, whether we acknowledge it or not, "orphans of history?"*[7]

Words like "orphan" arise within a certain construction of society, and differ from place to place. In some nations, this concept never existed until recently. The conditions must be created for it to make sense, and concepts are conditional upon the sense they make. Living in an orphanage, exiled from the idea of a nuclear family ideal, lends new meaning to the term orphan when we consider how we are imprisoned by that idea of what it means for a "nuclear family" to be elevated to a position of moral and social superiority.

Technically, I was not an orphan. My childhood in a nuclear family was intact and privileged when most were not, but it was not without the vicissitudes of my life and those times. As Mr. Akhan is Black Japanese, and of a similar generation born in Japan, I became interested in his story, something rarely seen in magazines and journals or on television. I was happy to see a mirror of myself without it being a case-study in some psychology journal or history textbook that relied on controlled ideas.

That particular orphanage for mixed-race children and babies in Japan after World War II received quite a bit of publicity because its founder, Miki Sawada, labored tirelessly so she could receive the necessary funds to get these children adopted into American and European homes.[8] They (we), the mixed-raced children,

Miki Sawada (center), founder of the Elizabeth Saunders Home for Mixed-Race Children in Oiso, Japan, with Amerasian orphaned children on an outing, circa 1950. Inspired by the story of the "Good Samaritan," Sawada founded the orphanage in 1948 to help mixed-race children, and named it in honor of her first donor. *Photo courtesy of Elizabeth Saunders Home, Japan.*

were all called *ainoko* (love-child, or child of an illegitimate union) or *konketsu-ji*—a supposedly more scientific word for mixed blood, which implied that mixed blood Japanese were not really Japanese and were disgusting alien objects.[9] The U.S. didn't want "mixed bloods" either. It still had its strong anti-miscegenation laws and cultural practices in place. During those times, and perhaps continuing even today, we—the so-called mixed bloods—were dangerous little bodies that threatened both Japanese and American purity and superiorities. Japan linked to and adopted its occupier's racism as we, the so-called mixing of two purities, were a threat to white supremacy in both places.

But this is still only a partial picture. Many American families wanted these children. Mr. Akhan says that the family that adopted him had to push Congress and adoption agencies three times before he could join his family. In an article about his visit to Japan in 2009, he recalled his childhood, and how he made peace with the struggle with his heritage and the past before eventually feeling empowered by it. Then it dawned on me. I was reading about him as if he was totally different from me. Although I was not adopted and raised by my family, those same anti-miscegenation laws affected me as well, not to mention Mama and Dad.

> *Ne-eh, Mama, onē-chan no namae nandatta no, oboeteru?*
> *mmm....nan dattan darou . . . . . oboetenai.*

Mama doesn't remember sister's name when I asked. She wonders what my dead sister's name was, trying to remember if she even named her.

> *Why does she remember the name of the planes that bombed her—the B-29s—but not my sister's name? But soon I would learn more. There are reasons.*

THE TRADITION OF DISPLACING histories and identities in the Pacific goes way back. Without minimizing each region's internal struggles—massacres and civil wars, genocides and the crushing of spirits and bodies—forming communal unity or nationalism usually requires a threat from the outside. Many in-between people live the reality of "Western" encroachment. So many controls construct the process of remembering and forgetting. In many cases, we refuse those memories because they cause us too much pain.

Before the Americans arrived in Japan to occupy it, the French, the British, the Dutch, the Germans, the Spanish and the Portuguese, all came to Japan to steal, exploit, plunder, rape, and legislate it, which created the ghosts of time. Before their arrival, there was no "map," and no such thing as "Pacific" until the first wave of Europeans arrived. What do these spiritual-historical entitlements to annex, displace, ruin, and kill do to people and their community? Or if it is carried elsewhere? Where do sadness and resentment reside? *Everywhere.*

When France came and transformed and colonized Indochina, another so-called "uncivilized" jungle of riches, many local women bore French, Cambodian, Laotian, and Vietnamese babies. When the Americans came to set up bases and run secret wars in Laos and Cambodia, American mixed blood babies were born. Unlike the Americans, however, the French mandated mixed-race children to be shipped to France. The jungle and countrysides of the Southeast Asian peninsula were combed for any mixed-race baby, white, black, or brown. The mothers had no say so in whether or not they wanted to keep their children.[10] Desperate cries rang throughout the country. French civilian, religious, and military personnel restrained Indochinese mothers as they removed their children. They were being used to prevent "traitors" from asserting that these mixed-race children were "French." Of course it didn't work out for either those mothers or the French. As is always the case, the children were either branded exotic, and used as mediators between colonial empires and their colonies, or as disgusting creatures. These ghosts continue to live today.

There are those children sired by Americans in Southeast Asia, saving their money for tickets or for traffickers in Thailand, Vietnam and Cambodia, in hopes of finding their fathers.[11]

*There is a companion missing.*

*My sister is here.* She has been here all along. She speaks to me, but I had not been listening. But she is not alone. There are many. They relate to me in a different way. They speak some things through me now. Time is but a chorus of ghosts we create to escape what we know we've killed, or want to face, or learn from.

"She sacrificed her life for you," Mama tells me.
A burden. Heavy and constant. For what possible reason?
She—my sister. She dreams us.
All this must be a dream that she dreams. 冒

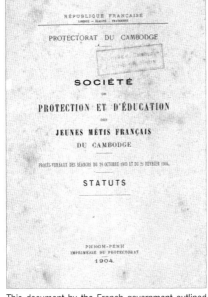

This document by the French government outlined their policies on the Métis (persons of mixed-race) in Indochina. *Courtesy of the National Archives of Cambodia.*

Children were forcibly taken from their homes and families in what is now Cambodia, Laos, and Vietnam, and into assimilation schools like this one in Cambodia. *Photo courtesy of the National Archives of Cambodia.*

1. Avery F. Gordon, *Ghostly Matters: Haunting and the Sociological Imagination* (Minneapolis: University of Minnesota Press, 2008).

2. I experienced this kind of situation a number of times, and was actually relieved that many people of American and Japanese descent have had similar experiences. See Teresa Kay Williams, Michael C. Thornton, "Social Construction of Ethnicity Versus Personal Experience: The Case of Afro-Amerasians," *Journal of Comparative Family Studies* 29, no. 2 (1988): 255.

3. "Blowback" is used to point to cultural realities of intended and unintended consequences of covert operations suffered by a civilian population. Its effects typically show themselves as random acts of political violence without a discernible, direct cause because the public—in whose name the operations were sanctioned—are ignorant of these secret attacks that provoke retaliation (counter-attack). I see parallels of this perspective in interpersonal relationships, where consequences of actions between groups and peoples, especially those differing in positions of power and hierarchy (known and unknown), are played out.

4. Sarah Kovner, *Occupying Power: Sex Workers and Servicemen in Postwar Japan* (CA: Stanford University Press, 2012), 9.

5. Zen Master Dōgen, *Mountains and Rivers Sutra* (山水經). My thinking is taken from this and his larger work, *Shōbōgenzō* (正法眼蔵). Compiled during the thirteenth century, Zen Master Dōgen (1200-1235) points to the reality after realizing the true nature of the self and reality as one, according to Zen Buddhism, when ecology/self are akin to solid mountains and flowing rivers. That moment when we perceive and are the universe, or "reality," thoroughly integrated, where everything becomes completely themselves, their "identities-already-connected, so they become themselves." There are many translations and versions of this particular sutra, and of the larger *Shōbōgenzō* collection. My favorite version is by Kazuaki Tanahashi, tr., *Moon in a Dewdrop: Writings of Zen Master Dōgen* (New York: North Point Press, 1995).

6. Mariko Kato, "Occupation Orphan Traces Roots," *Japan Times,* June 6, 2009. Accessed September 19, 2015. http://search.japantimes.co.jp/print/nn20090606f1.html

7. From "Book of the Times" by John Leonard, *New York Times,* April 23, 1981, a review of Salman Rushdie's, *Midnight's Children* (London: Jonathan Cape, 1991).

8. There are only two books in English, that I know of, that covers the Elizabeth Saunders Home for Mixed-Race Children, as well as information about Miki Sawada, the founder of the school: a dissertation by Robert A. Fish, *The heiress and the love children: Sawada Miki and the Elizabeth Saunders Home for mixed blood orphans in postwar Japan,* PhD dissertation (University of Hawai'i at Manoa, 2002), and a hard-to-find book by Elizabeth Anne Hemphill, *The Least*

*of These: Miki Sawada and Her Children* (Trumble, CT: Weatherhill, 1981). There are many articles and theses, however, that mention the institution or Miki Sawada.

9. This slightly differs from American thinking on inclusion/exclusion dynamics based on individual liberty. The Japanese intensify the notion of *naka/soto* or *uchi/soto* (中 / 外)inside/outside or insider/foreigner through systems of caste and clan. The notion of insider, the *naka* was constructed and solidified as an aspect of a "Japaneseness" during centuries of early nation-building, including contact with Western literatures from colonial periods up to the present.

10. For some of the best historical accounts in English of the French Indochina, and their actions and policies regarding mixed-race children during their colonial reign in Southeast Asia, see Christina Firpo, "Crises of Whiteness and Empire in Colonial Indochina: The Removal of Abandoned Eurasian Children From the Vietnamese Milieu, 1890-1956" *Journal of Social History* 43, no. 3 (2010): 587-613.

11. One of the few good books on the mixed-race issue in Indochina is by Emmanuelle Saada, *Empire's Children: Race, Filiation, and Citizenship in the French Colonies* (IL: University of Chicago Press, 2012). While Black-Viet Metis are not covered too broadly here, it does provide some pertinent information. Also, there is a touching documentary on this topic, *Indochina: Traces of a Mother*, directed by Idrissou Mora-Kpai (NY: Third World Newsreel, 2011), which has won quite a few awards.

# CHAPTER 7

# Apples in 1946 Shōwa Year 21
# リンゴ 1946年 昭和２１年

リンゴの花びらガ風に散ったよな
Apple petals, scattering into the winds

月夜に, 月夜に, そおっと　ええ…
into the night of the moon, into the night of the moon, softly, eh….

すがる娘は泣いたとさ…
They say the clinging young maiden cries…

美空ひばり、　リンゴ追分 [1]

— Misora Hibari, from the song,
*Ringo Oiwake ("Forked Road in the Apple Orchard")*

*I was walking on the veranda that wrapped along the edges of the garden, playing with my paddle and ball-on-a-string as I did in the mornings. The Noriko Awaya 淡谷のり子 song "Wakare no Buruuzu" 別れのブルーズ ("Break-up Blues"), played on the Victrola turntable. The chirping of morning birds, and the fragrance of cherry blossoms pierced the air. The huge, radiant deep red-gold apples dangling from the tree looked fun and smelled so good. The sliding doors seemed especially light this morning. I heard the faint sound of conversation along with the smell of genmai-cha and o-sembe. I softly approached.*

*Kā-san (stepmother) and her friend were talking and laughing. I almost never heard stepmother laugh. I always thought of her as a general, telling everyone what to do all the time like the kempeitai (military police) that were always in the neighborhood, keeping us safe. The only time*

*I saw Kā-san soften was when father came home. I secretly hated her. But I wanted to please her. Please love me. Please love me. Just once, I wanted her to hold me and say that she cared for me, that I wasn't as stupid as she always said I was.*

*When I calmed my ball-and-paddle down and held it against my side, sliding onto my knees to crouch by the sliding door, I overheard how they admired the apples that were on the tree in the garden. They were talking about all kinds of different dishes they could make from the apples, not just savoring their juiciness after plucking them from the ground after they had fallen. I suddenly thought that I needed to please her and see her smile at me!*

*I ran along, then jumped off of the veranda and into the green garden. I lifted my legs and grabbed onto the tree, hoisting my little legs around the tree, beginning the climb to fetch the apples for Kā-san. I was climbing up and up and up, breathing hard, climbing, grabbing, reaching. I had been drooling but I didn't know it. I had to get those apples. I would bring a bunch of them to Okā-san and she would be happy. I was now in reach of three. Let's see, I'd shake the branches and let the beautiful apples fall. I shook the branches, rustling and shaking. They were falling to the ground, not fast enough. Oh, fall faster, more and more. Elegantly they fell. I shook the branches with all my might. There should be more than enough to please us. Now I need to get down.*

*I froze. I couldn't move! Why couldn't I move?*

*I didn't know how to get down. I had gotten so far up but didn't remember how I did it. Now I didn't know where my short legs would reach or where my hands should grab to return to the ground. I was scared and desperate. Then I had to yell, "Tasukete! Tasukete!"*

*Nothing.*

*I screamed louder, "Tasukete!"*

*Soon I saw Kā-san and her friend running from the house and slipping into their outdoor slippers as they came off the veranda to see me, calling for help. I kept on shouting.*

She said, *"Damari-nasai! Kono baka na onna-no-ko wa."* (Shut up, you stupid little girl!)

I dreaded returning to the ground. Two men leaned a ladder against the tree and one of them told me to hold on to his neck and shoulders. He grabbed me and I held onto him for my life. I didn't want him to let me go. We descended from the tree. I tried to catch my breath between my sobs. Okā-san was, as usual, apologetic to the neighbors.

Bowing, apologizing for inconveniencing them, asked them if they wanted snacks and tea. The men left with a smile, feeling satisfied that they had helped the women in distress. As soon as they left the garden and closed the wooden gate behind them, she leaned into me to scold.

*"Kono baka na ko honto ni Ikareteru no ne."* (You're such a little idiot. You must be retarded).

She grabbed my ear and pulled. I cried out from pain. She then dragged me into the house as my little legs tried to move along. First, she took the cigarette that she had been smoking and pointed it toward me, pushing it into the right of my chest, twisting and burning me. I screamed. She then shoved me into the closet where the futon (beds) were kept, my body scrunched up between the closet wall and the shelving. The door slammed shut and I heard the scuffling of metal. She locked me in.

*"Konna baka na onna-no-ko wa hito ni wa miseru no ga honto ni hazukashii. Soko ni inasai."* (It's so embarrassing to have such a stupid little girl be seen by others. Stay there.)

In the darkness, I cried. I couldn't stop crying. It hurt so much. What I thought would please my mother became something I was punished for. I was so stupid. Why didn't she love me? Why couldn't I be the good little girl that she would admire and be kind to? It seemed like no day passed that I was not crying in a dark place. I could barely breathe while I sobbed. I became so tired. Soon I fell asleep.

When father returned later that evening, Okā-san related the whole story to him. Father felt sympathy for me, but scolded me for not thinking. Thinking *about what? All I was trying to do was make Kā-san love me. Father never knew I was put into the closet. I never said a word. It was normal for me to be put there sometimes. I felt so ashamed that I was glad she died while I was in America. I didn't shed a tear in front of Father.*

≋ ≋ ≋

THERE ARE DIFFERENT WARS. Sometimes related, sometimes not. They change place and position, hearts and landscapes. Women have fought and continue to fight wars against the legacies of child labor and trafficking, marriage dowries, and female servitude amid Japan's transition from feudal to imperial to postwar liberties. Cultures, genders, sexual relationships, and desires often combine and mutate into systems of assimilation. The concept of a single and uniformed Japaneseness in the Meiji era into the Tokugawa period did not prioritize a single-ethnicity nation, but a Japanese nation consisting of Taiwanese, Koreans, and Okinawans, among others. The single ethnic Japanese identity only became more acute, omnipresent and more intensely racialized before World War II and into the postwar. And the idea of America for most Japanese meant white. *White supremacy.*

Even as they tried to reinvent themselves as pure descendants from some natural mythology, Japanese viewed the U.S. as a country of mongrels with different racial groups intermingled together. The consequences of not doing so themselves meant being redefined by Western powers, since they had been previously defined as inferior.

The Japanese had to fight for their own vision to match the European and American images of superiority. These ideas persisted in new ways. Nations need race unification, or run the risk of being splintered, making it easier to be defeated, redefined and dominated. As a mother traversing through life, how did Mama make sense of things? She refused a life of subservience, something she foresaw in the Japan that was promised to her after the occupation. The only men she was willing to serve, at first, were her American husband, and me, her son. Freedom from bondage was her desire. But freedom always seemed to come at a cost and with different chains. 目

## CHAPTER NOTES

1. Misora Hibari (1937-1989) was and remains one of the greatest diva-extraordinaire entertainers of Japan. A national icon, Hibari was a powerful singer, actress and dancer from Japan's
wartime and postwar era until her death. In some people's eyes (including my own), we often
speak of her performances as an otherworldly experience. She almost single-handedly reflected
the mythology of Japanese national self-image through entertainment and wielded quite a bit
of power during the Shōwa period (1926–1989) into the Japan of today. In the latter years
after her death, it was disclosed that her paternal heritage was Korean—a fact some Japanese
vehemently protest.

# CHAPTER 8

# Names

"She makes complete her duration. As others have made complete theirs: rendered incessant, obsessive myth, rendered immortal their acts of leisure to examine whether the parts false the parts real according to History's revision."

— Theresa Hak Kyung Cha, *Dictee*[1]

WHEN I WAS IN MY MID-TO-LATE TWENTIES, I lived in Colorado for a time. It was the beginning of big hair, Cyndi Lauper, and Depeche Mode. Green Colorado, with its snow-capped mountains, beckoned me. It was a few months before my deepest, longest, and most traumatizing depression. Denver, for me, was the place where I would begin to really face who I was. Until then, I was plugging along, ignoring accumulated feelings and thoughts, pretending to be normal and strong, continuously recreating myself after failures and successes. Even though I was a well-known volleyball coach, and had trained athletes who received athletic scholarships, there was an emptiness. Success, for me, was being disturbed by ghosts I could not yet name.

In those days, I tried to visit Mama in Albuquerque as often as I could, about once or twice a year. On one of my visits that autumn, I sat listening to Mama and her friend Keiko-san laughing and chatting as I floated in and out of the room. Keiko-san had been my occasional caretaker and babysitter when I was young. She, too, had married an African American soldier, my Dad's best friend. But soon, he either died or divorced Keiko. I never found out. She was a connection to my life and Mama's, even now in Albuquerque, thousands of lifetimes away from postwar Japan. So Mama and Keiko caught up. It was comforting to hear them, transporting me back in time fragments.

65

Mama's immigrant ID card, laminated, legitimating her presence in the U.S. *Fredrick Cloyd Family Archive.*

As I was passing from my room into the small living room where Mama and Keiko-san were sitting, I was puzzled to hear Mama tell Keiko-san, *"Honto no tanjōbi wa shi-gatsu ja nakute Juu-ichi gatsu nano yo…"*

*WHAT?*

Mama's birthday wasn't in April as I had thought and celebrated all these years. Her birthday was actually in November. What?

I asked, *"Nani? Mama no tanjōbi wa shi-gatsu dattanjanakatta no?"*

She didn't wait for me to ask further. *"Mama no honto no namae wa Emiko nano. Hora, Dēri ga itsumo Emiko to yonda deshō? Kiyoko wa shinda one-e-chan no namae yo."*
(My real name is Emiko, really. Remember your Daddy would call me Emiko? Kiyoko is my dead older sister's name.)

Kiyoko, which Mama calls herself today, is then not really her name. I sat down as Mama continued, glancing at me.

*"Soshite, motto chiisai toki, itsumo An-na, An-na to yobarete ita no yo….An-na…An-na…"*
(And when I was even smaller, I was called An-na, An-na.)

Longingly she caressed that name: *An-na. An-na. Anna.* She repeated that a few more times. Keiko-san sat quietly, nodding empathetically. I could tell that she also had secrets that perhaps matched Mama's.

I had seen Mama practicing writing her name in English in my earliest memories, *K-i-y-o-k-o. K-i-y-o-k-o* over and over for six months. She started practicing way before I was born when she first learned that she needed a birth certificate to marry an American G.I. She practiced so she could learn to become her older sister and marry my Dad. *Kore, Mama no namae na no yo. (This is your Mama's name),* she'd tell me as I watched her write that name. I used to think she practiced only because she needed to write a different language, but it was more than that. She had to learn to become her sister. Her third name. Law, war, nation, woman and spirit intertwined. She became her sister's ghost. Maybe even her dreams. Death—her sister's death—was Mama's freedom. Anna…Emiko…Kiyoko. Step by step. Today, though, she says Kiyoko is her "real" name.

Her maternal grandfather was an Austro-Hungarian missionary, sent to China where he met her grandmother. They agreed to name their daughter Anna, but the war forced them to erase that name to guard them from being killed or ostracized by the Chinese. In Japan, Mama was *Emiko, no longer Anna.* Then she was Kiyoko, her sister. I called her Mama.

Her red-tinted hair was often blamed for the pain she suffered in China and Japan. When her sister died during the American bombings, so did the birth papers of almost the entire family. In order to marry an American, Mama had to assume the identity of the only papers that survived—her sister's. How many exclusions did Mama endure? Her own name displaced once again.

Whenever I visited Mama in our house in Albuquerque, we would fall back into comforting routines. This usually meant shopping at K-mart or at the mall, complete with eating in the food court: a Chinese restaurant, Pup-n-Taco, Vip's Big Boys, Lota Burger, or Dairy Queen. Mama would have one or two of her friends over, either to go shopping with us, or to sit and talk at home over *ocha* or Pepsi-Cola with *osembe* or Lay's Ruffles potato chips, or any kind of *otsumami* (finger food). *Kurimanju* (chestnut paste cakes) were my personal favorite. These things could only be found at this tiny little Japanese market in northern Albuquerque. As the years wore on, that market closed and we had less and less of my soul food.

Mama said laughingly that she was glad she was a November-born Scorpio and an Ox, and not her sister, who was an April-born Aries. Her interpretation was that Aries was a hard sign for a girl to be—too brash and assertive for the Japan of her times. I still sometimes forget to call her to wish her a happy birthday in November, rather than in April. Sometimes I do both. So where is her sister now?

"Hey, Amy!"

"C'mon, Amy!'"

Now I knew why Dad or Uncle Teruo alternated calling her Kiyo-chan and Emi-chan. The names were no longer a mystery, only ghosts that live. I began to understand that names are not just words, not just a single identity or idea.

*Silence.*

History is carried in names. Worlds.

They mark both, at the same space and time, a presence and absence. 冒

## CHAPTER NOTES

1. Theresa Hak Kyung Cha, *Dictee* (Berkeley: University of California Press, 2009). Initially published in 1982, *Dictee* is the best-known work of the versatile and important Korean American artist Theresa Hak Kyung Cha (1951-1982). A classic work of autobiography that transcends the self, *Dictee* is the story of several women: the Korean revolutionary Yu Guan Soon, Joan of Arc, Demeter and Persephone, Cha's mother Hyung Soon Huo (a Korean born in Manchuria to first-generation Korean exiles), and Cha herself. Cha died a week after the publication of *Dictee*; she was raped and killed, and suffered from a violent death.

# CHAPTER 9

# Unending July 1996 Heisei Year 8
## 終わらない平成8年7月

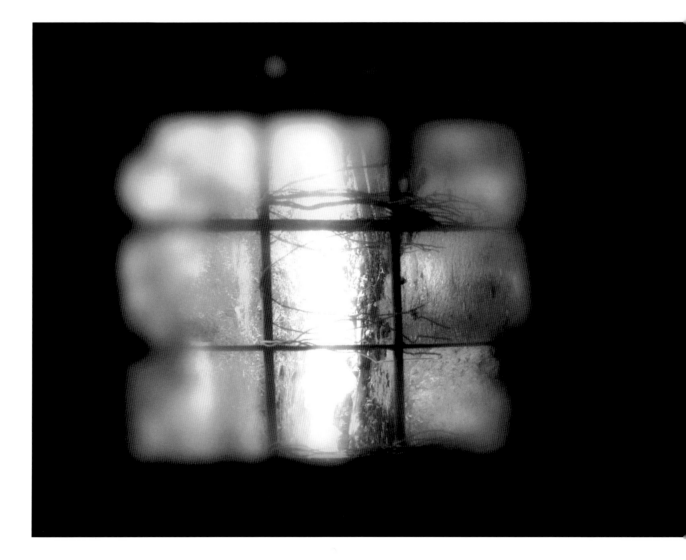

"So when you die of cancer, they don't write the name, just the number. When they do their reports on the people, they don't write our names, they only write our numbers."

— Quote by one of the many Rogelapese women effected by the Marshall Islands nuclear tests conducted by the U.S. between 1946 to 1962[1]

WHEN NORIHIKO KATŌ WROTE ABOUT war memory in Japan, he spoke of the political dynamics in postwar Japan that created a psychically schizophrenic and irresolvable contradiction from the legacy of defeat — incomplete spaces and times of mourning — to the bitter ironies of occupation *(sensō no kioku)*.[2] I felt Kato-san's words echoing in my head, with only Mama and I hearing them. *Echoes echo.* Are echoes heard? I don't know, but these sounds are thousands of years old.[3] The ghosts are speaking and I'm recording. When Mama is quiet, phantoms speak.

Even though our New Mexican adobe stucco house kept much of the heat outside, it was still oven-hot inside. Enough for a black guy, I often joked to myself, to have a big problem with this heat. After all, my African ancestors passed me this skin, right? I'm supposed to be better off in the heat. But this heat was like a furnace.

When I think of where Mama and I lived at this moment, it is ironic and twisted. This stucco house, this Albuquerque, is just two hours away from the Los Alamos laboratories. Los Alamos, where the great scientific minds of weaponry, democracy, and progress built and tested the atomic bomb that was designed to kill and devastate Japan, my mother's sister, and a Japanese sense of self. We live there — in the spaces between the bomb of

America's glory and Japan's devastation. An engineered "Pacific." Making Dad, Mama and me.

Yes—twisted by links. And living with links. Dad, Mama, and me, family, history—intimacies of mass destruction nurtured by the United States—1944, 1945, 1953, 1962 with Hiroshima, Nagasaki, Los Alamos, Enewetak, Bikini Atoll, Aga Point, Tonga, other Pacific places, peoples.[4] American soldiers and scientists polluted by their employers' radiation link with the lives of islanders and Asians, and Public Law 101-426—The Radiation Exposure Compensation Act of 1990. But Law 101—was cosmetic, hiding the absence of care for people and cultures.[5] Empire identities wind up no different from wartime imperialism. Dad, Mama, and I were forced to navigate through all of this, to no avail.[6]

Mama would usually wake up at noon or later. Her so-called insomnia jolted me back into my childhood and teenage routine, waking up alone and keeping busy, making myself something to eat, and watching *The Price is Right* on television. Before we arrived in the U.S., I remember when we watched the price-guessing daytime show *Zubari Atemashou!* in Japan. People would guess the prices on items like toasters and refrigerators and other things now manufactured in Japan after the war. I was then too young to realize how the Japanese price-guessing show was one of the ways in which intense American consumer culture began to take shape in the post-World War II period.

It isn't that Japan didn't desperately need spiritual, emotional, cultural, political, physical, mental and institutional resuscitation after being devastated from the war. However, Japanese postwar culture emerged out of ambiguity and contradiction under SCAP control. Movies, documentaries, songs, and shows were created, while other things were censored. American movies and magazines filled the screens and shelves. Complex intersections of democracy and domination are what forge nations. Japan was on its way to becoming one of the top three economic powers of the entire world, but only by way of its pre-American, identitarian[7] links to American global strategy.

Mama was still sleeping. Tired of watching men and women guessing prices, I decided to leave for a short walk.

*Walking.*

*Walking. Wandering.*

*Eyelids heavy. Heavier.*

*Glazed glass eyes. Swollen.*

*Anemic. Legs moving forward, lifting. Reaching, so slow and heavy.*

*I feel I need help making my feet move. Wandering. What is that smell? What do I do? Old woman reaches out her hand, wrinkled with age, but something is hanging. I see bone. Bone?*

*She looks at me. I at her.*

*Looking. Recognizing nothing. This ....wandering.*

*Hunger, hunger. Aching. Are these my feet? My stomach? My hunger? My eyes? My hair clings to my cheeks. Sticking. My cheeks feel like they're on fire. But are these my cheeks? Is this my neck?*

*Now what? Now what? Where do I go? What do I do? Stench. Wandering through Kita-katsuragi, Murayama, Shakudō, Shōwa, Atsugi, Tōkyō, Ōme, Yokosuka, Sendai, Ōsaka, Nara, Fuchū, Yokota, Tachikawa. . . . . .*

*kyodatsu jōtai* 虚脱状態
is the term for the all-pervasive psychological-spiritual-socio-physical despair-exhaustion-disorientation in postwar Japan.

To refuse this *kyodatsu* condition, Mama and her family insisted on walking quickly, doing things briskly.

*Sassa to arukinasai! (Walk quickly and briskly!).*
She always yelled at me for walking too slow.

The Japanese people from the rural areas would often distinguish those from the cities by saying that city people, especially those from Tōkyō, walked fast. The city people accused the rural Japanese of being mentally and physically "slow," making one way of walking "normal" and others not out of everyday *kyodatsu* life. Tōkyōites (*Edokko*) invented another point of superiority to other Japanese, even in the middle of the great death.

*"Ne-eh chigau. Sensou-chū, kempei-tai kara itsumo iwareta yo, mainichi, 'Sassa to arukinasai'-tte."*

(No not really. During war time, we were told everyday by the military police to walk fast.)

War effort. Let us all contribute to it.

It was a slogan developed to help the soldiers and the nation of Japan endure hardships during the war:

協力しましょう Let us contribute with our labor.

This same phrase was used after the war to rebuild Japan. Now this slogan from the war has become "Japanese," and applies to working hard to contribute to something bigger.

Continuity. Survival. The identity of "the industrial Japanese," all three moving forward.

When I walk now, I wonder who was walking then? What was Mama's walking after the war? Sometimes I feel like I am an aftermath of war. I'm an aftermath of imperial soldiers attacking me for walking too slow, or in the throes of a flatlining despair in the aftermath of defeat and devastation due to American bombs and occupiers. I am the despair and insanity of being an imperial soldier, torturing a foreign body and mind, knowing I must be destroyed.

Suddenly, there's a whisper when I walk: "Hey, Boy!"

I returned to the house after my walk. As usual, it was dark. The open windows brought in the constant and haunting fragrance and sounds of summer cicadas.

Mama said, *"Waaaa . . . honto ni Atsui!"* (Wow, it's really hot!)

After I changed, I asked Mama if she wanted a Pepsi or Sprite as I headed into the kitchen. She followed me and began heating up some rice as I pulled glasses off the shelf and poured the soda. I mentioned to her that I had gone through some hard times, some good times, and that I was surviving. She was happy that I had finally gotten my Bachelors' degree at Antioch University in Seattle, even if I was past forty years old. She mentioned that we were lucky to be in America where no one says much about going to college at forty. In Japan, she says, that would have been really hard because it would have been out-of-step with how it's supposed to be done. It brings abuse. Well, I told her, America has abuses too, for those who don't do what they "should" do. But she's right. America has more room for individualism.

I watched television while we talked, reminded of the occasional guilt I felt for not being in touch with her consistently all these years. There was a four-or five-year time in my life where I didn't call her. Later, there would be a six-year period where I didn't contact her. Secrets consumed Mama and me, leaving misunderstandings and separation. And secrets are not just about silences of choice.

I decided to tell her a secret I carried. After a swallow of Pepsi, I told her, *jisatsu shiyou to shita no*—in 1982, I tried to kill myself. Kill myself. *Jisatsu.*

Silence.

*Silence.*

I knew Mama had attempted suicide a few times herself. We had talked about those experiences extensively, and it made me hopeful that she would empathize with me and perhaps we could discuss *jisatsu*, a kind of bonding in misery and resilience. As I began telling her of my suicide attempt with pills in 1982, Persian Gulf War pictures flashed across the television screen, with reports of "terror" and U.S. bombs. Mama scrunched up her face in exasperation, and said, *"FFhhh! You were going to leave me alone, too, like everyone else in the world."* At that moment, I felt a huge gulf between us.

*Gulfs. Wide. Deep.*

I thought to myself: *oyakōkō zen zen dekinakute honto ni dame na musuko da yo ne. Oyakōkō*—a caring and reciprocal duty to our parents.[9] I felt sad over what I had become and what Mama was becoming, as if we were configured to become strangers in life. I also felt sad that Dad, who never heard these stories about us, would continue to be a stranger to us. And we would never know of his stories. But I think if all three of us were together now, it would be more of the same. Dislocated from any tradition, we would flounder.

Strangers becoming... stranger. 目

# CHAPTER NOTES

1. See Julian Aguon, *What We Bury at Night: Disposable Humanity* (Fort Lauderdale, FL; Blue Ocean Press, 2008).

2. Seraphim Franziska, *War Memory and Social Politics in Japan,* 1945-2005 (Harvard East Asian Monographs) (Boston: Harvard University Asia Center, 2008).

3. Theresa Hak Kyung Cha, *Audience Distant Relative. Exilee Temps Morts: Selected Works* (Berkeley: University of California Press, 2009). These are my own rendition of thoughts jumping out at me from Cha's work.

4. Holly M. Barker, *Bravo for the Marshallese: Regaining Control in a Post-nuclear, Post-colonial World* (Belmont, CA: Wadsworth Publishing, 2004). See also, Aguon, *What We Bury at Night: Disposable Humanity.*

5. For the law itself, see https://www.congress.gov/bill/101st-congress/house-bill/2372/text (Accessed September 12, 2017).

6. On February 1, 1990, the 63-year-old former governor of Guam—Ricardo Bordallo—shot himself in the head after draping himself in Guam's national flag and chaining himself to a statue of Chief Quipuha of Guam in a busy intersection. He had been convicted of bribery charges for accepting money from Japanese businessmen. For a book about Bordallo and the events, see Peter DeBenedittis, *Guam's Trial of the Century: News, Hegemony, and Rumor in an American Colony* (Westport, CT: Praeger, 1993).

7. The Identitarian movement is a pan-European socio-political movement that started in France in 2002 as a far-right youth movement deriving from the French nouvelle by Markus Willinger, *Generation Identitaire: Une Declaration de Guerre Contre les Soixante-Huitards* (London: Arktos Media Unlimted, 2013).

8. Refers to Public Law 101-426—The Radiation Exposure Compensation Act, passed by U.S. Congress in 1990, financially compensates those affected by nuclear explosion tests after 1945. I refer mainly to those of the Marshall Islands—Enewetak and Bikini Atoll. In relation to this is Aga Point—an area on the island of Guam, which to this day, the U.S. has ignored for inclusion in the act. For the law itself, see: https://www.congress.gov/bill/101st-congress/house-bill/2372/text (Accessed September 12, 2017) . To read about confirmation of Guam radiation, see: http://www.radioaustralia.net.au/international/radio/onairhighlights/researchers-confirm-radioactive-fallout-on-guam. For an April 2015 article on Guam and the delay, see: http://postguam.com/local/news/40253-decades-later-guam-still-waiting-for-inclusion-in-reca.html#.Vo8gxCfdz18 (Accessed September 12, 2017).

9. Oyakōkō (親孝行) is a tradition in Japanese culture, which is fast becoming a notion of the past. This entails the obligation and devotion of children to take care of the parents and elders when we reach adulthood, who took care of us. It is an aspect of filial piety.

# CHAPTER 10

# Quiet Drizzling Rain
## シトシトと 小雨 がふる

"LeMay said that 'If we'd lost the war, we'd all have been prosecuted as war criminals.' And I think he's right," says McNamara. 'He, and I'd say I, were behaving as war criminals.' .... LeMay recognized that what he was doing would be thought immoral if his side has lost. But what makes it immoral if you lose and not immoral if you win?"

— Commentary on the use of the atomic bomb on Japan
from the movie, *The Fog of War: Eleven Lessons from
the Life of Robert S. McNamara*[1]

AT FIRST, MAMA WAS NOT HAPPY about my attending a Zen Center in Denver in 1984. But on the one rare occasion she visited me in Denver and was persuaded to come to the Zen Center, she was comforted to know what I was doing. She had once thought of religion as an "opium of the people." Her experiences with proselytizing Buddhist sects in Japan had left a bad taste in her mouth, but what changed her mind was when she saw my eyes. She looked into my eyes and saw my 目つき *(metsuki),* and discovered someone present and much kinder. She knew I had radically changed in some way, though it was not readily apparent.

My Zen teacher, Roshi Philip Kapleau, had been a court reporter at the Tōkyō War trials, after working the Nuremburg War trials. His interest in Zen practice was fueled from his reporting days as he wondered why postwar Japanese behavior differed from the Germans. I secretly disagreed with many of his conclusions regarding the seemingly compliant and relatively accepting behavior of the Japanese compared to the arrogance and rationale of the Germans. I still feel that much of it had to do with racism—before, during and after the war—and how the Germans' actions

Bombs fall on Ōsaka, Japan, June 1, 1945. B-29 Superfortress bombers were ubiquitous in bombings over Japan. Its twin, the B-26, became so in the bombings over Korea. *Photo courtesy of the United States Air Force Historical Research Agency, Maxwell AFB AL.*

were dismissed as "bad ideology" while the Japanese were considered horrific and inhumane, through and through. Both countries were expected to adopt the U.S. as overlord, but the ways in which this was done, in relation to race and the aftermath of war, vastly differed on a global scale in everything from international finance to Orientalism and foreign policy.

My suicide attempt led me to find Zen practice. Contrary to the world telling me that I, as a mixed-race person, "must be confused," I was never confused with my identity. Other mixed-race people may have problems but I know who I am. My problem was figuring how to live in a world that projected its historical baggage onto me. There aren't paint brushes big enough to cover the multitude of these experiences. I knew who I was, but I didn't like the "position" in which I was always placed.

Mama and I never spoke of our respective issues, but while we did share some realities, her war experiences and my own from the residues of war, were both battles with different trajectories.

> *The noon siren started crooning all over the base. Mama cried out, suddenly rushing away from my side to the outer post of our porch. I shivered, and Mama looked at me, puzzled. Then she realized everything was okay. She was sweating and her face changed. Fear to relief to sadness, then defiance. Her eyes welled with tears while her face betrayed nothing but strength. "Kichigai ni narisou." (It's like I'm about to go insane).*
>
> *We went inside the house.*

Whether we were in Tachikawa, Yokosuka, Fuchū, Atsugi or Yokota bases, it was always like this—tense—in the few times I remember the noon-time siren sounding. Once or twice, she ran to a nearby corner of the room. I never asked her about it. Throughout most of lives together, Mama couldn't sleep at night and would pace the house, continuing to clean, or would make lists of the weather report for the week or chores for the day.

> *"Your mother has weird sleeping hours."*
> *"Why doesn't your mother sleep during the night like everybody else?"*

One neighbor's mother said directly that my Mama was lazy and that she should learn English and work like everyone else, even though she herself stayed at home. This woman told me that my Mama should keep regular hours like everyone else in

America. Regular hours? Why? Who cares? What, and who, is all this conformity for? What does conformity *erase? Allow? Just once I want cruelty and narrow-mindedness erased. Just once I want freedom and my differences to be left alone.*

Mama often had nightmares. She said she experienced *kowai yume,* but we never talked about those nightmares. And when I would be at school or outside playing, I never saw how so much of her life was a lonely burden. I used to ask myself why she did things so differently, but I never once thought they were "weird."

It was me and Mama, as we were. *Everyday.*

### April 18, 1944

MAMA'S FAMILY TOOK NOTE that it had been her birthday the other day. The trees were beginning to shed their leaves, some already gold and red. It was then that the first U.S. bombing of Tōkyo and Yokohama began.

The most intense, near-daily urban fire-bombing of Tōkyo began on November 17, 1944. In February of 1945, Americans began escalating their destructive will with a total of 174 B-29 superfortress bombers flying over Tōkyo. From March 17 through 19, the bombers rained 1,700 tons of explosives onto the city, from the bellies of 279 planes—so many that they darkened the sky. According to the Tōkyo Fire Department, over one million people became homeless, 124,000 injured, and 97,000 died in just this single first raid. The fires that began from these chemical incendiaries left Tōkyo smoldering.[2]

General Curtis LeMay, credited for designing bombing tactics that made the killing campaigns over Japan in 1945 much more desirable, had grown to realize that instead of the highly explosive bombs used by the U.S. against Germany, bombs that spread fire—firebombs—should be used exclusively on Japanese cities, as most of the homes and buildings were made of wood and paper. With the entire U.S. armed forces planning office waiting to hear of the success of the bombings, a total of 458 B-29s dropped over 2,890 tons of bombs onto Ōsaka in a daylight incendiary attack, on June 1, 1945.

On March 13, 1945, the first fire-bombing operation was ordered for Ōsaka. Between 274 and 306 B-29 bomber planes flew over Ōsaka, covering the sky for three-and-a-half hours. For three-and-a-half hour bombing raids. And just as in Tōkyo, the rain of bombs on Ōsaka were not only exploding to obliterate, but also created and spread chemical fires, releasing a fire storm lasting for days at a time.

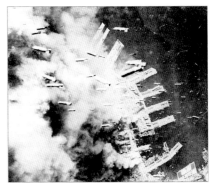

Kobe in World War II was part of the strategic bombing campaign waged by the U.S. against military and civilian targets during the Japanese home islands campaign in the closing stages of the war. Source: *WWII Database.*

Bodies charred from the American bombings are piled up to rebuild Japan. Tōkyo 1945. *Photo by Ishikawa Kōyō (1904-1989) circa March 10, 1945.*

The night was lit up with death, with putrid smells of charred flesh, deafening screams, and pounding explosions.

The bombings continued almost nightly.

*Bombs.*

More than sixty-six cities were bombed. *Sixty-six.*

There was more destruction and death from the air raids than from the atomic bombings combined. But hardly anyone remembers or cares. It was a scorched-earth policy.

Emiko, my Mama, and her family ran for their lives. After the first few days of fire storms, they moved to their home in Ōsaka before the bombings began there. Between 30 to 90 percent of each city was annihilated in a year. Mama eventually evacuated to the countryside where many of the schoolchildren were sent. The word *trauma* can hardly describe the effects.

The young girl, Emiko, became a *yakeato no ko* 焼け後の子 (girl from the traces of burned-out ruins).[3] Sleeping during the day became an act of survival.

## 1995

I BEGAN TO HEAR OF ONE GUY, two guys, another and another…dying. Dying terrible deaths. One friend told me that he didn't want to send me his partner's pictures because I wouldn't recognize him. I had not seen any of these friends in over ten years, having only kept in touch with their comings and goings, often through other friends who knew how they were. I had moved here and there as an adult, losing touch, and now they were dying. *Of AIDS.* It was too much for me to bear.

As I began thinking about AIDS in the scheme of American life, I couldn't help but feel suspicious, especially when I spoke to some activist friends at the forefront of the movement, and heard how American institutions and "the establishment" were handling it. From my own knowledge of the Tuskegee syphilis experiments,[4] malaria blankets,[5] and my father's stories of what happened to non-whites in the military, I was very suspicious. Although I was certain I myself would not be hit with a positive result, I got tested, and cleared myself. But this did not make me feel better. There were days when I couldn't get out of bed. I wouldn't cry. It was beyond sadness. *It went much deeper.* 冒

# CHAPTER NOTES

1. *The Fog of War: Eleven Lessons from the Life of Robert S. McNamara,* Errol Morris, Director (2003) is an American documentary film.

2. The statistics are from the Air Force Historical Studies Office, compiled by Kit C. Carter and Robert Mueller, U.S. *Army Air Forces in World War II: Combat Chronology,* March, 1945. Accessed September 19, 2015. http://www.afhso.af.mil/shared/media/document/AFD-100525-035.pdf; Freeman Dyson, "Part I: A Failure of Intelligence," *Technology Review* (MIT, 2006); David McNeill, "The night hell fell from the sky," *Japan Focus* (2005); Richard Rhodes, *The Making of the Atomic Bomb* (NY: Simon & Schuster, 1984), 599; Mark Selden, "A Forgotten Holocaust: U.S. Bombing Strategy, the Destruction of Japanese Cities and the American Way of War from the Pacific War to Iraq" *Japan Focus* (2007).

3. The term yake-ato (焼け跡) was first coined by Ishikawa Jun 石川淳 (1899-1987), a prominent author of the Shōwa period (1926–1989) in Japan. His work, *Yakeato no iesu* (焼け跡のイエス) was translated by William J. Tyler as *The Jesus of the Ruin* (1998). Often characterized as an experimental writer that was modernist in his approach, Jun used the term "Yake-ato Generation" (which comes from Yake-ato sedai (焼け跡世代) and Yake-ato jidai (焼け跡時代)), to describe the generation of Japanese who came of age during the bombing of Japan during World War II. The term "yake-ato" literally means "burnt-out ruins." A variation of Jun's initial definition has been paraphrased a number of ways. For example, *yakeato jidai* has been translated by Owen Griffiths as "the era of scorched earth," while Bruce Suttmeier has translated *yakeato sedai* as the "generation of the ashes."

4. The Tuskegee Syphilis Experiment, conducted by the U.S. Public Health Service between 1932 and 1972, was called "arguably the most infamous biomedical research study in U.S. history." Six hundred impoverished African American sharecroppers in Alabama who had syphilis were withheld treatment so that doctors could follow the natural progression of untreated syphilis to develop statistics and knowledge for the scientific community.

5. I am referring to the disputed fact that the U.S. Army purposefully distributed infected blankets to Native Americans during the 1830s as part of the U.S.' efforts to wipe-out their communities and brand the country as a white nation.

# CHAPTER 11

# Monsters 1950 Shōwa year 25
# 化け物 昭和 25 年

"[Japanese women] have been taught to hate you. They do as their men tell them, and many of them have been told to kill you. Sex is one of the oldest and most effective weapons in history. The Geisha girl knows how to wield it charmingly. She may entice you only to poison you. She may slit your throat. Stay away from the women of Japan, all of them."

— *Time Magazine,* August 27, 1945[1]

THIS QUOTE IS FROM A LEAFLET THE U.S. ARMED FORCES made available to the occupation soldiers during the most intense period of the implementation of anti-fraternization, which sought to discourage relations between Japanese women and occupation personnel.

What did these violent, racially motivated leaflets reinforce? Its goal was to promote and demote certain viewpoints, perceptions or agendas. In time, they succeeded in becoming the everyday norm, because they were designed to do so. For years. Does it stop when the leaflets stop? Or when bombs cease? Or when babies are born or when people marry? How long does it take when these words form lives?

### Mama, 1950

*American soldiers were around all the time. I was still afraid of them. My friend Mieko and I would talk about how the Japanese soldiers looked so handsome (kakko-ii) in their uniforms. My older brother was a soldier. He had fought in Burma and went through hardships there that he never spoke to me about. Now, instead of Japanese soldiers, we see Americans. Everywhere. Jeeps all over. Them walking around. They looked sexy too. Even the women soldiers. We'd never seen women soldiers before! I wanted to be around them all. They beat our soldiers. They won the war. I was afraid of them. We were told by some people in the neighborhood that the Americans were monsters and they would rape us. I wasn't scared but I had to believe it too.*

*One day, Mieko and I decided we would try to get closer to the Americans. When we were younger, we used to grab the candies and chocolates they threw from their jeeps, but now I wanted to see them in a different way. Closer. We knew about the U.S. military base that had been set up just a little walk from Mieko's house. So we walked with our arms linked so we wouldn't be kidnapped so easily. On this day we decided to go, there must have been something special going on.*

*As we reached a huge wire fence, we saw hundreds, thousands of American soldiers in straight lines. There were huge airplanes, tanks and jeeps everywhere. American soldiers everywhere in crisp uniforms. We heard some other soldiers in different uniforms—probably officers—screaming something at them. We didn't understand. There were hundreds of us Japanese girls there, leaning against the fence, peering through, staring, ogling and wondering in awe. We were attracted. But there was something very familiar. We watched our brothers and friends and uncles in similar lines with similar people yelling orders. So it must've been the same with Americans.*

*As we got closer, Mieko and I wondered, "Donna kao shiteru no ka ne, Amerika-jin wa?" (wonder what kind of [true] faces Americans have?).*

*We clung to each other as we leaned our faces through the spaces in the wiring, our noses sticking through, our eyes piercing and big. We looked to see American faces, the faces of the enemy my brothers and uncles went off to fight, the ones who killed my older sister in Hiroshima. Monsters. I noticed one soldier. He looks like he is my age, around sixteen. He's a boy! I see beads of sweat. I somehow see the look of fear in his eyes. I slowly work my stare down his body and notice that the hand holding his military rifle is trembling. Why? I turn to Mieko and ask her.*

*She says, "Kowai no yo, kitto. Amerika wa ima Chōsen de sensô shiteru no yo" (He's probably scared, you know, now America's fighting a war in Korea.) Then we both realized ... Americans were human too! This boy in his uniform was scared. I felt sorry for him.*

*Suddenly I felt different. I began to see all the soldiers' faces. They were all different now. They were boys like our soldiers, who went to war and never returned. The tanks, the jeeps, the planes, the rockets, the uniforms, the faces, the shaking, the sweat, the guns, all rolling and rolling, more and more, an endless parade.*

American bombs begin obliterating Wonsan, Korea in 1951. As in Japan, most of the major cities in Northern Korea (78 cities in total) were obliterated by American bombings, 30 percent of its population killed. Since the U.S. government called this a "limited" war, information on these bombings remained classified until recently to avoid public scrutiny. *Photo courtesy of the U.S. National Archives.*

## 1968

*Yuu Luv Neega Bitch!!??*

THEN THE THROWING OF whatever was near: cups, bowls, plates, forks and knives. They shattered all over the wall, the floor, the table, the chair. Dad would silently open the door to leave while he quietly, yet sternly told her, "Don't yell at me, woman."

Objects continued to fly at him in rapid succession.

*She neega bitch. Aguri neega bitch!*

She had found photos of beautiful black "women-friends" that Dad had hidden in the folds of the encyclopedia sets in our home. He must have thought that since Mama couldn't read them, the photos were safe there. But Mama cleaned every nook and cranny. She found them.

She often wondered why she was alone most of her life, in that house, raising me. Where was he every night? He was never home, even when he was supposed to be the father of the house. Sometimes I wouldn't see him for two or three days after a fight. This happened a couple times when I was a kid. Our home was hardly ever calm unless it was late at night or early in the morning, but Dad never raised his voice or hit or yelled. Mama did. The quieter Dad became, holding things in, the angrier Mama became. She wanted expressions, warmth, companionship. Something Dad couldn't give her. Dad was a charming man, who was peaceful and controlled. And when she would use the word "nigger" ... it was meant to hurt him. It also hurt me.

It may have been the only weapon she had to fight her battles with a man. An American man. Victor. Occupier. Class inferior. A warrior against the occupier white America. Although she didn't need to be a gentle geisha for Japanese men, she certainly was made to know her place as second-class, subservient to men's commands. In the postwar period, the protocols for "correct" Japanese woman-hood originally propagated by Japan's elite was now being deployed across the entire populace with the help of the Americans, British and Australians. Who were the monsters that now ran rampant in our home? Where were they from? What would love act like, look like, feel like?

I began to understand the complexity of race, marriage, sex and gender, even if I could not articulate it. Life was a not-so-simple thing. And as much as Mama was my caretaker and savior during those years, these times marked a beginning of my wanting spaces separate from her to deal with an aloneness that nothing could assuage. There was something, I thought for a while, that she hated about me. And Dad wasn't able to comfort me either. Whenever I did something he didn't like, he would always say to me, "You're your mother's son." He made me feel separate from him whenever I displeased him. A quiet exclusion. I began to know my place.

As much as I was loved, I became a symbol. Perhaps this is how love is demarcated. The three of us were a nexus displaced by nation, race, and gender. I was already defeated. Alongside, but not within, the same space as Mama. Or Dad.

But Mama had her own battles — those of having to be my mother.

## 1962

"You ain't nothin' but a nigger bitch!" the white woman sneered at Mama. Three of them were standing there with their shopping carts in the aisle. Mama had brought me with her to the PX to shop.

"You shut up!" Mama yelled.

The three white women came up to Mama.

Mama rolled up her sleeves, her face changing into a kind of monstrous expression that terrified me. Just then, a tall white man came and asked if anything was the matter. The three white women hurriedly left the aisle.

When Mama and I left the PX, she gripped my hand tightly and we stopped in our tracks. I looked up to see her looking all around, checking to see if those women were around.

They called her those names because they saw me.

They knew that my Dad, her husband, was black.

I was the cause of Mama's pain, I thought. 目

# CHAPTER 12

# Occupied

BEGINNING IN THE EIGHTEENTH CENTURY, blacks were called 黑鬼 *Hei Gui* (black devil, or black ghost) in China. Mixed-race Black-Chinese, born to local women and dark-skinned "non-Chinese" fathers (and almost always abandoned), were also called this name.

A man comments on my Hiroshima blog post:

*Your mother deserves to be bloody raped 6 million times. I wish 800 more atomic bombs were dropped on you. You're nothing but insects. All you motherfuckers should go to hell.*

I searched for the location of where that writer came from. *Korea.*

Mama remembers the term "B-29" but she doesn't remember my sister's name.

When do wars end? What and where are the markers of this "ending?" Do occupations die? What is occupation? People die, dreams die, ideas die, but do occupations? What happens to the citizens of a nation that have been occupied? Are nations themselves a form of occupation? What happens to the citizens of a nation occupied? We become *citizens.* What of "foreign" occupation? Even if the occupation has long ended, how do we carry on?

So the prevailing story of the Allied Occupation of Japan states: *the Japanese were the most compliant and gracious acceptors of the U.S. and Allied Occupation. There were virtually no incidents against the Occupation personnel.*

Of course, this view benefits the U.S. and Allied personnel. This positive image allows any group or institution more control and freedom to proceed with its works if the media is complacent. This image also assisted in intensifying Japanese elite control of

African American soldiers celebrate upon hearing of Japan's surrender in 1945, the end of a long war. *Photo courtesy of the U.S. National Archives.*

new Japan through their relationship with the Allied leadership. At the same time, both U.S. and Allied forces, and the Japanese elite would shift blame whenever there were serious problems, in order to avoid close scrutiny.

Japan was under almost complete censorship (nothing is ever "total"), contrary to the popular notion that the U.S. only "advised" the Japanese "toward democracy." From entertainment (theater and movie scripts, kabuki plays, movies, books), to education (speeches by teachers), to legislation (laws and amendments), all policies had to be approved by the Occupation administration (SCAP).[1]

Only African Americans were segregated into separate combat base units during the war, which continued during the Occupation. Separate base town areas of entertainment developed,[2] as both a consequence of black Occupation soldiers demanding their own spaces, as well as the reality of black servicemen and women being barred from, condescended to, violated and excluded from white establishments.

In World War II, black units experienced depression and "low morale" as a result of inferior equipment and attention. Then during the following Occupation, black units were housed further away from major cities and bases compared to their white counterparts in Japan. If any racial incidents occurred, black soldiers were almost always held responsible and punished more harshly than their white peers. Hostile and indifferent commanders and officials were commonplace. All aspects of Jim Crow were in effect.[3]

Off-base establishments in Japan offered black Occupation personnel a freedom and comfort from what they knew in the U.S. In general, the gracious and hospitable treatment they received from the Japanese people, contrasted against their experiences of intense racism in the U.S., led to positive views of Japan and Japanese women. Many blacks (of many ethnicities and nations, including South Asians who arrived with the Commonwealth Occupation Forces) sympathized with the Japanese and their status during the Occupation, while white American, British, and Australian soldiers were racial supremacists. However, there were also white Occupation soldiers who believed in equality and were peacemakers. Many were branded "nigger-lovers," in the eyes of their white brethren, traitors to white supremacy. Fights would break out between white American servicemen from this tension. The Japanese often observed these dynamics (peacemakers versus anti-black or anti-white Japanese), which would come to have a lasting effect in Japanese culture.

During the latter years of the official Occupation, with funds depleting rapidly, the officials who managed the stockades were ordered to reduce prison populations significantly. Black soldier-prisoners were among the first to be executed. Therese Svoboda, in *Black Glasses Like Clark Kent,* writes of her research into the suicide-deaths and the "silence" of the military police who witnessed these "secrets," including the "disappearance" of official records of events during this period.

In a 1989 interview, Kikkawa Ikimi spoke of her late husband, labeled "The First Atomic Bomb survivor" by the U.S. media, and insisted on noting how they both resented that label.[4] When Ikimi published his autobiography, the publisher completely omitted the story of his life prior to the bomb. The bomb became the centerpiece, and *the beginning of his history.* Fabricated beginnings and journeys. Creating identities of people, places, histories. I feel solidarity with Mr. Ikimi and his wife and the millions of others who criticize the way stories are written to distill life into a single dominating event. For many from Japan and the U.S., the atomic bomb *à la America* became the centerpiece of the Pacific War, Hiroshima, and Nagasaki. Now it is told as a tragic anomaly, while nuclear proliferation and warmongering continues in support of maintaining or constructing white supremacy (a "war on terror?"). To reveal disruptions and dislocations which destroy, produce, and forget, and to adapt and refuse history written by the dominant culture, what must be done? What is read by others and called *real* or *authentic* when there can only be that refusal of history? It is all the more political and messier than any one answer can establish. How does this exist in people's lives?

> *Yeah, yeah, yeah. War is bad, we all know. It's tragic.*
> *Yeah, yeah, yeah, let's move on. Humans are stupid. We suck! We're sinful.*
> *Yeah, yeah, yeah. Let's just move on.*
> *With such thoughts, ghosts come.*

Mama remembers the scores of Japanese children, including herself, who fought for the shower of candy and chocolates thrown from the backs of jeeps by generous American soldiers during the early period of the postwar. Many thought the Americans were superheroes just for that. Even the British and Australians envied the Americans for this tactic. For the Japanese, mired in defeat and desolation, the candy and the friendly American faces represented life.

Two Igorot children play in front of gawking Americans at the 1909 Alaska-Yukon-Pacific-Exposition, Seattle, Washington—one example of "human exhibits" (also known as "human zoos") where conquered indigenous people were exhibited next to the animal and plants exhibits by European, American, Australian and Japanese nations. The Igorot, pictured here, is the collective name of several Austronesian ethnic groups in the Philippines. *Photo courtesy of University of Washington Collection.*

*They won! And they had chocolates! We're the losers, and we don't have anything. We need you. You must be our savior. But you are also the enemy that killed my parents.*

The showering of chocolates was strategy concocted by American Occupation leaders that entrenched the image of Americans as saviors, victors, and benefactors that would defend against the coming Cold War, and the devastation of Korea, Southeast Asia, and Vietnam.

*But many of us despised you. Yet some of us could do nothing but depend on you for food. I knew we couldn't keep going the way we were going during the war. Japan was stupid. And soon we wanted the refrigerators, cars, televisions, and washing machines. Violence and benevolence, hand-in-hand.*

Like soldiers everywhere, they vow to kill your parents first, before they build your orphanages.[5]

Westerners began arriving onto Japanese shores and entered the social fabric of Japan long before the Occupation. During the sixteenth century, the Spanish, Portuguese, Dutch, and British, among others, arrived looking to exploit, as well as ally with the Japanese elite. The Western colonial powers brought African, Malay, and Gujrati slaves with them—all, of course, of the blacker body.[6] Commodore Perry bombed Tōkyō Bay, opening Japan for the u.s. These bombastic displays of "opening trade" were a show of demonstrating dominance and submission. Japan's modernization and westernization, which began primarily with Japan's elite was not yet wholly unified at this time. Internal wars had intensified along the lines of various Japanese political and military lines, especially those related to associating with the west. Western powers were also struggling for power amongst themselves. Early news of the British colonization of India, along with Southeast Asian colonization by the Dutch and the French, pushed some Japanese clans to band together for the purposes of acquiring military strength.

Commodore Perry landed in the Ryūkyū Islands (a chain of Japanese islands that include Okinawa, Miyako and Yaeyama today) before entering Japan on that fateful day. The entertainment that Commodore Perry provided for the Japanese, would deeply influence the nation's notion of color that would last into the present day. Minstrel shows by white men dressed up in blackface were performed for the Japanese. This was done while African and Black Pacific slaves served and obeyed Americans. There were many hostilities and friendships formed in this time and space.

Just after Perry's arrival in Okinawa, the first rape incident of Okinawan women by U.S. military personnel occurred. It was also the first incidence on record that did not view rape as a crime. Perry responded to his crew member's action by demanding the prosecution of the local men who had chased the rapist, a chase that resulted in the man's fall and death. While the local men were prosecuted and sentenced to banishment, he presented to the rape victim a gift of cotton cloth. Obviously, this was no resolution.

There is a memorial in Okinawa that exists for the man who fell to his death.[7] I question why and how a memorial was erected on his behalf. To remember who and for what? The Americans and the Okinawans today see that memorial in very different ways.

It was witnessing these interactions between white European slave owners and their black-bodied slaves that led Japanese elites to cultivate attitudes of black inferiority. This, coupled with early twentieth century European race science, helped Japan raise its social and industrial technologies of biopower toward an international model more ideologically linked to the elites. Linking a population to a concept of nation, race, and the world was now strongly tied to this sense of building "self."

It was similar to the question of who the laborers and slaves were in Japan and China, and who was considered "darker" in Japanese terms, like the underclasses from Burakumin, Koreans, Ryukyuan populations, and Southeast Asians. As European race science was foundational to rationalizing colonial expansion, Japanese intellectuals learned and adopted these theories, despite the presence of much resistance. The black body became a proxy between Japan's previous conception of ethnicity and nation-building, and proximities to arriving into the "modern world."

Occupation, regime-change, conquest, annexation, and civilization created the trappings of identity, love, silence, and rage. We are occupied as nations that have defined identity, power, race, worthiness, and hierarchy through wars and assimilation. We have made our bodies unrecognizable. And if we include the past and the dead and the grieving, we must also include the ghosts and dreams that lay in those spaces that live in and through us.

So Dad became a "new black"—a soldier in a new civil rights America while Mama—Emiko–in the imagination of the West and the Japanese nation, had become a "new" Japanese woman. Imagination was the unifying force in the alliance between former enemies.

Mama was positioned as subordinate, yet she resisted and became a new model of Japanese womanhood. The world refused to recognize her because she broke

One of many Nanban byobu (screen) paintings from the Edo period, 17th century Japan, depicting Portuguese traders with black slaves. Many, including this one, is attributed to Naizen Kanō 狩野 内膳 (1570 – 1616).

the mold. Like all of us, she too is marked. "She would become, herself, demarcations" (Hak Kyung Cha),[8] and becoming marked defined our lives. Mama carried burdens of history at the intersections of war, globalization, and culture, having witnessed Japan's displacement a number of times. Yet Japan was already displacing itself. She had to become "Japanese" and "woman"—ideas she lived with, and resisted her entire life—as Japan itself forged ahead from early to modern, from imperial to postwar and occupied, to the *Taisho*. America and the world occupied her with freedom and rage, through a redefined language constructed around concepts of race, nation, and gender. 冃

An American soldier handing out candy and chocolates to war-devastated Japanese children. As they transitioned from combat to occupation, in order to gain their trust, American troops showed goodwill towards a Japanese public as one publicity strategy as a way to bring Japan under U.S. client-ship. *Photo courtesy of U.S. Department of Defense.*

The bars in the districts frequented by Americans in the postwar, were segregated. "Blacks, whites and Japanese seldom frequented the same establishments. There were occasional exceptions but transgressions of the "rules" could and often would result in fights. For the most part, people stayed "where they belonged." This is a rare visit by a black man in "the Alley," quoted from *AP Alley: A Look at the Lost World of Sin and Fun in Cold War Japan of the 1960s*. *Photo courtesy of Tom Roach.*

Americans in formation at the Sugamo Prison, March 10, 1948. Built in 1895 and using the prisons of Europe as a model, Sugamo Prison in Tōkyō became known for housing political prisoners and allied spies. One of its most high profiled prisoners was Iva Toguri d'Aquino a/k/a "Tōkyō Rose." *Source: Occupied Tōkyō (Naha City, Japan, Gekkan-Okinawa Sha, 1958).*

# CHAPTER NOTES

1. Lindesay Parrott (1901-1987), a foreign correspondent and Tōkyō's bureau chief for the New York Times from 1945 to 1951, wrote in 1948, "As the fourth year of occupation begins, all major policy still is made by the Occupation authorities and even the most minor detail is checked and counter-checked on local levels by Military Government teams in all prefectures. Parliament remains largely a rubber stamp for the Cabinet it elects which in turn is a rubber stamp for the Occupation authorities." *New York Times, The Week in Review,* August, 1948, E4. Also quoted in Bernard Roehner, *Relations Between Allied Forces and the Population of Japan, Paris: Institute for Theoretical and High Energy Physics,* University of Paris 6 Laboratoire de Physique Théorique et Hautes Énergies, UPMC, Paris Working Report, 2009. This quote is accurate.

2. Many cities and towns around U.S. military bases located overseas develop a culture that is partially or mostly dependent on the base and its personnel. The locals almost always create their own hybrid language, and sell certain goods that cater to Americans, including, but not limited to, sex work, weapons trade, tourism, night entertainment and music. This is a global U.S. military base reality.

3. Reminiscence of Charles Bussey, a black officer stationed in Japan during the Occupation in Eiji Takemae, *Inside GHQ: The Allied Occupation of Japan and Its Legacy* (London, UK: Bloomsbury Publishing, 2002), 130.

4. There are several accounts of this. I used information primarily from the book by Yoneyama, *Hiroshima Traces,* 102.

5. This line: "First they kill your parents, then they build you orphanages" was told to me by one of the uncles of a Dersim-Alevi Kurdish friend (eastern Turkey) when he described how states pretend to act benevolently even though they created the problem in the first place. He spoke directly to the problem of assimilation and colonization used by elites globally.

6. See Arnold Rubin, *Black Nanban: Africans in Japan During the Sixteenth Century* (Indiana: African Study Program, Indiana University, Bloomington, 1974).

7. This story has been repeated in many publications. Some say rape, some say attempted rape of the Okinawan woman. See Wesley Uenten (上運天巖), "Rising up from a Sea of Discontent: The 1970 Koza Uprising in U.S.-Occupied Okinawa" in *Militarized Currents: Towards a Decolonized Future in Asia and the Pacific,* eds. Setsu Shigematsu and Keith L. Camacho (Minnesota: University of Minnesota Press, 2010); and Maria Höhn and Seungsook Moon, eds., *Over There: Living with the U.S. Military Empire from World War Two to the Present* (Durham, NC: Duke University Press, 2010).

8. Theresa Hak Kyung Cha, *Dictee* (California: University of California Press, 2001).

# CHAPTER 13

# 1945 昭和 19年

*I am a soldier of the United States, land of freedom's promise. I have come to help my single mother feed me and my three brothers, I've come to be a good man, I've come to survive, I've come to make myself participate in the American dream without that "black" thing holding me back, I've come to be a proud black.*

IT'S THE MIDDLE OF THE NIGHT. My notes come in a torrent:

### April 1, 1946

*"Major outbreak of smallpox and typhus in Japan, infecting approximately 60,000. There are over 3,000 deaths from these two diseases alone, not including others in Japan."*

— *The New York Times,* March 29, Chronology, Japan, 1945-1960)[1]

### August and September 1945

*The big ceremony of Japan's surrender brought 2,000 American B-29 bombers and fighter planes flying in ordered formation across the skies of Japan. Enormous battleships and destroyers docked in Tōkyō Bay. American flags flew overhead. Did it remind the ghosts of the bombing of Tōkyō Bay? After a most ferocious land battle, Okinawa became a strategic pawn, placed under U.S. military rule in exchange for eventual Japanese sovereignty, which allowed the U.S. to establish further control of the Pacific. The U.S. ordered the Japanese imperial police and military to continue controlling Korea. Villages in*

HARLEM PEACE MARCH, National Spring Mobilization to End the War in Vietnam, New York City, April 15, 1967. *Photo by Builder Levy.*

This was just another example of the empathy one oppressed group had for another because they both experienced racial discrimination in the U.S.

*Okinawa and rural Japan are bulldozed to make way for U.S. military bases. Some farmers and families are evicted at gunpoint. Many young American soldiers engage in all forms of crime, including petty theft, reckless driving, "disorderly conduct," vandalism, assault, arson, black marketeering, murder, rape and other sexual violence, especially during the early years of the Occupation. Many Japanese resist with individual attacks.*

*In Tōkyō alone, in the first three months of Occupation, over 1,000 people, mostly infants and children, died of malnutrition and starvation. Many Japanese were shot, imprisoned, or beaten by Occupation soldiers for scrounging through the garbage of the military bases, many searching for food or clothing. Occupation personnel lived in relative opulence. Resentment grew. A self-image of inferiority fed the national idea of "enduring hardships." Food and emergency aid made its way from the U.S. and Europe to Japan. However, it was not done "in kind." Japan now owes $2.14 billion dollars to the U.S. and Europe. Die or go into debt. All Japanese properties are handed over to the Allied powers. Most of the wealth and symbols of Japanese luxury were taken by Allied personnel for personal use. My grandfather's properties were included in this. Those who were spared from this were those working directly with SCAP.*

*Embassies and businesses tied to the rest of Asia were closed. For the Japanese, this meant starvation and perpetual injustice. Any person, institution, or group who didn't comply with Occupation policy or law, including the lack of reprisal for the crimes committed by Occupying personnel against the Japanese population, were threatened with military violence and severe punishment. All reports or statistics on crimes by the U.S. and Allied personnel, military or civilian, in Japan and Korea, were forbidden from being published. No mention of racist incidents between different American groups (mainly white and black), or between the Allies and the Japanese, were to be made in any way. Strict curfews were established. Criticism of SCAP was a crime punishable by heavy labor and imprisonment.*[2]

Emiko and her family searched.

They searched for her sister who was in Hiroshima when the atomic bomb came down. The *kyōdatsu* condition had taken hold of many Japanese. American soldiers were everywhere, riding freely in their jeeps. By 1952, the official end of the Occupation, Japan had begun seeing signs of 自力 a self-power.[3] However, Japan and the U.S. were forever bound by laws and cultural-corporate trade, as well as military agreements.

≋ ≋ ≋

IN 1950, MY DAD WAS IN HIS LATE TEENS living in Jim Crow America, when he joined the desegregating U.S. Air Force just as American bombs were falling on Emiko's home. My Dad's dreams rested on the death of Mama's country, but that isn't the entire picture. When I was young, Dad would tell me that he respected Japanese culture, having learned about the samurai warrior and the geisha as grand global cultural icons. He always told me I should be proud. Although I didn't know this at the time, many of Dad's relatives and friends who were fighting for civil rights in the U.S. looked to Japan to fight white supremacy. W. E. B. Du Bois, and other prominent African Americans, knew of Japan as the only nation to bring up "white supremacy" in their dealings at international conferences. Japan had won the Russo-Japanese War as well, and had given all non-white countries confidence in resisting global Western colonization.

Dad in his military police uniform in the 1960s. *Fredrick Cloyd Family Archive.*

*Mama Irma brought us up north by herself and we settled in Detroit. There were more economic opportunities. The Ku Klux Klan was all around Tennessee. We couldn't take it, I guess. I really don't remember those days because I was too little. All of us knew how to read. We were educated. Dad left us when I was six years old. Eventually Mama had to split us brothers up so we could all survive somehow. Some in Nashville, some in Cleveland. She had to raise me by herself. I quit high school to join the military. I had to do something respectable. I didn't want to become poor and useless like some of my friends. I had to be a man and do Mama some good. I didn't see anything respectable for me in American society. I could see the world in the military.*

It was also true that Dad admired Japanese women for their "obedient" behavior and professed that American women could learn from them. The change in this power dynamic provided black men in America a way to repossess their masculinity in a nation that often stripped them of dignity and community. Their relationships with Japanese women, coupled with the privileges of leading an American military

In the Philippines, children play in the aftermath of Japanese and American bombings during World War II. *Photo courtesy of John Tewell.*

life, gave black servicemen personal comforts that were longed for, but impossible on the mainland. Large homes with maids, for instance, gave black servicemen a taste of privilege while their own mothers worked as maids in America. Meanwhile, popular television shows like *Father Knows Best* and *Leave it to Beaver* circulated dominant American middle-class values of nuclear family bliss, with the woman's place clearly demarcated. These images and ideals were also widely circulated in most of the Pacific regions. They were taught in schools and on military bases in Japan. They learned from billboards, newspapers and magazines. Films were shown to teach these concepts to Japanese war brides, as well as to the Japanese movie industry, given their influence over culture. African Americans, in this context, often pursued dominant middle-class values in order to make themselves appear respectable to dominant American society.

My Dad and other American black men had found a way to escape the label of uncivilized "savage primitives." As middle-class white respectability is never described as anything other than "human," it remains unmarked. The construction of these concepts presume that being "civilized" ought to be the only goal of *all humans,* and that those outside of it will *die off.* It also assumes American superiority.

Japanese women became one ideal representing respectable ideological internationalism. So-called "equality" (newly intensified American globalizing jingo during the Cold War) became a way for many in the black community to gain entitlement, self-proclaimed superiority, and empowerment in their fight against the American racial order.

> *These Madame Butterflies (Cho-Cho-san) are lonely in America. We have to understand that we, as black in America, should be the last ones to discriminate against these Japanese brides in our community.*

Mama played her role strategically. She was not an obedient woman, but she knew that being a "Good and Wise Mother"—those duties drilled into girls in the schools of Japan—was important for her survival, but it was equally important for her to craft her own spaces.[4] The American bride schools instilled this value, promising democracy for women who were about to marry American soldiers.[5] Already Mama was being displaced even further. Mama for Dad. Dad for Mama. Black, white, man, woman, primitive, modern, Asia, America, military power and cultures—these dualities play out in life, often unnoticed. According to Dad, South Asians stationed in Japan—especially the Gurkhas[6] who arrived as part of the British delegation for the Occupation—sided with the Japanese or with the black soldiers in all matters of racial violence and racially-motivated disputes in Japan during this time. The old adversarial histories between the Americans, British and Australians also flared up, intensified by American domination over Commonwealth soldiers, which occasionally resulted in fights. Dark, white, and Asian roles were solidified, and was also made changeable in the postwar period.[7]

Dad also began to see, for the first time in his life, that he wasn't inferior because of his race. He saw a non-white people—the Japanese—as kind to him, and understood that some white soldiers were often supportive during racist incidents where other white soldiers or commanders were involved. He began to understand race differently, defining racism as a disposition that someone adopts, rather than as a natural fact. He also understood that systems could support an idea that demanded unilateral alignment, although unilateral alignment was impossible. Becoming anti-racist was possible for anyone, he thought, and no longer a lonely path the black man had to endure alone as some natural and pre-determined providence. He began to espouse a *humanism* as part of his personal philosophy. But what choice?

Mama was also no mere victim. Whenever her family traveled around Japan, many people would salute her and her father or brother when they passed official buildings, police stations, or schools. Emiko's father, my grandfather, worked for the Japanese government railways that played a crucial role in Japanese colonial expansion in China, largely through the creation of the state of 満州 *Manshū* (Manchuria). Our 柿並 *Kakinami* clan were of middle-elite status with several properties all over Japan and China, with an internationalist, aristocratic, high samurai class history.

Emiko was raised with housemaids who dressed her and cooked for her, whether in Szuchou, Manchuria, Nara, Hiroshima, Ōsaka or Tōkyō. Emiko's older brother Teruo was an officer in the Japanese army in Burma (Myanmar) during the war. He was also on the Japanese Olympic swimming team in the 1950s. An imperial family. Imperial eldest brother. National athlete, national soldier. The family did not starve during the Occupation. And during battle, Teruo Oji-chan—Uncle Teruo—was a commander who never had to fight for food like his subordinates. Despite their elite status, they also faced condemnation. Mama was used to being from the upper caste, and felt herself superior to Dad on many

South Asian, Nepalese and Tibetan Gurkhas as part of the British Commonwealth Occupation Force (BCOF), march through Japan in the early days of the Occupation. *Photo courtesy of Imperial War Museum / U.K.*

Me, taking in the sun on our veranda in our home in Ôme. *Fredrick Cloyd Family Archive.*

levels. Yet she also resisted the requirements that her father, stepmothers and older brother would push onto her. And because she was not "pure" Japanese, she had to attend the girls' school for non-Japanese. As much as she had friends who didn't share those attitudes, she became a target of general scorn and violence. Emiko Mama rebelled.

**Version One**

*So, you and your sister were Caesarean births. Your sister was born healthy, robust, big. You were born weaker and spent all of your first weeks in an oxygen-tent bed. We had to pay more attention to you. The doctors told me that you had a 50 percent chance of survival and you had to be watched. The doctors monitored you diligently day and night.*

*One week passed and there was no change.*

*One night, I was just about to fall asleep, when there was a cold wind that came through the room. There were no windows open. I suddenly needed to check on both my babies. When I checked your sister, there was no breathing. I called out to the nurses and doctor to come quickly. There was commotion. Your sister was dead. Within the same day, you gained weight and your color became healthy. Only one of you could live. Your sister gave her life for you. Your spirits negotiated and decided that you would be the one that should live. I'm glad you lived, and not your sister. The world is easier for boys.*

I think that, because of her life, Mama didn't like girls. When I asked Mama if she had any pictures of her, she said she burned them. In some old Japanese spiritual practices, it was best to burn pictures of the dead so that they wouldn't haunt.

**Version Two**

*"Dou shinda ka shiranai … mmmm oboetenai. Doushite darou? … zen zen oboetenai … honto ni kanashiku naru."*
"I don't know how she died … mmm, I don't remember. I wonder why? … I don't remember at all … I really get sad about this."

I FEEL GUILTY AND ANGRY at myself when I think, every once in a while, that Mama killed her daughter, my sister, like many mothers of mixed-race children did in Japan in those days. Crib death? Perhaps so. In any case, my sister became a water child. But I really don't know the "real" circumstances. The images of *oya-ko-shinju*, or parent-child murder-suicide pact, comes to me every so often because of memory.

According to my Dad, this was a few weeks after learning to walk, on the military base during one of his leaves to visit us, giving Mama confidence, who was still uncertain of his return from the United States, to receive us into America. *Fredrick Cloyd Family Archive.*

*Your mother gave birth to mixed Black Japanese twins just after World War II, under the U.S. and white colonized occupation of Mama's country. Traditions of killing little girls by their mothers' hands were still alive and well in postwar Japan, as well as in the most powerful nations around the world. Especially for girls born into poverty in nations that rely heavily on male superiority, the denial of girls' lives continues today.*

*In Japan, especially if the mother was alone and the father was an American, many Japanese found the child to have the face of the enemy. For you and these women who birthed babies of black American soldiers during those times, it was especially painful. If there were two, and if they were girls like your sister, they might have died and gone to the a-no-yo (other world) by the mother's hand. Most of the mothers left alone with their babies fathered by American soldiers left them in trains, wastebaskets, bathrooms, monasteries, and alleys, hoping for someone to take care of them or hoping the babies — like you and your sister — would die quietly and escape certain abuse. There were sensationalized cases where mothers would switch babies with any left unattended. Other mothers drowned their babies in bathtubs and rivers and canals.*

*Many mothers who wanted to keep their babies sent their mixed-race children and babies to their village relatives, away from the glare of the yakeato (burned-out ruins) people of the urban landscapes who had grown explosively bitter. They did not know what their own national soldiers had done in other Asian nations. Some mothers killed with intense openness while others did with a blank detachment. They didn't want to go insane. Out of their minds.*

*Many of these girls and boys who were like you grew up on the streets, sometimes taken care of by kind strangers and not-so-kind strangers. Some of them made their way by working for the yakuza[8] while others found a way to leave Japan. Others were kidnapped and trafficked for labor. Sometimes missionaries, social workers, or compassionate passersby who encountered them homeless in the streets took them to orphanages and Christian churches. Some mothers found out about these places and took their children there. It is true that many of these mixed Black Japanese babies were raised in black homes, soon to forget anything about Japaneseness; they lived various paths. Your parents both wanted you and they brought you to America to begin a different life from the one they knew may hold you hostage.*

*It's better if we weren't here. Isn't this clear? It's better if we weren't here. I'll let you go. I love you so much, I cannot bear to leave you alone in this hateful society.*

*Futari tomo ikiteirarenakatto no yo. Fretto ga ikiru tame shinjatta to omou. Nan ni shite mo, Fretto no ne-esan wa ikirarenakatto no.*
(The both of you weren't supposed to live. I think she died so you could live.)

*Gisei ni natta no yo.*
(In any case, your older sister wasn't supposed to live. She sacrificed for you.)

At one point, I asked Mama if she had killed my older sister, as if I were speaking about some far-off foreign being, and not a tiny girl Mama had carried in her body. She was devastated when I asked, crying as she said, *"Sonna koto-nanka shinai yo...."* (I'd never do such a thing). Then she rushed to her room sobbing, closing the door behind her. I never asked again. It was too cruel of me.

Mama and I share many ghosts. Ghosts of ways of living that are marred and changed, yet cling insistently. Many names mark our existence and the world. Mama and I have often agreed そうね, そうだな *sou ne / sou da na* that people are living in a 夢 dream state. Tonight, in the silence, I read and remembered something reminding me of another life, the crafted beginnings of other names that Mama and I are kin to strangers, yet so familiar. It reminds me of Mama's love and defiance, her commitment.

"While passing through Sekigahara in Gifu-prefecture, a long thin package wrapped in a purple *furoshiki* (similar to a large handkerchief) fell from the overhead luggage rack onto her lap. As she returned the package to the rack, the mobile police entered the car. Thinking that she might be carrying black market goods, they ordered her to take down the package and open it. She proceeded to put it on her lap and untie the *furoshiki*, revealing a pile of crumpled newspapers. She then removed the rubbish, and found a dead, half-black, half-Japanese baby in her lap." Sawada claims that God was sending her a message to care for these mixed-race children. This was the beginning, according to her, of her idea to create the school for mixed-race orphans.

—From Robert Fish: *The Heiress and the Love Children: Sawada Miki and the Elizabeth Saunders' Home for Mixed-Race Orphans in Postwar Japan*[9] 目

Newspapers from the Philippines continue to report the issue of Amerasian orphans and their need for dignity, rights, recognition, as evident in this article from the *Northern Luzon Inquirer,* July 5, 2011. *Courtesy of Inquirer Group of Companies.*

Margaret Bourke-White took some very famous photographs such as this one, of mixed-Japanese Amerasian children in one of many orphanages in postwar Japan. *Life Magazine, 1952. Photo courtesy of Getty Images.*

# CHAPTER NOTES

1. *The New York Times,* March 29, Chronology, Japan, 1945-1960.

2. The facts here are explored in numerous publications. A good place to start is Eiji Takemae, *Inside GHQ: The Allied Occupation of Japan and Its Legacy,* trans. Robert Ricketts and Sebastian Swann (NY: Continuum, 2002); and a popular book by John W. Dower, *Embracing Defeat: Japan in the Wake of World War II* (NY: W. W. Norton & Company, 2000).

3. This term *jiriki* (自力) refers to "self power" by Buddhist thinkers, and is often used to define the difference between a spiritual practice that prioritizes emphasis on deriving spiritual "help" or power on internal resources versus a spiritual practice emphasizing help from outside oneself—an "other power" *tariki* (他力) — often of Amitābha Buddha, the principal buddha in Pure Land Buddhism.

4. A "Good Wife, Wise Mother" (良妻賢母 *ryōsai kenbo*) was a political concept created and propagated beginning in the nineteenth century and solidified further into the "proper" role of women in imperial Japan. See Kathleen S. Uno, "The Death of Good Wife, Wise Mother" in *Postwar Japan as History,* ed. Andrew Gordon (Berkeley: University of California Press, 1993), 293-322. Although by the end of World War II, it lost its place as an ideology, elements of "Good Wife, Wise Mother" continued, first to train Japanese women who were marrying American servicemen, and later on, to solidify a woman's role in Japanese society. It was only by the late 1990s that this domestic and political-structural space began to break down. However, it had already begun assimilating a concept of "Japanese" women into the global Western system.

5. Brides' schools for Japanese women, numerous during the U.S. Occupation of Japan (1945-1952), were run mostly by organizations like the American Red Cross and used officers' wives to manage and teach the programs. They taught Japanese women how to speak English, cook American food, etiquette and proper manners, and all other aspects of American "house-wife" identity. English-speaking occupiers of Japan, such as the United Kingdom and Australia, also ran similar programs.

6. The Gurkhas are a people settled in Nepal and Northern India. Labeled a "martial people" by the British, who recognized their military nature and spirit, they were put to use as conscripted soldiers during Britain's colonial rule. They were prominent in World War II's Pacific campaign against the Japanese in Burma (now Myanmar).

7. The term "yellow" is a color metaphor for race that has been unfairly used to categorize people of East Asian descent. The label originated not in early travel texts or objective descriptions, but in the eighteenth and nineteenth century scientific discourses on race, when lighter-skinned Northern Europeans began making comparisons in skin coloration. Initially conceived by Kaiser Wilhelm II of Germany, by World War II, "Yellow Peril" became a hurtful epithet in the

context of war and occupation. Rooted in medieval fears of Genghis Khan and the Mongolian invasions of Europe, the term "Yellow Peril" combines racist terror of alien cultures, sexual anxieties and the belief that the West will be overpowered and enveloped by the irresistible, dark, occult forces of the East and a mortal danger to the rest of the world. The intensity of the racism that fueled World War II, can be read, for example, in Dower, *War Without Mercy: Race and Power in the Pacific War*, which speaks to a well-known notion of World War II as a "race war."

8.  *Yakuza* (ヤクザ) is a Japanese form of underground organized crime (much like the mafia).

9.  Miki Sawada's autobiography, *Kuroi Hada to Shiroi Kokoro: Sandāzu Hōmu e no Michi (Black Skin and White Heart: The Road to the Saunders Home)* (Tōkyō: Nihon Keizai Shinbunsha, 1963), 156-158, as translated by Robert Fish in *The Heiress and the Love Children*.

# CHAPTER 14

# Black Milkshake

*I come so far. In America now after long time. I won-der how mother and sisters are in my village close to Tar-lac. I send them money. The U.S.-Pilipino military camps around the village more and more and more. They train at camps for Clark Air Force Base business for the Americans. The Americans don't know my father. I ask and ask. You know when I go to city, sometimes Tagalog spit on me; call me "nognog" (charcoal) or "iniwan ng barko" (left by the ship). Mamban, Angeles City, Concepcion—you know, many places. My mother stop going because Tagalog call her many names. I had to go to city so I can feed my family. Our house was just grass and mud, wood and cement. We have some goats and pigs. My best memory was my friends, good times together. My mother was sad about father never coming back. Only five days together with mother in the village. I want to go to America to meet him. My heart hurts so much to meet him. I always ask American soldiers, "take me to Amerika, take me to Amerika. Do you know Mr. Lonnie?"[1]*

WHEN DAD RETURNED TO JAPAN after having been shipped away by the military, as was the common practice in those days for those who dared to fall in love with Japanese and Korean wom-en, we moved onto Tachikawa Air Base. A new hometown? Me? My life was entirely Japanese at that point. Small town Japanese. Thoroughly, even as an outsider, black, brown, kinky red-haired, different, enemy child. Now I was on a U.S. military base in Japan, a short train-ride away. Might as well have been a million miles. *Almost.*

The snack bar on Tachikawa Air Base as it was in the winter snows of the 1960s, where, as a kid, my friends and I would go for burgers and shakes. The base started life as an Imperial Japanese Army airfield. During the Occupation, it became a U.S. military base. *Photo courtesy of Mike Skidmore.*

It was through the gates of the Tachikawa Air Base that I became a hybrid. I began to learn English. Everyone spoke English except my mother and I. Mama and I lived in an American house on a spaciously arranged block of American style residential streets. Whenever we would leave the base to go shopping in downtown Tachikawa, we were reminded just how separate the worlds were. Japanese people stared at me whenever Mama and I left the base to be INSIDE Japan, off the base. Or OUTSIDE the base in Japan. We belonged INSIDE the base, OUTSIDE of Japan. Before moving, we were OUTSIDE the base, but also both inside and outside of Japan — marginal, but not yet part of American base culture.

Here, buildings were different. There were no more crowds. Our lives became decidedly more "modern" with amenities such as a washing machine, refrigerator, and Western furniture. Before, I sat on *tatami* and wore *geta*.[2] Now, I was wearing tennis shoes and singing the *Star Spangled Banner*. And my blackness was now blooming in an American way. My father was around. I barely knew him.

*My mixedness was now blooming.*

On the base, there were many mixed kids, so I didn't stand out.

I felt more comfortable, even though "Jap" and "nigger" were sometimes hurled at me from the mouths of parents or on the playgrounds at school, but this was a minor issue. There were those who helped me to enjoy life, so I no longer felt threatened or lonely. There were more friends who thought of those words as wrong. Milkshakes were that much more delicious to me, once I got ahold of one at the snack bar on the base.

One of my favorite things to do on the base was to feast at the snack bar. I'd always order a hamburger and french fries and different kinds of milk shakes or malts to go with it. Once in a while I would order a soda, but most often it was a milkshake. Strawberry milkshakes.

And not the kind common nowadays. Nowadays, it's more like melted sugar ice cream, thick and clumpy. In those days, the milk shakes were milkshakes — they were bubbly, shaken up, lighter, a bit more milky, subtle-tasting.

I was a black American outside of the house, and Japanese inside. Mama and I lived at home. Dad would take me with him out of the house to hobby shops or on his errands. Our visits to the snack bar were always full of glee, anticipation and tastiness. I became Black-American on the base, and my distance from my mother had begun, just as I began to develop a closeness with Dad. Milkshakes symbolized this.

Later, when we returned to Tachikawa in 1968, my friends in junior high school would still go to that same snack bar after school. I can still taste those milkshakes. It is attached to my earliest memories of Tachikawa Air Base, of becoming American. Boundaries were already entering my body, forming. With a strawberry milkshake taste. 目

CHAPTER NOTES

1. My friend introduced himself as "Lonnie," after his longed-for yet unknown father. I couldn't remember his Aeta name at the time of this writing. He came to the U.S. and worked odd jobs, and eventually began to sell drugs to make ends meet. When I first met him, I thought he was African American, but quickly learned he was one of the Aeta people (often referred to as one of the Negrito Asian tribes by many anthropologists). I only knew him for a few months, and I don't know where he is now.

2. *Geta* (下駄) is a traditional, centuries-old sandals made of wood, on short stilts.

# CHAPTER 15

# New Black[1]

"You, don't be afraid. I said that it was intended that you should perish in the ghetto, perish by never being allowed to go behind the white man's definitions, by never being allowed to spell your proper name."

— James Baldwin, *The Fire Next Time*[2]

THE GLOBAL DEPRESSION OF THE 1930S inspired many African Americans to climb out from under the residual conditions of slavery. During the First Great Migration (1916–1930), almost two million people moved from mostly rural areas to northern industrial cities, and the Second Great Migration (1940–1970) brought at least five million people—including many townspeople with urban skills—to northern and western states.

Joining the U.S. military was a way for many young blacks to earn a living, as well as prove their worth in the eyes of the American dream, even if the military was segregated. The U.S. military had discriminated against blacks since its creation. Ironically, during World War II, black enlistment was at an all-time high, with more than one million serving in the armed forces. For many African Americans, the war offered an opportunity to get out of the cycle of crushing rural poverty. Blacks joined the military in large numbers, escaping a decade of Depression and tenant farming in the South and Midwest. Yet, like the rest of America in the 1940s, the armed forces were segregated. When black men volunteered for duty or were drafted, they were assigned to segregated divisions and often given combat support roles, such as cook, quartermaster and grave-digging duties. When President Harry S. Truman signed Executive Order 9981

An African American contingent in formation before boarding the ships that would take them to the Pacific during World War II. *Photo courtesy of the U.S. National Archives.*

in 1948 to officially end segregation in the U.S. military, some forms of racial segregation continued until after the Korean War.

When black, Latino, and Native American soldiers returned, they found a country that still did not grant them full rights. Some black soldiers who had left farm jobs in the South decided not to return home. Instead, they moved to cities, looking for work similar to what they had learned in the armed forces. This movement represented an intensification of the black migration that began around the turn of the century. It was a movement that began to openly challenge Jim Crow and segregation. My Dad's family tackled this in their own way.

Dad left high school in the 1950s to become the new and envisioned black man by providing for his family and traveling the world. On this journey, he took along all that he had carried. Although the violences had been internalized, even with this escape, they would continue to revisit him. This would never end, not even in the U.S. military.

While the Korean War provided opportunities and hope, it was also a cauldron of ambiguity and violence. As the U.S. sought to desegregate the military during the Korean War, it was a process with very uneven results.

The imposition of color onto bodies of difference intensified in this liberalizing and homogenizing time in history. Prevailing notions of the inferior and subordinate status of blackness would not go away, and were sometimes painted onto bodies with very different histories, which both overlaid and engulfed people like myself who were equally puzzled by the foreignness of African Americanness.

I use the term "Amerasian" to point to mixed-Asian identities born out of postwar experiences. Most of the time, however, I am considered and treated as black. In invoking myself as "mixed Black Asian," I could not be considered a model minority or dominant "American," only racially inferior. As someone both black and raised in Japan, I was a particular body that Japan's dominant, mainstream laws and everyday perceptions did not know how to approach or handle.

In the U.S., black has been recategorized into "African American," a description that implements a "one-drop" ideology that ignores mixed-race people and lumps dark-skinned people into a general physiognomy and one category. As a result, this descriptor ignores the presence of native Africans as well as Black Asians, South Sea Islanders and Pacific Islanders. In Asia, anything darker and "African American-looking" is black, no matter what country or culture. In Europe, "black" primarily references African and South Asian, while, in Australia, it marks indigenous Aboriginal heritage. When mixed-race enters the conversation, the psycho-social relationship between how one looks (in relation to self, country, familiarity, and privilege), and the assumptions and perceptions that others have bought into becomes a disturbing dance. Navigating safety, love, violence and trust, as well as death, aloneness, and aliveness, becomes the ghost and dream of whoever is there, a set of borrowed gestures and movements from political war histories, educational institutions, and colonial identity formations which have formed culture and nation, which breaks—and makes—families and working relations in specific ways.

Bodies and words resound through certain terrains that can protect or violate identities in ways that often depends on what and how much one has internalized, what has transpired in their worlds including their past and the present, and how all of this is measured against our own experiences. Amerasian identity involves certain common "contact points" of experience shared among its various peoples.[3] We are an old yet new identity—a community constantly being repositioned in relation to silence and voice, dominance and resistance, ignorance and knowledge, care and apathy. The black/white binary paradigm remains intact and omnipresent as a racialized historical marker in America.

Even within the community, there are certain shared trajectories of history, which often contradict each other. Globalization—which I perceive as neocolonization— works as a system where "color, race, position, and historical amnesia" is increasingly globalized and normalized. Japan is a good example. Since the Occupation, images of African Americans and blacks have been proliferated primarily through the U.S. government and media. Its borrowed image of me and my father as American, yet performed in Japanese ways.

Color-based racial identity was introduced prolifically by the Chinese, who owned Black Asian slaves from Africa, the South Sea, and Pacific Islands, and who viewed black bodies as inferior. Japan began to replicate this racial identity. This belief of black inferiority, confirmed in the race science of Europe during its nation-making period, was confirmed again to the Japanese by the U.S. Occupation. In each case, as Amerasians were looked down upon as both black and inferior by many blacks themselves, Amerasian identity began to form. New struggles emerged, yet remained the same.

Amerasianness, linked with though separate from mixed-race identity, includes the ghosted quality of many prejudices and privileges, invented by various racialized histories, measured by its proximities to war and war-attitudes in relation to one's identity. It was also positioned alongside hierarchies of race, color,

Sigi Uming (1920-2016) of the Truku tribe in Taiwan, was one of the few tribal elders alive who could tell stories of tribal life, including oral histories that have been passed down from generations. There are likely fewer than three elders with tattoos still alive today. From the film, *Voices in the Clouds* (2010). *Photo courtesy of Tony Coolidge and Aaron Hosé*. Copyright © 2005. Aaron Hosé.

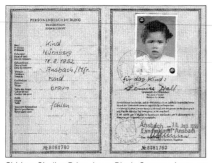

Shirley Gindler-Price is a Black-German born as one of the thousands abandoned by U.S. fathers in Germany after World War II. They were called "mischlingskinder" or "brown babies" in Germany. I had contacted her to connect our stories birthed in U.S. military occupation, racism, abandonment, children, and women. *Passport courtesy of Shirley Gindler-Price.*

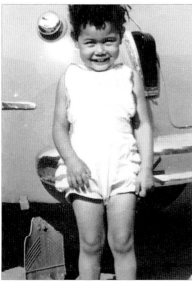

Shirley Gindler-Price as a child. *Courtesy of Shirley Gindler-Price.*

and class. It comes from unresolved dreams and the refusal of identities borne from national and gendered violences that have been condoned and excused. This is always changing, while the black/white paradigm of the U.S., which is in constant development, maintains its stronghold in American society. Some handwritten notes:

*The first mixed-race American-Japanese baby fathered by an American soldier is registered in Japan on June 1946. (Imagine the hundreds or thousands more, who weren't registered.)*

*By mid-1948, there were an estimated 4,000 babies of mixed-race, fathered by American and Allied soldiers in Japan. Into the 1960s, numbers are lost.*

*If an American father claimed paternity and registered the child, then both the child and the mother became citizens with rights and certain privileges. If there was no American man to claim parentage, both the mother and the child were considered non-Japanese, and as enemy alien by the U.S. military. It seems only fathers define these citizen-children, while mothers bear the brunt of societal exclusion.*

*During the postwar period, in both the U.S. and Japan, mixed-race babies were considered a danger to public health, welfare, and morality. This gave both nations the right to ignore, on the whole, issues of the babies' and mothers' health, welfare, and survival. Both nations joined forces to control and absolve themselves of blame with regards to the sexual intercourse that resulted in unwanted mixed-race children. Many policies were written in order to control this so-called "problem." Accordingly, I was a problem before I was born. The problem was the world. I did not exist at the time. This problem is made onto and against my body and my mother's before my body arrived. Racism, sexism, and nationalism were both actions and effects. Children whose fathers were black suffered more because of the idea of black inferiority present in both the U.S. and Japan. Of those not killed, abandoned, or forgotten, many of these babies were secretly taken to orphanages and churches. Most orphanages were not funded by either nations' governments and were poorly run and inadequate. Orphanage personnel often abused the children, considering them inferior. With some exceptions. One example was Miki Sawada's infamous orphanage, which became the*

*Elizabeth Saunders Home for Mixed-Race Children, along with several other Christian church-run orphanages. Even as Sawada was viewed as a hero of Amerasians, her racist views of black Amerasians were evident in how she "couldn't get the black" out of the children in "training" them to be good citizens (they were too expressive, too temperamental, too rhythmic).[4] Many survived in the streets. Thousands were adopted out to mostly African American and Brazilian families from the postwar period through the 1970s. This creation of subjugations, displacements and exclusions still persists in other Asia-Pacific nations where the U.S. military remains present.*

*Many GIs defied both SCAP and Japanese laws, marrying their sweethearts and bringing them to America, often after much waiting and pleading and bureaucracy, including pressuring Congress to pass legislation. While waiting, many single mothers in Japan committed suicide or gave their children away while some U.S.-Japanese couples committed suicide together. Some U.S. soldiers renounced their citizenship. Yet still, many children were raised by extended or nuclear families, or were adopted out of Japan and Okinawa.*

*During this time, Mama was unsure if Dad would return to Japan for her and me, as so many of her friends were left alone with their Black Japanese babies. But Dad did come back. Never losing touch with Mama, they often wrote letters. I was four years old when they married, as they had to wait until Mama could be included in the racial quota numbers to be able to come to America. Mama raised me alone in Japan for seven years, with help from her father and friends.*

DAD BROUGHT US TO THE UNITED STATES IN 1963. At the *Haneda Kūkō* (airport in Tōkyō), Mama and I had to leave about half of our things at the airport. Mama was furious and sad. She was furious that the U.S. Air Force had luggage weight restrictions and, of course, Dad loaded his own things first. Mama and I were forced to leave many memories and treasures at the airport. For Mama, this was a more significant severance of memory and family than she wanted. She always blamed Dad's "American selfishness" for this mistake. After a long ride in the Flying Tiger propeller-driven airliner, we arrived in Los Angeles. And then, be-

Mama and I sit with tumbleweeds at White Sands, an hour away from where the atomic bomb was developed, during our cross-country trip shortly after arriving in the U.S., amazed and uncertain. circa 1963. *Fredrick Cloyd Family Archive.*

Me and Grandma Irma during our family's Colorado excursion, circa 1970. *Fredrick Cloyd Family Archives*

cause he wanted to please me, we rode a *train* from Los Angeles to Albuquerque. He knew I had wanted to ride on a steam train, but, as he told me at Los Angeles Union Station as we waited for the train, there weren't any steam engines operating in 1963 in the U.S. anymore. Everything was diesel. We rode on the beautiful El Capitan of the Atchison, Topeka and Santa Fe Railroad. When it pulled into the station, with its glorious shiny and sleek silver carriage headed by its red and yellow diesel locomotive, I was mesmerized. I loved my Dad for this. Mama was also more comfortable on a train than on the plane. Even with this minor comfort, we were sad that many of our homeland comforts were gone. Mama and I were lost. Lost to English. Lost to Dad's way of loading the plane, Dad's thinking, the defeat of Mama's country and the Occupation. Lost to the vast expanse of the U.S.

Mama and I stared out of the window the entire time on the train. America was so enormous and expansive. Hours and hours and hours would pass without hardly any people. It was so unlike Japan. There were hours of mountains, fields of all kinds, forests and rivers and lakes. Forests, rivers, lakes. The train wound us through the deserts of Arizona and New Mexico, each with their distinctive colors and moods. Mama and I were amazed. We had seen nothing like it, and it appeared to have not seen us either. While Mama and I mentioned to each other how we wanted to eat *miso shiru* and rice or *rāmen*, none was to be found here, at least for awhile.

Dad took Mama and me on a cross-country trip in the family Volkswagen bug after about a month or so of living in Albuquerque. I began to hate long car rides on this trip; so did Mama. Mama preferred train and bus travel. She spent most of the plane ride vomiting or clutching to Dad's arm. Dad then took us on a car trip around the southern U.S., Midwest, and Colorado, so that Mama and I could understand our new country. Part of this involved visiting Dad's family and dearest friends.

When we arrived in Detroit, we drove into an area that was mostly African American. The houses were brick, with white or tan-colored wooden doors, all similar-looking. We arrived at a medium-sized house with a small lawn and a low stone wall with beautiful flowers. Dad told us that my grandmother, his mother, lived in this house. As Mama and I followed Dad's lead, getting out of the cramped Volkswagen, some of the neighbors saw us and stared. Dad waved at some folks and some said "hi." They were quite friendly. They were all black. But I didn't feel any camaraderie at the time. Community has little to do with color. It's more about collective experiences of oppressions. And I was too young to know or understand other lives or the history of blacks in the U.S. All I knew was that Mama and I had traveled across the Pacific Ocean to a strange and huge land where no one else spoke Japanese except Mama and me, and people behaved in ways unusual to us.

The three of us, with Dad leading, walked up to the front door where Grandmother was there to greet us with open arms and a big smile. Her name was Grandma Irma, and she was a husky, strong, jovial woman. And nothing could have prepared me and Mama for Grandma's love. Grandma grabbed Mama and hugged her, kissing her six, eight, ten times all around her cheeks and forehead, hugging and squeezing her and saying how beautiful she was and how glad she was to see her. Mama looked embarrassed as she smiled. This kind of greeting would be impossible in Japan! I became scared. *Kowai!* All of a sudden she was on me! Grandma Irma was kissing me all over my face and hugging me so tightly I thought I'd die. There was so much! Her kisses were a little wet, and I could feel a bit of a mustache. *Ugh! kowai!* It was funny and scary. But I was sensitive enough to know not to grimace in front of her. Or perhaps I did make a little face? When she finally let me go, my "new" uncles were laughing at me for making faces during the kissing binge. *Bareta!*[5] After I sat down next to Mama, I had time to wipe the wetness of the lightly-mustached kisses off my face. *Yuck! Ooooh, yuck!* But...I couldn't help but smile. I felt a love and warmth I had never felt before. Mama and I secretly loved the mustached-kisses and longed for them to never finish. *Never.* Mama and I looked at each other and giggled. *We had arrived.* Later that same year, Mama and I talked about Grandma Irma's kisses and hugs and we both giggled again. She told me that she had been surprised, but, at the same time, she felt guilty.

Mama sitting alone outside Dad's mother's home during our first visit to Detroit. She told me years later how lonely and scared she felt that day, circa 1964. *Fredrick Cloyd Family Archives*

≋ ≋ ≋

As mama and i began settling in at our home on Kirtland Air Force Base in Albuquerque, we began to understand ourselves as part of a large African American family lineage spread across the country. At the same time, we knew we were lucky because, in our travels through Dad's relatives, there were people and places we stayed away from, where we noticed faces of disdain or ridicule. Dad had protected us by befriending only his more "open" African American neighbors and relatives. His family was kind and respectful. Mama knew of some of her friends who were not quite as lucky. As we began to acclimate to American life, we were disoriented, displaced, and searching to find ourselves and how we were to live here as new and different people.

I was new at this. I began to understand myself as hybrid, but I also began to learn more about what "black" meant, and experienced new things. Nothing was as

Shinjuku Gyoen, Tōkyō, Japan, 1950. African American soldiers with their Japanese female partners. Velina Hasu Houston's mother and father, Lemo Houston and Takechi Setsuko (back row, far left). Her mother expressed discomfort about the event, stating that most of the Japanese women that she knew who had African American boyfriends had serious relationships and marriages, and the event that day seemed to be too casual for her. *Photo courtesy of The Velina Avisa Hasu Houston Family Trust.*

different, I thought, was the food I was used to on the streets of Japan, the *Tanmen* from old rāmen noodle carts along the side of the road with their outdoor stools and paper lanterns waving in the wind, the green soda with cherries and the *yaki-imo* and *kasutera* or the *katsudon*. The collard greens, pinto beans, hamhocks, and cornbread served by Grandma Irma's labor brought new pleasures, surprising me with their fragrances and tastes. Mama, on the other hand, questioned all this newness.

Here in America, I was gaining an advantage over Mama: I had begun to speak English first in the base schools on Tachikawa Air Base, and then in Albuquerque. My knowledge of it grew rapidly, given all the American television I had been watching, but my Japanese was still maintained with my mother. More than food and language, I was beginning to blossom in a different trajectory, a different self. Mama, however, faced a new set of psychic and cultural navigations in a land where she would largely be ignored, if not scorned or isolated, for decades. At the same time, she could celebrate those skills and aspects of herself that were scorned in Japan, but welcomed in America. Her past and present were intertwining into an intensified level. And I, in a relatively freer yet more isolated America, would experience different forms of happiness and violence as well. Yet in the back of my mind, there was something I could not articulate. Things that Mama and I could, perhaps, be haunted by.

> *Lemo Houston and Takechi Setsuko were married in the early 1950s. Unusual for those days, Setsuko was allowed to come to the U.S. to be with Lemo. They were visiting Lemo's extended family in New York City, but Lemo was soon called to Washington D.C. by his superiors, leaving his wife and two daughters behind with his family. Upon returning a few days later, he discovered his wife and daughters locked in the attic. According to his daughter, they were locked there so that the African American neighbors would not know that "they were harboring a Jap." Lemo, Setsuko and the two daughters left New York City immediately. He renounced his family and did not see them again. In later years, his daughters would connect with younger generations of his family.*[6]

I began to realize my privilege and my luck, alongside my pain. 目

My nuclear family, circa 1955. *Fredrick Cloyd Family Archive.*

# CHAPTER NOTES

1. It is only in recent years that scholarly works about the African American experience during and shortly after World War II have come to light, including books by Neil A. Wynn, *The Afro-American and the Second World War* (Teaneck, NJ: Holmes & Meier, 1993) originally published in 1976, and *The African American Experience During World War II* (Lanham, MD: Rowman & Littlefield, 2011); and Michael Cullen Green, *Black Yanks in the Pacific: Race in the Making of American Military Empire after World War II (The United States in the World)* (NY: Cornell University Press, 2010).

2. James Baldwin, *The Fire Next Time* (NY: Vintage, 1992).

3. See Bernard Scott Lucious, "In the Black Pacific: Testimonies of Vietnamese Afro-Amerasian Displacements," in *Displacements and Diasporas: Asians in the Americas,* eds. Wanni W. Anderson and Robert G. Lee (NJ: Rutgers University Press, 2005), an excellent piece on this topic. This was an important work that influenced much of my thought process when writing this book.

4. None of Miki Sawada's works have been translated in their entirety into English. Her book, 黒い肌と白い心：サンダース・ホームへの道 (*Black Skin and White Heart: The Path to the Saunders Home)*, is only available in Japanese, and is difficult to track down. She has two books about her in English, and she is the author of this book, only available in Japanese.

5. *Bareta* (ばれた) means "I've been found out!" or "oops I've been discovered."

6. Elfrieda Berthiaume Shukert and Barbara Smith Scibetta, *War Brides of World War II* (Novato, CA: Presidio Press, 1988), 225. This story was used with permission from Velina Hasu Houston (the author of the foreword of this book), whose family this story is about.

# CHAPTER 16

# Real or Imagined?

女は花か 男は蝶か,
Is a woman the flower, a man the butterfly?
森進一, 女と蝶 1967

— from the hit song, "Flower and Butterfly," 花と蝶
sung by Mori Shinichi (1967)

I WAS NOT PREPARED WHEN MAMA casually mentioned to me at dinner one evening, *"Goukan sareta no yo Mama. Yon kai mo."*

What … Raped?
Raped? … What?
Mama's been raped four times? Or …

I was twenty when she told me. A stream of questions tumbled through my mind: where was she raped? How? When? She said that when she was six, she was raped by a neighborhood boy; when she was ten, she had been raped in China by Japanese soldiers; and when she was hanging around the U.S. military bases just before she met Dad, she was raped by two white men. Raped in China when she was ten. What? It didn't make any sense as far as the sequence of what I knew of her life then. Why was Mama telling me this? Was it true? How could it be? She had not been living in China when she was six. According to what I knew, she had lived in Japan by the time she was three years old. Was she confused? And in the photographs and in memory, she couldn't have been thirty years old when I was born. What was this?

And then, at times in conversation with Mama, I would bring up how terrible it must have been to be raped and how she has had to learn to live with this in her life. But she would look at me, confused. *"Nanno hanashi sore?"* (What's that you're talking about?) Then she told me she'd never been raped and how lucky

133

she was that she hadn't suffered as many of her Chinese and Korean friends had at the hands of Japanese soldiers, or American soldiers. I knew how widespread a problem rape was. But hearing it as Mama's experience? I didn't know what to believe. *Perhaps a part of me didn't want to?*

I also knew that, in Japanese culture, like most other cultures, no one thought or cared too much about a woman being raped. It was the norm, especially between husband and wife. Rape considered as a crime is a relatively new phenomenon. So had it been a silent shame? Or was it something else? Was she raped? Or perhaps she confused it with her sister or a friend? *Was she making it up?*

For years, I thought about how she might have had to deal with being raped; at the same time, I wanted this far away from me. But there were never any other details. For a while, I told myself that they were lies. But which story is a lie? All of it or only some parts? She had made up stories before. Often there were reasons she made up stories — usually to cover up a deep and lasting shame that was ruining relationships between family and friends. There was also the Japanese shame that still configured many of Mama's moral behaviors.

Unbeknownst to me, for example, Mama told my youngest cousin Kō-chan when she came to visit in 1995: *"Kare shinjatta no yo"* (My husband died). When Mama told me years later what she had told Kō-chan, I understood, even though Dad was alive and well, living with another wife and other children in Texas. And when I returned to visit her in 1996, I hadn't seen any of the family photo albums in a while and asked to see them. In each picture, she had taken scissors to Dad, cutting him out of any photos with them together. Even him by himself. Mine were left intact. He was dead to her.

I began to think Mama was indeed raped and she had not talked about it because of trauma and shame. But then again, she was not in China when she was six, or eight, or ten. She had been in China when she was younger. Was it the other way around? Maybe she had mixed up the stories? Or maybe she was mis-remembering her friends' and dead sister's stories as her own? Who's to say that we only experience what we are objects of? What are the effects of this trajectory, this kind of life? Over the years, it began to matter less whether everything was accurate or "real" or not.

At the same time, I hated Mama for telling me. I felt burdened knowing of the multiple invasions of her body, on top of the ravages of bombs, militaristic schools, and seeing family and friends off to war. But who else could she tell? She was isolated in New Mexico, with no Japanese culture to speak of, and very few friends. Americans never bothered to know her. If she was raped even once, who else would know? What do I do with this knowledge? I could not shake it.

Since I was a child, I had a tendency to absorb everything. I had to work hard to detach and ignore things in order to function, but this had costs. This discomfiture helps when living in Japan and the U.S., I think. Masculinity is supposed to be rational, forgoing memory and emotion for the dominant cause/memory of nation, technology, and the progress and trappings of nuclear family stability and goodness, which alters our experiences so violently that it reorganizes everything into this good American "spiritual" self. To be a sensitive, questioning and caring man is often considered weak; a sissy, a fag, a queer, to be a lesser-man. All of these things and more: feminine, colored, and smaller, is inferior. One is expected to be strong, and in fact obligated to be strong under the dominant system so that it can maintain the status quo. They want us to be silent, to forget who we really are and be at peace with such ideas that have been made popular and normal by modern psychology and culture. If we don't comply, we do not belong. Or even worse—go insane.

Rage and depression are commonly medicated or criminalized, leaving many of us to venture into the world marked with national and historical issues that are not of our making. The world stays largely the same. This is not "life." Memory and culture, with nation intact and goodness as goal, is anti-life. It's a spectacle.

The intimacy between a child and a wartime mother in postwar occupation includes many stories which are often rendered almost completely silent—forgotten and pushed into an empty hole outside of memory—depending on the relationship between child and mother, between child and historical memory, or between nation, self, and survival. In my case, a son and a mother's connection is often thought of as weak and inappropriate unless the son carries on manly expectations. Gender construction has become one of many ways in which certain issues are pushed below the surface. And when those issues emerge, whether it's through an open door or a closed closet, they threaten the cultural foundation of a nations' hierarchy. Personal memories often need to be recovered, because they are an important part of our historical memory. Without them, we live in a void.

Historical memory contains the societal-historical violences that people internalize, which we then call "our own," or a "problem" from someone else, or "precious treasure," depending on culture or politics, which isolates individuals and families from the larger forces that create them. *Woman, nation, child, other.* Even the thought of occupation can refuse its own memory, and further accumulate trauma.

Soldiers marching up Montgomery Street in San Francisco's Presidio in 1930. From the Philippine War to the Vietnam war, the Presidio played a vital role in positioning the United States' military imperialism in the Pacific. Today, I live in San Francisco and walking these streets, I've experienced déjà vu that seems to trace back to ghosts of history. *Photo courtesy of National Park Service (USA).*

And in the case of Japan, Mama encountered Japan's rising world power through the everyday life of being a girl and woman there. There was life before occupation.

*Let it go! You need to move on. Why do you keep bringing it up? What's wrong with me? What's wrong with you? Forget it.*

*But the heart sometimes remembers, and clings on. Pounds on you. And some memories are prejudices that should be left to wash away.*

*Mama forgets. I forget. We both refuse to, yet we do. And we want to forget. We participate in turning things to dust.*

For me, if I forget (or erase and refuse) Mama's life, I refuse Japaneseness in my mixedness. I refuse my childhood, and my whole existence. I refuse the moments of her soft hands comforting me where rocks were thrown at me and split my skin, the moments of her lovingly making my soft white rice and miso soup. At the same time, if something blinds us from moving into a life that mindfully honors ethics and social justice, then we must force ourselves to move forward and take the risk. Remember, to empower remembering. Forget? No. Conscious letting go and remembering? Yes. But in a land called America, we move on and on and on and remember to forget.

*There are all kinds of rape.*

**Further Notes:**

*During the Spanish-American/Philippine-American War, when the notion of "Amerasian" mixed-race children was first being popularized, it came at the height of America's racial divide. So much so that, during all wars, letters from home to the battlefield were monitored and censored. This way, the war and racial divides could continue without interruption by discussions calling for reexamination. Orders to "kill every native in sight" was the norm during America's four wars in Asia. One soldier's letter, similar to so many written during this time, says: "I am probably growing hard-hearted, for I am in my glory when I can sight my gun on some dark skin and pull the trigger." All soldiers whose letters had these words were ordered to retract them. If they refused, they faced court-martial.[1]*

*August 18, 1945: The u.s.-Japan Securities Bureau establishes official prostitution houses with the governing administrative body named the Recre-*

*ation and Amusement Association (RAA). The association actively recruited war widows, bar hostesses, homeless women and girls, high school students, and orphans drafted for labor during the war.[2] The city of Tachikawa, where I spent my childhood and early adolescence, was intensely populated by prostitution businesses during this time. The official record of prostitutes in all of Japan in 1946 numbers 70,000. The actual number was far greater, and increased well into the 1950s. Any attempts at self-defense through legal, physical and/or verbal complaint were severely punished by the U.S. ruling power. No criticism of the Occupation was allowed. There were severe consequences for those who violated this, from forced labor on the bases to imprisonment and beatings.*

*In the first ten days of Occupation alone, 1,336 rapes by Allied personnel against Japanese women and girls were reported in Kanagawa prefecture alone. "No Japanese Allowed" signs and "Indigenous People Keep Out" signs were placed in most Occupied buildings and recreational sites throughout Japan, with military bases walled or fenced off from the Japanese people. Special trains and busses, many half-empty, were intended for Occupation personnel use only. Meanwhile, the Japanese crowded into packed buses and trains to travel for food and clothing. Curfews were immediately instituted.[3]* 目

# CHAPTER NOTES

1. Calvin Sims, "3 Dead Marines and a Secret of Wartime Okinawa," *New York Times,* June 1, 2000. Accessed September 19, 2015. http://www.nytimes.com/2000/06/01/world/3-dead-marines-and-a-secret-of-wartime-okinawa.html

2. Excerpt from a letter from a New York-born soldier in the Philippines War from a book by Stuart Creighton Miller, *Benevolent Assimilation: The American Conquest of the Philippines, 1899-1903* (New Haven, CT: Yale University Press, 1982), 243.

3. See Dower, *Embracing Defeat* 127-31; Takemae, *Inside GHQ* 68-9; and Kovner, *Occupying Power* 22-4.

Named "Buffalo Soldiers," the 9th Calvary of African American soldiers pose for a photo in the Presidio of San Francisco in 1900, just before their departure for The Philippine–American War. *Photo courtesy of National Park Service (USA).*

# CHAPTER 17

# Leaving

*I was in high school when I met Mieko. It was a few months after the war ended. She was my best friend. I met her after I decided not to hang around the bad girls as much. Even though I felt good being bad, having people get out of the way when I wanted and telling other people off when I wanted and not feeling scared because I knew my girls would back me up … I knew I wasn't me anymore. It was tiring. Mieko was nice, but she was like me—an outcast. Her mother is Korean and father Japanese. She told me once that their entire family changed their names into Japanese names so they could do better in Japan. We Japanese didn't consider Koreans (Zain-ichi)[1] to be civilized, or to have the right manners. But we all had Korean friends. Most times, we didn't know they were Korean until after a few years. She taught me a few Korean phrases and we would hang out together and go window shopping for hours, riding trains all over. She and I were so much alike, like sisters. One other thing we had in common was that we both hated life.*

*We would often compare scars we got from our mothers or fathers or schoolmates, or neighbors. My cigarette burns were always ugly. Mother was smart, because she made me take off my kimono or blouse before she would twist her cigarettes into me to hear me cry. Mieko would sometimes have bandages from her mother hitting her too hard and drawing blood.*

*We often talked about killing ourselves. The key was to be creative in how we'd do it. We didn't like messiness. We were too afraid of using knives. Besides, we knew other*

141

girls who had tried killing themselves with knives who had survived and had scars and went through tremendous pain. It wasn't final enough.

A short time before my nineteenth birthday, Mieko and I decided that dying would be better than living. What was left was nothing but going to school and helping our mothers and being unable to have our own dreams, except as wives to some man. To please ourselves, we thought, perhaps we needed to leave this world. So we decided to try and kill ourselves together. After all, our sisters and brothers and friends had died in wars killed by people who were children.

Americans were all around, and, one day, we saw some of the American soldiers throwing our friend into the canal, or forcing our friends' parents to give something to them and laughing at them. We hated the Americans, but, at the same time, we wanted to know more about them. But we felt distant from the girls who hung around the American GIs, even though both Mieko and I became two more of "those" girls later—another way to make ourselves "bad." Our own families were nothing but cruel to us, and nothing was ever explained to us, just demanded while insinuating that we were stupid. What were we girls supposed to do? What's the point of living? People were poor, trying to get onto the American bases to steal food from the full garbage cans, and then chased by the GIs, or taken to jail. We were nothing.

We didn't want to die in pain and blood, so we knew that knives were not going to work for us. We wanted it final and painless. Mieko had read somewhere that hair dye was poisonous. I trusted her. She was a really knowledgeable friend. That's what I liked about her. We were pals. So we could die together. We planned one day to get together after we went to the store and found the right hair dye, planning the right time and place where we wouldn't lose our nerve or be distracted or caught.

The next week, Mieko and I brought the money we saved from the allowances our parents had given us to buy the hair dye. We went to Mieko's house before her younger sister came home from school while her parents were both away at work. We carefully followed the directions for the jet-black-with-a-hint-of-brown hair-dye mixture, mixing in extra powder to *ensure instant death. When we were done, we quietly gathered ourselves and sat staring at the dye mixture in its nice blue bowl with the chopsticks we had used to mix it. The enclosed Buddha-shrine stood across the room in the now-open wooden altar, looking at us while we quietly and nervously watched the hair dye.*

*We could hear our own breathing along with the ticking of the huge Chinese clock. We looked at each other and said good-bye, and may we see each other in the next world. We cried. Gathering our energy, together we bent our heads back swallowed the cups of hair dye. Ahhhhh! Our throats were BURNING! BURNING! We gagged, and were on fire. We were spitting and writhing and coughing and gagging. Then our voices stopped, nothing coming out, and we grabbed at our throats. We couldn't scream. We writhed on the floor, our legs flailing. Hair dye splattered around the room. We rolled around and tried screaming, but nothing would come. Oh, what to do, what to do. Rolling, writhing. We somehow got up and out of the house as we gasped and coughed, delirious. Some passersby came and soon a policeman came to us. He flagged someone down to take us to the hospital.*

*The other world would have to wait for us. We were such idiots, for real!*

≋ ≋ ≋

TODAY, MAMA HAS SOME THROAT TROUBLES. Sometimes her voice barely comes out unless she drinks some soda. She constantly massages her throat. I haven't noticed her massaging her throat in the last decade or so, although anytime she coughs, it is still painful. And the cigarette burn scars remain on her upper body underneath her shirt, out of sight from most people. 目

## CHAPTER NOTES

1. *Zainichi* (在日?)is a term used to identify ethnic Korean residents of Japan. More than half a million ethnic Koreans live in Japan today, mostly as a result of Imperial Japan's colonial rule over the Korean Peninsula. While many are fourth and even fifth generation with little connections to Korean culture or language, this distinction is still made.

# CHAPTER 18

# Today

"But that nonsense aside, I see you have an astonishing number of scars and almost all of them look as if you made them yourself, am I right?"

— Kenzaburo Ōe,
*The Day He Himself Shall Wipe My Tears Away*
大江健三郎 みずから我が涙をぬぐいたまう日 (1972)[1]

*Stepmother was married to my father through an arranged marriage. It was the case of a poorer woman being sold by their family to my father; you know, it was common in Japan in those days. Father had three wives that I knew of. Stepmother did not particularly like my father, but liking or not liking doesn't have much to do with traditional Japanese marriages arranged between families. Our family's caste was higher than stepmother's and, for that, she had to defer to him even more than someone in a same-caste marriage. The war made these arrangements even more desperate, clearly demarcating who was to rule or not, even though the women usually had more control in most households. But for those like stepmother, it wasn't that way because of her family caste. For this, sometimes the maids in our family treated her unkindly too. One of my sisters was sold to the family against stepmother's will. But stepmother began to like her more than me. Nowadays, when I think of it, it must have created a pain in stepmother's heart [kokoro] to be forced into a marriage because her family was poor. I was later promised to a wealthy son of a friend of the family. I liked him, although he was killed in the war. One time I heard from onē-chan (older sister) that*

145

"Blackbirding" by Australians in the so-called Frontier Wars, was used to build Australia. It involved "rounding-up" Aborigines like hunted cattle and chaining them together like animals. Sovereign Union of First Nations and Peoples in Australia. *Photo courtesy of Michael Anderson Ghillar.*

*Stepmother was jealous of all of us. I didn't know why. But even so, I still wanted her to be kind to me in those days. But I was a child.*

*After having you, I raised you with as much freedom as I wanted you to have, not like my own childhood. That's all I could do. I tried to give you as much freedom as you could get, without me nagging you all the time, ordering you to do this or that. But you were an easy child to raise, gentle and kind, compared to me, a rebellious and selfish sort. So I was tormented often, by Stepmother. The cigarette-burns on my body ... here, look.*

SHE LIFTED UP HER LIGHT BLUE SWEATER. It was snowing outside. The furnace warmed the house as huge snowflakes fell, blanketing the landscape in a haunting white and silver. I saw wrinkled round marks—seven or eight of them, dotted around her upper arms, chest, and belly. The scars left on her body from her stepmother crushing lit cigarettes on her body. Signs of stepmother's wrath and cruelty, anger and resentment. *"Kawai sou ne, Mama."* (I am sorry for you, Mama.) She slowly and quietly glanced down, looking into her distant, yet always present, past.

### San Francisco, 2014

I WALKED INTO THE FLEA MARKET at the Civic Center. It was a typical Sunday in the spring, sunny and bright. I approached the vegetable stand, looking through my shopping list.

An elderly Asian couple stood next to me at the stand. I heard them talking. They were Vietnamese. With a disgusted look, the man shoved me with his forearm and says,

*"Bui doi Black."*

Startled, yet defiant, I said, "Why don't you shut up!"

The elderly couple walked away. I turned to see a young Latina girl, working behind the stand. She looked at me with fear. She thought I was the problem.

*It always works this way. The game is rigged.*

The name he called me was a mix of Vietnamese and English. *Bui Doi* is a pejorative term that means "mixed-race." He adds "black," which he has learned to say in English. I was surprised to hear it in the U.S., but I wouldn't stand for it, even if they were immigrants who were struggling.

*First, he was taken from his tribe. Crammed onto ships with others of my tribe, other tribes, with people who looked like U.S. but weren't. They called us nee-gahs and chained us to each other at our wrists and waists. The waves were huge, rocking us. The white man talked to us but we understood nothing. It was not our language. At first, he seemed pleasant but he would return time and time again, growing angry, screaming at us. After a day, we arrived at an island and were herded off like animals onto the land. We walked for a half a day to a large building where another white man and other people like us, who spoke other languages, stood beside him and guided us into the building. They washed us off with buckets of water then dried us off, gave us these pieces of clothing. White man's clothing. The next day, we began strenuous labor, cutting the large plants and loading and unloading them. If we failed to work, we were beaten.* [2]

The Black Wars, as they were called in Australian history, devastated Tasmania at first.[3] Some historians label the entire history of the founding of Australia the Black Wars, given the series of forced assimilations through schools, massacres, and policies that broke the spirit and communities of the existing Aboriginal tribes in the South Sea Islands, New Zealand, and Australia. Most of this history has been hidden. The tribal members were called "niggers." There were also African slaves, brought with European colonizers, who were thrown together with them and considered "the same." Even today, very few people outside of Australia and New Zealand consider the black tribes of the South Seas, Southeast Asia, and the Pacific Islands. They are often called "African." Dark-skinned people who look relatively similar were often treated as coming from Africa, called the same pejorative names. The Pacific slave trade was the most intense *after* the end of the U.S. Civil War when slavery became illegal in much of Europe and the U.S.

*The Black Pacific began for me in this dream.*
*Today, and the future, is my dream time.*

The uneasiness and longing I feel began before I was born. In many shapes. No, the scars that I have, that my mother has, where my sister has returned to, are not caused by us. 目

A newspaper article (1934) about the Darwin House seeking homes for orphaned mixed-race children. Written comments on this clipping reads: "I like the little girl in centre of group, but if taken by anyone else, any of the others would do, as long as they are strong." Australian newspapers advertised requests for people to adopt aboriginal and mixed-aboriginal infants and children from orphanages populated by children kidnapped from their families to be assimilated into Australian culture, which was a state policy and system until 1969. *Courtesy of the National Archives of Australia.*

Assimilation schools, like the one shown here (circa 1920s), were made for Australian aboriginal and mixed-race children. Today, that period of history is called the "Stolen Generations." From the 1880s, children were forcibly removed from their families by government agencies, to be brought up in institutions or fostered out to white families. *Photo courtesy of State Library of Queensland / AU.*

Mama and I on our front porch n Albuquerque, circa 1971. *Fredrick Clpyd Family Archives..*

1. Kenzaburo Ōe, *The Day He Himself Shall Wipe My Tears Away* 大江健三郎 みずから我が涙をぬぐいたまう日 (1972)

2. Many stories of the shredding of Aboriginal culture in the founding of Australia and New Zealand are available. This sequence is a composite. One of my favorite books is by Anna Haebich, *Broken Circles: Fragmenting Indigenous Families, 1800-2000* (Freemantle, WA: Fremantle Press, 2000).

3. For starters, see Nicholas Clement, *The Black War: Fear, Sex and Resistance in Tasmania* (Australia: University of Queensland Press, 2014); Robert Kirk, *Paradise Past: The Transformation of the South Pacific, 1520-1920* (Jefferson, NC: McFarland, 2012); Henry Evans Maude, *Slavers in Paradise: The Peruvian Slave Trade in Polynesia, 1862-1864* (California: Stanford University Press, 1982); and A. Dirk Moses, *Genocide and Settler Society: Frontier Violence and Stolen Indigenous Children in Australian History* (War and Genocide) (NY: Berghahn Books, 2004).

# CHAPTER 19

# Kurombo Shōwa Year 34 (1959)
# Black Sambo/Nigger/ 黒んぼ 昭和 34年

"Sometimes I go about in pity for myself, and all the while a great wind is bearing me across the sky."
— Native American Ojibwa (Chippewa/Mississauga/Saulteaux) saying

MY EARLIEST MEMORIES OF LIFE In Japan were that I played mostly...alone. But not always. In 青梅 Ōme, my birthplace in Tōkyō prefecture near the sea, I played with friends during that time, although, most times, I was alone. I longed for the company of those friends more intensely in my desire to forget loneliness. Playing became a deeply lonely thing, and as a result, people in general were something I learned to distrust and fear at an early age.

Ōme is a memory dream of humans and animals enveloped in a deep green forest with kind shopkeepers and dirt roads. Tall trees crowded over us, covering the sky. A river creek a few minutes away was where Mama and I would go to wash our clothes. Temple bells pierced the air with their low and haunting tones, echoing through the branches across the sky, lingering. The smell of incense would cling to our *hanten*[1] while deer wandered unhindered as the cicadas cried. We lived in one of Jiichan's (grandfather's) properties—one of the only ones not seized by the U.S. government.

Several times a day, the echoes of passing steam trains comforted me even as they shook the house as they flew past. This was when I began an intense lifelong love of trains. Steam trains were powerful, filling my imagination with the thought of being taken to other places. I saw them as elegant and ugly, simple and complex at the same time.

Simultaneously, tens of thousands of Japanese women were giving birth to, or raising, children of U.S. soldiers stationed in Japan. Since my father was in the U.S. and not to be seen, I was

153

Me distracted while playing with Chaco-chan near our house in my hometown, circa 1960. *Fredrick Cloyd Family Archives*

called *Ai-no-ko,* a term meant to exclude and demean. It is a name used against anyone who was a so-called "half-breed," meaning illegitimate love-child or child of an illegitimate union. *Kurombo* means "black sambo" or "blackie" with more of the meaning, tone, and intention of the cruel American term "nigger," and was also used against me. *Konketsuji* was used in the same way later. Sometimes I would be enjoying myself in my own world when sometimes, and suddenly, stones began pummeling me. I would run as fast as I could to hiding places, forcing me to always be on the alert for other Japanese kids who came to hurt me and my kind. I knew I wasn't wanted. My predicament at the time was unknown to me. From the standpoint of society's social structure, I was neither wanted by the U.S. government, the military or Japanese schools. Some parents' associations in Japan had recommended an island where mixed-race children could be raised. I knew of no such things then. All these things were enacted in the stones, glances, silences, and words that were constantly being hurled at me.

Sunlight, piercing through the dense forest tree branches as crows called, became my calm. On other days, it was the slow and gentle drizzling rain, the thick and haunting fog, or the gentle snow. There were no people in my calm, save for an elderly woman with a white headscarf tied behind her head, in a thick blue *happi,* pulling a cart full of vegetables behind her, smiling and bowing at me as she pulled. Wherever people appeared, there was both this intense pain of suspicion alongside the powerful desire to be loved. Sometimes it seemed like every single day I had to run from the stones and cries of *"Kurombo da!"* and *"Ainoko da!"* When it first started, I would cry. Later, I would cry less and resolve to not ever cry again. I would sit sometimes on a large rock in front of the temple, running my fingers through the fur of a deer as it grazed.

I had three friends. Seiko-chan, Chako-chan and Jirō-kun, two girls and a boy. They were my only friends. They played with me only when their mothers couldn't see them. We could only play away from their homes so they wouldn't be punished for playing with the *kurombo* (the black dirty one), or *ainoko* (the non-Japanese love-child, the one with the American seed, the former enemy, the dominator, the white, the black, the blond, the kinky-haired... whatever). Mama had exchanged words with the parents that I don't remember. They never spoke again after those words and basically ignored each other. Mama never stopped me, though, from playing with any friends.

I was four years old. Mama had just bought me the train set I wanted. I was playing alone in the forest that afternoon as I often did.

A group of tall boys wandering from down the mountain path came towards me. They stopped and smiled at me. They must have been around thirteen or fourteen-years-old, I thought. They offered me some apples and candies that they carried in a box wrapped in a *furoshiki* (a large handkerchief). After a bit of joking around, they asked: "おい,

緒に来ないか、緒にこないか、秘密の遊び場所のところえ？
(Hey, why don't you come with us to a secret play area we know?)

Wow. I was so happy! New friends!

"野球のやり方をおしえてあげようか？" they said.
(We'll teach you how to play baseball.)

I so appreciated the chance to make new friends. I wanted to learn to play the game that we saw on television all the time in those days. They told me to follow them and so I did. Ecstatic! We began walking. Walking and walking, with the trail wandering through the tall forest trees. I heard them talking amongst themselves as I followed, only seeing their backs as I trailed along. We came to a riverbed clearing with only a light stream of clear water. I felt a sense of foreboding.

Two of them grabbed my arms from behind my back. *Ah! Shimatta!* I struggled to get loose, but they dug into my shoulders and arms, pinning me in place. The tallest and slenderest of the three, who stood in front of me, pulled out a wooden baseball bat from nowhere and sneered:

"お前の汚い血は本当に僕らのように赤いのか？"
(Is your dirty blood red like ours, for real?)

It was futile to run away. I just stood there, my arms at my side. The bat struck at full speed on the right side of my head with a loud crack. A sting! Then lightheaded, lightheaded. CRACK! A ringing in my head. An array of ringing colors, then white light. Dizzy.

Another CRACK! Warm, hot, sounds blurred, everything turning white, glowing. Dark ....dark.

*We moved across the sky. We saw you. You were alone in a huge field. Your body lay there in the expanse of grass and trees, sprawled, your head and face unrecognizable with blood, your face disfigured. You lay limp, lonely,*

Me (center) and my two cousins, Kou-chan (left) and Kazu-chan (right), in the backyard of Uncle Teruo's compound in Shakudo near Kyōto in Japan, summer of 1961. *Fredrick Cloyd Family Archive.*

*small, vulnerable. All was quiet, save the sound of our wings and our calls. You were alone. We see. Wake up. We'll guide you home.*

I woke up with the smell of wet dirt and river water and grass overwhelming me. The big sky, pink and blue and yellow, came into focus. I couldn't feel my body at first, falling at the first few attempts to stand. When I was able to stand upright, I felt very light. There were birds flying above me. I looked at them. They flew towards my right. So I began walking, following their lead, looking up at them as well as the road ahead.

I don't know how I got home. It was nighttime by then, with a hint of pink and orange in the distance. I came home like I usually did. *"Tadaima!"* I felt very light.

Mama came out to greet me. When she saw me, she screamed, then quickly ran out of the room. *"Dou shita no, Fretto!?"* she asked from the other room. I couldn't tell her what happened. I didn't remember. She returned a moment later with a big towel as I removed my shoes and sat down on the floor, feeling light but tired. I remember feeling the towel, soft and cool around my head. She didn't say a word as she guided me to the room with the running water. I wanted to look in the mirror to see why she screamed when she saw me. She wouldn't let me near one. In many Japanese homes in those days, there were no sinks and flushing toilets. Bathrooms were rooms with dirt floors covered with wooden planking, with a large tub and a well pump. She held my head under the cool water as she wiped me down.

After a while, she wrapped me in a warm blanket and led me to the room with the futon. I laid down and she covered me with the *mo-ofu* (woolen blanket) and began singing me gentle songs *(O do ma, bon-giri bon-giri, bonkara sakya orando, bon ga hayō kurya hayō modoru)* I fell asleep. I felt comfort.

When I was twenty-three years old, on another one of my visits, Mama and I were talking. I had since moved to Los Angeles to devote myself to collegiate volleyball, having become somewhat detached from my past and Mama. She suddenly asked:

*"Furetto, oboeteru? Ano hi chidarake de kaettekita toki? Daredaka waka-ranai hodo kao ga tsubusarete..."*
(Do you remember that day you came home and you were completely covered in blood and your face was so crushed up I almost didn't recognize you?)

I responded, nodding. I remembered that day and now I learned how she saw me as I was that bloody day.

My mother continued: "Well, I found out a couple of years later when this family came to visit me and two of the boys apologized for beating you that day. So I found out who did it. I cussed the family out that day. I got a bad reputation with the town after that. But I had a bad reputation before that anyway."

I loved my mother for this, but I knew it caused her so much pain. In some ways, I felt that I was the cause of her misery. I had dreamt about that experience off and on throughout my life, but attached no feeling to it except contempt toward life. But now, I choose to remember it as a moment of courage for both Mama and myself.

She told me that she dared not take me to a hospital. Without hesitation, she decided to keep me home to heal me. She said she didn't trust Japanese doctors or the Americans training them.[2] She kept me warm and snuggly and still, singing songs to me, wiping me with the soft towel. I found out later that her distrust of hospitals came from the fact that she was a medical student who had observed Western domination of Japanese doctors she respected. She told me that she didn't like how Western doctors didn't let Japanese doctors express their knowledge and would make them lose face in front of other staff. Mama mentioned she didn't trust Japanese doctors with mixed-children and she was sure that the doctors and nurses might have killed me somehow under the guise of an accident. One of the first times I tried to talk with a teacher in Albuquerque about our family problems—the problems between Mama and Dad—they told me that I should learn to accept it, that this was the problem with people from different races coming together. I knew of plenty of people who were happy, or at least getting along, who were mixed Japanese and American, or Mexican and Indian, or some other difference. Many of them were friends of ours. At other times, some of these adult Americans made my parents sound like crazy people with no manners or intelligence, but surely they were, I thought, because these adults had never met my parents. These teachers were like parrots, repeating things they read or heard with condescension, or even hate. All violent. *Civilized.*

Another teacher (or perhaps school counselor) who I confided in told me that black people's passions and Japanese women's obedience made marriage very difficult. I shut up. I thought these people were nuts. The last thing Mama could be called was obedient. And I never considered Dad a passionate person. Although little kids are not meant to know things, they do pick up on things, so as I began figuring things out I kept things to myself. But it was no use. Islands and whole

Me going solo for awhile, at a neighborhood store in Ome, my birthtown in Japan. *Fredrick Cloyd Family Archive.*

countries formed without Mama, or Dad, or me there, but we played our part. It was that moment, that time, that I learned to always look for and expect danger. Really look. To see smiles as invitations for danger. It is a blessing in many ways, seeing beyond the surface of people, I learned to survive in the coming days, months, and years. 自

# CHAPTER NOTES

1.  *Hanten* (半纏) and *Happi* (法被) are traditional jacket styles.. *Mompe* (もんぺ) are women's traditional baggy trousers popular since pre-war days in Japan, usually of blue *kasuri* (絣) material.

2.  During the postwar, there was rumored knowledge among some Japanese that it was dangerous to deal with the medical establishment. Americans and Japanese authorities were rumored to experiment, and do research on the Japanese, either dead or alive. I have personally spoken with three Amerasians from Japan and one from Korea, about their experiences being forcibly drugged during their months at their respective orphanages in the postwar periods in Japan and Korea. They do not want their names or identities published. Such articles as: "High Anxiety: LSD in the Cold War" by Raffi Khatchadourian, in *The New Yorker,* December 15, 2012, or "The Hidden Tragedy of the CIA's Experiments on Children" by Dr. Jeffrey S. Kaye and H.P. Albarelli, Jr. in *Truthout*, August 11, 2010. Besides the biomedical experiments on humans conducted by the Japanese Imperial Army that are now infamous, one book gives a hint at CIA programs, by Allen M. Hornblum, Judith Lynn Newman, Gregory J. Dober, *Against Their Will: The Secret History of Medical Experimentation on Children in Cold War America* (NY: St. Martin's Press, June 2013). The literature does not include any notes on orphanages, but one must imagine the possibility.

# CHAPTER 20

# The Constant King

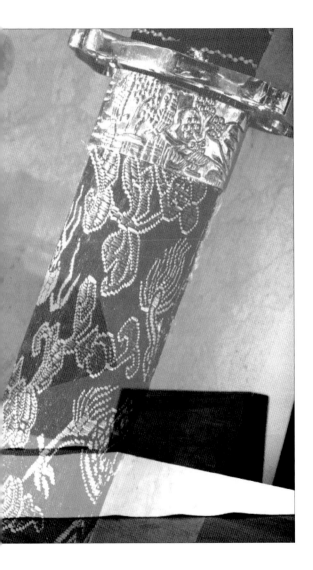

*Mama and Dad and myself at the dinner table.*

*It was really the first full year that Dad sat at the dinner table with Mama and me for a meal or two.*

*In the past, he had been out of the country. When I was born the military didn't like that he was with us. At least this wasn't how Mama explained those days of their marriage/non-marriage to me. So he was in America and Korea. In America in 1963, only a couple of months after we arrived, he was sent to the battlefields of Vietnam. In Hawai'i, when he was living with us, he was rarely home. In 1964, two years after our family had moved from Japan to America with no official housing due to U.S. military scheduling, we began to settle. In Albuquerque, we moved from apartments of my Dad's friends into a nice brick house on the east side of Kirtland Air Force Base. I was eleven. Dad was out with his friends every night or building furniture at hobby shops. The only time I saw him was for about two hours around dinnertime. Although I enjoyed his presence, he was still a bit of a stranger to me.*

*One evening, Mama had just put the rice on the table as Dad and I were called to the table to eat. After Mama set the rice down, she rushed back and forth to bring the plates loaded with well-done pork chops, which she had learned to cook because Dad loved them. I loved them immediately too. She brought a large bowl of boiled spinach with bonito flakes and sweet shōyu, followed by a plate of buns and green beans, and some brown gravy in a Japanese serving bowl*

161

Mama and Dad on their first date in Tōkyō, 1952. Mama is wearing a Chinese Mandarin dress, passed down from her family. Note the A-1 Sauce, ketchup, and other American goods that were already circulating from the military base PX. *Fredrick Cloyd Family Archive.*

*a few seconds later. Oishi sou! And Coca-Cola and genmai-cha that we all loved. Mama did most of the cooking, although sometimes Dad would cook so that she could rest. That's what Mama loved about him. He tried as hard as he could to think of her.*

As usual, Dad was silent during dinner. He wasn't icy or cold, but quiet, charming. Sometimes he would tell a joke or ask how our day was. I knew that, like me, Dad enjoyed eating. For him, it was also a time for the family to be together without distraction. It was something ingrained in him since his childhood in Nashville and Detroit when his mother would call him and his brothers together for a meal, a rarity given his mother's two jobs. Mealtime was important for family to come together, to be grateful to have good food, and to enjoy the sensuality of eating.

Our mealtimes were usually silent if we didn't have Dad's friends over. The television would be off, then turned back on after we were done eating. Mama was busy running around making everything perfect. In typical old Japanese fashion, she ate last. Dad would be reading the evening newspaper at the dinner table, putting it away only once everything was set and Mama sat at the table. As a teenager, I wasn't used to his presence. After years of living with just Mama, she didn't have rules at the dinner table. But that probably wasn't fair to say. It was more like I ate Japanese. My way of eating was something I learned organically in Japan. But it seemed that my Dad, like most of my American friends' families at dinner, had a lot of rules: don't put your elbows on the table; don't burp; don't fart; don't fidget; pass the food before you eat; sit up straight; don't use your fingers to push your food; and so on, and so on, and so on.

*Eventually, I learned and it would no longer be a problem.*

Eating was almost as much of a chore as a joy in those days when eating with Dad. But he loved food. That was something he and I had in common. Mama did not like food so much and always ate sparingly. Later, I learned that it had much to do with her experience in wartime and postwar Japan when food was scarce. She felt guilty for being in an upper caste family where food was abundant while many of her friends were constantly on the brink of hunger or starvation. In Albuquerque, Mama was always attracted to soup kitchens that served the homeless. It was a wartime image that she chose to remember as a way of feeling thankful for her life in the face of all her difficulties. For me, it was an emotional comfort and a way of preserving a distinct cultural self-memory within a foreign environment.

Mama carefully served us. When it seemed appropriate, I picked up the bowl of miso soup and began drinking it as usual. Then Dad slapped my hand, knocking the bowl out! It flew a foot or so, spilling onto the table, running over the front of my part of the table.

"Who taught you to eat like that?" he said intensely to me (my father never yelled), blaming Mama indirectly, and putting us both in our place according to his view of a proper American way of eating.

I was silent. Mostly because I didn't even know what the hell Dad was talking about.

"You don't pick up the bowl to eat like some kind of savage."

It took me a moment to understand that I was supposed to use a spoon to eat all soups, as he held a spoon in front of my face. In Japan, I had learned that you drink soup by picking up the bowl (unless it is a large bowl).

Dad turned to Mama, and said, "Did you teach him to eat like that?"

Mama was silent, glancing down and looking at the floor, ashamed. I turned to look at Mama for either support or an answer. She glanced at me with disapproval. I stayed silent.

Dad continued, "Pick up the bowl and clean this mess up!"

I complied.

I felt alone.

I knew that Mama did also.

I also felt betrayed (selfishly speaking as an eleven-year-old, I expected her to answer that this was how we usually drank miso and other soup). I cleaned up the soup.

Mama helped.

*There was a long silence.*

Today, as I reflect, I think my mother was in a hard position. Cultural differences. But not only that. This moment introduced worlds, time, nation, postwar occupation. We were with the *man of the house*. A new *man of the house*. Occupier, occupied. The victorious and the defeated. The modern and democratic versus the child-country, the uncivilized, the *on-the-way-to-becoming-democratic* object. The man-king, the woman-made-docile. The arrangement of nation, race and gender, be it adult or child had been stipulated and demanded. We were just supposed to obey. For Dad, living with the intimidating and brutal subjugations of the transition from Jim Crow to what exists today—a more underground racism—being the master of the house was a triumph he needed. It wasn't enough to be the boss.

*It was his "duty" and "right."*

As a child, I remember that moment when I realized I never wanted to be like him. I respected and admired him in many ways, but his behavior around us wasn't something that Mama and I should bear. *Why should we eat his way?* I kept it to myself. He wasn't around all that much, so I would listen to him and do what he told me while he was around. But most of the time, he wasn't. So I didn't make a fuss. At the same time, I didn't want to be like Mama either. Later in life, I changed my mind about this.

And what could I say anyway? As the years went on, Mama learned to become more vocal in her disapprovals and disagreements with Dad. It was not psychological, as Americans might think. From the context of Japanese culture, this was part of an expected trajectory of waiting for time to level the playing field through the division of certain domains (house, work, money, etc.). At dinner, Mama learned not to shame her husband and to teach her son deference to his father. And now I eat at American dinner tables without my elbows on the table, and drink soup with a spoon, except for whenever I eat Asian soups in small to medium bowls. I didn't need the soup spilled on my lap or Mama being humiliated by the person who was never home. I had separated.

How, then, are manhood, fatherhood, and hierarchies constructed in this? It's not just one thing.

*You're too young to remember, I think. One time I was giving you a bath. It was at our house in Ōme. Your Dad came to Japan to see how we were doing, a year after he was here for your birth. We were still waiting for the American government to let us marry. Until then, your father could visit us only once a year. I was putting you in the bath and your father came in. He saw this huge blue mark on your butt. He asked me what this was. I told him it was the mark left by his hand when he spanked you. You'd peed in your pants or something earlier that day and he spanked you. You were a year-old, I think. When he saw the mark of his hand, he pulled you close to him and hugged you with so much tenderness. It seemed like he couldn't believe it. He told me "never again." And your father never hit you again, for any reason. I loved your father for that. He is a kind man. You should appreciate your father.*

What toll does this take when sitting at the dinner table with Mama and me even as he was experiencing some of the worst racism on u.s. military bases? What stories of death and destruction he could not tell, or even find the words for? What had accumulated from his young soldier days stationed in Korea after fleeing the Ku Klux Klan as a child in Tennessee? What internalizations did he have in order to survive the battles with racist white superiors on the bases of Japan, Korea, and Vietnam? What had his relationship to Asia and the Pacific become? How about himself? How did he relate to Mama and me? He said over and over through the years, that people everywhere were equal. What does this say about identity? Self?

When I was in my thirties, Mama told me that Dad was sent back to the U.S. after his helicopter was shot down in Vietnam and he was injured. He continued to stay in the U.S. Air Force into the 1970s. He wanted to rise higher in the ranks. This was possible only to a very small degree. Blacks were never promoted higher than a certain rank. Dad found out the hard way. In Korea, Japan, and Vietnam, the military considered him "good with local Asians," even though he could not speak their languages. Dad understood himself to be a *humanist*. He brought home Japanese American *(Nissei)* U.S. soldiers and Puerto Rican soldier friends to our home, even in the early days. What role does marrying a Japanese woman play? How do the violences and destruction of Asians—the constant experiences of life in subjugation—play out in his imagination and actions? Where would his frustrations, self-displacements, and rage go? He was a man of peace. He never yelled, threw things, raised his voice or showed anything out-of-line in our house. But there were lines that were not to be crossed. How would this play out at dinners and family outings? What becomes important or not? How would Mama's life and dreams play out? What would I come to value in this?

So I saved notes from my research on Japanese War Brides. There aren't many, but whatever I found, I took notes:

*1924 Immigration Exclusion Act or Chinese Exclusion Act (U.S.A.) targeted Asians especially. In 1945 and 1946, the U.S. Congress passed special laws for war brides, but not for Japanese brides.*

*Public Law 213 allowed spouses of U.S. citizens thirty days to sign all papers to immigrate to the U.S. with their American husbands from July 22, 1947 on. Massive paperwork, investigation of Japanese women's backgrounds, and required permission from immediate commanders prevent the majority of women from even qualifying, as they first needed to understand these words, concepts, and policies, and find out what, where, and when they could be obtained. By that time...*

*Frustrated U.S. soldiers petitioned Congress for relief. Many Japanese women, along with a few U.S. soldiers, committed suicide, after years and years of fighting their commanders and the U.S. government. Many GIs renounced their U.S. citizenship. Others were married by Shinto priests in Japan, even though Shinto is not recognized as legitimate during the U.S. Occupation. For the couples, it was legitimate. Of course, these statistics were never gathered. No one knows how many were married or died.*

*In the United States, between 1941 and 1951, approximately 200 private bills were passed to allow all sorts of controls on racial exclusions.*

*June 27, 1952, the Immigration and Nationality Act revokes the 1924 Exclusion Act.*

*Before 1952, approximately 819 Japanese brides were admitted to the U.S. Most were Japanese American Issei (first generation Japanese Americans) who had petitioned Congress.*

*At the time, most Issei and Nisei (second generation Japanese Americans) despised any Japanese women who married U.S. servicemen and treated them (like my Mama who came to the U.S. as late as the 1960s) accordingly.*

*In 1952, 4,220 were able to immigrate. For each year, a quota limit was established as to the number of brides allowed. Dad came as a young teenage soldier to Japan after this period when many American military men had begun laying the groundwork against anti-miscegenation laws to be able to marry whomever they pleased.*

*In late 1962, Mama was one of the 2,749 brides named in the immigration statistics as being allowed to immigrate to the U.S. I was seven. Dad and Mama was granted permission to marry after four years of pleading and waiting. Dad found a minister in Minnesota to marry them. Mama was able to leave behind the graves of her friends, who had perished in the mire of desire and racist military law.*

In Mama's photo album, I see one of her when she is young. She is dressed in Western style lingerie, sitting on the bed with her back to the lens, turning her head and face to the camera smiling. Toward the top of the photo, in my Dad's handwriting, is written: "To my darling Emiko, my sweetheart." Dad and Mama exchanged many letters while the armed forces tried to keep them separated. They kept writing letters, encouraging each other, waiting.

For Mama, especially, these were the years of hoping and dreaming, wrapped in the dream of freedom from the confines of Japanese hierarchies of womanhood into a "new" history. For Dad, it was not just desire for one person, but a way to express his "equality of all humanity." *Black internationalism.* 目

# CHAPTER 21

# Men and Flowers 1961
# 男と花 1961年

**Tripler**

MY STRONGEST ATTRACTIONS in life began in Hawai'i when I was ten years old. My earliest crushes and desires became real and physical, making me think of someone for days, weeks, and months wanting to be near them, to hold and be held by them. When my attraction for others became more evident to me, evident enough to reflect upon and consider, it was scary. All around me, the comments made by friends and classmates and neighbors, and in physical education classes, became clear: I desired both girls and boys. I soon understood and experienced this as *not good* in terms of being accepted in society. Yet amid the palm trees and bright blue skies, the ukuleles and battleships, there were terms like *mahu* (muff)—a Hawai'ian local term for "fag," a pejorative term for "sissy," an effeminate boy or man—that were spoken with implied disgust about homosexuals. I was in the seventh grade, attending Aiea Middle School. It wasn't until I was in my thirties when I realized there is a lack of valorization and prioritization of heterosexual and heterosexist systems in many indigenous cultures.

Socially dominant ideas aren't primordial. When circulated constantly, these ideas become normal, operating as deep truths like smoldering desire, an escape, a glance, a need. These desires, needs, and escapes circulate in our lives, first appearing when we are young and formulating our identities and worldviews. The nations in which we are born and raised, the cultures that inform our parents and communities' values, are how nationalism, sexism, and racism weave through our lives. In this construct, the effects of identity-branding, culture and nation formation inform our lives, events and memories, killing diversity in the name of a globalizing neocolonization that violentizes.[1]

Me on my new bicycle on Tachikawa Air Base, circa 1962. *Fredrick Cloyd Family Archive.*

In Hawai'i, when I visited Samoan and Tahitian friends in their neighborhoods and villages, I saw very effeminate men and boys and very masculine girls and women, who were not attacked or ostracized. It was only in school that I felt menaced. Years later, when our family moved to the mainland U.S., I noticed a stronger division between male and female expectations, and the threatening and violent attitudes towards non-heterosexual "effeminate" men and "masculine" women that was even more intense and all-encompassing.

It was also in my Samoan, Filipino and native Hawai'ian friends' homes that I discovered that terms like *mahu* (which they saw as colonial terms invented by the *haole* (white people)) and that *before they came* (third- and fourth-gendered people) were not ostracized or ridiculed. This, I learned in conversation with the elders, caused tension between the elders and young people. I, conscious of this dynamic as a mixed-Black Japanese male with different desires, began to understand in a deeper way how there were internal battles being formed within us that were not of our making.

When I think back, my earliest sexual feelings were for movie stars on Japanese television. There were two or three male stars and one female star that I had feelings for. My first experimentations took place when I was ten years old, on Tachikawa Air Base, with two of the neighborhood boys, who were both affectionate and secretive.

In Hawai'i, sexual experimentation was fairly easy. My physical education teacher at Aiea Middle School, an older Japanese American man, was particularly obsessed with teaching us about "homosexual evils" and would point out newspaper articles about those people he thought were *homo mahu,* to make sure we didn't turn out that way. I thought he was dangerous, and ignored everything he said in class, which angered him. Hawai'i was a pivotal time for me. It was, after all, during my pre-teen adolescence when I began thinking most intensely about my sexual desires.

THERE WAS A DOWNPOUR THAT MORNING. *That day, classes were backgrounded by the pounding raindrops and the deep damp smell of grass and wet palm trees.* Soon, the rains stopped and a little ray of sun gleamed through our window. I forget which class I was in. Most of us were not paying attention to the teacher. Then someone from the back of the room yelled, "It's Tripler!"

*What, or who, was Tripler? I knew it was the name of the hospital I stayed in for my surgery. Tripler Hospital. But this couldn't be that.* Then, almost all the students quickly rose from their desks and filed outside. The class bell rang, the teacher still collecting his things as we rushed out the door. I still didn't know who this was. Everyone seemed excited. As we stepped out into the clean, misty morning, shining after the morning rain, a small group of people headed toward us from across the school courtyard. There was a guy in the center of the group, flanked by the others who were hovering, following him around. All of their attention was on him. As they approached, I felt a pang of desire. He was beautiful.

I asked, "Who's he?"

This other guy answered, "It's Tripler, he's so cool! He had some kind of accident and we haven't seen him around but here he is!"

So this was Tripler.

A couple of girls swooned, *He's soooooo sexy!*

And the kid who told me who he was turned and added, "Yeah, we all want to be like him. He's a real man."

Yes. He was sexy—as sexy as a seventh grader in 1967 could think. Tripler was an eighth grader, soon to be an adult in high school, or so we were all thinking. I was enamored with him. I could see why people liked just looking at him. He wasn't beautiful in a mainstream sort of way, but more locally so, a kind of Pacific Island look—scruffy, graceful, tender, muscular, and jolly.

I couldn't take my eyes off of him. I wanted him to have eyes only for me. I was surprised at how strong my feelings were. Other students started coming out to watch him, to greet him and say hello, to touch him. Tripler knew he was popular and maximized that.

I continued to experience his spell. I was also puzzled and amazed, not just because of my desire, but that he was able to cast a spell on everyone. Even some of the teachers liked him and came out to shake his hand. Then the sun rays disappeared and a few sprinkles of rain dropped. The bell rang.

Many students stayed outside but the majority had to go to their next class. We went. All I could think about during class was to see Tripler again and to watch him walk, to feel a tingle of arousal, my heart palpitate, my lips quiver and my eyes glow. Staring, smiling. When I ran outside, the courtyard had become muddy. After scanning through all the people, I spotted him. I went towards him, sitting beside him on a bench where some other students were.

Suddenly, a frog croaked. Some of us turned and saw its small frame, sitting underneath one of the low palm leaves.

Tripler approached the frog as others followed. Then it happened. He kicked it into the air. It landed upside down on the sidewalk, turning itself upright and looking afraid. Tripler came and kicked it again. My heart sank below the earth. My lips now quivered with disgust. My eyes narrowed. I was sad. A frog. Just living, beautiful in the rain and mud. Tripler destroyed it. Soon we saw blood. The other boys and girls were apparently amused at this violence. The frog laid lifeless. A couple of girls covered their mouths and ducked out of the crowd. Could they have been as horrified as I was? The bubble of desire that momentarily consumed my world had burst. Was this someone to be admired and desired? Then, as now, I could never stand by someone who hurts life.

I learned that day to no longer trust my initial desires because they could betray me. I also learned that we can desire someone without knowing another's true self (as if we ever could). I could not tolerate how the others kept following Tripler around as he kept kicking the frog until its death. It was not just Tripler. It was the whole thing. A man? I guess he was a man. He's *that* kind of man. So typical. So adored. So allowed. I was, in a slight moment of deranged confusion and disgust, glad not to be like *them*. If this is what a real man was, I wanted nothing to do with it.

≋ ≋ ≋

**Men and Flowers**

IN A SUNLIT CLASSROOM IN 1963 at Tachikawa Air Base, surrounded mostly by the white sons of officers and servicemen, with a few Japanese and one black boy, there was a lesson being taught on how boys and girls should behave in the world. The teacher asked the class: "What do you think good boys should do?"

That year, for the first time, I understood my name to be "Fredrick," and not my Japanese name. Mama had prepared me by telling me over and over again that my name was *Fredrick*. Almost a year had gone by since I transferred into the U.S. military base in Japan and began attending school there. I spoke a little English by then and, while I didn't understand everything, I sort of understood the teacher's question.

She called on a few other kids to respond and I don't much remember their answers. Then the teacher pointed to me. Without thinking, I answered. "Boys sword fight, make beautiful flower designs, make haiku, and make good food." Suddenly the classroom filled with laughter. I understood that the laughter was not just about something "funny" I said, but that they were laughing at me.

"No," the teacher said. "Boys don't play with flowers. Only sissies do."

I was put in place. Even as I remember the humiliation I felt, I also remember how, for the rest of the year, both boys and girls would tease me, calling me a sissy. I knew it wasn't a good word. I knew what they meant after the teacher told me I wasn't the right kind of boy because of flowers. This was my lesson.

How many lessons are borne from pain? How many lessons come from the repositionings of self from a known past and culture to an unknown subordinate and abnormal one—adjusting, succumbing, internalizing, resisting? First it was color and occupier-nation identity, and now it was something else.

It started before the Occupation. *I was becoming the Occupation.*

It started hundreds of years ago. It started when a small group decided that all of us belonged to this nation, remaking the globe according to that minority's ideas. Even as I was learning to be "Fredrick"—learning English and how to be an American—I was also learning how *to be* a boy. *How not to be a boy.* A particular kind of boy, one with American white Christian secular values—never complete or total—but always fragile, always full of resistance. *Boy isn't just boy. It's about a boy being caught in the middle of a nation's cultural and gender roles, and its resistance against anyone that resists those roles and behaves differently.*

The teacher and students not only challenged my "boyness," they also questioned my Japaneseness and my former life. *My survival, compromised.* In Japan and Okinawa, where more than 150 U.S. military installations still existed, manhood must be seen within this perspective of occupation and defeat. When one reads about indigenous cultures in the Pacific and in the continents in general, it is clear that their systems of living were more diverse and egalitarian than our modern nations. In many cases, gender divides weren't as severe or were almost nonexistent, and not all communities were patriarchal and run by straight white men. For example, homosexual and transgender individuals were common among pre-conquest civilizations in Latin America (such as the Aztecs, Mayan and Quechuas) and were treated equally in their respective communities. Even today, matriarchal communities remain intact in indigenous communities in China, Africa, Iceland and Albania.[2] Extreme patriarchal communities are often connected with violence and dominance, and often seen as militaristic societies.

Japan's crafting of nation depended upon a violent militarism which could rival European and colonial powers. Militarism requires a construction of internal and outer "enemies" to dehumanize and to destroy the "other." For nations to unify, a diverse populace must think of themselves as "belonging" to one idea, requiring various forms of suppression and violence.

Japan's so-called Meiji Restoration[3] brought enormous changes and a purposeful westernization of its ideas of "self" (of nation) in order to compete within the world and, in the process, changed its existing views of sex, gender and masculinity to become much more politicized. However, poetry, floral arrangement, and brush calligraphy were still an important aspect of warrior training, a residual idea from Japan's samurai heritage that remains present in Japanese culture today. In a way, the warrior spirit was being naturalized in order to craft a technique of nation-making, a set of values that inspired a warring nation, a defensive nation, to match and rival the European codification of their racisms. In time, national visions became a part of pop culture and everyday life everywhere. Japanese nationalists came to use these images of warriors who could write poetry and practice floral arrangement as things to be saved, as part of the Japanese soul, in order to resist the onslaught of the "whitening" of their world. At the same time, others believed it was outdated. *These ideas remain internally contested.*

Through all of this, I understood and appreciated the aesthetics of beauty and art. I found no equivalent appreciation of such things in America among men (except as a form of "self-expression" for female and male artists). This, along with the teacher's words and the never-ending malicious comments and pointed laughter by my classmates, "trained" me to hide and diminish aspects of my heritage as I knew them. Behavior, desire, language, my quietness, and my physical looks were wrong for everyone.

In this American military base classroom of 1961 in Japan, nation, race, gender, and culture played out onto and through my body, mind and spirit as it displaced my heritage ideologically and physically, literally and figuratively. From this place within my memory, I crafted a life dotted with self-degradation and notions of integrity and pride while killing the "internal enemy" created by an American or Japanese nation. I learned all this from a young age. *My childhood, compromised.*

This not only happened in the classroom, but outside of it. Some white kids who initially befriended me in the neighborhood on Tachikawa were soon nowhere to be found. There were four or five boys I remember as my friends who stopped talking to me without reason. I was deeply hurt. When I approached them and asked why, they would walk faster and move away from me. But one time, one of them didn't run, and he told me, "My parents don't want me to hang around you because you're a nigger." A year later, just before our family left Tachikawa Air Base for the U.S., another friend told me that his parents didn't want him to be around me because "Fred's a sissy, a homo."

As a boy living on military bases, I realized that my friends who attended my school and lived off-base were, more often than not, marginalized themselves. As I reflect, I realize this is no surprise.

I remember visiting one of my friends at his home when his father called him a sissy, causing my friend to become sad and sullen. I sometimes sat with him in quiet, just being with him without saying anything, sometimes putting my arm around his shoulders as we sat side-by-side. In this sense, I was very lucky. My parents did not attack me for my apparent lack of masculinity or lack of interest in chasing sexually desired friends. Dad once found a book I had borrowed from the school library on "male homosexuality." I was afraid that he would treat me like my friend's father did, but all he said was, "If you have questions, just ask. But don't you think you're too young for this?" He did not use an angry tone. I responded, "No," so he put the book back into my drawer and told me that dinner would be ready soon.

In my research, I encountered stories of effeminate black men who were stationed in Gifu military camps in Japan, which were comprised of African American troops, who were treated in a friendly manner by most of the servicemen, and, of course, approached for sexual favors at night when the lights were turned off. This interaction collided with the growing tensions arising between African American servicemen and white commanding officers who felt uncomfortable about how punishments were continually given out—to no avail.[4] Race, nation, religion, and disappearing cultures in Japan and the United States intersected where sexuality and gender were being colonized by dominant cultural and religious forces. Nowadays, if I bring this up with African American heterosexually-identified men, it disturbs them, sometimes inviting outright hostility. To forget and repress a different African American relationship regarding sexuality and gender requires more time.

A few times, Mama took me to my favorite adult bookstores. She confided in me that sometimes she was attracted to certain women, especially women in uniform. These conversations were meant to be private and intimate between us, and were not meant to be seen as some kind of branding of self. But in both Japan and the United States, both of my parents understood that to be true to one's self, or to live truly free, could be dangerous. For my father, this was especially true given his military career both saved him and molded him. For my mother, keeping quiet about such matters represented another way that others could ostracize her for her racial-cultural differences. For me, many of the same reasons rang true.

As I grew into adulthood, gay-identified men would be "grossed out" by my attraction to both men and women, and my interests did not lie in many of the mainstream "gay" interests. For all intents and purposes, I never relied on the structures of these formed communities: black or Japanese, straight or gay. I always found friends who were nonconforming in ways that challenged the spaces I lived in and through. Being a man brings up the question of how this conformity is determined. Militarized masculinities inform nation-building and a nation's sense of self, as well as individual relationships to difference. In vastly different cultures such as the older Japan and, to some extent, the U.S., I can look back at the formative years of my selfhood; as difficult as it has been, it has also been an empowering journey to live out my desires on my own terms. I, having grown-up in direct contact with nation-building in relation to global dominance, militarism, and occupation, refused to adopt these terms.

I wanted to be clear to myself about how this race-gender-sex-class connection was trying to define me. I learned to understand the racial and sexual categories created by European and white American scientists that have been used to control social hierarchy and culture normalization in their nation states. These categories would not be much of an issue if it wasn't for the violence that constructs these labels into weapons for people to kill each other—socially, physically, emotionally...spiritually, really.

*Nevertheless, the ghosts of nation—as they relate to race, color, gender, sexuality, and war—live in the ways we interact, in the ways we desire, and the ways we show up and think of the world.*

Developing identities often embody the markers of oppression. Oppression is inescapable. *Identities rule boundaries.* Those children's laughter has been etched in my mind forever. It is not particularly painful anymore, except when I reflect and remember. Now it is just a part of me.

Men and flowers can coexist. But I'm afraid that, here in the U.S., it is by choice. It is not taught to soldiers that protect the nation. It is not taught to young boys who are growing into manhood. Masculinity is a delicate flower. "Real" men are made, not born—so goes the conventional wisdom. In other words, manhood is a social status earned historically through brutal tests of physical endurance or other risky demonstrations of toughness that mark the transition from boyhood to manhood. Once earned, men have to continue proving their worth through "manly" actions.

In modern society, this may no longer mean clubbing meaty prey, but instead, we witness equivalent displays of masculinity such as earning a decent living or protecting one's family or space. One misstep — losing a job, for instance, or showing compassion in a way that is defined as effeminate — and a man's gender identity is compromised.

I am not sure who said flowers, a natural and earthly element are considered "feminine," but when you look at this both factually and symbolically, I am thankful that more and more men around the globe are pushing back against this hypermasculinity that society has tried to enforce upon us, especially in the U.S. We need to shred this image of what a "boy" should and should not be. A boy can grow into a man that can become many things, really whatever he wants, and he should not be judged by the type of man he chooses to be. And the people he chooses to love. There is nothing wrong with being emotional and caring. There is nothing wrong with being affectionate, for men to hug and lean on each other. And there is nothing wrong with men loving flowers. It's from this perspective of colonial domination by the west that has proliferated these Western notions of masculinity inscribed within the nation-state, the globalizing world. In this, the non-Western nations have always been considered less civilized, more primitive, Orientalized, and effeminate. Dreams are born from this. Flowers are arranged and designed in these places and times. *Time moves, creates, takes away.* Men are also arranged and designed in these places and times.

In recovering my learned Japanese relationship to manhood and flowers, I had to battle dominant American masculinity that is against men and flowers. But as American men lay flowers on the graves of fallen soldiers, will they, perhaps, become a "non-man" and allow for those moments of grief and connection, remembering and hoping? Are they girl and woman? Perhaps, in that moment, the natural and normal world we live in may rest. The ghosts can rest as they remind us of our folly. Identity may, in the experience of being with flowers, suspend its wars of truth and domination. *Release them.* Mothers and little boys and girls, may, in these moments, become themselves instead of the ghosts of globalizing regimes.

Oppression is the ghost-maker. If one claims to not be oppressed, or to not know ghosts, then that person is hiding, or cannot see or feel. Denial, ignorance, and refusal "protect" oppressions through privilege and/or shame, but are also ghosts that cry and grieve, going unnamed. Complicity is the engine of maintaining cultural, national, gendered violence. *Yes, Ghosts haunt us all.*

I wait for the time of men and flowers. 冒

A scene from the narrative experimental film, *The Woman, the Orphan, and the Tiger* (2010), which tells the stories of three generations of women: the former comfort women who were subjected to military sexual slavery during by the Japanese Army in the 1930s and 1940s, women from Korea and the Phillippines who served the US military in Korea, and transnational adoptees who were sent to various countries in the aftermath of the Korean War. Hetero-masculinities play out through the vital roles women's bodies play in the militarizing power of U.S. presence in the Pacific. *Photo courtesy of Jane Jin Kaisen and Guston Sondin-Kung, Copyright © 2010.*

# CHAPTER NOTES

1. Acts and processes of making violent. For starting an examination of Pacific sexualities and gender, see Lee Wallace, *Sexual Encounters: Pacific Texts, Modern Sexualities* (Ithaca: Cornell Univ. Press, 2003); and Stephen O. Murray, *Pacific Homosexualities* (San Jose: Writers Club Press, 2002).

2. Christian Koch, "Where women rule the world: Matriarchal communities from Albania to China," *Metro UK*, March 5, 2013. Accessed on September 12, 2017, http://metro.co.uk/2013/03/05/where-women-rule-the-world-matriarchal-communities-from-albania-to-china-3525234/

3. Meiji Restoration (1868-1912) in Japanese history is the political revolution that came to be identified with the subsequent era of major political, economic, and social change that brought about the modernization and westernization of the country.

   This idea of naming the Meiji movement as a "restoration" is controversial, and not an accurate depiction of what actually occurred. Japan's "westernization" has been noted to have begun intensely and successfully at this point in its history. Use of this term provided nationalists in Japan with confidence in its "re-alignment" into a colonizing, globalizing world, as well as its national strength being a threat to white, Western powers.

4. See, Yasuhiro Okada, "Race, Masculinity, and Military Occupation: African American Soldiers' Encounters with the Japanese at Camp Gifu, 1947-1951." *The Journal of African American History* 96, no. 2 (2011): 179-203.

# CHAPTER 22

# Tree of Death, Tree of Life 1965
## 死の木、命 の木 1965 年

"I remember a day when I took leave of this place.
I left.
It was all out in the open."

ATTENDING KIRTLAND AIR FORCE BASE elementary school in Albuquerque, was an experience that paralleled my experience in Japan. In Albuquerque, there were nice teachers I could tell my troubles to in order to alleviate some of my loneliness. I also met a few kids who would play with me at recess and after school without needing to keep it secret. Yet some of the boys called me "Jap boy," "nigger boy," or "mutt," purposefully knocking books out of my arms in the hallways or shoving me against the walls to provoke a fight. "Sissy" and "sissy-boy" were names I was called because I was quiet and didn't play the rougher sports with the other boys at recess. There were always a few boys and girls who tormented me, but I kept to myself. Girls often teased me about my handwriting *being like a girl's*—which, I guess, was supposed to be *bad*. Even Coach Crabtree, the P.E. teacher, called me "girlie." I grew to dislike P.E. classes because of it, even though I was talented in some of the sports, like track and field. Left alone, but growing used to it, I wandered around the large dirt playground, watching all the others play different games.

In the fourth grade, a group of white boys I didn't know approached me while I was on the playground during recess. It had been the first day since my friend Kathy and her friend Debbie were no longer at the school, and I was very lonely. Kathy had moved, and Debbie had transferred schools. My friend Don moved away that year as well. Besides them, I didn't have anyone else. As they chatted with me, one of the boys invited me to join them. I declined. After lunch, those same boys found me again, sitting on the fence near the school parking lot, playing with ladybugs on the branch of a large tree. They asked if I wanted to join them for some fun after school. This time, I agreed, thinking I really wanted some friends. Besides, they didn't call me any names.

We agreed to meet after school at the far end of the playground in the opposite direction from where I lived. There were about seven boys waiting. We walked through the residential area of the base, where most of the houses look alike, while they quizzed me about my mother and where I was from. After a little time, we arrived at one of the guys' homes. In the backyard area, shared by all the neighbors, he said, "So we need you to stay close to this big tree here and we're going to pretend to tie you to it." There was a large tree protruding from a dirt area in a courtyard-like space.

They began to circle the tree. Slowly, like in some American Western movie. I soon noticed they were carrying a long rope. I was pretty dense. After a few minutes, I realized they were tying me to the tree. I flashed back to the baseball bat in Ōme. As I tried to loosen myself, they began running faster and faster, wrapping and tightening the rope around me against the tree. "Hey!" I said, "What are you doing?!"

Two of them held me against the tree while the rope began chafing my arms, burning me. They were all smiling, having a good time. As I struggled, one of them hit me on the back of my head.

"You're a goddamn ching-chong China-man. You're a Jap."

Another boy spat, "Naaah. He's a nigger." He leaned close to my face. "You probably eat watermelon with chopsticks like a retard."

Then almost in unison, all of them contorted their faces: jutting their jaws to bare their front teeth out to feign bucked teeth, fingers pressing on each side of their eyes to slant them, signifying my "Oriental" ugliness to them. I began to hate myself for wanting friends so strongly and being such an easy mark.

There was a crushing pain on the right side of my leg. Then another one against my stomach. They were laughing as they kept attacking me. After a while, I became numb. I could feel nothing. I was blank. The most excruciating and volcanic loneliness welled up inside me. At first, I felt a sob, but then I began to quiver violently. Crying became an enormous tidal wave of wailing, engulfing everything. I think I became like a monster. The boys circling me grew scared. They ran off. I wailed, and kept wailing. I don't know how long. I became an enormous wound.

*I see a little brown boy smoothly and quickly unraveling the ropes from around his body. The ropes fall to the ground in a heap. The brown boy leaves. He doesn't look back at me. He runs. I try to reach out to him, trying to stop him. I can't reach him. He runs and runs. His figure grows smaller. Now he's out of my sight.*

忘れないで *don't forget me.* 忘れないで *don't forget me.*

As the sun began to set, the sky was turning pink and purple, some people came running from one of the neighboring houses. They must've seen or heard me. I felt like a limp slave-body, dangling. In reality, I was still as a stone, too tired for any muscle to move. A nice older white couple untied me. A crowd formed, asking questions. I could tell them nothing.

I was blank, desolate, weak, detached. I felt dark, empty. The woman caressed me, her head nestling against the top of my head as she held me close. I felt their warmth and care. My body shook as I was loosened from the tree, falling into the woman's arms like a rag doll as the man rushed to help her hold me up. They brought me to their home and took me inside, laying me down on their pink-flowered white sofa. I heard birds. Was it the birds that brought me the warm tea? A warm, white wool blanket covered me as the orange-pink rays shot through the window.

Apparently, I had been there for hours. The kind woman wiped my face with a warm cloth, and asked where I lived. I told them that I didn't want anyone to know where I lived and could get home on my own. They told me they wanted to call the ambulance, but I refused. I didn't want to be seen or noticed. I rose, walked to the door, and thanked them. It was night when I began walking home. My body ached. My mind was blank. I felt tears well up in my eyes, wiping them dry as I walked.

I didn't want my mother to go through this. She had been through enough. This was now my problem. My world. There was nothing she could do. It had all come crashing down. I arrived home, greeting Mama *("Tadaima!")* as she was reading in her bedroom, and shuffled quickly to my room to get under the covers of my bed.

Mama opened the door slightly and asked if I wanted anything.

I told her no.

She repeated, *"Honto ni nannimo iranai no? Jaa shimeru yo."*

The door closed behind her once she made sure that I didn't need anything. I laid on my side, staring at the HO scale model train layout beside my bed. Tears fell.

For about two months after, I hid the purple and black bruises that marked my tan skin so that Mama would not see them. I made sure to dress and undress out of her sight, taking care to bathe when she wasn't around. One of the bruises on my chest took over two months to stop hurting. In aching, I began to think I deserved them. And, over the years, some people have told me that I did. No way. *Masaka.* No. Please, no. Decades later, I learned that Mama had hidden her pains from me as well, as life sometimes makes us do. 言

# CHAPTER 23

# Ritchie and His Sister

"Finally no one is ours. You then will belong
To no one, too — not even me, your executioner.
You of course have known this all along?" [1]

— Agha Shahid Ali, *The Country Without a Post Office*

MAMA'S MEMORIES AND MINE are linked by unforgettable conditions, people, and times. When we lived in Japan, only one of the three or four other Black Japanese families that Mama maintained relations with lived nearby, in the next town. Whether our home was in 青梅 Ōme, 村山 Murayama, 立川 Tachikawa, or on 立川ベース Tachikawa Air Base, every four or five months, we'd manage a visit, whether at their home or ours. My good friend リッチ Ritchie, was in one of these families. Our mothers had known each other for a long time. Since the war. Ritchie was one of the very few friends I had who loved trains as much as I did. Together, we would play with our beloved toy trains. I always loved being around him as he was joyful, compared with my more quiet demeanor. And our mothers talked for hours, laughing and laughing as they made some of the best food in all of Japan — no, the world! I always looked forward to their visits, and so did Mama. They always talked on the phone when they could. Both of our fathers — Ritchie's and mine — were in the U.S. I don't know if they knew each other or not, but I assumed they did. In those years, it was still common practice for the U.S. military to discourage American servicemen from being with or marrying their Japanese girlfriends. Ritchie's mother was similar in temperament to Mama — quick to anger; quick to smile; and quick to speak. After three years of friendship, one summer passed when Ritchie and his family didn't visit. We hadn't visited them

185

either. Or heard from them. Mama didn't know what happened — or, at least, that is what she told me. I didn't find out until years later what had happened.

As was usual, many American soldier-dads left their Japanese girlfriends or one-night affairs (and their children) to fend for themselves. Some were forced or manipulated to leave their girlfriends by U.S. military commanders. Others thought of Japanese women as sexual playthings. Those Americans interested in returning, or at least intended to be responsible, would send monthly checks to their families in Japan. Many felt financially responsible, or wanted to do the honorable thing.

*In the springtime, just after Ritchie's family visited that year, checks stopped coming to their family. Their mother was worried. After three months, they were getting low on funds and she could not find out where her husband was. She found out later, after many delay tactics by the military, that he was in Thailand. The Air Force was finally convinced to contact him to suggest he phone his family. When he did, he said he had been sending the money, and didn't know what was wrong.*

*She began tending bar in a local dive where U.S. soldiers would come and regularly get drunk and/or take Japanese women home with them. One night, as she was walking home in the rain, she tripped. She tore ligaments in her ankle and could not work. There was no money.*

*There was no mail for months. Five months passed. She became despondent and the children, Ritchie and his little sister, began asking neighbors for food. The food ran out. The Japanese government provided no services for "their kind." She became more ashamed. She could not protect Ritchie and his sister from the abuse of some of the adults and other kids in the neighborhood. They were called kurombo, ainoko, konketsuji, nigger, foreign dirty illegitimate mixed-race babies, mixed (dirty)-blood. She was also targeted. Some called her "yoru no onna" (woman of the night/prostitute). Shopkeepers would sometimes refuse her service and kids would harass her as she arrived home from shopping, far away from her normal routines. She began working the night shift at a different bar. It was the only job she could find to support her family. Sometimes her boss would not pay her on time. The housing officials began harassing her. She worked longer hours and still wasn't paid. She received an eviction notice. No relatives would help her.*

*Her only other friend besides Mama had committed suicide the year before. The prospect of living on the streets became real. She didn't want to give her children up to an orphanage.*

*On a particularly lonely night, she decided to end their suffering. She was tired, hurt, hungry, and growing desperate. Too ashamed to go to my mother or her own family for help.*

*She had run away from her family to marry the U.S. soldier. Now, look.*

*She gathered her strength and resolve.*

*Grabbing a big kitchen knife from where it hung near the refrigerator and stove, she walked past the moonlit windows to where her children were sleeping. She stabbed them as hard and fast as she could, over and over. Blood everywhere. When she was sure they could not survive, she stabbed herself in the chest.*

*The neighbors found Ritchie, his sister, and their mother a week later when they went to check on her. The women of the neighborhood knew parts of the story and cried for her and her children as the police and ambulance gathered their bodies. I was always angry thinking of the neighbors crying when so many of them were at fault, complicit in her death. Where were they when she needed them? The crevice of "pariah" goes deep, as deeply as genocide. Mama told me that Ritchie's father became so depressed he eventually left the armed services and became a very heavy alcoholic. We don't know where he is now.*

*Perhaps because we loved each other's families, so we can never forget this. Certainly not the love. But memory attends with love alongside death.*

Mama had known that family suffered. She kept these sorrows from me, as she believed that I wouldn't have understood. What provokes different responses to different situations? The Japan of those days was poor and didn't respond kindly to the faces of those considered so close to the former enemy and present occupier — the *konketsuji* and their mothers.

The term *konketsuji* (meaning mixed blood), with its more "scientific" definition, became popular in Japan in an attempt to replace the pejorative word *ainoko* (love child). Well, that so-called "scientific" word didn't eliminate any of the stigma. It was used in the same way as *ainoko.* Was it a surprise? Yet there were many teachers and leaders across Japan who felt strongly that Japanese society needed to stop abusing us *konketsuji,* and stop the discrimination. Some Christian organizations in Japan opened specifically to take care of mixed-race children while other schools attempted to integrate the Amerasians into the Japanese public school system. But these social welfare programs and religious organizations were largely intended for orphans, brought to them by family members or officials who found them living on the streets. For those like Mama and Ritchie's mother, who weren't interested in giving us away, what would they do? There were no laws and organizations protecting mothers like mine or Ritchie's. My mother was fortunate to have a father and older brother who did not ostracize us.

Sorrow, grief, rage and suffering are not only caused by individual actions and thoughts.[2] Who and what causes the killing of dreams and the toil that follows? In many nations where mothers of mixed-race children are blamed for suffering, is only the mother to blame, if at all? Who and what wants us dead? There is dying, and there is being killed, killing. Death—*being killed*—was meant for me as well as Ritchie. Mama as well. But we lived. We survived. It was another war. Something kills. *Oyako shinju,* or parent-child killing, was thought of as a way for parents and children to unite in the other world instead of enduring impossible hardship and spiritual separation in *this* one. A parent dying alone would be considered a form of child abandonment. Further, abuses by orphanage caretakers were also well-known, intensifying the need for mothers to protect their children from society; better than the torments they would have to endure keeping the child in the family and witness their exclusion.

IN THE CONTEXT OF POSTWAR JAPAN, America's nuclear family ideals were a brand of social engineering that led to death (just as it did for indigenous communities). To suddenly have people and policies in place in ways foreign to what was established before that break in time/space/power was jarring. In the twentieth century, *Oyako-shinju* (parent-child killings) was the most common term for parent-child suicide in Japan, resurrected from earlier centuries that intensified in the 1920s into World War II. Most occurred after severe economic depressions brought on by global economic collapse.

With the rise of the U.S. as a global military power, U.S. favoritism towards China also influenced the number of deaths. Unlike Theodore Roosevelt, who ignored China, Franklin D. Roosevelt favored that nation in his personal life, which showed politically when he cut Japan off from the United States and established economic sanctions, which only intensified anti-American sentiment and desperation. Japan began to think the only way to survive was through military might, vesting its survival strategy with further encroachment into China, Southeast Asia, and the South Seas, in order to foster nationalistic empowerment after their victory against the Russians. The Japanese reasoned that America was willfully standing in the way of the nation's ability to obtain resources to feed itself, so food must be taken, lest Japan be swallowed whole by the white nations.

National military might create discipline and austerity amid economic embargo. Poverty and survival, linked with death, intensified in those times. In Japan, the divisions between the wealthy elite and the servile clans gradually expanded in the modernizing period of Japan's history. Western moralities began to replace traditional communal processes of childbearing. Japan openly stated that it needed to mimic the West in order to survive and empower itself. In my mind, the United States played a major role in the increase of parent-child killings and suicides in Japan and China. As citizens of nations, we all internalize *the nation,* whatever that may be. Parent-child killing is not inborn to a people, but represents social forces that are far-reaching, spanning beyond the personal, communal, or even national. This is only one facet of a process linking war, the rise of imperialism as national unification, and the need to survive.

The American occupation forced a reorganization of wealth (by extracting it from the wealthy, and displacing clans and entire villages, etc.), which stripped much of Japanese society of their former social structures, leaving mothers particularly vulnerable. In the wake of dead Japanese fathers or absent American ones, mothers faced an intense isolation without any known social or institutional models to rely on. Whereas the Japanese previously had their own structures for caretaking, albeit abusive ones dependent on Tokugawa and Meiji caste-system regimes and the slavery of the poor, particularly girls, they now had nothing. In this desolate terrain, death loomed just over the horizon, and killing became more of an act of compassion that dominant Western perspectives did not understand.[3]

Furthermore, parent-child suicide pacts were an act against child abandonment, and a way for children to be with their mothers in the afterlife rather than fending for themselves in a society not yet equipped to socialize them within a nuclear family environment. Although there may have been alternative solutions, the impact of extreme and unbearable hardship created this enlivening of ghosts. These disjointed ways of resisting trauma, isolation, poverty, and shame are borne of the ghostly constructions of society. And these forces that create the acts become identity in motion, across space and time, across various modes of violence and compassion, becoming transcultural and transnational in globalization.

**1985**

*Japanese woman in Santa Monica, California is dragged from the waters of the beach after "drowning her two children in the water" after attempting to die alongside them as an act of being together in the afterlife where suffering had ended. Instead, she is pulled from the waters and charged with first-degree murder. For the Japanese in Japan, it revealed America's lack of compassion. For Americans, it was a shocking act of a mother's abuse and evidence of insanity.* [4]

≋ ≋ ≋

THERE WERE MANY NICE JAPANESE friends and neighbors who supported Mama and I while we lived in 1950s Japan. It was not all bleak. Mama herself was tough, alternating between quick escapes and verbal retaliation when people would enact their prejudices against her or me. And Mama's family or friends were usually around. Sometimes, when speaking with Americans about my memories of Ritchie, I'm told to forget because it is too depressing. *I refuse.* Yet my grief and Mama's grief were separate, isolated. Our griefs were related to the entirety of our remembered history of those times, not confined to particular people and moments in our lives.

*A communal grief needs to exist, to lament, to honor struggle, to honor love.*

I am alive and my friends are gone. Their deaths allowed my life. I must pay them tribute. 畺

## CHAPTER NOTES

1. Agha Shahid Ali, "A Fate's Brief Memoir," *The Country Without a Post Office: Poems* (New York: W. W. Norton & Company, 1998), 61.

2. As of this writing, in Okinawa, Korea, the Philippines, Vietnam and other areas of the Asia-Pacific, American soldiers and/or their superiors continue these traditions of abandonment. In many places, including Japan, only certain kinds of women are eligible for many rights and services as the children are not considered citizens otherwise. Asian women left behind with their mixed-American children are considered impure, tainted by the outsider/enemy. These babies are largely unwanted by American men and legally ignored by the U.S. government. The Asia-Pacific sex-industry for the American military, along with businessmen and women of wealthier Asian and European nations, is a leading industry in the Pacific. So these children become officially "stateless." What choices are left?

3. See Shigehiro Takahashi, "Child-Murder/Mother-Suicides in Japan," *PHP* 8/5 (1977): 61-76; and Mamoru Iga, *The Thorn in the Chrysanthemum: Suicide and Economic Success in Modern Japan* (California: University of California Press, 1986).

4. See Maura Dolan, "Two Cultures Collide Over Act of Despair: Mother Facing Charges in Ceremonial Drowning," *Los Angeles Times,* February 24, 1985; "Mother Placed on Probation in 2 Drownings," *Los Angeles Times,* November 21, 1985; Janet Rae-Dupree and Jack Jones, "Children in Arms: Mother's Trek Into Sea Stuns Her Neighbors," *Los Angeles Times,* January 31, 1985; and David Reyes, "Officers Are Baffled by Murder-Suicide," *Los Angeles Times,* July 16, 1985. See also the play by Velina Hasu Houston, *Kokoro* (Dramatists Play Service, Inc., 2011), based on this moment.

# CHAPTER 24

# Who Injures?

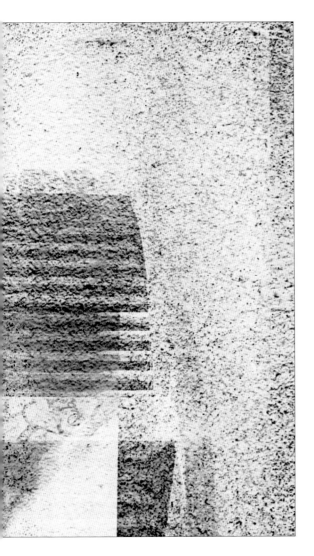

In 2007, Mama was diagnosed with a mild case of dementia. One of her neighbors, Tim, helped me by looking in on her, and mentioned to me that he thought Mama was living with a brain injury. I had told him about some of the things that had happened to her, as well as her occasional bouts of violence— throwing, kicking, biting and cursing out anyone in the vicinity when she lost her temper. For a small woman, she could really hurt big bodies. She lost friends because they did not understand. When I was younger, she would remember these incidents with regret and fall silent for days. As she got older, she did not remember any of these events, but when we would tell her what she had done, she would be genuinely surprised and remorseful, sometimes crying.

Tim and his partner were kind-hearted, working-class Republican neighbors, who were taking care of my mother while I lived away. At first, Tim and his girlfriend had a difficult time believing any stories about Mama's capacity for violence. They were not privy to any incidents, and Mama was generally charming, interesting, wise, and funny. *I also think that it was partly due to white people's conception of Japanese and "all" Asian women. You know—gentle, obedient, giving, self-sacrificing, bowing all the time, self-effacing. Ugh.*

When Tim began experiencing Mama's violent outbursts himself, he noticed that she didn't remember any of it afterwards. So he decided to record her on his cell phone during one of her outbursts. In one incident, where she had almost cut his face with a pair of scissors she had thrown at him, she remembered nothing afterward. So he played it back for her.

She was shocked. She began to weep, apologizing over and over.

It became increasingly painful for her to live with herself. When I was growing up, I would often protect myself from her by hiding in my room where she would never chase me. She would stay away, perhaps wondering where her violence came from. Yet this would be accompanied with a barrage of name-calling and put-downs. During my high school days, sometimes she would tell me that she wanted to kill me. If we were in the kitchen, she would sometimes pull a knife from the drawer. I would run to my room. Her monstrous face of anger would remain for a few minutes, then tone down. I was mostly afraid of her taking her own life. These outbursts were infrequent, but nevertheless violent. Sometimes, if I were in my room for hours after her temper flared, I was afraid I'd find her dead, gone, or disappeared, having run away from it all in some way.

Perhaps the outbursts were due to some brain injury, something just now becoming more well-known and well-researched. It wouldn't have surprised me, given Mama's suicide attempts and the daily bombings she endured. Or perhaps the bursts of rage came from a shame and memory from war and occupation? Or maybe just flat-out rage.

In the rush to "cure" people of their emotions and rationalize the world, making it controllable and manageable, we run away from things that we need to address. Control and manageability, both rational and scientific, also kills diversity. Why would I want to "fix" her? What would be lost? Why are we hiding the perpetrators of violence and injustice by "fixing" those who carry these memories? Social histories are fraught with violence. Laws, and the normalized values of our lives, carry the structures built by perpetrators. This does not excuse, heal, or justify violence, but since these perpetrations are embedded, they are often not named or acknowledged as "violent." Who and what makes pain? Who injures? What do the injured do when the injury is not named? If I am going to fix anything, it's going to be the world that does this to all of us. *Not my mother.* 目

# CHAPTER 25

# Future Teachers of America

WHEN I ATTENDED YAMATO HIGH SCHOOL on Yamato Air Station a service base attached to Tachikawa Air Base, I became a member of Future Teachers of America (FTA)[1] in the ninth grade. It was 1969-1970. It was our family's second life in Japan, having moved from Hawai'i before our return to Albuquerque. Japan had changed drastically since we left. Although we never visited the old neighborhood again, we did return to my birth town to visit one of Mama's old friends. The streets were no longer dirt roads as I remembered, but were now paved. Some of the buildings were re-done and old shops and restaurants had mostly disappeared. Japan was becoming more like the U.S. in its own way.

Returning to Japan was a way for both Mama and I to heal and learn anew, forming a different relationship to our home country. For both of us, Japan was where our language had meaning and form. Even today, English is still foreign to us both, even as we forget our Japanese language. Even though my English is fluent. I don't feel as expressive in English as I do speaking in Japanese.

And somewhat surprisingly, the violent prejudices I experienced in my earlier years in Japan were non-existent now. If I did experience racism in Japan, it was less physically violent now and more evident in attitudes. In the mainstream, Japanese people were now more fascinated with people such as Mama and me. Books had since been published about brides of American soldiers in Japan. When I was a child, the books and articles available then scorned those like Mama, who were looked upon as traitors who went against the grain of Japanese womanhood. Now, there were books that wrote of Japanese women who lived in America as American wives, courageous and enduring women, admirable yet "non-Japanese." Mama wanted nothing to do with any of these

197

The Tachikawa Air Base main gate, circa 1959-60, which faces the main Tachikawa city. Mama and I always looked forward to going to the city to shop, eat, and visit friends. Every time we crossed those gates, it always reminded me of boundaries of self, culture and society. *Photo courtesy of Mac Hayes.*

perceptions. She thought of them as machinations bent on controlling women, but she was, at least in our conversations, glad to no longer have to fight the glares and insults around the neighborhoods, shops, and streets where she walked. She felt freer. In Albuquerque, she had been experiencing anti-Asian and anti-Japanese hatred by older white Americans, but not by a majority, as it was in her early years in Japan. She felt that, in some way, she was being prepared for changes.

While this reflected some of the changing attitudes of Japanese society from the 1940s in relation to mixed-race kids, it was a contradiction for me.[2] I was in the Future Teachers of America group at the time, along with six others who became close friends of mine. One of them — Francis — and his brother were Caucasians who grew up almost entirely in Japan, and had been adopted by a Japanese woman. They were fluent in Japanese and English, like myself, but had never left Japan. There were also a few other mixed white Japanese guys in our group of friends, plus two Japanese girls who were adopted into a white American family on the base. All of them had some relation with the FTA group. In fact, as I found out later, this reflected an administrative move by the FTA to encourage bilingual mixed blood Japanese to join FTA organizations in Japan. This was part of a larger administrative move by the U.S. government to encourage international studies organizations and schools to use mixed bloods in order to foster more skilled intercultural relations, or so it was alleged.

When our FTA group traveled to Japanese middle schools and high schools to give talks and put us on display, we were not considered Japanese, but foreigners, even though we were all Japanese citizens. Japanese middle school kids would talk with each other about us in front of us, and were shocked to discover that we understood every word and could respond back. And their questions about America would often center on cultures.

"Did the Indian raids in New Mexico still trouble you?" one student asked me after I had announced that our family lived in Albuquerque before living in Japan. Why didn't they ask about Europeans stealing and killing the Indians instead? What were these kids learning in their schools? It began to sink in, more and more, that the education in Japan resembled that of the United States, and that much of it was meant to keep people in line with a national version, which included keeping us ignorant.

Indian raids, John Wayne, and the civilizing of the natives; the glory of Iwo Jima and Okinawa and Pearl Harbor and the A-bomb — this is world history. For the Japanese, all things American were fascinating. Although all things Western had served as an object of fascination from the eighteenth century, modern American culture had been pushed onto the Japanese during the Occupation. It made me sick in the classrooms in Albuquerque, and it made me sick in front of the students in Japan.

At the same time, I enjoyed it immensely. It gave me pride to represent the Future Teachers of America. For me, the question of what was sacrificed and forgotten and assumed in the name of becoming a global economic power was a process Japan was beginning to undergo by adopting a corporate mentality of tall buildings, urbanization, individualism and elitism, which began before Western contact, and intensified from the colonial period to the present. This was what the original Japanese elite nationalists wanted for Japan before the arrival of the Americans. A perfect match.

In the Highland High School classrooms in Albuquerque, I would be the lone "representative" of all Japan in the classrooms. Teachers would ask me to talk to the class about Japan and Pearl Harbor, and about the Japanese perspective. That would always be a problem when there were Japanese Americans or Japanese expats in the room who didn't consider me Japanese. Indeed, some of the white Japanese mixed kids would taunt me and gang up on me. In both Japan and the U.S., any access to dominant whiteness (or yellowness) was sought by non-dominant people who suffered under it. Mimicry is one way.

Sometimes, these teachers would tell the class, without asking me in particular, that mixed-race Japanese were a tragic group and that their social exclusion was why *they* had come to the U.S. I realized, whether in Japan, the U.S., or anywhere, that teachers often represent knowledge alongside their own opinions and prejudices, circulating inaccurate statements and passing them off as "valid," making use of their institutionally-sanctioned position. So many people supposedly knew about Japan. They knew facts that were "real." But what did they *know?* What, then, is *true? You know nothing. Nothing, mon amour.* Now, in Japan, I represented something else—a wagon-train New Mexico, a monumental and fascinating "other," the American, the former occupier. *Not Japan.*

In 1970, as a fifteen year-old, I considered what I needed to do and be in order to become a teacher. Up until then, I didn't feel like there were many true teachers. What's a true teacher? Where are they, if they exist? What is it that is taught? Who is it that actually learns? Learns what? Who benefits? How? For whom and why?

In 1969 and 1970, mama and i noticed that there were more mixed white Japanese singers and entertainers on television. Stories of the insubordination of these *konketsuji* were also quite common. I recall the singer Aoyama Michi 青山ミチ, who is Black Japanese. I loved her songs. My favorite was *Shikaranaide* 叱らないで ("Don't Scold Her"). I recognized her as being like myself, having Black-American and Japanese heritage, even though it was not blatantly announced. Publicly, in those days, these things were never mentioned. Michi's life was difficult. As one trying to carve her way into Japanese entertainment and society in the 1960s when upward mobility required kowtowing to the superior so-called full-bloods, she walked a courageous and treacherous path. In general, entertainment (for women and effeminate men) and sports (for masculine men) were the two places that mixed blood outsiders (such as *Zainichi* Korean, Okinawans, Buraku, etc.) could break into mainstream Japan, often enduring extreme forms of humiliation, racism, and exclusion.

As an aspiring singer in Japan, Michi was often written off as troublesome, and was even jailed for a time. Daily humiliations are commonplace against an "other" who is considered socially unacceptable. What about rage and sadness and loneliness? Where do they go? Where does preservation of honor and dignity go against a violent dominant that acts with impunity while the "other" is forced into positions that reinforce them as objects of scorn? Those who are impure in a nation's cultural eyes are thought to have something intrinsic to their *otherness*. Any prejudice and scorn is then that victim's making, and not their own society's fault. How could this be?

I immediately recognized and empathized with Michi's soulful voice and her ballads. When she came on the television to sing, Mama would watch, disgusted. Did Mama not understand how her disdain of Michi's background affected me? If I responded to her that I didn't like what she did, she always said that she didn't consider me to be the same as her. How? What does this mean when we think of my own life now, and what is required for social justice and change? Still, I knew that Mama loved and cared for me. That was not a question. As people become hybrid, what becomes of us all?

So in 1970, I found I could now navigate more easily in Japan. But this "easy navigation" of myself could only happen as a *foreigner*. I was now an exotic mantlepiece that somehow knew Japanese ways and language. Not only this. In reflection, I learned that the link between the u.s. bombings of Japan, the changing of Japan's national policies via u.s. Occupation, and the u.s.-Japan Security

Pacts reinforced Japan's position as submissive on the international global level, a Geisha to white U.S. muscle.

In the 1980s, when I was coaching volleyball, I was one of two designated Americans selected as guides for the Japanese Men's Olympic Team tour around Denver. My host partner was a Japanese American *Nissei* (second generation Japanese on U.S. soil). The local volleyball delegation thought this would make the Japanese team feel more "comfortable." I spoke Japanese. My friend Alan, who is Japanese American and looks "more Japanese" could not speak any form of the Japanese language. The Japanese team was a fun bunch. And they would often join us during meals, when there was time to talk. Some of the team members expressed surprise and confusion, occasionally speaking to me while looking at Alan (as if I was a puppet master voicing Alan's lips), when they realized I could speak fluently. They thought of me as Hawai'ian or Jamaican while Alan looked Japanese. Yet he couldn't understand a word of what was being said. I explained to them our backgrounds when they asked. I felt happy in disturbing their dominant notion of Japaneseness, in loosening its grip, even a little, on what constructs single ethnicity nationality as legitimate. At the same time, they decided that I was foreign. I could never *be* Japanese. Being accepted as an American has had its problems too. And who has the power to accept? Or not? What are the consequences and effects on either side of accepter and accepted?

## Rochester, New York, 1990

Two friends and I decided to eat at a Japanese restaurant. We found one that looked decent. We were seated and looked through the menu. The waitress came to our table. I guessed her to be about twenty-four years old and Japanese from listening to her speak with some Japanese customers and the cooks. She approached us and asked in slightly accented English, "May I take your order?"

I began to order in Japanese.

She interrupted me and said, "You should order in English. You're not Japanese."

I immediately asked her to get the manager. *She refused.*

I stood up as my friend sat in the booth, looking shocked at the events unfolding. I said sternly in Japanese: *"Anata mitai na onna-no-hito wa Nihon ni kaetta hou ga iin ja nai? Koko Amerika desu yo."* (Women like you should return to Japan. This is America).

I talked to the manager, and I heard him scold her politely in Japanese. *I secretly hoped that she was fired.*

I had learned to covet a superior Americanness, repeating the violence I often experienced and abhorred. Japan also needs to acknowledge and reflect on its multicultural heritage. I recognized that saying that she should go back to Japan was not magnanimous or useful, and would preserve Japanese internalized oppressions (Japan is not civilized enough) and prejudices (mixed-race people do not fit into Japan as Japanese). In remembering that moment, I knew that I had a long way to go to become a teacher. I had to stop reacting through my known divisions and learned patterns. I had to speak differently, respond differently. I had to learn effective ways to go beyond the dualities and divisions of Japaneseness, Americanness, blackness and whiteness. *The sexism.* 冒

# CHAPTER NOTES

1.  FTA (Future Teachers of America) is now known as Future Educators Association (FEA). It was once a program under the National Education Association (NEA), but in 1994, Phi Delta Kappa International took the lead on FEA, and in 2005, changed their name to more accurately reflect the international nature of the organization. FEA's mission is to encourage young people to become educators.

2.  For me, contradictions are not a problem or a puzzle, only patterns of thinking that are not compatible. Incompatibility is a fact of life, and nothing needs to be fixed. If it is, one or more sides are assimilated into becoming compatible—which I firmly believe is an act of violence.

# CHAPTER 26

# The Depths of Wounds/Love

"What does it mean to be haunted by a history of division and destruction, then to migrate and become assimilated into a country that had an active role in creating and maintaining that division?"

— Grace Cho, *Haunting the Korean Diaspora*[1]

MAMA, DAD, AND I BEGAN LIVING TOGETHER again in our second life in Japan in the late 1960s. We left Japan in 1963, and returned in 1968. It had changed tremendously in those years we lived in the U.S., now becoming more open to mixed-race people. Mama and I hardly encountered any open prejudice. New prejudices, instead, were directed at people who were fat, or too shy, for instance. Increasingly, murders of teachers at the hands of bands of students were in the news. Yet this did not mean that all had changed. All the old hatreds still persisted. It was now the individual who was increasingly the marker of success or failure, not the culture or government system.

As Japan developed, the taller buildings seemed to parallel more wealth in the general population. The Shinkansen train had long topped the world in speed records for rail travel. I began settling into my everyday life, spending time with school friends, watching television, and pursuing more of my own interests.

At thirteen, I was always out with friends, or listening to 45s in my room, blaring out The Supremes, The Temptations, The Association, The Beatles, 黛ジュン Mayuzumi Jun, ザ。スパイダーズ the Spiders, 森進一 Mori Shinichi, or ザ。シューベルツ The Shoebelts, or 美空ひばり Misora Hibari and many others, all on my personal turntable that Dad bought for me.

205

Dad often took me around the bases in Japan, showing me off to his friends. One of his friends took this photo of U.S. on Yokota Air Base. I was close to two years old. *Fredrick Cloyd Family Archive.*

In those days, Mama always made home perfect for Dad's arrival from work. In earlier times, it was few and far between, given how seldom he was home. He had been in Thailand and Vietnam for most of the time Mama and I were in Albuquerque. Now, while Dad lived with us, Mama was determined to be the good wife. Through phone calls with Dad, with both speaking the wartime U.S. military-in-Asia base town pidgin slang, she would find out what time he was coming home for the evening. She would clean, organize, and return everything to its proper place. A couple of hours before Dad came home, she began cooking, chopping vegetables and preparing the sauces.

I was sometimes there when she started this routine. There was pleasure, devotion, and purpose to life in this way of giving. Isn't this what the good wife must do? Yet it wasn't so much a sacrifice as it was a reciprocal contract for Japanese people. However, this wasn't how American men viewed this relationship. Through the eyes of Orientalism and heterosexism, they saw this as Japanese women sacrificing and being dutiful to the men, which was something intrinsic, something of "the soul" of Japanese women, seen through the eyes of Orientalism.[2] In Japanese culture, it was anticipated that the man would then reciprocate with certain actions, but for Dad, an African American man, struggling in the black and white U.S.A., this was how he fantasized about being treated. Becoming the occupier-king, a role opened to him through his entrance into Occupied Japan and a whitening Pacific as an American soldier. Mama had no thought of those things then. She would just get to it, working thoughtfully and carefully 協力しましょう！(Let us be productive! Do our duties!).

In the early days, she played her role with joy. But as she spent more days alone and isolation crept in, her joy began to diminish. It wasn't just from the absence of a husband/man who was supposed to take care of her, she became isolated because she could not speak English. On the base, many other Japanese women spoke more English. Some were wives who had attended the wives' training courses offered on base. Mama didn't attend them. Certainly none of the American women paid any attention to her, nor did any of the Japanese wives of servicemen. Sometimes a few of those American women called her Jap. I used to think, "You're in Japan now. How could you call the people here with a pejorative term, and treat us like we're foreign? I wish you all would leave."

My mother knew that word "Jap" well – she had heard it a thousand times out of the mouths of American soldiers in Japan, and from American women in Albuquerque. Mama would curse them under her breath. She became more aware of how difficult it was to socialize with white American women, but she remained popular with all kinds of men of all ages. Some of the Japanese wives of servicemen looked down on Mama because she didn't speak English, and on Dad because their husbands were ranked higher than he was. Other Japanese women with white husbands looked down on those married to Latino or black servicemen. Mama picked and chose her friends carefully. So her aloneness was an accumulation, fragmenting the dreams she built in her *kokoro* (true heart-mind). She was a woman of the *kichi* (base town), that longed to escape to America with an American man, away from her war-torn subservient existence to a society, the Occupation told her, that was far more democratic for women.

When I was in high school, the mother of a friend of mine in Albuquerque, also the wife of an American military serviceman, tried to "set me straight" and correct me (in her eyes, but not mine): "Oh, come on, Fred! You're a military family. All military wives go through this. Wives don't have normal *Leave it to Beaver* lives in the military. Your Mom should've expected as much. And seeing as she's foreign and Oriental, she shouldn't complain anyway. And isn't she used to sacrificing anyway?"

I could understand her ideas on the lives of military families. But, for her other views in that moment, I hated her.

When we moved onto the military base in Japan, from Ōme City, it was the first time that Dad lived with us, even though I only remember seeing him once or twice a week. I was too young to know then that the Air Force was sending him on assignments, and that my parents' marriage had been discouraged by both governments. But Dad wasted no time in trying to bond with me. There was no doubt that he was proud of his son.

I remember huge Christmas trees decorated with a thousand lights and spooky fake snow, dressed with a huge woman at the top that I was later told was "an angel." What was Christmas? A day when kids got gifts and toys! I remember that first Christmas on base. I woke up and found the living room floor covered with toys. Although I don't remember, my parents told me that I was a strange child because I only chose to open three or four packages and left ten or twelve of the others unopened, even a week later. I became obsessed with the one red wagon, one toy truck, and three toy trains. After two Christmases, the many toys became a few. I think they knew that I didn't want a lot and my tastes were particular. Certainly the gigantic Santa Claus images pasted around Tachikawa and Ōme didn't make sense to most of the people, at first. Still, the Americans pushed them up and onto the Japanese city and townscapes.

My parents attended the Armed Forces Day festivities. For me, these days were long and boring. Dad would bring Mama and me to the airfield where most of the military families from around Japan came to enjoy the ceremonies. The kids would climb all over the tanks, airplanes and helicopters, and peer at the different guns on display. I fell in love with the airplanes. So many aircraft carriers and fighter jets! But when one of Dad's friends offered to take me up in a jet, I said no. I was too afraid. I didn't like flying. Earlier in the day, I said "yes" to a helicopter ride and almost vomited as we lifted off the ground.

Then there was the parade. On the second or third year of the Armed Forces Day parade, Dad was the flag-bearer. It was something he was proud of. But I hated parades. Mama seemed to enjoy watching the men march and seeing Dad carrying the flag. Perhaps for my parents, this was their bond. Military uniforms, hardware, parades, and glory. Pride.

*I was bored.*

Mama was always quiet on those days. She followed wherever my Dad and I went. She was not so interested in the weapons and the ceremony, but she was proud of my Dad as he carried the flag in the parade or see him being honored. When I think of it now, I think the Armed Forces Day and its displays brought her bitter memories of death, devastation, hunger, and loss — Japan's subjugation. It brought the reality of subjugation through American military weapons and technologies into our family life directly. Whenever Dad would ask her if she wanted to see this thing or that thing, or go to this exhibit or that, Mama always quietly declined.

So Dad would take us wherever he thought would be enjoyable for me.

Later when I asked Dad to buy me a model airplane, I wanted a B-17 bomber or a P-17 fighter jet model. These planes were used in the European part of World War II. I didn't want any B-29s because they played a major role in Mama's memory of destruction, but I did want models of the Japanese Zero fighter-plane, and had a few of those.

Mama never commented on my choices and let me be. Dad became proud that I was becoming a boy, no longer content to play jump-rope with the girls at school and now playing with so-called "boy toys." He seemed proud of me when I'd beautifully assemble a model plane. And later, I bought army men and comic books of World War II.

When I'd play "war games" with other boys in the neighborhood, I'd always want to play a "Kraut" (German) or a Jap soldier. Never American. Why was that? And why did I copy the American television shows that portrayed Japanese soldiers who only knew these three phrases: "Yankee devil die!" or "Hail to Emperor!" or "My name is Hashimoto"? And in cowboy-and-Indian games, I always wanted to be the Indian, never the cowboy. If I did play a cowboy, I wanted to be Jesse James.[3] An outsider. The few times I did want to be American, my American friends wouldn't allow it. *Why is that?*

Sometimes I asked Mama questions, I realized later, she didn't want to answer. I asked her if everyone in the Japanese army yelled "banzai!" (hail to the emperor!) when they died—mimicking what I saw on American media. I wanted to find out, so I could be realistic in my army games with the other boys. I had become very American.

At the time, I was a child and did not understand or consider Mama's position. This must have been painful for her, but she never spoke of it. "No," she said, "Japanese boys who died as kamikaze pilots usually died saying good-bye to their mothers or fathers." She said that books, even in Japanese, that reprinted their death letters, were, of course, those that showed loyalty to the nation. *It had to be.* She also said that when they published the diaries of kamikaze pilots, they often chose nationalistic ones, but the majority of them did not exclaim "banzai" when they were about to die. Mama said that, often, what was portrayed wasn't what was actually going on. She said that the literature after the Occupation was closer to, or was, propaganda. Still, in those days, she liked to read the new women's magazines where letters from returned soldiers would often be reprinted. Later, she couldn't bear to read anything having to do with the war.

*How long will we all participate in this dream?*

≋ ≋ ≋

ONE NIGHT, THE TONE INSIDE OF OUR HOME suddenly changed. Mama had begun her routine as she always did. The fragrances from the stove began making my mouth water, and the bath water she prepared was the temperature Dad liked. The steam could be seen through the hallways, warming the entire house as the fragrance of the food enveloped us. Our long grandfather clock ticked loudly on the wall.

A half-hour passed. Mama turned the water off and walked to the kitchen to turn off the stove. The fragrance of the food lingered yet colder, and the steam slowly disappeared and the house became quiet... quiet... and then the grandfather clock was the only thing existing.

TICK ...TICK ...TICK...

Nine o'clock in the evening. Dad wasn't home.

Then ...I heard my mother weeping in their bedroom.

I didn't know what to do, what to think. I left her alone, as I was alone, feeling vulnerable, helpless, and keeping to myself in my room. Listening. That night changed our family.

*Wasn't he supposed to take care of me? Wasn't America caring? Wasn't this the land where freedom and democracy created paradise? Wasn't he my American husband? He is supposed to care for me.*

*The American women here hardly speak to me. I am different from them. And now, he has better things to do. And the other Japanese largely look down on me because I am married to my husband. I don't know how to live.* 目

# CHAPTER NOTES

1. Grace M. Cho, *Haunting the Korean Diaspora: Shame, Secrecy, and the Forgotten War* (Minneapolis: University of Minnesota Press, 2008). The quote speaks to the division of North and South Korea, implemented by the Western nations at the end of the Korean War (1953), dividing families and systems, cultures and norms. It was painful. For me, this quote can also apply to many cultural-political situations as well. For me, it was the specter of the U.S. Occupation and the Cold War, as well as the reality of race and racism in East Asia and the United States — the dividers of times, places, bodies, communities. For an excellent view of the North and South divide that occupies Koreans today, see also Bruce Cumings' works, particularly, *The Korean War: A History* (Modern Library; Reprint edition, 2011)

2. I use the term here as defined by Palestinian American literary theorist and public intellectual Edward Said (1935-2003), to describe a pervasive Western repetition, both academic and artistic, of creating "the East" in the present, from the Euro-imperialist attitudes of the eighteenth and nineteenth centuries. In other words, the dominance of the West, the so-called "Occident," was a way for Europeans to construct and make monolithic the European self against a construction of an "strange and alluring" other. Europe would become "rational" and therefore superior, while the Orient was made "exotic," emotional, and "feminine inferior."

3. Jesse James (1847-1882) was a famous outlaw in the American West who committed major robberies from the late 1860s until his death in 1882.

# CHAPTER 27

# 許し Forgive Mid-July 1969
# Shōwa Year 44 昭和 44年 7月中

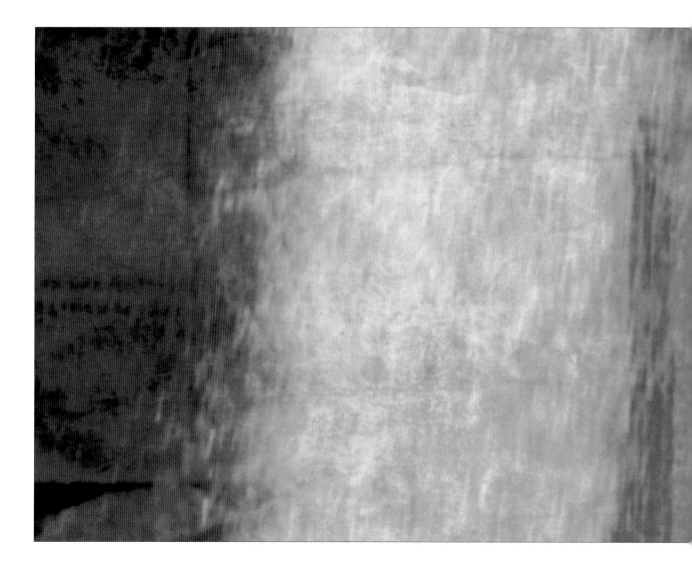

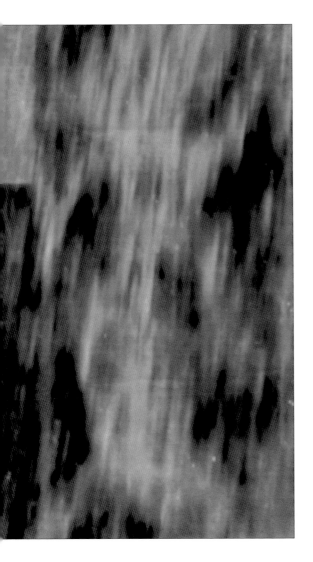

Uncle teruo, or teruo oji-chan as I called him, lived near Nara in a neighborhood called Shakudō, with his wife. My uncle and cousins, Kō-chan and Kazuko-chan, visited us from Shakudō in the summer of 1969. We rode the common commuter train through the steep green mountains of my town, switching onto the swift modern 中央線 *Chūō* commuter train that took us into the great 公園 park where Mama and I were to meet them along with one of her friends. It was the annual 七夕 *Tanabata* festival and fireworks. This year, they were coming with Mama and I back to Tachikawa. The previous summer, we had visited them in Shakudō. I never understood why Dad never came with us on these trips when he was in Japan.

I had just begun my obsession with volleyball in those days. It was the middle of the *Barêbōru Bûmu* バレーボール ブーム, a big volleyball boom after both the women's and men's national teams had won Olympic medals. I was sucked in.

That evening, I was watching one of the women's matches on television when my two cousins were engrossed in their summer homework. I was always relieved that I didn't go to a Japanese school. Japanese schools were intense and Japanese students were almost always studying. I, on the other hand, attended American military base schools, which allowed for a lot of free time. That night, I overheard Mama speaking with Teruo-oji-chan about some girl that had died and something about forgiving her *("Maa, mou shindankara yurushitōtara e-eyan ka?")*. For a moment I wondered who they were talking about before I returned to watch television.

I imagined this person who needed to be forgiven was a family friend or an ex-wife. I knew he had been separated from his first

213

Uncle Teruo and I on the front porch of our second Tachikawa Air Base home. *Fredrick Cloyd Family Archive.*

wife, which was taboo in those days. It was also possible that it was a former mistress or second wife too, as was common before the Occupation. I was too engrossed in the volleyball match to listen carefully, and barely cared. This person they were speaking of was dead. But why was Uncle Teruo forgiving them and why was Mama unwilling to?

Teruo, the former military officer who fought against British, American and Indian troops in Burma (now called Myanmar), and remembered the brutality of his fellow soldiers against the local populations and their enemies, became a lawyer. When he was in Burma, he told me of the brutality of his commanders who used to hit them, their own soldiers, and constantly chastised them. This was an old Japanese way of teaching obedience when obedience meant acquiescing to dominance. Things were beaten into people as a way of making an "old weak spirit" die to revive a strong spirit and to internalize the current order of things.[1] Mama told me that when Teruo came back to Japan on leave one summer, he wouldn't eat the おにぎり *onigiri* (rice balls) or any of the other food that the women of the family painstakingly made for him. They thought that he was physically sick. Two years after the war, Teruo told them that he couldn't eat anything in those days, not because he didn't have an appetite, but because the beatings by his commanding officers in the war were so brutal that the inside of his mouth was riddled with cuts, making it excruciatingly painful to eat. On top of that, his commanding officers often ate hefty portions of food, starving the enlisted soldiers in the battle-field. He was disgusted with the food, despite desperately wanting to eat.

I often saw the hazings of the U.S. military on television, and understood that they needed to harden men and women to be willing to face, or better yet, become numb and superior to the enemy in order to be able to kill them. Machines kill without thought. In war, people are trained to become like those machines. Japan had their way in training their soldiers as all powerful nations do. After all, Japan had gone through several hundred years of civil war in order to build their nation (just like all the others). Whole nations mobilize their citizenry through whatever means necessary to get them to believe in the killing mission in order to provide the resources needed to build the machines and care for their leaders and soldiers. Military tactics fused with corporations to control foreign economies. The link between those wielding the weaponry (and abuse), and those without were never far apart. In this, people are born.

Despite experiencing brutality as both perpetrator and victim, to his commanders, to the Japanese imperial project, and towards women, Teruo had always been an internationalist. When the war ended, he had no trouble accepting and admiring Americans. It was perhaps easier for him because his duties in the military involved dealing with British and South Asian armies, and his life before the military was in the upper classes where contact with Westerners was commonplace. At first, he and the entire family initially objected to Mama dating Americans, but they later relaxed on this notion. Their race was, apparently, not a concern. However, many of Mama's friends were ostracized by their families that resulted in poverty, prejudice, and violence. Even as SCAP removed family homes from the privileged, resulting in many of the concubine-families losing their homes and being left to starve, they felt it was something they had to endure just to survive. Teruo had been very kind to me. I truly felt like part of the family, and was never treated as an outsider. My cousins called me ニーちゃん *nii-chan*—big brother—and treated me no different from any other older boy in the family.

That particular summer, Mama and her older brother were getting along, but they would also argue. Mama was one of the rebel girls of the family, as I was beginning to learn. One night, I waited until my cousins and Teruo Jiichan had gone to sleep. I took a chance to ask her what they were talking about: *"Ne-eh, kyō Teruo to Mama dare no koto hanashite ta no?"*

Mama became quiet, reflecting on how she should respond.

*"Motto okiku nattara itsuka tsutaete ageru kedo, ima wa mou ammari iitaku nai yo. Ii ne?"* (I don't want to speak about it until you're older.)

The woman I lived with became a ghost. When I looked at my mother, working away in the house without speaking to me, deep in her own thoughts, I understood she was not ignoring me. I knew that she had many ghosts in her life. A hard life. It was something I, being a boy in a U.S. military high school with mostly American friends, did not know how to process. I never resented it, nor did I ever feel that she disliked me. In many ways, she was giving me lots of room and freedom, something she felt she never had in Japan. 目

## CHAPTER NOTES

1.  The brutality of the orders given by the military and the state, including language and forms of discourse underlying our words and values, are discussed and traced by Michel Foucault, notably in *The Order of Things: An Archaeology of the Human Sciences* (New York: Vintage, 1994).

# CHAPTER 28

# Military Brats 1968

*Americans had to learn to hate Germans, but hating Japs comes natural — as natural as fighting Indians once was.*

— *Life Magazine,* May 21, 1945[1]


*The natural enemy of every American man, woman and child, is every Japanese man, woman, and child.*

— *The New Republic,* 1944[2]

THIS WEEK, CABLE NEWS HAS BEEN PLAYING NONSTOP footage of the devastating earthquake and tsunami in northeastern Japan. The Fukushima and Sendai areas are in turmoil amid the fifth strongest recorded earthquake in Japan's recorded history (since 1900). It's 2011.

As of April 11, 2011 at 3:00 p.m., a total of 13,228 people were confirmed dead by Japan's National Police Agency with 14,529 missing. In tweets and online communications, Americans said that this was God's retribution against Japan for Pearl Harbor. Others remembered Japanese atrocities in their home villages, towns and fields, and thought, "Good. The Japanese should suffer like my relatives suffered." Elders in Japan, of various ethnicities, remember and continue to live with the aftermath of the atomic bombings of Nagasaki and Hiroshima, and treaties signed between the U.S. corporate military and Japanese elites in 1951 and 1960, which ensured the "security" of nuclear weapons in our world. Apparently, the atomic bombs were not enough retribution. And the sixty-six cities bombed by the U.S. during the war were not enough killing and killing-wishes. Ill-wishes for people and nations born from the past: *Alive and pulsating.*

Mama and me by our house, circa 1956. Notice the railroad tracks and the mountain in the background, that became consistently loved themes and interests for me throughout my life. *Fredrick Cloyd Family Archive.*

*The past is not past.* The past is past. There is no past (we move on). *The past is not past.* We make the past the reason for our present. Thirty or a hundred or thousands of years…how long does this go on? This is no accident or act of nature, or something inherent in people. I think that we can change these thoughts of violence and death, if we are able and willing to grasp what is going on.

During my only year of high school in Japan — my freshman year — I had to take the blue and white school bus from our neighborhood to get to classes at the high school on Yamato Air Station. It was a pleasant enough ride through the narrow streets outside the base, where I often fantasized that I was on one of the beautiful blue express trains pulled by a powerful C62 or C57 steam locomotive. My love of trains had continued since childhood. My fantasies during my junior and senior years, living behind the fences and walls that divided the U.S. military from the rest of Japan, helped me escape my fear and loathing of most people as well as my longing for them.

On the very first day, there were certain kids I learned to hate. One was quite popular. He used to play a game with some of the other boys on the bus where they would see how many old ladies they could spit on during their bus ride. When we stopped at a stop light, the boys would stick their head out to look for the old ladies, who would be walking slowly, scrunched over from years of working in the fields or surviving the war years, dressed in their gray or dark blue *kimono* and *hakata*, often walking *zōri* or *geta* and leaning on their canes as they walked to the market or to visit a friend or relative.

All the school bus drivers on U.S. military base were Japanese men. With white gloves and discipline, they drove us back and forth to school. In fact, on all the base schools I attended or visited, and all the base clubs Dad took me to, most of the food servers, bus and taxi drivers, janitors and office clerks, were primarily made up of Japanese, Filipino, or enlisted blacks. Simply put, the Americans, who took up considerable real estate with their bases and off-base businesses became the overlord, and the Japanese needed jobs in postwar Japan.

Usually, on our way to school, our bus driver would stop somewhere to get his little bottle of *yōguruto* (yogurt) or to pick up his *bentō* lunch box. He would see the white boys spitting from the windows and he would ignore them. I heard later on that he was punished by his superiors for complaining about the American boys' behavior, and was told to *gaman shinasai* (endure or bear it), and that it was inevitable *(shikata ga nai).* So was the Occupation over or not? While the Japanese men did not look happy, they were happy to have steady work to feed their families.

During one of the stops, the boys on the bus would lean out their windows making sexual innuendos at passing girls and women below, laughing and ridiculing them. Some of them used the word "Jap." When one of the Japanese American girls mentioned these actions to a white teacher (the only kind), he answered: "Well, you know, they're dumb boys. They'll get over it later. Let them be."

I felt attacked by all this. "Letting it be" allows and empowers those who attack people like me. It is a moral binary that seems to remain unequivocally intact. Let the bad people be bad; let the good people be good. *That's it?*

There were also about five other mixed-white Japanese boys on the bus. Three of them sometimes participated with the white boys in these games. And some of the white and black girls would laugh along with them. Other mixed-white Japanese and white kids would stay silent, perhaps feeling as I did. I never believed this was a stage of life that kids went through. If that was so, every single one of us would've participated in this. But there were about ten or twelve of us on that bus, who sat silently and waited for the bus ride to be over.

My friend Chris reported the spitting game to the teachers and the principals. Nothing ever happened, as far as I could tell. But some of those guys found out and threatened him. None of us really said much to anyone about these things after that. We quickly learned that the world belonged to bullies, whether white, black, Japanese, or mixed. And today, not much has changed. It's unnatural. But we make it normal and natural. In the most civilized nations, the system favors the bully-boys and bully-girls, while the rest of us remain invisible. 訁

## CHAPTER NOTES

1. "On To Tōkyō and What?: The Proof of our victory will be a Reborn China," Editorial, *Life Magazine,* May 21, 1945.

2. Tsuyoshi Hasegawa, "Were the Atomic Bombings of Hiroshima and Nagasaki Justified?," in *Bombing Civilians: A Twentieth Century History,* eds. Yuki Tanaka and Marilyn B. Young (NY: New Press, 2009) 118-9.

# CHAPTER 29

# September 1985 Shōwa Year 60
# 昭和 60 年 9 月

*[Pan-pan girls are] squalid tribe of harpies, loud, without manners and somehow contrive to be more degraded than any European whore.*

— Honor Tracy, *Kakemono: a Sketchbook of Postwar Japan*[1]

MAMA HAD JUST FINISHED MAKING her famous *Hamu chā-han* (ham fried rice) when I was visiting her from Denver. *The Phil Donahue Show* was airing a program on forgiveness. I flashed back for a second to that conversation regarding that woman in Uncle Teruo and Mama's life who needed to be forgiven.

As she often did, Mama asked me what the television show was saying. I explained to her that, on this show, this man could not forgive his daughter for a wrong-doing. Mama became very quiet, watching more intensely. I took this opportunity to ask her about the woman that she and Uncle Teruo once argued about. Mama began telling me a few details.

She had two other sisters. I have never been clear whether they were blood sisters or sisters bought from poor families, as was the frequent method in Japan of dealing with poverty. Mama had many sisters of different mothers. All of the women and children lived comfortably, as they were wealthy and upper class. Otō-san, my grandfather, had Mama's mother and another wife in China. There was her older sister Kiyoko who had died in the atomic bomb blast. This sister, then, was Mama's sister from her other mother. Her father also had two other wives (that I knew of) in Japan. This was quite common until it was forbidden under U.S. Occupation law. One of the women lived in a village in northern Japan. Apparently, they had a child together. Another

221

Dad, Teruo and Mama, out for a party a few months before our nuclear family exodus to the United States. *Fredrick Cloyd Family Archive.*

daughter. In the United States, we would call her "half-sister." But again, stories would change.

*Sometimes the stories I am told of these sisters changed.*
*Sometimes they were non-existent.*

### Version One

THIS SISTER — the subject of Emiko's argument with Teruo — was taken from a northern Japanese village to China as a sex-worker for the Japanese army. When she returned, she could not find work as she was too emotionally abused, and was shamed by the women in the family. With no work available, and already considered a whore, she became a prostitute in one of the other *kichi* (U.S. military base towns) in Japan.[2] She killed herself two or three years later, a few years before I was born. Emiko, her younger sister, did not forgive her for being a prostitute. I thought this very odd. I could not understand why she could not forgive her sister. Mama always cried openly about other people's sorrows, especially for women who suffered, and took their own lives. She understood. But she could not forgive.

When Mama finished telling me this story, her disgust was evident in her wrinkled and disapproving face. After a few minutes, she began to cry. Being the inept and distant boy that I was at the time, I felt sad, but didn't know what to do. My eyes teared.

The women often dressed in the Western styles of those days, wearing ankle-length plaid skirts with white bobby-socks. They were called *pan-pan girls.* Reviled but envied. The accumulation of food and cigarettes were abundant from the American commissary, stores on the military base, and around the *kichi*. Women who dressed in more modern styles were more expressive than mainstream Japanese society wanted. Pan-pan culture became the primary subject of many newspaper and magazine articles, garnering the admiration of artists, singers, and writers, because it represented the general feeling in Japanese society at the time that they were servicing the Americans in order to be free. On the other hand, there were those who thought of it as symbolic rape. However, the way they were personally treated was another issue.[3]

At first, when Mama and I used to see Japanese women with Americans in the PX or at the commissary, she would keep me away from them. I soon realized that Mama wanted to keep me away from her past. These women catered to American servicemen as a strategy to survive postwar hunger and desolation. Mama had been like this with many men, Japanese and American. Power was possible there, but so was the possibility of being disfavored, which would cast her as impure.

I learned that Tachikawa was home to one of the most popular pan-pan houses in the area, filled with fifteen- and sixteen-year-old girls (some even younger), who helped their families get food by flirting with servicemen. Most of them went into it with a sense of freedom, pleasure and power because it went against the grain of Japanese society. And while many of these "flirtations" were sexual favors in exchange for money or goods, there was a grayer category of what were sometimes referred to as *onrii* (from "only" or "only one"), women who engaged in serial, ostensibly monogamous relationships with "only one" uniformed lover at a time, and received various forms of material compensation in return.[4]

Although Mama tried to trick me with secret names and silence, we would occasionally run into one or two of her former friends, and I would piece together some of their conversations. It must have been hard for her because being seen with them meant other more "respectable" women might consider Mama to be one of them. Rumors would bring ostracization. To be separated from friends was hard, but to be seen speaking with them, some of them her former childhood friends, was even harder.

Mama didn't go hungry, except for a two-week stint in Tōkyō after the war. She was from a wealthy and upper-class family, yet this added to her feelings of shame. What were the thoughts and feelings that reeled and receded through Mama and her relationships with these sister-friends? It was something I would never know.

Many girls sought favors at the bars and *mizu-shōbai* (night-entertainment businesses including the so-called red-light districts) of the base towns that were almost always jam-packed with American servicemen. These women were not technically pan-pan or geisha. Some girls participated on occasion so they could acquire food and status symbols, such as lipstick, nylons, cigarettes, and clothes. Was the only difference between them and us the location? The license? Anyone associating with American servicemen, whether sexually or not, were considered whores as their bodies were being given to former enemies and current occupiers. In some public discussions, even women and girls who were forcibly taken from Korea, the Philippines, and Japanese rural areas to provide sexual comfort to the Japanese Imperial soldiers, were considered "those" women. It was said by some that the pan-pan girls willingly "volunteered" and were therefore unchaste. The pariahs among the pariahs. I question this notion of "volunteer" and this notion of "choice," espe-

Mama and her friend in 1946, after they had run away from her family home. *Fredrick Cloyd Family Archive.*

cially in a war-torn and so-called postwar life in the context of poverty, loss, emptiness, exhaustion, destruction, disease, and defeat.

In addition, there was the question of position and class within families in Japan. Some of the sisters were half-sisters sold into a clan or family from a poorer clan or family, as was the tradition in Japan before the war. How much of this had to do with the way our family talked about certain people in the recess of memories, where secrets, mourning, desire, regrets and longings are kept in the crevices of a caste system?

**Version Two (Three, Four . . .)**

OVER THE YEARS, I would ask Mama how she felt about her sister (or was it a friend?) who had committed suicide. In each case when I asked about her sisters, she denied having another sister except for the one who died in Hiroshima. At other times, she would tell me of another who was given away to another family during the war, who she had lost track of, or surprised that I thought she had another sister who was one of the 慰安婦 *(ianfu)* comfort women.

I was perplexed (and still am). Her sister or sisters, or friend? Dead? Killed? Suicide? Or…? How many sisters did she have? Or were they close friends? Cousins, maybe, that she called sister? Since Japan was not a nuclear family nation before SCAP's mandate, how were these histories reinterpreted, and made mandate in Japan? What disruptions and new hierarchies formed in the process? How is a Japanese citizen formed? What oppressions, then, pass as part of "Japanese culture?"

Because of new depictions on television, radio, and magazines, the idea of how to be a proper, and therefore superior, Japanese became closer to what America imagined. In this process of self-subordination, how did women relocate themselves and each other? How do we live with pain and dislocation, shame and trauma?

I often wish that I never asked Mama. It must have been painful for her to be asked. While Mama is the last person that wants pity, I think she needed solace and care, something she rarely received in life. Simultaneously, because of the paths we took, she made it difficult for me to provide her solace. However, it was too much, too little, too late. What ghosts did she produce and how many were produced for her and through her? I realized that, in many ways, Mama and I had become ghosts to each other. 目

# CHAPTER NOTES

1.  "Pan-pan" is a Japanese onomatopoeia used during the Occupation and post-Occupation days to mean "prostitute that caters to foreign military men."

2.  Prostitutes in most places around the world are often categorized by the kind of prostitute they are and where they work. Street prostitutes were worse off than the Pan-pan girls, who were not as good as the ones from the RAA (Recreation and Amusement Association (特殊慰安施設協会), as they were protected by Japanese organizations sanctioned by the SCAP administration. Many of the RAA women were oftentimes tricked by brokers or sold into indentured sexual servitude by their own impoverished families. This was also in the context of extreme poverty and hunger, in contrast to wealthier areas where the military bases stood (called base towns or camp towns). The RAA served as a "female floodwall" (*onna no bōhatei* 女の防波堤), allegedly protecting the pure women of Japan's middle- and upper-classes. Clearly, the RAA was, from the outset, steeped in an ideology of nationalism (and let us not forget, commerce) that pursued the systematic exploitation of women left destitute after the war. It was only after the rapid rise in venereal disease among Occupation personnel in its first few months of operation that SCAP declared all RAA establishments off limits, and the RAA eventually disbanded. Of course, prostitution continued to prevail in brothels, hotels, restaurants, bars, and dance halls in the "recreation" and "red-light" districts of base towns during the postwar.

3.  In Japanese postwar culture, Pan-pan was integrated into a changing Japanese culture, especially in artistic sensibilities. A form of westernizing, for instance, where sexuality is made Western (such as the way sexual acts are openly depicted) is mixed with empowerment and modernization.

4.  On prostitution as well as onrii, see: John Dower, "Chapter 4; Takemae," *Embracing Defeat: Japan in the Wake of World War II* (NY: W. W. Norton and Co., 1999), 68-71; Sarah Kovner, *Occupying Power: Sex Workers and Servicemen in Postwar Japan* (Palo Alto: Stanford University Press, 2012).

# CHAPTER 30

# Neighbors/Next door となり

These expressions are extremely crude and regional, and have a rustic air; middle-class Tokyo residents would laugh at their provincial quaintness.

— Dorinne Kondo[1]

## MAMA REMEMBERS 1940:

*We were obviously not* 江戸っ子 *Edokko.*[2] *People reminded us that we were foreign and other, even though we were Japanese. In the elite world, people treated us with sophistication and as people who were cultured and* インターナショナル *[cosmopolitan]. In the neighborhoods, we were often considered more degraded. Older sister spoke louder than other girls and liked to be around the girls who were always in trouble at school. The ones who were poor and rough.*

*I was too young to know, one way or another, what I wanted, but I knew that we were wealthy.*

*Okā-san (mother) was always in the house. She and father wanted us to speak upperclass Japanese, not the benjo-guchi (toilet-mouth) Japanese that older sister spoke. But Otō-san, Okā-san and Teruo spoke Ōsaka-ben (Ōsaka dialect) at home, while I spoke the Edokko Tōkyō language. When Okā-san went out, she would put on a wig that looked like a maiko-san (apprentice geisha), and she'd put on a kimono. But she was always really noticeable as she was at least a head taller than all the other women [Chinese people were known then to be generally taller than the Japanese].*

227

The maids would dress me. Our maids were poor Japanese, Chinese, and Korean women. In China, many of my neighbors had Japanese maids too. But that changed after a while. I think, because of the war. First, the maids would bathe me in the mornings, and then, when they would dry me, I would stick my arms straight out from the sides of my body, and the maids would dress me for the day. But Okā-san would dress herself, and she was always in a hurry. She came to our house later, after our family had been in Japan for a long time. She came from China after we had arrived with Otō-san (Father) and Onē-san (older sister).

My younger half-sister was away in a village somewhere in the North. I hardly ever saw her. There was some kind of family problem and Father did not want Imōto (younger sister) to be here. So Onē-san took care of me when Okā-san would go shopping. She would go shopping with two men who usually came over. They were very nice, I remember.

Otō-san did not want us to associate too much with the neighbors. The neighbors were always talking about other people, passing leaflets around and inviting us to meetings. I hated those meetings. I didn't understand what they were talking about. They would argue. And sometimes one of the neighbors would be taken away by the kempeitai (military police). These kempeitai, and a few of the neighbors, made sure that everything was orderly in the town. Whenever something controversial happened, one of the neighbors would be there. If it weren't for the neighbors, the kempeitai would never come, I think. There were always four or five who were especially passionate in their duties to enforce their opinion that we should all be unified and "good Japanese," no matter if everyone thought differently about what that was. Besides, being Japanese was not our only way of seeing ourselves. It was more important to refer to clan, region, city, status, jobs, rather than calling ourselves Nippon-jin. We had to support the army. Of course Teruo-nii-chan (older brother Teruo) was a high-ranked soldier so it was assumed that we were in support. We were proud of him. We went to the train station and watched him go as the smoke, steam and clanking of the trains took him away to war. Okā-san would always cry and be sad for hours afterward.

One day, a group of about ten to twelve neighbors, I think, came to our house.

*"Gomenkudasai!" they shouted as they entered the house [the standard Japanese greeting when you enter a home] but their politeness was more like a command. Onē-san and Otō-san (older sister and father) went to answer. I was a child so I couldn't understand everything. But they were asking about mother. Lots of questions. They wanted her to come out. Otō-san and Onē-san told them that she was unavailable and was not at home. I don't remember well, but I used to ask why Okā-san was hiding all the time. Why did she have to? What was happening? I remember feeling that we couldn't trust our neighbors, and that this was why Father told us not to associate too much with them, or tell them about our family or what we did, or where we were from. I was too young to understand what was happening.*

*I don't quite remember, but I think it was about a month later or so... I heard sister screaming from the furo-ba (bathtub room). I ran to where I heard the scream, but I don't remember this part. I think Otō-san was speaking with someone. There were many people in the house. I think I was taken to our sleeping quarters. Later that evening, Otō-san sat me and Onē-san down and told us that Okā-san was dead. That's all I remember.*

*I guess, from what I remember, she died from overheating in the ofuro. Actually, I don't know. I don't remember. I wonder why? I wonder if I was ever told? It happens a lot, you know — people dying in the ofuro. Japanese baths are so hot and people stay in too long. I remember I cried and cried and cried. Okā-san was gone to A-no-yo (the other-world).*

Kempeitai (military police) on a train in 1935.
*Source: Shōwa History Vol. 7: February 26 Incident, published by Mainichi Newspapers Company.*

Okay. This needs review.

The neighbors, as well as Mama's family, in her story, were not just people or neighbors. Let's include history. To me, this is an example of how our world views can change according to a knowledge of history and ways to think, and what we remember or don't remember.

### Tonari gumi 隣組 Neighborhood Association Groups

IT WAS JAPAN in the 1930s and 1940s. *Tonari gumi* associations were first formed by the ruling government during the Edo and Tokugawa periods as a form of neighborhood civil participation and national unity. This became more intense when the Edo government (and those subsequent to World War II) demanded

The Kempeitai (pictured above, in formation, 1938), was the military police arm of the Imperial Japanese Army's Tokkō Special Forces, from 1881 to 1945. Operating much like Nazi Germany's Gestapo, throughout Japanese neighborhoods, many Japanese citizens feared them, including Mama. *Source JACAR, Japan Center for Asian Historical.*

general security assistance. They were essentially "mutual aid" oriented, although their roles changed many times leading into the postwar period and into the 1980s and 1990s.

On September 11, 1940, the *Tonari gumi* were reorganized by the imperial government into neighborhood watches to assist in disaster relief, civil defense, and to enforce strict moral and ethical codes. This type of local organizing helped spread propaganda nationally. This system of national culture-making was not unique to Japan. A nation needs to be strong, especially when preparing for war. Unity is paramount for a nation's existence, so it must be manufactured. Many of these groups were ordered to perform "national spiritual unity" propaganda everyday, through the infiltration of ideas and covert operators.

During World War II, the neighborhood associations also assisted the special police *(Tokkō Police - Tokkō Keisatsu)* as informants. During this period, the *tonari-gumi* groups raised suspicions against their Japanese, Chinese, and Koreans neighbors and accused many of them of being spies or having anti-Japanese sentiment. This made it even more dangerous and precarious throughout Japan, raising local tensions everywhere during the war. If a neighbor didn't like someone, they would accuse them of being spies. Hardly any proof was necessary for an informant to accuse someone of anti-Japanese sentiment. Prejudice would win. Since it was mandatory, the Kakinami family participated, though, due to their status, they were not hassled as much. Apparently, grandfather was known to have thrown out the more nosey and stubbornly nationalist neighbor-informants out of the house on more than one occasion.

All this talk about culture and race and political climate — where do these things begin and end? What things protect and also harm us? What helps surveillance and who is the one that surveils? What becomes of our life and death when memory is fractured and ambivalent? To a little girl like my Mama, these were nosey neighbors. But a complex nexus of government-created squads and patriotic and dutiful neighbors were in place, even as others, like my mother's family, resisted to varying degrees. What happens when differences shape or reshape Mama's memories (forgetting and remembering)? Or yours? Or mine? How does ignorance play a role in our differences? Since we are borne into different histories, how does this affect how we name people, places or things and enact power (or disempower)? Can't we handle our minds and assumptions differently from the norm? This is all that we have. Having a sense of history and its effects on our lives — the silences, the violence, the structures of how cultures develop — is necessary if we are to remain awake and aware.

*We aren't just different. There are reasons.*

And just because there is a likeness in appearance or sound does not mean it is "the same."

*Histories must be located.*

### Albuquerque 1971

ON A CRISP FALL DAY, I had just returned home from Highland High School and as usual, Mama was reading a book. *Okairinasai!* She would say in the typical Japanese greeting for those of us coming home. But since she's been in the U.S., she didn't come running out of her room to greet me, instead she stayed in her room reading and chuckling to herself as I went to my room to put my schoolbooks away and then go to the kitchen for some *osembe* and Pepsi. Then there was a knock at the door.

Both my mother and I stopped what we were doing and walked to the screen door, where two white women with clipboards stood with quiet smiles.

"We're sorry to bother you but we are here to ask if you have heard of Our Lord Jesus Christ."

I translated to Mama that Christians were once again at the door. Mama hated proselytizers. She couldn't stand the *Sōka Gakkai* in Japan, doing the same thing in the Japanese neighborhoods she grew up in, snooping around, and she distrusted religions of any kind.

"We especially wanted to make sure that as Japanese Americans, you would be interested in learning more about Our Lord our Savior."

My mother and I had a brief and sort of annoyed conversation about how we were not Nisei, so what are they talking about?

"We're not interested. And also.... we're not Japanese Americans. We're from Japan."

The two women looked puzzled.

"We're sorry, perhaps you misunderstood. We are interested in hearing more about your Japanese American heritage and how…"

"We're not interested. And we're not Japanese American," I responded again.

"Your English is very good,"

By now, inwardly, I was so annoyed. Mama returned to her room to read. I didn't want to close the door on these two women, but I felt they were intruding while they are doing what they felt are "good works."

"We understand that perhaps your Mother's experiences in internment camps, may have introduced her to the churches in those awful places and we were…."

*I closed the door.*

From someone else's viewpoint and limited worldview, we often think that other people are such-and-such people, a label we learned and are used to, have heard somewhere, or were taught to believe. We are all like that. And as individuals, we have varying degrees of resisting, rebelling, claiming, or believing in different identities and hierarchies that are attached to whatever we encounter. Sometimes and often, we do it without ever thinking about it.

I learned very early in life not to make too many judgments about other people. This is because our family moved from place to place, and more often than not, places that were dissimilar to each other. Although I was open to difference in an unconscious way, I was always bothered by both American and Japanese mainstream cultural ways of constantly judging everything. Still, it didn't mean that I didn't become entrenched in certain kinds of things. In locating our inter-relational pitfalls (with our institutions, nations, cultures, partners, friends, selves and moralities), we need to acknowledge how we are educated in histories of war and domination, victory and defeat, and systems of control. No matter how "free" we think we are. This is not a pitfall, really. I believe it is the quintessence of being human. In life, our encounter with one another, intimate or not, institutional or personal, in ways big or or small, always wind up being some sort of confrontation with this exact point—a level of nationalism, history, cultural hierarchies and universal worldviews we apply to everything and everyone. We need to locate our histories, so we can develop a true relationship with who we are, who others are, and what our nations do to us. 目

# CHAPTER NOTES

1.  See Dorinne Kondo, "The Narrative Production of 'Home,' Community, and Political Identity in Asian American Theater" in *Displacement, Diaspora, and Geographies of Identity,* eds. Smadar Lavie and Ted Swedenburg (Durham, NC: Duke University Press, 1996).

2.  *Edokko* (江戸っ子) a traditional term rarely used today, which, at first, referred to people whose family clan and heritage is from Edo (the former name for Tōkyō). On the other hand, Tōkyōites were not traditional because they were more outspoken, individualistic and direct than the traditional Japanese. Gradually, the term moved from a mere labeling of urban Tōkyō residents and lineages to the preferred way of being Japanese—representing individualistic (and more Western) Japan, in line with modernization. By the 1970s, it gradually became more of a pejorative word to mean something akin to the old American term, "country bumpkin," signifying an uneducated, unsophisticated commoner, but without a connection to Tōkyō.

# CHAPTER 31

# Diz

Mama's and my first life together, in my memory, crossed mountain towns, urban cities, and the surrounding villages of Tōkyō and Nara. In 1962, Dad came and we moved onto Tachikawa Air Base. We began our lives inside of those walls where different signs separated occupier and the occupied.

Even while Mama and I lived outside of those military walls and fences guarded by the impeccably-uniformed military men and women, we acquired the privilege of being Americans in Japan. No longer Japanese to the Japanese, we were foreign on our own soil. We were saluted by soldiers at the gates who, with blinding white gloves, would wave us through while Dad drove. I don't remember understanding much English, but it felt nice for all three of us to be saluted. Soon after we started living inside the base, we moved freely inside and outside the fences. It wasn't until years later that I began to understand why some Japanese living just outside the base would give us looks of contempt when they saw us leaving and entering the base, whether it be Tachikawa, Yokosuka, Atsugi, or Fuchū. Those looks directed at us were no longer just about my being a *kurombo* in their eyes. Now they could plainly see that we had freedoms they did not have.

The culture immediately surrounding the bases often relied on U.S. military personnel business. The resentment from knowing that Japan was depending on the U.S. was also a ghost that created the looks they gave us.

As our lives began adjusting to military base life, our friendships were among the major things that began to change. We saw less of Mama's friends, and less of my friend Ritchie and his sister. Now I began making new friends who were not Japanese. Some

Mama in her Mandarin dress in Albuquerque, 1964, shortly after we moved there, when Dad took her out on a night on the town. Whenever she wore this dress, she was quite joyful and later confessed she felt more attractive. She never wanted to wear a kimono. *Fredrick Cloyd Family Archive.*

were Black-American, but most were white American or Mexican American, where no Japanese language or mothers could be found.

My life and friendships began separating from Mama's. Mama was also growing quieter and smiling less. At the time, I had no consciousness of thinking Mama's life was being disrupted. My life was becoming more diverse. I was learning English for the first time. Also, I was making friends with a black boy about my age. He was called Diz. He was the son of one of Dad's friends.

Mama and I would tag along with Dad to their home for dinner one or two evenings every month. From the first, I liked him, even though I didn't understand much of what he was saying, as my English was barely developed. All I knew was that he wasn't mean to me. We laughed a lot. He didn't exclude me from his other friends or his brothers. He shared things with me. I had a warm welcome into American friendship, into a "black" friendship, but this wasn't always the case. Some things in my life intensified my longing to be with Diz. I learned in those first months living on the base that it wasn't just the Japanese who could be ridiculous or cruel. And I began to understand that my defenses were not that strongly developed. I was still sensitive, tender, and vulnerable when it came to human abuse, no matter how slight or strong or annihilating. While other boys chose violence as a way to deal with other boys, I began to defend my sensitivity to verbal teasing by telling myself that the bullies were *ikareteru* (crazy, idiotic, ridiculous).

≋ ≋ ≋

ON ANOTHER NIGHT, we visited another family friend of Dad's.

"You Hawai'ian or somethin'?" the two black guys asked me.

*Does this mean I'm not American? Why ask? Who gave you these trigger-words?*

They were sons of my Dad's friends. They hadn't seen my mother come into the house, and were in their rooms with the door closed. Their dad led me to their room. Dad was taking Mama and I around to meet his friends, and to introduce us to folks in Albuquerque. It had been tiring moving from Japan to New Mexico. It was weird not being surrounded by wooden and paper houses and shops, all scrunched together; and I missed the winding neon-light streets heavy with the fragrance of *charumera rāmen-ya* and sounds of joyful laughing businessmen at bars after work. It was so quiet. Hardly anyone around day or night. Do people live around here? There was hardly any green. All browns and reds and oranges, dirt and rolling weeds. But the sky was so big.

I realized that I needed to answer these guys with the little American English I knew. "We're Japanese."

"You're no Jap. Wait...yeah, you kinda look like a gook with them slanted eyes an' all. Your Dad went an' got himself married to a chink! Shit!" They laughed. "They didn't kill all of y'all yet?" Their laughing became hysterical.

I swallowed. "Well, we're American too."

I'm thinking to myself *Kono gaki tachi baka ja nakarou ka?*[1] I'm glad I didn't know how to say it in English at the time, or I would have been beaten to death. I didn't want to ask them not to call me Jap. It would have been an unwinnable fight. I didn't like the two brothers. "We better be careful. He's gonna do some judo on us!"

I rolled my eyes but I had to smile (good racist joke!). But the third brother, the older one, was nicer. He came into the room and told them to leave. After watching him studying me, not saying much, but not showing any menace either, he and I returned to the living room with the adults. I sat next to Mama on the sofa while Dad talked. Mama, I could tell, was trying to be quiet and respectable as the men and the boys chatted. The mother was nice to Mama. The women went into the kitchen, and their mother began talking with Mama, trying to share in cooking duties. Mama tried to understand as much as she could. I retreated to the bedroom with the three boys.

"So what do you eat at home? Chop suey?"[2] the two brothers asked me, laughing. I felt awful and small, like a circus exhibit. In some way, I was a ghost to them, a dream, like water. They spoke about things they'd heard and read but there was no me—a "Fretto" or "Fredrick"—in their questions. Were they even interested?

The eldest brother, then, got mad at them, and said, "Y'all better shut up! I'm gonna tell Dad that you're talkin' like that!" He somehow understood. I liked him. I felt protected with him there.

"Did you boys have a good time?" their dad and my Dad asked as we were about to leave (after the incredible dinner of meatloaf, mashed potatoes, greens, and biscuits).

"Yes," I replied as we put on our jackets, and were saying our good-byes. I ignored the two brothers, thinking to myself that I was getting better at lying to keep peace. The dinner was fantastic though.

Dad and I, being cool at White Sands National Monument in 1963. *Fredrick Cloyd Family Archive.*

After our family had moved across the waters, onto Kirtland Air Force Base in Albuquerque, New Mexico, I thought of Diz.

I remember sitting with Dad in his favorite reclining chair, as I often did, to watch his favorite television shows. The times I spent sitting with Dad in his chair were some of my most cherished moments with him. He was usually in his *yukata* (casual kimono-like robe), and Mama would make us *sencha* or *genmai-cha*. I would already be in my pajamas (which I never liked being in). We would watch one or two of Dad's favorite shows—*Combat, The Rifleman, Gunsmoke, Rawhide, Bonanza,* or *Twelve-o-clock High*—which were all popular at that time. My favorite show we watched together was *The Big Valley.* After such frustrating evenings spent in private rage and loneliness, an evening close to Dad without any worries, with the comfort of television and with Mama relaxing, were some of my favorite moments growing up.

Yet, often, during those times, my mind would drift off, thinking about Diz. He didn't say things that were *ikareteru*. He didn't hurt me intentionally. We watched our favorite shows together: the new anime *Tetsuan Atomu* 鉄案アトム *(Atom Boy)* or the *Gojira* movies ゴジラ *(Godzilla)*. And we both loved our samurai sword fighting movies チャンバラ! But Diz didn't understand or speak hardly any Japanese. He just watched and enjoyed what he could. He was one of the best African American guy-friends I've had throughout my life. Yet after our family left Japan for Albuquerque, I slowly began to forget about him. 冒

# CHAPTER NOTES

1.  Translation: "Are these brats idiots or what?"

2.  From the 1940s through the 1970s, terms like "chop suey" and "fried rice" were often used pejoratively in American society to describe anyone Asian. These and other such stereotypes became manifested in American culture, media, literature, theater and other forms of expressions. Although some would say they do not intend anything condescending, it was already so.

# CHAPTER 32

# Allegiances 1962

IN FIRST GRADE, DURING MY FIRST DAYS in school on the American military base in Japan, we were made to say words after the teacher greeted us and before we began lessons, we placed our right hand over our hearts.

*"I pledge allegiance to the flag of the United States of America. And to the republic…"*

At the time, I didn't understand the meaning at all since my first language was Japanese. So I just moved my mouth along with others, copying. Later, as I began to understand, I was still hesitant. I suspected it had something to do with being married to the American flag. And later, when Mama had to take her citizenship test, I understood it as ridiculous. It was much harder for her than it was for me. But as a kid, new to the U.S. military base schools, I had to learn what was going on. *Nothing made sense.*

After a month or so, when the morning recitation of the pledge was happening and I was mouthing without voicing, Tommy, the kid who sat net to me in class but bullied me all the time, pointed at me while signaling the teacher. I kept mouthing the pledge. The pretty brunette white woman, our teacher, began walking down the aisle towards me. Everyone kept reciting. When she reached me, she stopped. "…and justice for all."

*It was quiet.*

The teacher said, "Why aren't you learning the pledge? You have to learn the pledge." I told her I didn't want to recite it; I didn't know what it meant. She started to explain to me about being a loyal American. Unclear how to respond, I shook my head no, and kept saying I didn't want to.

*After all, I didn't have the words to express this at seven years old with limited English.*

She grabbed my left ear hard.

I cried out.

She pulled me by the ear through the aisle. I had to follow. "You're going to the principal's office. You're a [something-something] child."

I don't remember her exact words. I winced as I stumbled along behind her, not wanting my ear to be torn off. I was pulled out of the room and down the hall for what seemed like an eternity. She said something at a door and the door opened, then closed behind me. I couldn't focus on anything besides the pain. She spoke to someone — a man behind a desk. Two American flags stood on each end of the desk. A large one on a pole stood in the corner behind him.

I didn't know if he was the principal, the assistant, or a counselor. I didn't know him. He looked stern as he finished up some work at his desk. After a few minutes, he leaned towards me, pointing his index finger an inch from my nose. "Do you know how to follow instructions? Kids who don't do the pledge are communists. Are you a *communist?*"

I remembered that word because it sounded so interesting that I wanted to tell Mama about it when I got home. Of course I had no idea what he was talking about. I didn't even know what the United States was, except that it was somehow an imaginary thing, different from where I was standing.

The principal lectured me, telling me that if I wanted to be a good kid, I needed to pledge my allegiance and learn the words. I just sat there.

"Don't be a *communist,*" he told me. "Be a *good* boy."

*Nani kore?* Why did I need to be loyal? Loyal to what? Why did I need to be good (whatever "good" was)? What was a communist? All kinds of questions rose in my body-mind. In Japanese kindergarten, when we were scolded, we were told that we shouldn't do things that would embarrass our parents or make us stand out from others. I did not understand being American was "being good." At the time, I was terrified, I kept still and quiet. But I understood that I had broken a rule and had displeased people. What did the recitation of the pledge have to do with anything? I was confused. But I knew that "communist" was something unacceptable. And I knew that I was supposed to say these things about America and the flag.

In the next few months following this incident, after listening closely in social studies lessons and movies we would watch about "American" things and "communist" things, it occurred to me that I was not anywhere in the world, except in an interior created by forces from the outside. So I was to be loyal to a United States? Okay, I'd do it, even though it was strange, even though I had, again, become a "not-me." And I began understanding what this "good" was. It was being a certain way in order to be complimented for a learned normalcy, and to act that way regardless of anything else. Be obedient and docile. *Present no difference.* No discomfort, and no emotion except for smiles. *Comply.* No difference and no discomfort, no matter how uncomfortable or disfigured we were. Present no difference. Present no difference. *Good.* I had come to understand that I was being taught to *embody a nation.*

American military cargo planes fly over protesters in Sunagawa in 1956, a base town near Tachikawa. Across Japan, protests such as this against the U.S.-Japan Security Treaty, became intense, with perhaps the most violence culminating in 1960 when the Japanese leaders, under U.S. orders, sent special military police forces to squash the protests, which resulted in the most violent demonstrations in Japan since the Marxist-inspired May Day riots of 1952. *Photo by Genten Fushō.*

And years later, as I reflected on the difference between the Japan of my youth and the Japan I knew nowadays from people I met and television shows, I realized that, in my youth, children were disciplined by being told that they were doing something embarrassing or that others would be angry with them or laugh at them. It was a social requisite, not a personal morality. I never heard "you are bad" or "you are good" in the Japan of my youth (not that it was never said, just that it was not prevalent). Now, in 2011, I hear it said by Japanese more often, *"Warui ko desu ne!"* (You are a bad kid, aren't you?). Languages are now occupied. It may be mere "change" or even "progress," but I view it as more problematic than those sanitized and historical comments.

Language is more than mere words. It changes the location of self and shapes the ways in which a person or nation considers change. Now, more Japanese think problems are inside of them or inside others, as Americans think. It was not always so. Now, more people can tell themselves not to be communist because it makes more sense, as conditions have been created for it to make sense. For me, it was something I had to internalize.

Mama ignored me. She finished her citizenship test, and thought only of how to relate to neighbors and friends without a man behind a desk with flags. While I refused to recite it, and detached myself from its recitation in school, my mother worked hard to learn the pledge, in order to live with her husband in this new land.

For her, there were histories with Marxism in Japan, losing friends in the Anpō riots of the 1960s, and student riots of 全学連 *zengakuren* (student resistance groups that began in 1948) — which were directly connected to the 1955 system and the CIA.[1] These groups were almost completely wiped out and criminalized by the American-Japanese link in relation to the demonization of Marxism in the Cold War. Although she may have wanted to say and to defend, in the context of the woman she was becoming, she disassociated herself from any relationship or affinity to those groups. The memory of the death of her friends in the name of resistance to Americanism, and the fact that American values may change Japan's cultural system away from some of the older values, was a contradiction she struggled with.

I remember Dad saying he did not believe that the communists were particularly evil, but they were supposedly more prone to accepting dictators and didn't want as much freedom as democratic America. Being the "black humanist" that he saw himself, and a stout believer in individual freedom, I could see why he thought these things.

Me, I would make up my own mind as my life went along.

*Places become feelings, memory, allegiances—forced or not.*
*And these places are forms of Self.*

In many ways, young me was vibrant, yet emptied, stolen (occupied).
I acted. I got through.
Like Mama had to. 目

# CHAPTER NOTE

1. Anpō Jōyaku 安保条約, or Anpō 安保 for short, is the name for the U.S.-Japan Securities Treaty, which in 1960, aroused the largest full-scale riots in modern Japan. Many students were jailed and killed. Many socialist groups were shut down during this time, while university professors and artists were banned and jailed as well. Linda Hoaglund has a wonderful documentary called, *Anpō: Art X War*, which was the result of her research and thinking on the past in the present and the role of those protests in U.S.-Japan history. The documentary is in Japanese with English subtitles. Of course it is thought of as "Japanese," when this is an extension of Japan's one-party rule and their alignment with the CIA.

# CHAPTER 33

# Peace

ON A YOUTUBE VIDEO I FOUND in my search for videos about Pearl Harbor, there were comments by viewers that mirrored those made about Hiroshima 1945. It's 2011. Some have commented on my website and said the Japanese deserved the atomic bomb. This echoes thoughts and sentiments expressed by many others I've known from the Philippines, Korea, Vietnam, and other places where Japanese imperial forces committed atrocities. The past is not gone. *It lives in the present.*

When I was eleven and twelve, our family lived in Hawai'i, in the *Halawa* (the "w" pronounced like the English "v") neighborhood, near Honolulu proper. Recently, I've heard that a sports stadium stands where our neighborhood used to be. So I think of those times even more intensely now as a way to remember the beauty and horror of times past. From the time I was born until 1967, we frequently moved between Japan and the United States. During these moves, I remember Mama growing despondent and quiet. There had been many things that had broken her dreams and disturbed what she thought to be a path to freedom and desire. But those moments became something else.

Our time in Hawai'i, however, brought Mama's social life alive again with Japanese radio and television programs, and a neighborhood community that took care of each other. It was different from what she knew on the mainland. Here in Hawai'i, all around us were families of Portuguese, Samoan, Caucasian, Japanese-Hawai'ian, Hawai'ian, Puerto Rican, black, and other heritages that defied the notion of separate and divided. They always visited and invited Mama to different events or to dinner at their homes. Mama began smiling so much more. I became happier too. The lonely Albuquerque life became a memory.

Queen Lili'uokalani (September 2, 1838 – November 11, 1917), pictured here in London in 1891, reigned over the Kingdom of Hawai'i from 1891 and was overthrown by the U.S. government in 1893. Photo by Walery. *Courtesy of Hawai'i State Archives, Queen Liliuokalani Collection, PP-98-11-013,*

Our immediate neighbors, whose front doors were not even a meter apart from ours, were the Aiu family. Mother Aiu or her kids would always be over to our house and we'd always have fun. I was close with the four kids. Mrs. Aiu was from a white family on the mainland, but had lived in Hawai'i for most of her life. She was very friendly and kind. Her husband was a native Hawai'ian and always away on business. I remember she came over frequently to help Mama adjust to life in our new home.

On the morning of December 7, 1941, the day the Japanese planes came to bomb Pearl Harbor, Mrs. Aiu was a teenager. The entire area around the bay, including where our compound was, had been under attack. She was here, not far from the building that day. When I asked her about that day in 1941, she said how terrifying it was, describing how they ran into the bomb shelters near the house. Our housing complex had survived that attack and remnants of it could still be seen in the bullet holes and craters marked in our housing complex. The pillbox nestled in the green across from the west corner of our building held the remnants of a machine-gun turret used to return fire at Japanese planes.

One early afternoon, after I heard Mama getting up and making hot water for the morning *sencha* before returning to her room in silence, I thought I heard her crying. I went to see what was happening and asked through the closed door if she was okay. She answered, *"Nandemo nai yo."*

But I knew something was wrong. I was afraid and sad. As an eleven year-old boy, I didn't know what to do when Mama cried. It didn't happen often, but when it did, she tried to isolate herself. While I was in my room, hiding and confused, I heard our screen-door screech open. Mrs. Aiu called out to us. "Hello! Are you in?"

In those days, Hawai'ians rarely knocked on doors of friends. Just as it had been when I was a child in Japan, we just opened the door and announced our presence.

I told Mrs. Aiu that Mama was crying in her room and I didn't know what was wrong.

She carefully went into Mama's room to find her in bed with the covers pulled up close to her ears, crying. I peeked in from behind Mrs. Aiu's hips. She didn't seem like she was physically hurt. Mrs. Aiu asked her what was wrong as she pulled back the blankets, cradling Mama's head gently against her chest and rocking her like a child in her arms, stroking her head. Mama cried quietly. I felt sad and relieved. Mama's loneliness as a military bride in the U.S. had not registered with me yet, much less what the constant and sudden movement meant for her.

I barely understood my own loneliness. At the time, I was blossoming with the neighbor kids and enjoying life. I rarely considered that Mama barely spoke English, and was limited in who she would want to speak to. There were also other bewildering cultural adjustments.

An hour later, Mrs. Aiu returned with a steaming pot, the lid clanking. She carried this into Mama's room and opened the lid. It was *oka-yu*, or, as my mother called it, *okai-san* (rice gruel). Mrs. Aiu had also placed an *umeboshi* (fermented Japanese plum) in the middle of the *oka-yu*, with its distinct purple pink color. My mother began to sob loudly and Mrs. Aiu held her for a while.

"That's okay. Everything will be okay."

I remember this as a photo in my memory. And soon, Mrs. Aiu began to feed the *oka-yu* to my mother with the chopsticks and spoon as they both cried and ate. My mother thanked her in her broken English, "Sank yuu...Sank yuu..." her voice cracking through the tears.

I asked Mrs. Aiu weeks later why she was so nice to us since she was a white American who had been bombed by the Japanese. My encounters with white parents in Albuquerque had largely been tense and unfriendly. Most of them refused to speak to me, or if they did, spoke to me in a condescending manner. But in Hawai'i, amid the palm trees and the Pearl Harbor pillboxes and USS Arizona memorials, I recognized Mrs. Aiu's care. Her difference. She told me that governments and militaries play war games with people, but that is no reason to hate whole groups of people. She said that my mother did not create the war and did not make any hatreds on her own. She found Mama to be a lovely woman. It was the first time I had ever heard someone speak of Mama in this way. These words warmed my heart.

Pearl Harbor, the genocidal bombing of Nagasaki and Hiroshima in 1945, the ethnocidal daily fire-bombings of sixty-six major Japanese cities, the ferocious Japanese aggression and rape of the Philippine Archipelago, Vietnam, Thailand, Cambodia, Korea, Okinawa, China, and colonization of Guam, Fiji, the South Seas Islands, Australia, Burma and more — the devastation was on all sides of the Pacific. And it did not begin in 1941 or 1939 or 1925. Dates are only markers that render certain stories. What is told in textbooks or by politicians and magazines and news outlets dominates the stories told by people like Mama or Mrs. Aiu, or countless others.

Mostly, I remember Mrs. Aiu's kindness and her thoughtful actions. Not only did she cradle Mama, but she thought to make *oka-yu*. *Oka-yu* is something Japanese people feed to the ill to make them feel better. No one but Mrs. Aiu made Mama *oka-yu*. Mama had made me *oka-yu* many times when I was sick, and it always made me feel good and better. But as a child — or perhaps the kind of child I had become — I could not think of Mama's pain, or her longing for home and love. She felt alone.

For Mrs. Aiu, the memories of December 7 were lived with increasing self-reflection, self-education, thought, and care across difference. If she had brought my mother chicken soup, it would not have been as healing as the *oka-yu*. War-memory is not like a box inside someone's head, but an aspect of identity that cannot be isolated. The war-memories Mama carried the remainder of her life are not those that live in textbooks. One can argue that when they are told, they appear as anecdotes to the glory and naturalness of war or demure stories of "Oriental women."

How will we move forward in the world? It is easy for those who are cut off from their own histories to forget, to not understand. Who would admonish others to forget and "be peaceful" (and therefore "good") in order to continue with a refusal to question and remember? To me, this is violent. The honorable, the valiant, the inescapable and carefully constructed links between valor and violence need to be undone. In memory, can we construct different memories? *Tender and robust memories not conceived through battle.* 目

CHAPTER 34
# Wars 戦争

### Battle 1 戦い1

*[Nation-building/identity-making] redraws its frontiers in the menacing, agonistic boundary of cultural difference that never quite adds up, always less than one nation [always] double.*

— Homi Bhabha, *DissemiNation*

*Law 836 — Lu Chun, the appointed governor of Canton, China, in the year 836 A.D., created a law forbidding locals to have any relationships with "darker people." This primarily referred to Malays, Persians, Indians, and Arabs, as well as African and Aboriginal peoples, who came as traders and explorers. Local people of various ethnicities with darker skin tones were also included in this "illegal" category.*

*China, in the nineteenth century was not "unified." Many different factions and ethnic groups vied for supremacy through an adoption of European race science. Intermarriages between the Han and other groups became legal, but those deemed "illegal" were off-limits. Today, Han-identified people control the identity discourse of the entire nation called "China." Undoubtedly, this influenced Japan's own adoption of race science, as well as the rise of fascism at the turn of the twentieth century. This would provide legitimacy to the Occupiers as white supremacists. Yellow supremacy would intensify in response to this approach.[2]*

253

*Where do our ideas of "unity" develop their concepts, reasoning, and methods of unifying? What then is nationality, ethnicity, or race and racism?*

*Mama said:*

*I started to like black men more when I saw the way some white soldiers treated them. My feelings were sometimes confused when some of my friends sided with white soldiers, who joined in making fun of the black men and humiliating them, while other friends sided with the black men. We all wanted to be loyal to whomever we saw ourselves with. I remember one time when two white soldiers were telling the young black soldier to lick his boot! We girls got so enraged!*

*When fights broke out, it wasn't just the white men and the black men against each other. We women would join in. Sometimes we would start fights. I didn't like fighting anymore like I did when I was a child. Punching, kicking, pulling hair, gouging eyes, and twisting arms. We'd have to be separated from each other by the American* MPs *(military police). Most of us Japanese hated the* MPs, *but, at the same time, we wanted them, even though I met your father later, and others who were* MPs *that were suteki. The nice American soldiers were black, white, and some Mexicans. But most of us knew that black men were nicer to us.*

*Many of my girlfriends' white boyfriends beat them. Some of them didn't, but there were more white ones who beat my friends than black ones. But we would hear about all kinds of Americans and Australians, especially those who raped Japanese women. One time, we girls started kicking and punching the* MPs *when they tried to hold some of our friends back at the train station when our friends were being shipped to the Korean front. We wanted to see our boyfriends off. The white* MPs *and officers didn't want us to be there. But after the first two or three times, there weren't any incidents, and they let us stay on the platform with our guys. We chased the train, crying as our boyfriends left for the war. Most of us never saw them again.*[3]

*And the Occupation leaders wouldn't publish anything that Japanese writers wrote in the local newspapers. We were mad at the American Occupation rulers just as much as the Japanese government. After hearing about democracy, democracy, democracy, we found out what that really meant. It* meant that whoever was the leader decided what was said or not, just like Japan was before.

There were so many things going on between the American soldiers and us Japanese, especially the Japanese men. I think there were a lot of Japanese men that hated the Americans. There were some that wanted to become Americans. There were lots of friendships too. But none of our concerns could be published in our magazines or books or newspapers. At the same time, I wanted to be with an American. And to be honest, I married your father to get out of Japan. After all, what had Japan done for me?

And these clubs we'd go to, they were fun. Sometimes, just like Japanese clubs, the Americans would have fights. There were lots of times they were drunk and we'd be with four or five other girls under some soldier's arms. But I just wanted to be in love. Many of my friends became onrii (only) too, not like the others who flitted around like butterflies and prostitutes. I was reading somewhere about how the Japanese had whorehouses with Korean girls working.[4]

Well, they weren't all Korean.

The Occupation forces were telling the Japanese to close these houses. But they wouldn't close the places that the Occupation kept frequenting, which were also full of prostitutes. It was hypocritical. Ichi Doru Kurabu (one-dollar-girl clubs) were everywhere. Always crowded. But I didn't like the clubs and stayed away.

I met your father on a train. It was an accident. I was going to learn English every day and I would see your father.

And people who didn't like us girls who wanted to be with American men would just call us pan-pan whores. Some girls didn't care if they were called that, while others would just punch whoever called them that. Others would try to be as secretive as they could. But being with an American soldier in secret was almost impossible. I looked up to some of the older girls who were with Americans a lot. They would go to the PX, commissary, and get so many new clothes and so much food, cigarettes, and chocolate. They wore lipstick and Western clothes. They were so "in," akogarete ita (enamored). So I easily fit into that life. And whenever black women came around, we had to *compete with them for the black men. We learned to dislike them and talk about black women in a bad way.*

*Although black men were generally nicer than the white soldiers, there were rapes by both black and white soldiers. That wasn't any different. One of my friends was a secretary assistant in the SCAP office. She got pregnant because her American boss threatened to have her job cut if she didn't sleep with him. That's why I was so happy to meet your father. He was a nice man. Most of us needed the Americans for food and other things that we couldn't get so easily without them.*

*I don't like to talk about these things because it is humiliating. And I feel ashamed by some things I did. But I was just trying to live, to not just go along with things. We were hungry. I was trying to survive and not cause my family so much trouble. Even now, people think we were all prostitutes. I don't like being a woman. We are mean and ridiculous. The world doesn't take us seriously, no matter how much we try. In America, I love it, because we are free. I can fart anytime I want. We can fart and wear bananas in our bras or dye our hair purple and be outrageous and nobody bothers us. But America is a lonelier place. Nothing is what I've ever wanted. Dreams change into something else in life. And now I hear Japan is much more like America. I think sometimes that's a good thing. But I know that not everything in America should be copied.*

## Battles 戦い 2

*I remember one time my friends and I went to Yokohoma to run around for the weekend. We stayed at my friend's relative's house. We were there to go to the bars and to meet black soldiers. There were many black women soldiers (black WAACs) in Yokohama. Women soldiers, no matter what color or country, are very attractive. And many of us always were attracted to people in uniform, man or woman. But we didn't want those women to be taking our American men away. Americans were here now, of their own choosing. They were in our country. We should do what we want. Sometimes the black women would come and taunt us, call us prostitutes, "Yellow Bitch," and other nasty names. Some of them were very nice to us.*

*We just called the ones that made fun of us "Bitch! Bitch!" and "Agurii manki woman!" (ugly monkey woman). Some of the girls thought they had tails. Some white American men would tell us they did. And some Japanese books we had in wartime had drawings of black women and men with tails like monkeys.*

*That weekend, a few of us got into two or three fights with black women. They accused us of taking their men and told us that foreign Jap women should stay away from their men because their men didn't want yellow pussy. They could be in America and find plenty of men. There weren't enough good Japanese men around in Japan. And American men were much nicer than Japanese men. Besides, what kind of Japanese would want us now after being around the bases with the soldiers all the time? We had to take care of ourselves. We were forever dirty. No one was going to keep us from getting an American, and all the things they could give us. We always knew two or three girls who were beaten up by their American boy-friends, but there were only a couple of times this happened with black men. White men wanted to own us like Japanese men did. Of course I'm speaking broadly. There were son-of-a-bitch black men and wonderful white men. And Japanese too. I'm only speaking broadly. In any case, the black girls were not going to have any advantage over us Japanese.*

≋ ≋ ≋

U.S. PUBLICATIONS REPORTING RACE-RELATIONS in Occupied Japan, and in particular, black publications such as the *Baltimore Afro-American*,[5] provided varying views on the relationship between black American Occupation soldiers and Japanese women, which created an uproar in the U.S. mainland and on bases in the Pacific. Some reports covered Japanese girls going head-to-head in brawls with black female WAAC personnel as well as with servicemen or MPS. Some articles blamed black soldiers for dating Japanese girls, continuing the uneven relationship between the conqueror and the conquered, to the "immorality" of Japanese girls compared to well-behaved American servicewomen. It was a tangled web of subordination, racism, and heterosexual norms of gender and sex intensified by the caste structure.[6]

U.S. Military Police at Misawa Air Force Base in Aomori, Japan, in the 1960s. *Photo courtesy of Tom Roach.*

### My Notes

*American soldiers, regardless of race, appealed to the victor's sense of militarized masculinity through sexual conquest and subjugation of the native women in occupied Japan.*

*Black women served by enlisting in the Women's Auxiliary Army Corps (WAAC), and were often labeled "ten percenters" because they made up 10 percent of the women recruited. Although black WAAC officers received officer cadet training in integrated units and enjoyed some luxurious lifestyles attendant to the privileged (like hiring Japanese maids), like black servicemen, all other aspects of life in the corps were segregated.*

*A little known fact during World War II: The Japanese created Negro Propaganda Operations as a way to attack Anglo-Saxon racism in the U.S. The Japanese used their own radio announcers and African American POWs, focusing on U.S. news stories involving racial tension, such as the Detroit race riots and lynchings. While many see propaganda as biased information intended to promote a particular political cause or view, some scholars believe that the Negro Propaganda Operations, "evoked a variety of responses within the black community and the sum total of these reactions forced America's government to improve conditions for Blacks in the military and society."[7]*

Mama's thoughts on African American women was influenced by other ideas that rarely came from a single place, space, idea, or moment. When I was nine years-old living in Albuquerque, I was looking through some of my Dad's books when I found a nice big photograph of a beautiful woman, an African American woman with curly flowing hair in a beautiful dress. I asked Mama who it was. She looked at it, disgusted, and told me to put it away.

Later that evening, after Dad had come home and we had eaten dinner, I asked him about the photograph I found, pulling it from the space between two sets of encyclopedias that decorated our shelves. When he told me her name (which I have forgotten), his expression changed. He said this was a friend. This was in 1969. But in the early 1970s, when I mentioned that photograph again inadvertently to Mama, she said that it was Dad's girlfriend. She had thrown things at him, yelled and cursed at him. This woman was someone Dad had fallen in love with while Mom and I were in Japan before we came to the U.S. Mama had found the photograph before I did that day, and put it back where she found it.

I understood that Dad's black heritage was important to him. The woman in the photograph was, perhaps, one way for him to hold on to his black culture in a world that largely hated or demoted blacks. As an African American teenager in the U.S. armed forces occupying Japan, Dad had gained certain privileges and was empowered more than he had ever experienced in America.

Dad and Mom dated, and later created me, but his heart was often divided between cultural-racial-national loyalties, dominant white and African American compulsory manhoods, and a history of multiple oppressions. There was also the reality of being sixteen and seventeen in the Korean War fields, and on the military bases in Japan. Dad was learning how to be a man.

*But how?*

When Mama and I began meeting Dad's family over the years in the U.S., Mama grew to love and respect them. As I loved the kindness and humor of Grandmother Irma and Aunt Doris and others, I became curious about what black women were going through in America during the Cold War years. In her younger years during Occupation, Mama had internalized competitive feelings for survival, and racial and gender conflicts that elevated her to a better life. By the time we arrived in the U.S., America had already begun to popularize *Father Knows Best* as a benchmark for a thing called "the ideal nuclear family," which was not a mainstream ideal in the Japanese cultural imagination. Interestingly, after World War II, images of military woman were seen as a contradiction between those values of homemaker and individual liberty. This could also be said about the native women in Occupied Japan.

The intensity and loneliness of black women in Japan in the immediate postwar days mirrored the escalating and intense division between the African American genders along lines of class and nation.[8] Many African American men drew upon dominant white notions of Japanese women as submissive and docile. Some often compared black women to Japanese women, and were critical of black women. Quite a few African American men used to say, "I like Japanese women better than most black women." This kind of desire and exclusion is very complex in its historical-political structure. More importantly, most Japanese women understood their docility and obedience to men as a role, not as an identity.

According to Mama, Japanese women jockeyed their "docility" and "obedience" to vie for the affections of black servicemen. She said that most women did that with Japanese men as well, although some women wholeheartedly embraced their constructed inferiority. Some did this to satisfy their curiosity about Americans and, in particular, black men, or to escape poverty, or to gain favors in order to survive.

Many Americans, both men and women (of all colors), read about Japanese women in the pages of *Time, Life Magazine, Readers' Digest,* or black publications like *Ebony, Jet,* or local newspapers like the *Baltimore Afro American,* and saw Japanese women depicted as obedient, and their controlled behaviors as a form of slavery, a mark of primitiveness. Indeed, this type of reporting was supported by the patriarchal and sexist social structures that existed during this era. For American women, it was a reminder of their own histories of gendered sexual subserviency. Perhaps this was also why some African American women wanted nothing to do with Mama and the other war brides and their children, who suddenly became part of their African American families after the war. But this was not the entire story either.

Writers in those days often wrote of G.I. Joe rescuing the geisha from the rice paddies that confined her to Japanese patriarchy. Some wrote how Japanese women were playing American G.I.s for suckers.[9] So who is exploiting whom in the context of occupation and inequality? But not all Japanese, nor all black women and men, played out these dynamics. There were also many black women and black communities who welcomed Japanese war brides with open arms when they came to the U.S., as was the case with Dad's family. And in Occupied Japan, many enduring friendships developed between Japanese women and African American women. But in most cases, relationships formed with differences in city, town, state, rank, race, and socioeconomic status in multiple configurations. In my mother's case, for instance, like many people on all sides of an Occupied territory, the American soldier and nation became the key centerpiece. In some ways, everything else could be degraded in the service toward that goal.[10]

How the varying links between race, gender, caste, and nation were constructed to prevent solidarity and compassion is something I have questioned for most of my life. It is my way of questioning social justice. There are many who try to ignore them, and pretend these webs do not exist, or are things of the past. This does not help those who face conflicts, threats of death, and assimilation. These questions were marked on all Japanese women, black women, mixed Black Japanese children's bodies. And in this lapse and violent separation from solidarities and compassions, what makes life? How do we wind up conceiving life? Through what histories do we act? I have found that resistance and liberation comes through struggle. It is possible and can be done, even in the most difficult spaces.

One year, my Dad and his brothers organized a family reunion. The year Mama and I went, it was held in San Antonio where Dad lived. It was a particularly lively reunion, partly because they had found their long-lost father, who they had not seen since Dad was six-years-old. Because their father was attending, Grandma Irma didn't want to go because he abandoned her years ago, but she eventually did attend. It seemed like a rather pleasant reunion. Since I did not know how Mama felt about being around black women so closely since she had left Japan, I asked her about it after we returned to our house in Albuquerque.

Family reunion photo, summer of 1972 in San Antonio, Texas. Mama's exuberance, loneliness and troubles hide behind her calm smile. *Fredrick Cloyd Family Archive.*

*Your father's family is so lovely and nice. They are all good-looking. Your father's mother is wonderful. She shows her love so physically. I love your father's young half-sister Doris. She is funny and beautiful. I saw her putting a teaspoon of instant coffee into a full cup of gin at breakfast. I always wondered why she was so happy all the time! She is hilarious! I love those kinds of black women! She is attractive and smart and fun. If you marry a black woman, you should marry someone like her.* 目

# CHAPTER NOTES

1. Homi K. Bhabha, *Nation and Narration* (London and New York: Routledge, 1990)

2. China, known as an advanced society, was a huge influence in the world until the Western world overcame pre-modern growth constraints and emerged during the nineteenth century as the dominant population. Japan and other Pacific nations also adopted China's racism and ethnic prejudice among minorities within the nation state. See books by Frank Dikötter, *The Construction of Racial Identities in China and Japan: Historical and Contemporary Perspectives.* (Hawai'i: University of Hawai'i Press, 1997); and *The Discourse of Race in Modern China* (London, U.K.: Oxford University Press, 1992).

3. The parting of Japanese girlfriends and fiancées from their military boyfriends at the train station was a trope of the star-crossed lovers, saying goodbye and not knowing whether they would ever see each other again. Popular photographs, films, and songs mirrored this scene, the parting of lovers at railroad stations, saying their goodbyes as they faced an unknown future. I always felt that the difference between how Mama and I felt about trains was gender-specific. For example, my love of trains symbolized a longing to leave present circumstances for something new, and a love of the aesthetic power that steam trains showed. For my mother, of course, this was not the case.

4. Different categories of girls developed in and around the U.S. military bases in Japan, whether they were professional or amateur prostitutes, or women who occasionally dated G.I.s for food, cigarettes and treats. *Onrii* (only) girls favored being with one American man, akin to monogamy (although what they said and what they truly believed were often two different things). There were other terms for differently-configured relationships. These subcultures and unique languages were part of a general base town culture that developed – a base town pidgin which had many similar words across the Pacific. For instance, *Mama-san,* which is a combination of Spanish/English and Japanese honorifics, was a term used by American soldiers and base town residents in Korea, the Philippines, Cambodia, Guam, and Vietnam.

5. Matthews, "Wacs and Pom Poms Wage War in Yokohama," *Baltimore Afro-American,* September 22, 1951.

6. See Rumi Sakamoto, "Pan-pan Girls: Humiliating Liberation in Postwar Japanese Literature," *PORTAL: Journal of Multidisciplinary International Studies* 7, no. 2 (2010): 1.

7. Masaharu, Sato, and Barak Kushner, "'Negro propaganda operations': Japan's short-wave radio broadcasts for World War II Black Americans." *Historical Journal of Film, Radio and Television* 19, no. 1 (1999): 5-26,

8. Elaine Tyler May, *Homeward Bound: American Families in the Cold War Era,* (NY: Basic Books, 2008). May discusses the creation of American gender ideology in the Cold War, espe-

cially in the Introduction and in the first chapter of the book. See also Megan Taylor Shock-ley, "Looking Ahead: Middle-Class Women's Activities in the Postwar World," "We, Too, Are Americans": *African American Women in Detroit and Richmond, 1940-54* (Champaign,: University of Illinois Press, 2003), 103-136, where Shockley shows the domestic ideology of African American gender politics (was internalized from the dominant society), which began affecting civilian and military life through an idea of "responsible patriotism." See also Victoria W. Wolcott, *Remaking Respectability: African American Women in Interwar Detroit* (Chapel Hill, NC: University of North Carolina Press, 2001).

9. For example, see Ethel Payne, "Says Japanese Girls Playing GIs For Suckers: 'Chocolate Joe' Used, Amused, Confused," *Chicago Defender,* November 18, 1950.

10. See Yasuhiro Okada, "Gendering the 'Black Pacific': Race Consciousness, National Identity, and the Masculine/Feminine Empowerment Among African Americans in Japan Under U.S. Military Occupation, 1945-1952" (PhD diss., Michigan State University, 2008), one of the most well-rounded studies that I know of on this subject, at the time of this writing.

# CHAPTER 35

# Woman That Sees

THERE ARE SOME PEOPLE WHO HAVE BEEN displaced in victory or defeat, displacement or destruction, desire or need. For women, this displacement is greater because of the chauvinism that exists in most nation states. What aspects of Mama were suppressed and pushed out of existence? Some people cannot endure the pain, not because they are weak, but because there are forces out there that work to extinguish them, making it unbearable for them to endure. This invisiblizing and forced erasure is certainly unnatural and sometimes inevitable, but it is always political, based on domination and survival coupled with the repositioning of causes and conditions.

*When I was a teenager . . . around 1950, I went with Stepmother to visit old friends in Tōkyō. Those friends were so much fun; I liked them because they were all outspoken and foul-mouthed. Anyway, I had to use the benjo (toilet) at least once a night while I slept. You know me. I'm always kind of half-asleep when I go to the o-benjo.[1] Remember the old-time obenjo we used to have? That one was in a sort-of closet that you went into in the bathing room with the wooden plank floors and coal-burning tub. (Yes, I remember. How could I forget? My earliest memories of our bathrooms in our homes were this type of benjo.) So when you take a bath, you rinse with the water outside the tub. You go into the tub to soak (Yes, Mama.) So I remember that first night at our friends' place. I got up in the middle of the night to go to the toilet. So I'm stumbling while I walk fast, so I could get back to the futon . . . and*

Mama in Albuquerque, circa 1976. *Fredrick Cloyd Family Archive.*

*this woman, sitting on the small stool outside the bathtub, is pouring the water over herself gently, rinsing herself. I remember saying, "Sumimasen," (excuse me), then sliding open the toilet room door (o-benjo no tokoro no to), and going in. I finished going, then stumbled back into bed.*

*In the morning, my friends and I were just talking about all kinds of things, when I mentioned the woman who was rinsing in the bathing space, and asked them who it was. Then they said, "What? You must've been dreaming, Emi-chan. A woman? There's no one else here." Then we all screamed. "Kowai! (That's scary!)" And I remember we all ran into the other room where the adults were and told them what happened. I remember father telling us about a Korean woman who used to live in this house before they moved here. He said that she killed herself by hanging herself outside of the bathtub after killing her children. "Oh, no. Not again!" I thought. I had been visited by this woman. I've been visited yet again by someone others can't see.*

MAMA UNDERSTOOD WHY KOREAN GIRLS often committed suicide in Japan. She empathized with her five Korean friends who committed suicide. She knew what it was like because Mama also tried to kill herself. She, along with her Korean and Okinawan friends, were ostracized as being non-Japanese when they attended schools for foreigners. Mama was not only looked down upon because of her own ethnic national background, but also, as a member of the upper-class, she was looked upon with disgust alongside forced respect. But in the hierarchies there is usually one or the other form of status that wins out. Recently, when I talked to her about the official laws that barred Koreans from retaining their Korean names, my mother became angry. She could not believe Japan would behave this way.

Her friends are ghosts who visit her. She did not like the idea of being visited. She did not feel that these visits could help them or herself. She had her own troubles. She felt this was a burden she had to endure.

Mama told me that she had this ability "to see" since she was a small child, but didn't want these abilities, much less acknowledge them. Yet she had always done palm readings for her friends in Albuquerque. If she had learned English, she could have made money as a credible psychic. I was sometimes afraid of how accurate her readings were. Sometimes I interpreted for her when my friends came over, wanting my mother to read their palms. She stopped doing them after she predicted her friend Yoshiko's car accident, and it came true. She had warned her to be careful, but nevertheless, one of Yoshiko's limbs had to be amputated. Even today, Mama has sleepless nights. Remembering.

*Sometimes they are remembering. Sometimes the visitors come to her.*

Sometimes you can't sleep. I don't mean to make you afraid. The world forgets us. I just don't want you to forget me. You know me. So I visit you. 冒

# CHAPTER 36

# Self Sistas

THE "SELF," CONTINUALLY ASSEMBLING itself through our everyday lives, is made up of things we create and things we suppress, things we resist and things we forget. By internalizing the world, we make ourselves in it. No other way is possible. I began to realize that unless I could think and reflect on some of the things that happened to me, I would continue to be a ghost to myself. Mama was acutely aware of this as well. This shared self-reflexivity comes with strife, but is necessary for survival.

I never wanted to become "Japanese" the way dominant wartime Japan designated Japanese culture, or accept the way U.S. Occupied Japan expected Japanese women to behave. I didn't want this but this dominant behavior became normalized with time. Rules became the norm. Before the war, a student could be punished for not being Japanese enough, or not supporting their army. But during Occupation, it was confusing in a different way. There were too many changes taking place, especially as Japan had been bombed into nothingness. The Japanese felt empty and desolate, inferior and without ground. We also felt that American culture had ways that could improve Japan even though America was the enemy; we were enamored by them, even as some of us denounced their attitudes of superiority over the Japanese. This is why some people, whether Japanese or whatever identity or culture, make me sick. They are so willing to go along with whatever is required of them while they self-efface, and going along with their own status as inferior in Japanese society, while demanding that other women do the same. Their self-effacement appears as silence and collusion with a dominance—and violence—that needs to change. This is why I had so many Japanese friends who were also a little different, who were labeled "troubled spirits" in Japanese society. This

269

"trouble" means they were embodying the ostracization and humiliation of being outside the norm.

**My Notes**

*In the early 1950s, a poll was taken of sixth graders in Japan by a Japanese national research project. They were asked what nationality they preferred to be born: 53 percent American, 22 percent Swiss, and 16 percent Japanese. Most Japanese, of any age, did not have a compelling answer to the question of what made them identify as Japanese.[1]*

*The Meiji government began intensifying their efforts to unify Japan into a single ideological identity, but because it was not a singular race, they tried to make Japan into a singular people (nation). Most Japanese had relatives from China, Korea, Okinawa, and other places. In U.S. anthropological records, it was shown that Japan's population, like any other nation, consisted of diverse peoples. The British were more aware of this fact in the way they saw the Japanese. Some Brits noted how Americans homogenized the Japanese, seeing them only as one ethnic group.[2]*

*In creating a national identity, homogenization is both an action and an effect. The Japanese used this to great effect. It is my experience that when meeting university students and younger Japanese, they think of themselves as a single ethnic and racial group. During my mother's generation, this complete homogenization was not so prevalent. The Okinawans still referred to the Japanese as Yamato people, much like the Han people are the dominant group called "Chinese" in China. Forgetting is not passive. It is constructed.*

*Into the 1970s, people in Japan who divulged any Korean ancestry risked ending their careers or, worse, being lynched. It is an increasingly controversial topic today as many famous singers, including Misora Hibari and Miyako Harumi, among others, who are at least partially of Korean ancestry. How would this be a controversy if hybridity were accepted as national identity?*

*Through these and other ways of losing time, place, space and traditional ways of relating with each other after the war, identity was often expressed through a developing music scene in postwar Japan, which made longing and sadness a pervasive theme for decades. This is contrasted starkly with, but nevertheless linked to, the movement in the 1980s to reorient Japanese culture, including its popular music, toward brightness, happiness, and superficiality. Thus, the beginnings of Japan's "search for its identity" created new questions. And with it came reflections on the Shōwa period of its history, which some have called "Japan's American century."*

## Coloring Self

It is a monumental moment whenever I meet another Black Japanese or Black Okinawan person. Not because there are so few of us, but because for whatever reason, a Black Japanese community doesn't really exist. We are fragmented and dislocated, so it makes finding each other somewhat difficult. But meeting black Asians in general is also exciting, at least initially. Today, I have been meeting more and more of them, as the world becomes "smaller," and more people are traveling and crossing boundaries into countries that have been restructured since the end of the wars. The Pacific War does not loom as large with an enemy or occupier dynamic as it once did during the 1940s to 1970s, although new dynamics have emerged from America's hegemonic role in the Asia-Pacific today.

Yet differences among black Asians do exist: differences in our war experiences, an experience of first-hand cultural devastation, whether we experienced occupation or not, whether we lived in the Asian nation of a parent's birth, had access to and can speak fluently an Asian language, or have had steady access to supportive Asian communities. How close are we to a specific African or African American community? Do we socialize or interact with those comunities, or do we ignore them? All of this marks the spaces and times of how we interact with each other.

The eight or nine Black Japanese I met in the United States beginning in my mid-40s (circa early 1990s) were mostly raised in America. Almost all of them, save one, considered themselves black first. The extent of their Japaneseness was perhaps the few words of Japanese they would speak with their mothers or grandmothers, or the Japanese food they ate and loved. Most hardly knew anything about Japan, and weren't too interested in Japan except as a land where one of their parents came from. From my limited perspective at the time, and since I was raised in Japan, I thought their relationship with Japan was primarily colonial and exoticized. *So you eat sushi. How exotic. How else could it be?*

Proximity plays a role. But what exactly emerges as knowledge or as an authentic "self" depends on one's proximity to communal, national, or cultural experience. Sometimes people fill those empty spaces with inaccurate depictions from the media, rumors, or fictional family stories passed down to replace real stories. Shame is sometimes a culprit.

In some ways, I was annoyed when some Black Japanese brothers and sisters I knew seemed to exoticize their Japaneseness, or had decidedly taken on Americanized views of that aspect of themselves. Nowadays, what I find really annoying is this universal Americanized view of a single ethnicity, a racialized heritage that does not include Japan as it was and how it is today, and often includes wartime caricatures of Asians. In addition, those like myself, living on the margins of Japanese society, have encountered other issues. I had to overcome my struggle to communicate difference. But it was also petty of me to think this way. From their point of view, I was annoying because I wouldn't let them be "completely black." Blackness, in its American form, offers spaces of resistance in the U.S., and the dynamics of a black/white binary paradigm rife with sociological ghosts such as racism, discrimination, social bondage, and forms of historical slavery.

For so many whites and non-whites alike that have experienced hardships in both dominant U.S. and Japanese cultures, black culture offers resistance to this supremacy. If a Black Japanese Amerasian leaves Japan at an early age, or is born in the U.S., or grows up in an orphanage, or on a U.S. military base in Japan, or has experience living in different countries and socioeconomic classes, their world views differ drastically. When one lives in an orphanage in Japan, or on a base with a nuclear family in Atlanta, Georgia, or on the streets of Tōkyō, how does Black Japaneseness show up? Often, it shows up as "race" only, because skin color dictates identity. Identity, in our present globalizing condition, has been overly racialized. So it's tempting to erase one's Japaneseness when blackness can provide a safe space of belonging, while Japaneseness becomes invisible within the American "model minority" Asian social myth.

There is no one way of perceiving blackness or Japaneseness and mixedness unless one adopts the meaning of something that came from other sources and memories. For Irish, Greek, Polish, Jewish or Russian white Americans, whiteness locates itself dominantly, but is replete with its own resistances as well, due to their European historical lineages of oppressions and dominance, accesses and exclusions. These symbolic and identity-based beliefs play a critical role in what a person thinks, feels, sees or experiences.[3]

However, proximities to Asianness depends on one's proximity to nation or culture. This idea of Asianness has many meanings, but hinges on whether one plays up the internal diversity in that word, or the externalized sameness imposed through that word. While Asians are highly diverse ethnically and religiously, there remains in our society an insistence that they share something in common that gets summarized in the term "Asian." For example, many Japanese do not consider themselves Asian. To them, that term applies to the Chinese, Southeast Asians, and Koreans. And, from my point of view, proximities to war, war-culture and experiences of superiority, form our relationship to the identities that the dominant society has assigned us. In another example, in the United States, it is common for non-Asians, to think of Asians and Asian Americans as the same, when they are vastly different from each other for the reasons I mentioned earlier.

One problem I have with the social construct of Black Japanese identity is its being rendered dualistically—either as a non-community, a thrown-together combination of race, ethnicity, nation, and culture; or one "community" with a single way of perceiving and doing. For example, Mama and her friends, and other Japanese people called white Americans "American" but call Black-Americans "black." What is that all about and why? These markers serve to remind people of the transnational migration of concepts of race and racialization in the Pacific, both in and from various conjoined histories. Any sexual union between races and nations becomes magnified. *Sushi and chitlins. Teriyaki and hamhocks. Hiphop chopsticks. Exotic.* But what is black? What is African? Africans (from Africa) cannot relate to this at all. There are Africans married to Japanese women who exist outside of how Americans see blackness. There are African Americans who have not lived what is considered "African American" culture. The domination of American cultural practices looms large in how people see themselves and how they are seen by others. In short, in the mainstream, "black" is a foregone conclusion with certain characteristics. Japanese is a foregone conclusion, with certain characteristics.

In any life, I suppose, individuals subscribe to some kind of mythos that resonates with particular histories and goals, shaping a person's behavior, character and personality, ethics and morality. I'm not interested in embracing a readily available mythos that limits creative possibilities for a different world, simply because it's easier for others. My mother is mixed Japanese and my father is mixed African American. I was born and raised in Occupied Japan. I speak Japanese fluently and thoroughly understand the customs and traditions of Japan, but do not necessarily ascribe to or act on them. Once I immigrated to the U.S., I learned and acknowledged my African American ancestry through Dad and his family, but it never occurred to me to subjugate my Japanese heritage to white Americanness and African American blackness, yet many Black Japanese have done just that. Why? Because it fits into America's neat and tidy American racial paradigm, one of the most rigid constructs that obfuscates and distorts and maintains social hierarchy by maintaining white supremacy and systemic hierarchies of color, race, gender, and class. Some mixed-race people become confused when they have internalized the need to fit into the categories neatly and find that when the boundaries are blurred, they become contradictory or exist violently in conflict.

For myself, this confusion has not happened. I questioned the world and its machinations, not who I was. I questioned why the world was this way or that, what people and institutions did to make me feel unwanted, questioned my belonging in the world, what gave people the right to humiliate me, and try to kill my spirit. Throughout my childhood, I was never confused about who I was. I thank my parents and my relatives for this.

There are no obvious Black Japanese social worlds, communities, or ghettos. These worlds are largely individualized and dislocated, ambivalent precisely because they are disconnected. This is no different from any other identity. It's the dominant society which tries to force us into forgetting our histories, and tries to dictate who and what we are. Why, in the twenty-first century, is there a necessity for a separate school for Amerasians? What populations are served in the passage of time in places such as this? In places occupied by the United States, such as Okinawa, Japan, the Philippines, and Korea, laws and policies creating and affecting the citizenship status of mixed-race children in the global arena mimic those of the U.S. For example, there have been a recent series of court cases (circa 2006) where mixed Filipino-Japanese sued the Japanese for civil rights violations in relation to citizenship.[4] What other way can people survive if there is no other recourse, no other way to take steps toward justice?

How do we participate in our own erasure?[5] Not doing so requires a strength that forces us to enter spaces of discomfort where dominant nations claim and maintain their continuity through countless wars and genocides, through labelling the miscreants and the tortured, the special and exotic, the should-be-ignored and the moronic. When we erase ourselves, fear and loathing takes over and nurtures militarism, valor, and superiority. In any case, wealthy nations invest in creating and recreating certain ghosts for history. Certainly the *buraku* ghettos of Japan, the prisons, the bars and entertainment centers, as well as the coal mines, prostitution houses, sports teams, music industries, and modeling agencies, are filled with the bodies of Black Asians. So what does empowerment look like for me?

In 1979, having moved to Long Beach, California, I sorely missed Japanese culture. When I traveled around the country coaching or playing volleyball, I sought Japanese restaurants and stores. Even if I knew I couldn't visit these places, I would look them up. I sought store owners and sushi chefs who would speak to me in Japanese. I sought Japanese language teachers at language schools where I worked, or Japanese culture professors at universities. In the many places I've lived, Japanese establishments were non-existent or hidden, save for a few Japanese restaurants, often run by Koreans.

When I heard that my college would be starting a Japanese student club, I quickly took the opportunity to show up. After a brief moment of hope, one of the organizers said to me, *"I'm sorry, but you're not Japanese enough."* It was so disappointing. Another sign of un-belonging. While I didn't feel like ignoring him, I also didn't feel like fighting over my identity. What was interesting was that none of the nine students that showed up to that meeting spoke Japanese, and only one of them had been to Japan on a vacation with his parents. I was the only Japanese one, I thought. *Who were these people?* But it confirmed to me that being Japanese, American, black, or any other label, is oftentimes a joke for me. There were moments when I was becoming unrecognizable to myself, but still, I knew who I was.

This "not recognizing ourselves" has different ways of being enacted. The moments of unrecognizability were when I would attempt to change myself to get along with others, to split, to shift, in ways that were, now, recognized as unnecessary. But perhaps this is the nature of growing as a person, to make changes and learn the boundaries of the self. Not recognizing the self is so prevalent in diasporic and transnational communities borne of war, where identities are crafted out of necessity, but not our deepest longings. So these memories of growing and acknowledging are not just memories. Memory is who we become, as beings in the world. As victims, we often learn to perpetrate in defense. Most of the time, it isn't conscious. At a Zen Buddhist retreat in Upstate New York in 1987, a memory I had not considered for twenty years came suddenly and intensely. I had to find ways to heal, to combat the internalized violence that I was unable to see, much less acknowledge. During this journey I struggled to find acts of atonement, as

Unknown Korean women with black GI.s at a base town club, possibly in Daegu, Korea in the late 1960s. *Photo courtesy of Shirley Gindler-Price.*

In Korean cities and villages—such as this one in Yon Sul Gol in 1961, like Japan, and the Philippines, Guam, Hawai'i, Vietnam, Thailand, and other U.S. military locations, prostitution thrived and built economies of survival around them. *Courtesy of René Burri/Magnum Photos*

well as ways to undercut those links between sociological violence and personal triumph. This was abhorrent to me. I have committed many acts of violence, as most of us do in life, unknowingly sometimes. There is one memory I want to mention here.

### Couldn't Recognize My Sistas: How I was Violence

IN ALBUQUERQUE IN 1966, a few months before our family would move to Hawai'i, I was ten. Mama had befriended a Korean woman she met through a Japanese friend of hers, who was in town for a couple of weeks before their family moved overseas. Her name was Dat. Dat was a dynamo. She was expressive, swaggering, and almost masculine in her ways. She powered her way around wherever she went with a strong gait, expressive gestures, and her loud talk. She was hilarious and fierce, outspoken and direct. Mama admired her, I think, in many ways. I also think that she saw herself in Dat. Dat was desired as a friend by Mama, because she was nostalgic, reminding Mama—Emiko, of her past self.

Mama and Dat would go out to the clubs along with some of their other friends. Dad was in Vietnam at the time. Although Dat's African American husband was also doing his duty in Vietnam, Dat did not hide her distaste for staying home and waiting around, doing "housewife" things. She spoke in a heavily accented, broken U.S. military-based Korean-English pidgin slang, which she used to communicate with her daughters and with Mama. Mama used the same kind of slang, except the Japanese version. There were many military slang-words in that language of Pan-Asian war brides which made it easy for them to communicate with each other—all coming from contact with American base cultures.

U.S. military-base slang had many parallels across the entire Pacific. Since Japan colonized Korea, some Japanese words were understood by Koreans and became part of the Korean lexicon. The language was forced upon Koreans, as all occupations do in occupied lands. Dat and Mama knew some of the same terms: *Mama-san* (middle-aged Asian woman that sometimes meant woman bar-owner or prostitution-house owner), *neh-bah hap-pun!* ("never happen!" meaning "no way!"), *runpen* (homeless bum/beggar), *Chah-ree* (Charlie: soldier man) – an endless list, really.

In Vietnam, the Vietnamese enemy were called "gooks." Gooks had been the pejorative name for Koreans in the Korean War, and now Vietnamese were being called gooks. The term was first used against Filipinos fighting against the Americans during American massacres in the Philippines in the Spanish-American War, similar to the way "nigger" was used against black slaves in the United States. The Cold War intensified and maintained the position of Oriental-as-enemy without differentiation, transferring it to whomever the enemy was at the time. Mama, too, also carried much of the prejudice against Koreans she had learned in her days in Japan, sometimes saying condescending things about Dat to me.

When she was with Dat, Mama traveled back in time, perhaps feeling like a single woman from the base towns of Japan again – the days of relative freedom, empowerment and rebelliousness. Mama was happy to have a social life outside the projected boundaries of "proper Japanese war bride." When Dat came over, there would be heightened spirits and energy, the air crackling with action and laughter, and I cherished the food we ate that they often prepared together – mixtures of Korean and Japanese: *kimchi* and rice, *takuan* and *bulgogi,* seaweed and *yakimandu.* Her two daughters were often eating rice with room-temperature water in a bowl, along with fish cakes and *kimchi*. However, Dat wouldn't cook too much because she felt it was a way that men enslaved women. But she cooked enough for us to enjoy her country's food. *"No like cook!"*

For *sleh-bu!*

Mama knew nothing of Japanese dominance in Korea, nor why her Korean friends in Japan had Japanese names while her Korean friends in the U.S. had Korean or American "white" names. She once told me that Koreans "wanted" to become Japanese, and it was all voluntary because it was natural for them to feel inferior to Japanese people. Nationalist training always works, no matter where: Japan, Korea, the U.S., everywhere. In time, Mama acknowledged Japanese prejudice against Koreans, noting that Koreans had a hard time in Japan. But in her mind, Japan must have had to subjugate Koreans. She was told they were more "primitive," "washing their bodies in the same water that they defecated in." They were "dirty."

It was always interesting that Mama spoke of villagers in Japan in the same way. Her nationalism and upper-class status always came through, even though her vernacular and behavior contradicted her status. These renditions of Koreans were often published in American military journals and magazine articles.[6] I used to distance myself from her prejudices as much as possible, even as these prejudices often contradicted her other thoughts and behaviors.

She reminded me of certain friends I had, either white, black or Japanese, who I liked, but who she knew held me in low esteem. I also think she was jealous of Dat because she was more "free," without understanding that rebelliousness comes

These photos of Korean Amerasians at an orphanage in Bu-Pyung, Korea, were taken between 1979 and 1981 during one of many visits by Americans for International Aid, to transport orphans to their newly adoptive parents in the United States. *Photo courtesy of Jeannie Hatcherson/Corawill, Inc.*

from resistance to subjugation. Dat's expressive, powerful, defiant demeanor grew more unlike Mama's as the years wore on. These traits were not "Korean." There were plenty of Japanese women, some of my mother's friends among them, who were bold like Dat.

I was around eleven when Dat would come over, pushing Mama to go out to the clubs with her. They would leave me alone with her two daughters. When I was alone with them, I felt contradictory emotions. I felt very close to them, like looking in a mirror, but at the same time, I felt resentful. I also realized that I had power over them as a boy. They looked to me as my cousins in Japan did, as an older brother. I couldn't fulfill that role. I wanted to play by myself. As cute Black Korean girls, they were mirrors for me and yet not at all.

Although Dat and Mama entrusted me with them, I did not see myself as responsible for them.

Laura was around three, while Cheryl was five. The nights alone with them passed peacefully. One night, as they played their own games while they sat beside me, watching me play with my trains and my trucks on the floor, I suddenly became annoyed with their presence. I pulled the top blue blanket from my bed and covered Laura with it, hiding her underneath it. She began to cry. Then Cheryl began to cry.

I was never one to hit, but I did threaten them with another blanket. Cheryl tried to uncover Laura. I told her I would cover her too if she took Laura's blanket off. It was my own cruel game. The big brother showing who he could be. It seemed like a half hour passed. The girls kept crying. I kept the blanket over Laura. After a while, I became bored and uncovered Laura. They began to calm down. Laura, tired from crying, fell asleep. I pulled out some Ken dolls and army men that I had, offering them to join me in playing. We played together until Dat and Mama came home. No one spoke of what I had done.

The best I can do now is to write this lament about my black Korean sisters. I did not know or even considered that we were sisters and brothers of a humanity that needed care. I had inherited prejudices, although, at eleven, I didn't consciously think Korean, Japanese, black, or how this population or that population should be treated. If you, Laura, if you, Cheryl, if you, Dat, are somewhere reading this, feeling this, I know it is too late and the damage has been done. I wish in that moment I had not become violence. My loneliness could have made Cheryl and Laura my sisters. Instead, I violated the longing in myself and in them. I am sorry. It was what I had learned to be.

Learning to be a person at any given moment is unconscious. This so-called unconsciousness is connected to the culture, history, and power that surrounds us. I must live with this, as I have made Laura and Cheryl live with my violence. Black bodies of the Pacific of postwar Japan, Korea, Vietnam, and the Philippines need a solace that is impossible to comprehend.

Even now, as Black Pacific bodies toil with the laws and prejudices that energize much of our world, I wish to eradicate these prejudices and process our isolated pains and sorrows to understand who we are as human beings through the exploration of self.

When I read about the *Ukishima Maru* 浮島丸 [7] and the role of hiding, manipulating, silencing and killing in the name of ideals, I think I have learned to struggle against my internalized nationalism, sexism, and patriarchal entitlements. But as a boy, there was no such analysis. There was only my mind and body, making their worlds ugly. I turned against my sisters, and perhaps made them hate me. I have had to learn to see this in order to resolve this struggle within myself. It'll never be perfect, but I continue to take small steps. Again and again. Searching for self. 昌

# CHAPTER NOTES

1. See John Lie, *Multiethnic Japan* (Boston: Harvard University Press, 2001).

2. Hugh Cortazzi, a British Diplomat, was assigned to Japan for the Occupation, and in later years wrote many articles and a number of books about Japanese society. See Hugh Cortazzi, *Japan Experiences: Fifty Years, One Hundred Views: Post-war Japan through British Eyes 1945-2000* (Japan Library, 2001), where he shares many of his observations about the differences between American and British attitudes towards the Japanese.

3. See Patrick Brantlinger's book: *Dark Vanishings: Discourses on the Extinction of Primitive Races, 1800-1930.* (NY: Cornell University Press, 2003) where Brantlinger presents the idea of progress as a way of justifying annihilation.

4. See "Filipinos abandoned during war sue for Japanese citizenship," *Japan Times,* September 1, 2006. Accessed September 19, 2015. http://search.japantimes.co.jp/cgi-bin/nn20060901a7. html. See also Center for Japanese Filipino Families. Accessed September 19, 2015. http://home. att.ne.jp/banana/cjff/homepage.htm

5. One of my favorite lines/questions from Anne Anlin Cheng, *The Melancholy of Race: Psychoanalysis, Assimilation and Hidden Grief* (London, UK: Oxford University Press, 2001),

6. For one example, see Milton A. Smith, "GIs Spurn Korean Gals, Wait For Jap Lassies," *Chicago Defender,* December 16, 1950, where the elevation of Japanese womanhood helped render newly-formed Japanese nation during the U.S. Occupation of Japan (1945-1952), and their superiority to other Asian nations through Orientalist notions of the submissive Japanese (compared to the Koreans). For an excellent study on this, see Yasuhiro Okada's Ph.D. dissertation, "Gendering the Black Pacific: Race Consciousness, National Identity and the Masculine/ Feminine Empowerment Among African Americans in Japan Under U.S. Military Occupation 1945-1952" (Michigan State University, 2008), 197-8 contains the section on the creation of hierarchy between Japanese and Korean women in the minds of American soldiers. My father, as well, told me some of the exact same lines about them when I asked.

7. The *Ukishima Maru* (浮島丸) was a Japanese naval ship built in 1937. On August 24, 1945, the Ukishima Maru exploded in Maizuru Port in Japan. Varying stories and records have been created, of course. One version was that the ship carrying 3,725 Korean laborers, most of whom were Korean women and their families who were forced to work as "comfort women" for the Japanese army, exploded and sank in the port of Maizuru on its way to the Korean port of Busan. The cause was never determined. Some say it was a suicide bombing ordered by military personnel on board — to prevent a controversy over responsibility for Korean prostitutes in Japan; officials say that the ship hit either a U.S. or Japanese mine. According to Japanese government figures, the incident cost 524 Korean and Japanese lives, however that number remains in dispute to this day since officially, the number and names of the deceased remain unknown. Japanese fatalities were treated as deaths in combat and the bereaved families received pensions,

but the Korean victims were ignored. In 1992, some eighty surviving passengers and relatives of those who died on the ship filed a lawsuit seeking an apology and compensation. In 2001, the Kyōto District Court recognized a breach of duty and ordered compensation, although a demand for an official apology was rejected. However, in a stunning reversal, the Ōsaka High Court reversed the judgment in 2003 and upheld the government's position that the state was not responsible and that one cannot oppose the Navy's views. See Grace Cho, *Haunting the Korean Diaspora: Shame, Secrecy and the Forgotten War* (University of Minnesota Press, 2008), 169-72.

# CHAPTER 37

# Familiar 1966

I ASKED MAMA ABOUT KOREAN-BLACK PEOPLE ONE DAY. She said that they went through similar things in Korea and the U.S. as with the Japanese. Of course she never thought of them as equal to the Japanese, even though our sufferings were very much the same.

Dat and the Korean women who had relations with American G.I.s, and were impregnated by them, had romances or married during and after the Korean War, had as many bad names hurled at them as their sisters in Japan, the Philippines, and post-colonial Southeast Asia. Women in these places who gave their love or bodies to white and black foreigners, forced or not, were the targets of local hatred. Even today, in Korea, Okinawa, and the Philippines, these names have not gone away.

The U.S. military bases still carry an entitlement to humiliate and exclude certain people that have remained in place by the U.S. and the locals. "Juicy Girl" is a name for Filipino women who are with American military men. *Yanggongju* is the pejorative term for a "child of the Western princess" in Korea. *Kkamdungi* is the "nigger," the mixed-race Black Korean child. *Yanggalbo, Dong-a-ilbo,* among others, is the Korean "whore" who sleeps with the American devil. Like those before her, any Asian woman living near the U.S. military base lives on the precipice of place, personhood, acceptance, history, and survival (bodily and discursively). When you look at all the names of women who have relationships with foreigners or who are raped by them, and the children who are born from these moments, we can and must acknowledge the continuities.

In the Philippines, kids like me are called: *iniwan ng barko* (left by the ship); bye bye daddy; bamboo shoot; half-dollar; *uling,*

283

*baluga, nog-nog* (charcoal); *Kulot* (curly). So many names birthed in the heat of night, linked across time, events, and place. Parallel heartbreak and strengths.

≋ ≋ ≋

BY THE TIME OUR FAMILY lived in Albuquerque for a few years, most of the kids in the neighborhood knew me. The Flicks, the white family that lived across the street from us, were a large family. I liked playing with all of the children. There was an older brother about a year older than me, a sister two years younger, and two other sisters and a younger brother. I never saw their father. Mrs. Flick was always home, cooking, cleaning, and being with her kids. They hardly ever invited me to their house except on a couple of occasions. And they seemed afraid to come inside our house.

One day, as I was on the Flick family porch, playing with the children, we could see Mrs. Flick cooking through the window, listening to us.

When the subject of making plans to do something the next day came up, I told them that I probably couldn't because it was Wednesday. Mrs. Flick yelled, "It's Tuesday, not Wednesday!"

I was sure it was Wednesday because there were certain television shows I would watch and I knew which shows were on and when. It was *Combat, The Man from U.N.C.L.E.* and then *Petticoat Junction* that were on last night.

"No, I really think it's Wednesday, so I should go check with Mama…"

Before I could finish the sentence, Mrs. Flick yelled, "God, you're so stupid! You should learn the American calendar! It's you nigger kids, or Jap kids, whatever you are, who come here and say stupid things. My kids know what day it is. You're a nigger. What do you know?!" I was disgusted with her. I looked at the Flick kids sitting in front of me. They were silent, embarrassed. I just wanted to get the hell out of there. In fact, I remember that the Flicks could no longer come across the street to my yard. If I wanted to play with them, I had to cross the street to their yard. As if they were going to catch something. When I asked them what it was all about, they just rolled their eyes and became quiet.

Someone told me that Mrs. Flick's mother was Mexican. Although I could never be sure of people's stories, I considered it: she had lighter skin than all of my Mexican friends and their parents, so I didn't think of her heritage as anything other than white. If she was Mexican, or of Mexican heritage, she must have had to train herself to think of herself white, forgetting her own self, her own mother's heritage. I understand how this could happen, given the way America and Japan are.

And in that forgetting, she crafted her venomous weapons of domination and abuse. There are plenty of people like her. People who occupy positions of power and influence, who mask the same kind of thoughts she spewed that day. She revealed herself to me, but only after a year. Until then, she was a mother, cooking and cleaning for her children. That day, everything changed. I didn't play with the Flicks anymore. What do women's histories turn into? What of the children? Who and what crafts these histories? 目

# CHAPTER 38

# Manchuria, Ōsaka
# 満州、大阪

AS I GREW OLDER, I reflected on how rough a person Mama was. As much as she was tender, graceful, gorgeous and outrageously funny in a twisted sort of way, her roughness was raw, open and unhidden most of the time. I remember it from my early memories of us in Japan. She hadn't become tougher. I think that it was something she struggled with, and it had always been an aspect of her that helped her survive. I become angry now when people refer to her as mentally ill, or worse, "too outspoken and expressive for an Asian." It was just as bad as hearing how nice and gentle she was, according to the Western definition of Japanese women as geisha (intensified by Japanese male elites negotiating this image as a necessary "ethnic" quality). *If they only knew the violent training geishas receive to become demure. That demure refinement takes incredible amounts of violent discipline and resilience.*

From the beginning, Mama refused the geisha image because she did not see herself in it, while some of her friends, perhaps, were. In a rapidly unifying postwar Japan, where the ideal Japanese woman was made dominant and all-cultural, she could play some of its roles to survive, but her only goal was to obtain unconditional love to undo the violence that claimed her youth, ravaged her family, and marked her body. She told me I shouldn't care too much about following everyone else's ways, but always think of what to show and what not to show.

Mama's ancestry was Austro-Hungarian, Chinese, and Japanese. She told me that Uncle Teruo remembers their mother speaking German, Mandarin, and Japanese. Even before Mama — Emiko or Kiyoko — was born, the family members were alternately respected for their status and closeness with Europeans, yet ostracized because the matriarch bore a child with a

Mama and her best friends at the time, on a rooftop in Tōkyō, circa 1951. *Fredrick Cloyd Family Archive.*

Christian missionary from Europe. Even though they were an elite family, their non-Japanese purity still bore bitter fruit.

Mama and the rest of the girls in the family were pushed into *jogakkō* (girls' boarding school) but not the socially acceptable kind. A couple of the girls escaped and ran away, according to Mama. When they did attend to their education, they were made to attend the *jogakkō* for non-Japanese for students. There, the neighborhood tough girls would beat them up and mercilessly tease them, saying terrible things about their mothers and routinely calling them whores or かぼちゃ頭 *kabocha atama,* pumpkin-head (something they called Chinese people sometimes). During the war years, the boys were taught by soldier-teachers to fight with *katana* (swords) and guns. The girls were taught *naginata* 薙刀, the art of fighting using a long stick with a blade on the end. Everyone in Japan was prepared to face the Americans when they landed in Japan.[1] This toughened up the girls.

Mama / Emiko became a nuisance for the family when she started hanging out with the tough girls at her school. In the atmosphere of wartime Japan, streets increasingly displayed the divisions, violence, and unhappy realities of sacrifice for an unseen, unknown nation still in the process of formation, with all its virulent changes, myth-making, conformities, and resistances. Emiko had now become one of the tough girls. She could now make the girls she hated, or deemed inferior, get out of her way when she walked down the hall. If anyone said anything, they would band together to beat those girls up, pull out their hair, attempt to drown them in a bucket of water on the playground, throw stones at their houses, or call them names and spread vicious rumors about their families. She was in a girl gang.

Emiko reminds me that this is not like the gangs we see on American television nowadays, with guns and tattoos. This was Japan in the 1940s. To be more "modern" and "respected," you wore Western clothes, bright lipstick and bobby socks. The dresses or skirts were a little shorter than the school headmasters wanted, but still long from our modern perspective. When they walked down the hall, they snapped their fingers in unison. They smoked cigarettes and listened to European and American music—markers of high status and "being hip." Mama would say that during this time in her life, she was violent and acted superior to survive other girls' constant violence against her, as well as doing so in a group to protect herself. Everyone in and around the school knew when they were coming and cleared the halls when they heard the snapping of their fingers. They felt they were respected, but in reality, they were just feared. What other way was there? Pleading with the abusers or keeping silent never helped. Violence was the only language. The groups were tightly-knit but also short-tempered. The boss-girls within the group controlled who was in and who was out. They were usually the tougher, bigger girls:

> *We used to tease each other. Sometimes we'd sit a girl down and say, "You know those trucks that carry the pumpkins and watermelons and other fruit to the store from the farms? You know how sometimes the pumpkins would be on the back of the trucks, rolling around and around, bumping into things and breaking and cracking and getting bruised? Pretty soon the jostling around would make the pumpkins lose their shape and their clean orange and green colors and look battered and worn out and broken up and ugly. Well, that's what your face looks like!" We'd laugh and laugh.*

But soon, she said, the girls were becoming more violent, teasing girls who were fat, Korean, Okinawan, or poor. She didn't care for it and grew more despondent. She herself had Korean and Japanese friends who committed suicide, so she could no longer pretend that she didn't care. And as a girl of this region, even though she spoke the dominant and proper Tōkyō version of Japanese language, they were teased when they went to Tōkyō, as they were from Ōsaka or Kyōto.

Emiko's older brother and father spoke in the Ōsaka language of the Kansai district that was supposedly inferior to Tōkyō's "proper" and national language. Their dialect was considered sweeter yet more primitive, uneducated, and "rural." Typically, most modern nations prioritize the urban in the hierarchy of national image. This fragmentation of herself was too much. Along with the discipline of her father and stepmother, this convinced her to stop hanging out with the gang, but she said she'll never forget the power she felt in resisting the norms. Her own status as a girl from a former samurai family created spaces of guilt, as well as negotiation in her navigation of an increasingly fragmented world.

When she was angry with me, she became frightening. For a small woman, she was strong like Hercules. But she never beat me up like she would some neighborhood girl that had teased the gang-girls. She would give me a whack, or threaten to kill me with a knife. She would only do it when I did something that displeased her. Sometimes after a tantrum, she questioned her own violent behavior and felt remorseful. Somehow, I understood this and never felt resentful.

However, as I grew older and bigger, that didn't work anymore. I could use my physical presence to remind her that I didn't like the violence, although I never threatened her. Even when I knew she was right, I could still use my maleness against her.

In our home in Ōme, Japan, Mama (right) and Keiko-san (left) the wife of a good friend of my Dad, who was also an African American soldier. Looking closely at Mama here, you can see a glimpse of her rebel personality. *Fredrick Cloyd Family Archives.*

Male dominance works between a son and the mother who raises him. I would run to my room, and Mama would grow quiet. Separation was the best way. In a nuclear family, this meant isolation.

Today, in Japan, the U.S., and Britain, bullying is an epidemic, as my mother and I have always known it to be. People considered within mainstream societies, who have little understanding, or lack reflection, become aware of "bullying" as a special phenomenon, some "new" epidemic that hadn't mattered before and was previously "tolerable." Mama and I talked about how, in Japan and the U.S., being bullied and bullying were how those countries formed. Neighborhood associations that spied on and reported their neighbors, Commodore Matthew C. Perry's Tōkyō Bay, the rapes, mutilations and aggressions of Japan in Asia during the war— is all of this related to bullying? Why do older Koreans and Taiwanese understand Japanese language? What are fire-bombings? What are the scars inside my Uncle Teruo's mouth? Why are Japanese wearing Western clothing, but hardly any Westerners wearing Asian clothing except as "costume?" Who becomes wealthy from the treaties and deals of international institutions and various wars? Aren't these forms of bullying? Mama has lived through and engaged these questions and endured. But shouldn't living her life be more than just enduring? I'm afraid that this enduring is romanticized and valorized, allowing us to ignore the problems of "enduring" life. 冒

## CHAPTER NOTES

1. Right before the war ended, the Okinawans or Uchinanchu (うちなーんちゅ in Okinawan; ウチナーンチュ in Japanese), were prepared to fight both the Americans, as well as the colonizing Japanese they called "the Yamato People."

# CHAPTER 39

# Ōme and Tachikawa 1959
# 青梅と立川 1959 年

MAMA AND I THOROUGHLY ENJOYED going into town to shop and eat together, either with or without friends. Going to eat and people-watch and shop was a favorite pastime for us. In Japan, it was particularly exciting in the *Isetan depāto* 伊勢丹デパート (Isentan department store), as well as in the local shops, especially the bookstores. Since Japan was very crowded, the department stores grew upward into the sky, unlike the American malls and department stores I grew to know later, which grew outward and took up space. And in most cases, there was an amusement park on the roofs of these *depāto*. I would always enjoy Mama taking me all the way up to the roof, going from one amusement park ride to another and eating 弁当 おべんとー or *bentō* lunch box or *aisu kuriimu* アイスクリーム ice cream. When I was smaller, she would take me *onbu* on her back, or hand-in-hand when I was able. Sometimes she would have difficulty at shops because some of the people were mean to her (because of me being there). They may have been friendly at first, but when they noticed me, their expressions would change from pleasant to disgust, or there would be an argument. And later, as I became able to walk, I would go off by myself and meet my parents later — something American parents nowadays wouldn't even consider. But Mama held onto me longer than other mothers allowed. It was because of who we were. As the years went on, it became less and less necessary as people became more used to people like us. Mama was sharp, though, so we went to great lengths to go to specific places where the shopkeepers and customers were nice and friendly.

One of the first incidents I remember when I was little was in a bookstore. We were often in bookstores as Mama loved to read. [1] Japanese were encouraged to read in those days, especially dur-

293

This is a photo of the train station platform sign for Ōme and Tachikawa, 2007. I was surprised and delighted when I found this photo, which I remembered my Mama and I looking at during our many trips into Tōkyō when I was a child. The station has been preserved as a landmark in Japan. *Photo courtesy of Laurel Wilson.*

ing the occupation when the nation would recreate its identity through words and images. In the store, I walked a few paces and was looking at train books (in those days, what else?) when I felt legs and a hip next to me. I heard a voice, and turned my face up to a woman's disgusted face.

She said, "何よ、 この黒んぼ, こんな所に突っ立って、 じゃまですよ"
*What the hell are you—a sambo—doing, standing in the way?*

I ran and found Mama in the next aisle. I was too shaken up to say anything. When we returned home, and she was unpacking the bags of books and groceries we had bought, I mentioned to her about that woman at the bookstore. Mama did not hesitate. She took my hand and said, "何処にいるのその人？" (Where is that person?)

She grabbed my hand and marched us back out the door, walking briskly to the train station. We rode the train, then walked to the bookstore. I didn't think this woman would still be there but she was. Then again, I wasn't sure. I pointed to one woman who I thought was the same woman. Mama walked over to her and stopped a few inches short of her face, screaming at her.

"何よ！この女め！私の子供を黒んぼと呼ぶならぶっ飛ばして やるぞ！"
*(What the hell, you damn woman! If you're going to call my child a sambo, then I'll beat you into nothing!)*

At first, I felt surprised and proud. How strong my mother is, I thought. How much she wanted to protect me. I was so comforted by her protection. The woman was slightly heavy, I remember. In all of it, I felt terrible for the woman who had niggered me, put me down, hated me for what I was, an object of whatever she was taught to think. She was also the object of Mama's wrath. Not much was dealt with, except for affirming Mama's strength in protecting and defending. And I wasn't even sure if it was the right woman I had pointed out. I felt terrible for us all.

As a kid, I just wanted to hide, regretting I told Mama anything at the same time that I was proud of her. But soon I learned that silence was best. I became the quiet, gentle child. But I don't know if I became that for my own good, or for others. There was a cost for being silent. Being quiet and letting things go, it turns out, is the most uncompassionate act, for someone like me and the histories that produced me.

**Notes**

*The New York Times* writes on November 19, 1945:

> "A G.I. and his girlfriend were murdered in Japan. *The bodies of an American soldier and a Japanese girl evidently beaten to death with a club have been found near Ōsaka. A public relations officer of the Sixth Army described the deaths as a double murder. (p. 3).*

It was never just one thing affecting Mama. What she had to think about, what she had to drown out, what she had to endure, what she had to fight, what she had to pay attention to... all this was her life. Perhaps she knew those people killed, or knew someone who did. Perhaps she felt the emptiness, loss, rage, and loneliness. What she thought, how she was to raise me, what she was to think, was influenced by these goings-on in Japan.

By the late 1950s and 1960s, many mixed-race children from Miki Sawada's orphanage went on to become members of Japanese society without much fanfare, but not without difficulty. Many of the women married and became housewives of *sararii-man* ("salary-man," a Japanese term for businessmen). Many of the mixed Black Japanese people who grew up in the orphanages became social welfare workers, or ran businesses in the entertainment districts of cities. Many of them have had to battle substance abuse, incarceration, or homelessness.

> *She looked at her arms as she rolled up her sleeves. I couldn't believe it. So many scars. They were from her history of cutting herself. When she left the orphanage as a teenager, she began to do it. She would feel relieved when she cut the pain out of her body.* [2]

> "*In a recent triple murder in Japan, a fourteen-year-old orphan with a Negro father hacked three girls to death because, he told police, he was tired of being ridiculed about his kinky hair. At the other extreme are part-Negro boys like Akitoyo whose intelligence and likeable personality have earned him the friendship and respect of his classmates.*" [3]

Make one ugly, impure, a body of crime. Make the other an angel that does the normal and socially acceptable things — and is therefore ignored. The socially-acceptable things create ugliness, but everyone wants to embrace an angelic position, forgetting and demoting those who carry society's — your — forgotten woes;

those who would kill aspects of themselves to make themselves more acceptable in society. Perpetrating impulses into "other" bodies as the disciplinable, the inferior, the not-quite-civilized, the exotic, the Oriental, the dark, the civilized. 目

## CHAPTER NOTES

1. The proliferation of reading materials, bookstores and libraries in Japan exploded during the postwar period (after 1952). One reason for this is that books, and all media, were the primary ways in how the SCAP administration propagated ideas for the new Japan, as both a client of the U.S. and its position in a global setting.

2. I befriended a Black Japanese girl in 1969, who was adopted by a white military family and we attended the same school. I think I was the only one in the school who knew her "secret."

2. Kenneth Ishii, Associated Press, "War Babies of Mixed blood Come of Age," *Standard Times,* January 21, 1968.

# CHAPTER 40

# Faith

WHEN I WAS IN HIGH SCHOOL IN ALBUQUERQUE, I came home one day with a friend. He and I enjoyed each other's company, sometimes cutting classes to go to Pup-n-Taco for tacos and chili fries, or over to his house while his parents were gone to look at comic books and argue about dinosaurs or watch television. We seemed to click. It was an easy friendship.

We stepped into the house where Mama was doing laundry in the kitchen. My friend Don followed behind me quietly to my room after we greeted Mama. Once we were in my room, Don smiled slyly and said, "So...your dad's a nigger and your mother's a slant-eye..." I shoved him hard against the wall. My chest and heart burned with all the shock and anger accumulated over the years. I held him against the wall, wanting him to disappear, but I didn't hit or choke or kick. I squeezed him against the wall harder and harder, wanting him to disappear into it. He started slugging me all over my back, head and face.

I yelled, "Get the hell out! OUT!"

All of the affection I felt for him vanished. Familiar terrains. Then Mama dashed into the room, wielding a broom, swinging at Don with full-strength. By then, Don had pinned me to the bed. Her blows hit him hard across his back and he yelled, jumping up and sprinting out of the house with Mama chasing him with the broom, screaming after him, *"Maza fakah! Yuu maza fakah!"* Mama knew those words. How could she be around drunken U.S. military men and not? *"Daijobu?"* Mama asked, as she entered my room and flung the broom onto the floor, sitting on my bed to pull me closer.

I nodded, and began to cry. Mama held me for awhile. She understood betrayal. The small bruises on my face took months to completely heal. I met and made true friends with others as time passed. I learned to expect betrayal, but never grew used to it. I learned to appear cold and dissociated. After all, smiling was not a guarantee of pleasantry or happiness. And at that moment of betrayal and aloneness, I wondered if darkness and betrayal were my destiny.

IN 1985, I BECAME INTERESTED IN what I could find out about my Cherokee heritage. Not much came of finding Cherokee relatives on my Dad's side of the family. Those who would remember more about our Cherokee history had died. Most of it was an oral history, as most histories of people of color in the U.S. tend to be. In my search, I found out about a Cherokee spiritual leader, who was called a shaman, who was well known in Colorado and around the southwest. I sought his advice when I found out that he was visiting a new age spirituality store that a friend of mine managed in those days. In 1985, I had begun Zen Buddhist practice, which sent me on a path of discovering different spiritual practices, including Native American spiritualities. This visit with the Cherokee teacher, I thought, would be helpful. During the visit, the teacher did a Bear Clan astrological reading for me.[1]

> *Your spirit-keeper is the Shawnodese. A flicker, a woodpecker, symbol of the Frog clan. You are a nurturer and of great importance in the world, to teach. But your path is not easy because your ways are not well-understood by mainstream cultures, as you are also a trickster and have knowledge that can seem strange, immoral, or misplaced — or so it may seem. Only you know. This makes you alone. This makes your life difficult because you are a messenger for the earth archives. This makes you annoying — like the constant pecking noise you would make as a woodpecker against a tree. You tell the stories people do not want to hear, much less listen to or learn from. You must become a walking stick for history in order to give The Great Care. You will leave a body of writing for the world.*
>
> *Be strong on this path, as this is the reason you are here in this world. You do not trust your deep self, and many trials come to teach you to believe in the deep self. You must learn to listen to yourself. This is a difficult path. You may not be able to carry its highest ideals, but no matter what you think, you must*

*keep on. You yourself may not understand what must happen but things unfold through you. You must trust. You must annoy. You must teach.*

At the time, I felt that his words rang true, but he had no concept of my path in life. I never thought of myself as writing anything in particular. I understood this through volleyball coaching and training, where much of a path as teacher already rang true. Little did I know that sports was just the beginning for me. 目

CHAPTER NOTES

1.  See Sun Bear and Wabun Wind, *Medicine Wheel: Earth Astrology* (NY: Touchstone, 1980), for more information on the postmodern form of the Native American Bear Clan Medicine Wheel astrology.

# CHAPTER 41

# Running

EMIKO'S RAGE WAS INVISIBLE TO MANY. Rage can be internalized. Rage is also survival. Surviving is not recognized as a skill by those who do not understand. Docile obedience serves an agenda of the elite who want to maintain control. There are those, like my mother, who carry the rage and displacement of mothers and nations internally.

She lived amid the abuse and death of so many people in her life, first during wartime Japan's militaristic rule, and then in the U.S., where immigrant isolation and forced assimilation was normal. The so-called unification of Japan rested on certain rules of behavior that enabled assimilation and ambivalence. Mama loved her brother and father, who both worked for the nation, yet hated the strict domineering government whose prejudices she had to endure. It was a relief when the war ended, and the Americans brought new possibilities. Yet she hated the way Americans imposed themselves upon her and the nation.

Those watch groups, the *tonari gumi,* who reported on their neighbors were rewarded. In *yakeato,* bomb-ruined Japan, where people were desperate and starving, it became extremely difficult as much as it was saddening and crippling to bear witness to how the nation state treated its citizenry.

The Americans were bombing daily. What could anyone think except that the Americans were the monsters of whom they were warned? During one bomb-raid, Emiko was with a group of friends, one of them a boy from the neighborhood she had grown up in. They held each other's hands as they ran towards the bomb shelter amid the sickening stench and smoke that burned their eyes, and the screams and panic of everyone around them. The

303

B-29s roared directly above them. Dead bodies and burning pieces of wood began tumbling around her. She ran as fast as she could.

She arrived at the shelter and climbed down the steps and into the shelter. Others began screaming when they saw her. Women covered their eyes while some children began crying more intensely. Emiko wondered why. Her stepmother, who had been running just ahead of them, approached her and gently lifted Emiko's right hand, which had been holding her friend's hand while they ran. It was only the hand. He had been blown away without her knowing. She remembers screaming for what seemed like hours. She cursed the Americans.

In 1951, during the last year of the official u.s. and Allied Occupation of Japan, Emiko was enrolled into one of the top medical schools in Japan.[1] She was fourteen-years-old. This meant that she needed to deal with medical students in her class who were in their late teens or twenties. Emiko did not want to go to the school and would have preferred hanging around the American military base with her friends, but her aptitude in medicine was tremendous, with abilities that surpassed her classmates. It was too much responsibility and too much abuse for her to endure as a fourteen year-old, but her father and older brother demanded that she do it, given that opportunities like this were rare, and would give her a chance to redeem herself in the community. She had no choice.

It did not help that Emiko's stepmother would lie to Emiko's father. She hated her daughter and wanted her to go away so that she wouldn't have to constantly apologize to people, as if she were a problem. Although Emiko had stopped hanging out with the bad-girls and wasn't bringing any attention to the family, she was hanging out where the American soldiers caroused at night, where many of her friends did 水商売 *mizu shōbai* in the kichi around American military bases. The family did not want her exposed to that kind of life. By then, it had been established that any girls hanging out around the bases were "whores," whether they were sex-workers or simply working for a living in the bars that American and other Allied soldiers frequented. Her stepmother wanted to protect their status, and while her father wanted the same, he understood that Emiko was an impatient teenager full of anxiety, angst and curiosity.

In medical school, Emiko experienced the ways in which the Western medical establishment reinforced their superiority. Japanese doctors and scientists were routinely shamed in front of students and peers, ridiculed with condescending laughter by the American and European medical personnel who were there to "civilize" Japanese medicine. Hospitals became sanitized white places with white walls and sanitized ways of thinking and working with patients. Instead of exchanging dialogue between doctors and patients, the doctor was the sole expert.

Emiko felt resentment toward the Westerners.

After a few months of this, along with the abusive behavior she suffered from her older classmates and being isolated from the life she preferred, she decided to escape school. Again, she sought to escape the domination of the men in her life as well as her stepmother. She wanted to be free to decide her own fate. One night, her friend met her in town and she ran away to Tōkyō. She lived with her friend for a while, sometimes on the streets. As their family had connections, they were shortly found and she was allowed to stay with a relative in Tōkyō. In the coming months, she decided that the best thing to do was to marry an American and get away from it all. She then felt that, in the land of the big white men, she could experience freedom, away from the devastated place she sometimes called *"Namida no Kuni" (The Land of Tears).* 🗒

## CHAPTER NOTES

1. There are many, including myself, who would say that the Occupation has not ended. Even after the official Occupation dates, the U.S. government, corporations and military, maintain a heavy presence and influence in policy-making since the U.S. Occupation of Japan (1945-1952). Furthermore, if we are to question the number of U.S. military bases in Japan and the Pacific region, in so-called "sovereign" countries, then we can begin to be curious about what is hidden and/or ignored in our idea of occupation and its effects after the official dates. For me, I was born in 1955. This was after the Occupation. The U.S. maintained some control over the Japanese in matters of crime, the existence of the U.S. military and the continued training of the Japanese defense forces, and the co-leadership and rulership over the Okinawan islands. Certainly the U.S.-Japan Security Pact and the 1955 System instituted that year, enforces partnerships between U.S. global corporations and government policies and Japanese culture and nation.

CHAPTER 42
# Enemy / Lover

I WAS ABOUT FIVE. This was one memory etched stronger than bone and burned in my marrow. I remember it then, as I do now, as a strange event. It was around 1959 or 1960. I was singing along with Misora Hibari and Hashi Yukio on the radio. I remember the temples, the tall trees—green and inviting in the misty mornings and the caw! caw! of crows. I remember quiet, and the sound of deer, steam trains chugging along and echoing across the mountainside. The flapping of little ひな祭り *Hina Matsuri* flags watching me as I left the house to play. There were plenty of *mochi* and mochi-pounding ceremonies in the neighborhood, and I was impatient to grab a few to eat. There was energetic laughter and gossip, and conversations among Mama and her friends around the house.

We lived in a large wooden house, sparsely furnished with detailed moldings that showed family crests, signifying the clan's history and position in society. There was also a garden I loved. Since my mother's family came from relative wealth, I assumed our garden was fairly large. But on days when Mama's friends visited, it seemed the house was only a backdrop.

That late afternoon, six of Mama's friends were chatting loudly, their arms and faces gesturing and mimicking whomever, something I knew Japanese men frowned upon in those times. Here, the rude-talk was private between the deep wood and paper of our home. Women seemed to be freer in our house than when they walked the streets. But today was different.

*Something was strange.*

I felt that there was some kind of trouble as I came back in for our *o-den* dinner. Women were talking without smiling. As we sat, eating *osembe,* one of the women was talking on and on, saying with a tone of malice, *"Koroshite yaru."* (I'm going to kill [him]). I knew that all of these women were either married to American soldiers, or were friends of my mother. I know now that Japanese women who married U.S. soldiers were deemed crazy, rebellious, and impure, yet were thought to be living an exalted life. During this visit, there was another kind of trouble.

*"Koroshite yaru!"* she kept saying. As a child, that's all I could hear. She said it in a very manly drawl, complete with a rolled "r." In Japanese, rolled r's was considered manly, something women shouldn't do.

Outcast women gravitated to marrying Americans just after the war, especially American soldiers. I learned about my Dad from my mother, and he was, as far as I was concerned, a ghost that would someday become a reality. I felt his presence as a gentle man that she loved, as she often told me *"Dēri, sugu ni kaettekuru yo" (Daddy is coming home sometime soon).* But that day, this woman with the manly drawl, sitting opposite Mama at the table, was not speaking of her man in a tender or dreamy fashion. I was afraid. I stayed close to my mother as this woman suddenly shot up from the *kotatsu* table where we all sat drinking tea, and made her way to the kitchen. All of us shot up and chased after her.

The front door in the next room slid open, and a man said, *"Gomen kudasai."* We heard the door slide shut. We greeted a Black-American man in a tan U.S. military uniform. He removed his hat and shoes. I remember he spoke very good Japanese. Aside from pictures of my Dad, I had only seen non-Japanese in their military jeeps and trucks around town, or walking in groups. I thought that he seemed kind.

Suddenly, the woman reappeared, gripping a large kitchen knife above her head, which she pointed at the American man. The man began saying something in English to her with his arms out, interspersed with Japanese, trying to calm her down.

She lunged at him with a loud cry and began trying to plunge the knife into his chest. The man blocked her knife-wielding arm, grabbing her wrist, while his other hand grabbed her around the waist. As they wrestled, tumbling to the floor, I jolted up and yelled.

*"Yamete!" (Stop it!)*

Mama pulled me next to her. All of the women sat in a row by the front entrance as the two of them fell struggling onto the floor. He pleaded for her to stop as they wrestled.

*"Yamenasai!"*

*"Yamete!"*

I forced myself to stay calm.

Mama drew me to her tightly, clutching my arm into her body. I looked around to see the other women remaining seated, all of us watching the wrestling couple as if we were watching a theater play. There was no movement to stop it. Soon there were tiny splatters of blood as she scratched his face with her fingernails. The knife in her hand flew out, skidding across the floor as he held both her hands against the floor. The knife tumbled and landed near the front doorway. One of the women now stood, running to take it. I thought, is this what men and women do? Why doesn't anyone do anything?

*Then there was quiet.*

Their heavy breathing filled the room. The woman's chest heaved with heavy breath. No one was killed or seriously injured. At least, not physically. We froze, waiting for the next moment.

The man got up slowly, putting his hat back on, making his way to the foyer to put on his shoes, and leave. He was weeping. We all watched him leave without a word. After the door closed behind him, we turned our attention to the woman lying on the floor. It felt like an eternity.

She began to cry.

Then wail.

She was making sounds I had never heard before but understood deeply. I started to cry. Some of the women had already begun weeping, hiding their faces with their hands. I did not know why I was crying. When I think of it now, I remember it felt like a ritual, some kind of strange ceremony.

Mama and the women began to stand up. All of them eventually ended up sitting around this woman. They leaned over her, comforting her. I didn't know what to do. I sat there, wondering, shivering from fear and anxiety. I had learned something. I didn't know what then. I watched and listened as Mama and the others consoled her.

*Don't worry. There are other men.*

I had so many questions I didn't know how to ask. Why did she want to kill him? What was their story? Why didn't anyone attempt to stop it? What was going on?

Since then, I have never intervened physically to help someone. I would call others to do so. I think this inaction is linked to that day of the knife—to indifference, intensity, terror, struggle, blood, cry, peaceful repression, and observance. Were my mother and the other women crazy?

*Was the man and the woman crazy?*

*Needs and desires. Complexity ensues.*

An African American soldier and a Japanese woman, legacies of family love and family violence, legacies of rage against men, unnamed oppressions against women, legacies of betrayal, of feeling insignificant, of shame—what becomes peace? What are its contours? Is inaction or calm a sign of death? This was not just a freak moment. *What of your legacies?* 目

# CHAPTER 43

# Kinpatsu 金髪

星の流れに身をうらなって‥‥‥‥
泣けて涙も枯れはてた
こんな女に誰がした？

*After I left my body's fate to the flow of the stars‥‥‥‥*
*In being able to cry, even my tears have all dried out*
*So who has made me into this kind of woman?*

— from the eternally popular hit song from 1947,
星の流れに "In the Flow of Stars"

## 1986

MY FRIEND ERIC DROVE US TO VISIT MAMA in Albuquerque on our way to visit the Santa Fe Zen Center, before heading on to the Rochester Zen Center where we would formally train with the *rōshi* (elder teacher). Eric was young, vibrant, and good-looking. We drove from Denver, where we had both begun our training. We had been accepted as formal students of Philip Kapleau Roshi at the Rochester Zen Center, with whom the Denver center was then affiliated.

I was eager for Eric to meet Mama. He was a fun travel-mate who was open to new experiences. He was from a small town in Nebraska, now seeing a world new to him, not to mention beginning Zen training in order to settle the "unsettled matter of life and death" that Zen teachers speak of.

As Eric drove us to my house in Albuquerque, Mama was there, having anticipated our arrival, stepping onto the porch with a big smile. Alongside her was Rob, a friend of mine from the University of New Mexico, who was living there and taking care of her. I noticed that Mama began staring at Eric, not removing her eyes from him as we approached the front of the house

The Yasuura House, located in a large seaport base in Yokosuka, was one of many prostitution stations that catered to American servicemen, sanctioned by the RAA (Recreation and Amusement Association). The officially sponsored brothels were ordered closed in 1946 by General Douglas MacArthur, due to the human rights violations of women. However, it was privately acknowledged that the main reason for closing the brothels was the increase of venereal disease among U.S. soldiers. *Photo courtesy of Yokosuka City Council.*

with our bags. Rob came out to take one of the bags left from the car. Mama kept staring. As we began putting our bags down inside the house, she asked what his name was. I told her. She nodded, looking embarrassed. I introduced everyone and we stepped into the house. I thought, perhaps, that she was attracted to him. But I didn't think anything more of it then.

THE U.S. AND ALLIED OCCUPATION began in 1946 and officially ended in 1952. Although the occupation of Japan was an Allied Occupation, with British, Australian, New Zealander, and Indian Commonwealth military personnel, the Americans had become the undisputed leaders of the Occupation. Alongside the military, many civilians were hired to do things the military could not do. It was messy, and unquestionably contentious.

During wartime, radio broadcasts told the Japanese that the Americans were monsters. Now, as tanks and jeeps carried thousands of American and other soldiers around Japan as if they were kings through the streets of Kobe, Yokohama, Tōkyō, Ōsaka, and the rest of Japan, these monsters were now occupiers. The wealth of the Americans attracted many Japanese women and children. The soldiers were part of America's marketing effort, driving their jeeps through the streets of Japan, handing out candy and chocolate to throngs of Japanese children.

Many soldiers had their good times with Japanese women, leaving them with children to raise in a country not yet prepared to deal with them. Many Japanese men took advantage in order for their families to survive, baiting and ordering many of their sisters or younger siblings to befriend the Americans to get things from them, including food. But there were also many Americans who were not quite ready to be friendly with their former enemy that had, only two weeks earlier, been the yellow peril monster that they had been instructed to kill. Now, instead of killing them, they were responsible for infiltrating American culture into Japan.[1] The sex work business that the Japanese government and U.S. Occupation established separately was initially a buffer, meant to appease the fear of rape that circulated throughout Japanese neighborhoods.

At first, the Allied command went along. Because of rising venereal disease and tens of thousands of mixed-race children being born, Douglas MacArthur ordered the brothels closed. Emiko wholeheartedly embraced the king-like image of MacArthur that was publicized. Even though MacArthur himself held a decidely paternalistic and racist attitude toward Asians and other non-whites,[2] and didn't think they could become democratic (as if the Americans themselves were), he followed the orders of the government in his own way, displeasing them in other ways. Emiko continued to admire him, even as Japan became violent in its erasure of what had existed in the minds and hearts of the Japanese before the war. Many of her friends gave birth to American-fathered babies who never returned to see them. Other friends abandoned their American-fathered babies in alleys, trash cans, and monasteries, or ran to rural areas to escape intense scrutiny from city officials or neighbors. Emiko wanted to believe that the American dream would transform Japan into a new Japanese dream.

When she had just turned sixteen she fell in love with a white American army man. It was love at first sight. She always spoke about him angelically. He was a beautiful blond man, who she thought was the nicest man in the world. They began seeing each other secretly. It was illegal for them to be married, but they wanted to marry so badly. This blond man and Emiko were the centers of each other's worlds from the first day they met.

Mama's family, of prominent samurai lineage, was an international family whose legacies included the shame of a half-sister who was a sex-slave for the Japanese imperial army and another who was part white and Chinese (Emiko), giving the Kakinami clan plenty to worry about, including the fear of being ostracized. This nurtured rebelliousness in some of the children. Although Emiko was a very proper Japanese girl in many ways, she became more outspoken, rebellious, and individualistic than most Japanese women allowed themselves to be, and there were many like her. But because she was not "pure Japanese," she was targeted. This made her even more outspoken and tough. But her beauty allowed her to use her charm to make her way through many troubles. And now, she was in love with an American serviceman, she was stepping into another space where she defied proper Japaneseness. For many Japanese, the Americans were still the enemy. Many of the women who associated with American soldiers were scorned, ridiculed, or ostracized. But for thousands of Japanese women, there were instant desires and attractions to the Allied soldiers for many reasons.

Emiko met the 金髪 *Kinpatsu* (the blond one) that year. He was so kind and loving to her that Mama considered him to be her greatest love. He was from one of the wealthiest families in middle-America at the time, and his family had a proud diplomatic and military lineage. His father worked for the U.S. government, hated Japan and Asians, and aligned with Douglas MacArthur regarding

Club Coral Reef and Jimmy Bar East Tachikawa City, 1957. "Penicillin shops," like the ones beside the Club Coral Reef in this photo, were numerous on side streets and alleys – often called "VD Alley" – where bars crowded with Occupation soldiers and Japanese base town girls thrived. *Photo courtesy of Ray Metzger.*

the Japanese. Not surprisingly, both of his parents forbade him from seeing her. His commanding officer followed suit. And of course, the more his parents and his commander pressed him, the more he refused. Both of their families traveled extensively in the U.S., China, and Europe, and were educated. But a few in the family, including Teruo's new wife, didn't want anything to do with any Japanese who married an American. This caused tension in the family.

Nothing could hold back their desire for each other. After four months of secret meetings, the lovers decided to run away together—a way to solidify their commitment and express defiance (as young lovers in a taboo affair). After he had overheard a conversation in which his father threatened to ship him out of Japan and away from her, he went AWOL.[3] They stayed in some of Emiko's father's friends' homes, moving every couple of days.

After a few weeks, the American military police found him and jailed him. While in jail, he found out his parents had succeeded in shipping him off to Europe, which happened to many U.S. soldiers who wanted to marry local women in Asia. Although the War Brides Act of 1945 was modified by President Harry S. Truman with the Soldier Brides Act of 1947, whereby wives of American citizens could not be kept out of the U.S. because of race, the military made interracial marriage difficult by creating bureaucratic policies that could rarely be followed. This didn't stop thousands from applying for marriage when marriages were allowed. Some U.S. servicemen married their Japanese girls at Shinto and Buddhist shrines, although neither government recognized these marriages.

This blond, under the strong command of his father who felt stifled in the U.S., was finally experiencing a freedom he had always wished for, which intensified his desire and romantic notions. Now, in Japan, he had a chance to control his life. Emiko was his life.

When he was finally released, he paid a friend off to let him go alone, and ran to Emiko's side. They spent one night in each other's arms, vowing to be together forever. But in the morning, as they lay in the dark corner of the small room together, they came to an understanding. The only way they could be together was for them to kill themselves. According to official records, there had already been a few dual suicides by American soldiers and their Japanese girlfriends during this time.

Because they wanted their death to be private, they had to think of where they could go without attracting attention. They decided to drive off one of the highest peaks of Japan. That day, they drove up and up and up the hill in the rented military jeep. Mama doesn't remember what kind, but she said that she and her lover took some drugs that made them feel relaxed and elated. Up the winding dirt road, up the steep mountain. When they approached what seemed to be the perfect place, he began accelerating. As he accelerated, he released the wheel and turned to her, both of them clinging tightly to each other as they launched into the blue sky, over the cliff.

Flying down.

Down.

They flew into the sky together, meeting for a final yet eternal kiss.

Oblivion.

Quiet.

The officials soon found the wreckage. The blond one died instantly. The jeep had gone into flames. His body was in it, charred. Emiko, however, was unconscious, left dangling from a tree. She had been thrown on impact. Her head hit one of the jagged rocks as she flew into a protruding tree branch. The right side of her face was crushed. She was in a coma for three days.

When she awoke, she said, "彼 . . . . どこにいるの？彼 . . . . 死んだの？"

(Where … is he? … Did he … die?)

She wept when they told her. She remembered her father and brother comforting her, and told me that she wished she had died and not him, because she was good for nothing while he had big dreams and talent for the world.

Nowadays, Mama, with partial dementia, doesn't remember anything she cooked for me. But she will never forget him. She doesn't want to see videos of anything that reminds her of Japan. It hurts her body. The memory tears at her from the inside. But she doesn't remember much of our lives growing up. And once, when we had been revisiting her story of the blond one, she jokingly said:

*"Omoshiroi ne. Wasuretai mono o wasurerarenai de, wasuretakunai mono o isshō wasurete yuku. Honto ni bakarashii jinsei ne. Atama ni kuru!"*
(It's funny huh? There's things I want to forget, but I can't forget. And things I don't want to forget, I forget for a lifetime. Life is really idiotic, huh? Really pisses me off!)

We laughed and laughed.

忘れないで don't forget me. 忘れないで don't forget me.

Then yesterday, Mama asks, "

*"Neh Furetto … Erikku wa konogoro doushiteru?"*
(Fred, what's Eric up to these days?) 昌

# CHAPTER NOTES

1. For an example on a civilian Commonwealth Occupation worker in Japan, see Cortazzi's book, *Japan Experiences—Fifty Years, One Hundred Views: Post-War Japan Through British Eyes,* (Routledge 2001).

2. There is an often-quoted statement by Douglas MacArthur, where he says that the Japanese are basically equal to twelve-year-old boys compared to "mature" Americans and Germans, which is from his statement at his Senate hearings of 1951. I refer to it from Dower, John, *War Without Mercy: Race and Power in the Pacific War,* p. 303. (Random House, 1986).

   To begin reading about MacArthur's attitude and behavior toward Asians and others, and his "civilizing mission" during the Occupation of the Asia-Pacific, see "Chapter Six: Neocolonial Revolution," pp. 203-224, in John Dower's classic book, *Embracing Defeat: Japan in the Wake of World War II* (W.W. Norton & Company, 1999) and also another classic on the Occupation of Japan by Eiji Takemae, *Inside GHQ: The Alied Occupation of Japan and Its Legacy,* chapter 1, pp. 3-8: *The Pacific War and the Origins of GHQ.*

3. AWOL is a military criminal acronym, meaning, "Absent Without Official Leave."

# CHAPTER 44

# Monk
## 雲水 Unsui

*First, I tried taking pills and Kaa-chan found me. At the hospital, I was drained of the pills. Kaa-chan found another reason to call me baka-na-ko (stupid child) for months on end. I tried cutting myself with the razor Kaa-chan used to shave my legs. I bled and bled and screamed, and Kaa-chan had to take me to the hospital again. She twisted her cigarette into me a few times and slapped me for being ridiculous and causing so much trouble for the family. I got with the girl gangs after that, enjoying some of the slapping and bullying I could get away with toward those I wanted to punish. After that, it became boring. I met Mieko. She and I tried to kill ourselves with the hair-dye. But that didn't let me go. Over and over in life, I used to question why I couldn't go away to where I wanted, and instead must endure pain. I could see if my life was worth something. But I don't know what that is even now.*

*Then I met an American soldier. He was a beautiful boy. We started to see each other as often as we could. But his parents forbade it. And his commanding officer didn't like it. So we tried to kill ourselves, and went off the hills together in his stolen jeep. I woke up later, but he died in the jeep. I was left alone again. Mieko finally did commit suicide alone and she left me. Everyone leaves me. My sister went to the other world in the Hiroshima bomb. Hide-san died as a kamikaze pilot during the war. What good am I in life? Nothing. And in those days, there was always a part of my kokoro that wondered when the next time and opportunity would come for me to leave this world and go to the other world.*

321

*One day a Zen monk (Obō-san) came to visit father. He would visit two or three times a year to discuss things with father. I never knew what they talked about. I ignored them. The monk wore a robe and seemed smart and wise. But in Japan, all women seem to do is follow orders. We were punished or ostracized if we didn't. Even when I do what I want to do, things seem meaningless.*

*But one day, when the monk visited us, father wanted me in the room with them. As usual, I greeted the monk, along with my father, as he arrived and came into the house where I had prepared special tea for us, along with a plate of special cut asparagus, eggplant slices, and some yōkan (sweet bean cakes).*

*I was off in my own world, pretending to listen as they spoke. Then, when father put his hand on my head to get my attention, I looked up to see the monk staring kindly at me, his eyes gentle and steady, piercing through me. He said,*

"エミ子、もう自殺をする気持ちをあきらめたらどう？もう４回しようと思って出来なかったんだろう？神様達はエミちゃんは大切な人間だから死なせないと決めてるんじゃないか？生きると決心すればいいと思うよ"。
*(Emiko, don't you think your attempts to commit suicide should stop? You've wanted to die four times, and you tried, but couldn't, right? The gods of this world think of you as precious so they are making it so you won't die, couldn't that be so? I really think you should make up your mind to live.)*

*Was the monk kind? I don't know. But I didn't try again.*

IN 2004, I FOUND OUT THAT New Mexico was trying to take possession of our house in Albuquerque. Medicaid stuff. She was barely able to keep up with the tax payments, although the mortgage had been paid off. And over the years, as she became physically weaker and more frail, she lapsed in the care of the house. She suffered emergency visits to the hospital, but she was still quite vibrant, although isolated. Most of the three or four Japanese friends she had in Albuquerque were ill, dead, or relocated. She could no longer drive, as her license had been suspended due to her bad vision. She was too embarrassed to tell me. I had been living in San Francisco, trying to stay afloat, and getting worse myself.

Mama didn't understand the circumstances. She didn't understand that the state was coming to take possession, as they do with those who cannot afford payments. Tim, Mama's neighbor, had been kind enough to work with the legal system, taking the best care he could of the place. He asked me to translate what was going on with the house. When she understood, she answered, defiantly:

*This is my house. I have worked different jobs, and lived a life protecting the only thing in this world that I have—You, and this house. I have nowhere to go. There is nothing in life but this. If the state demands that they want this house, I will slit my wrists on the state building steps and see how they like it. I'll show them. They have no right.*

I understood her completely. In Japan, *jisatsu* (suicide) was, in Mama's younger years, not only a form of escape and weakness, as it is seen in Western cultures, but also a way of recapturing honor and protesting authority. Nowadays, suicide has begun to increasingly be defined along Western lines—as a psychological illness or just plain stupid—but the remnants of older Japanese thinking remains. The general rise in the standard of living creates privileges that shield people from confronting privilege itself, or those who are constantly marginalized because of it.

For Mama, *jisatsu* was a way to protest with one's life. I was tired of Americans making this story focus on her "Japanese" will for suicide instead of its protest. It is enough to know that we continue to keep Mama's and my property going while she is still in the elder care facility today. She still asks about the house. I tell her that we are renting it out, and earning a little income. It's in poor shape.

≋ ≋ ≋

I BECAME A STAFF MEMBER at the Rochester Zen Center, in New York, after two years at the affiliate center in Denver. Zen Buddhism appealed to me for its direct responses to my questions about the meaning of life. I had once tried to take my own life. As I hadn't died, I felt that there must be a reason that I was still here, living. I didn't think there was anything wrong with me. I felt that I didn't belong here in the world. 目

# CHAPTER 45

# Peace Intruder

THE AMERICAN MILITARY MAINTAINED its presence and influence after the official dates of Occupation in different ways. Today, this is most intensely felt in the Ryūkyū Islands (Okinawa) where the Japanese and American governments continue to work together to subjugate Okinawans. Okinawa has been a colony of Japan for centuries, in the face of continued resistance by the locals. As a matter of course, the United States uses Japan as a bulwark in the Pacific, which includes its surrounding islands with its laws, bases, and personnel. For many young people, this is no big deal as they have grown up with it, alongside the ignorance, apathy, and identity-forms of subjugation which are normally enjoyed. Okinawa is a geopolitical post in our global reality-game of constant war, and Japan was necessary in order to play this game. Dad and Mama came together during this game. Desires were formed for this game. My body was born from this game.

When I was a kid, I didn't know the word *occupation*. What I remember is running from the stones the other Japanese kids would throw, playing with friends in the places where we knew the other kids wouldn't bother us. I enjoyed shopping with Mama in downtown Tachikawa. I remember what I see in the photo albums, being carried *onbu* on Mama's back everywhere. I remember once Mama getting angry with me for being such a nonchalant, slow walker, and that she had to train me to walk faster. She said it was because she didn't want to walk slow enough to see the looks of disgust or confusion on people's faces. I remember that she would sometimes yell at anyone, usually women, who would look at us funny.

There were other things. I remember American jeeps. Everywhere. There would sometimes be huge tanks, battleships and airplanes nearer to the airports or seaports. But outside the bases, American soldiers were everywhere. Sometimes, you saw them with Japanese women. There were a few times when fights would break out between Japanese and American men. I'd see others laughing and talking together as well, but mostly, they ignored each other.

Mama and I were walking outside the train station one day when we arrived in Yokosuka for a visit to one of her friends who lived on the base there. We had to take a bus from the train station. As we wound our way through the streets, Mama grabbed me and pulled me to her. I glanced out the corner of my eye, and saw what seemed like hundreds of Japanese men, shirtless with white *hachimaki* (bandanas) tied around their heads. Most of them carried baseball bats and sticks. I leaned further out from the corner of the building and saw that the men were headed toward some American soldiers. Soon, men were swinging at each other. Mama clutched me to her tighter.

A tall, blond American soldier, young with a pretty face, came to the alley where Mama and I, and a few other women and children, had run to at the start of the riot. He said something I couldn't understand, as I didn't speak English then. Mama answered him after he spoke. He stood in the alley, a rifle held up vertically above his shoulder. I thought he was protecting us. Who is he? What's going on?

I heard whistles and the intense sounds of more jeeps and trucks arriving from every direction, and the squealing of wheels and brakes. Then quiet. The blond soldier lowered his rifle and turned to us. Mama released me from her tight grip, and we walked. We arrived at her friend's house.

*"Daijobu, Furetto?"* she asks.

I was okay.

In 2009, as I read accounts of the peaceful postwar Japanese occupation, I know it to be a lie. The racism that existed made militant resistance a reality. Mama remembers that yes, that kind of thinking, "never surrendering," was publicized and pushed onto the Japanese citizenry. But most people were ambivalent to that kind of ideology, or thought it outright stupid. So while the Americans expected some kind of continuous war from the Japanese, there was violence and resistance against the Occupation by everyday citizens.

Intensifying this situation, many Japanese soldiers who returned from the war wanted their Japanese commanders dead more than the Americans.[1] Even my Zen teacher in Upstate New York used to speak to the difference between the Germans and the Japanese after the war. Although he did not specifically mention the postwar condition in Japan, there was widespread belief that the Japanese peacefully accepted their fate. In reality, the story wasn't that simple.

In American textbooks, the U.S. Occupation of Japan was a triumph, the Japanese hospitable and feminine, civilizing themselves into America's vision. During my early childhood, I remember two violent incidents between groups of Japanese and Americans, and a few other assaults and scuffles in the streets. I also remember the mix of nice and respectful Americans with the bullish, violent, and arrogant ones. And these were considered minor incidents in an otherwise amicable situation of occupation.

Really? Are occupations amicable? And these group violences, which are labeled "riots," I would call uprisings and resistance. From the perspective of dominant states, a "riot" connotes primitiveness and wildness — something "civilized" people aren't supposed to possess. Most often, these eruptions of violence were about the favoritism many Japanese showed to the Americans at the cost of the locals. American soldiers did not have to adhere to Japanese laws, and therefore lived with impunity for crimes committed against Japanese people. Japanese male chauvinism and imperial attitudes also played their part in this game.

Someone like the American blond soldier, taking care to guard U.S. citizens from violence, did his duty. He protected us. But he was an occupier in a war-torn, depressed, starving Japan. Japan had to be stopped from its imperial aggressions and abuses, but for the occupiers to say Mama and all others like her should've died, what is that? No one ever said that about the Germans or the Italians, but it was always acceptable to say this about the Japanese. *What is this monster that speaks about Mama and those like her in this annihilating way?* Depending upon the community and its laws, the past encounters the present and future in multiple ways to different effect. Those wounds of war and abuse go deep. Words favor and/or show a certain kind of strategy, disposition, betrayal, privilege and suffering. Rarely does it tell the truth. 目

## CHAPTER NOTES

1.  My uncle (Teruo) and Ojī-chan (grandfather), who served in the military, were sometimes targeted by soldiers who blamed them and the officers for plunging into war. However, (according to my family) both were generally loved and admired by their men. For an intense documentary on a crusader who wants justice in Japan, for the war crimes of his superiors, see *The Emperor's Naked Army Marches on (Yukite Shingun)*. Directed by Kazuo Hara. (Japan: Imamura Productions, Shisso Production, Zanzou-sha, 1987, Japanese with English subtitles), where Hara investigates his own interpretation of former military commanders during the 1980s through his protagonist, and his subsequent entrance into prison after he commits murder.

# CHAPTER 46

# Becoming Well 1967

AS MAMA AND I BLOOMED IN HALAWA, I grew fond of listening to Motown records. Many of us kids became obsessed with The Temptations and The Supremes, The Young Rascals, Van Morrison and The Association. My obsession with the great Misora Hibari subsided as the Motown sound took over. Still, one sunny Hawai'ian day, Mama called to me when she heard Misora Hibari's new song on the Hawai'ian radio: 真っ赤な太陽 *Makka na Taiyō* (The Red-Hot Sun), which she sang with the rock group, The Blue Comets. I have many fond and fun memories living in Hawai'i.

One evening, Dad and Mama sat me down to tell me that I needed to go to the hospital. I needed an operation to lower a testicle that had not dropped down completely. I learned that, for kids around my age, this procedure was safe and very common, so I felt comfortable.[1] But I did ask a few questions. Why did I have this problem? Where did it come from? Responses were varied, but one nurse's opinion stuck with me most: it was common for the male twin of two-gender twin children to have this. *My twin.*

At that time, I didn't know what she was talking about. I didn't know I had a twin. After the operation, I could not leave my bed without help. I had a buzzer attached to tall railings that enclosed me, and my groin was covered in contraptions and bandages. It was painful and awkward to walk for a long while. I was being fed through an intravenous tube for a day or so, before transitioning to regular hospital Jell-O and other food. Mama and Dad visited me every day. Other than getting tired of Jell-O and craving Mama's cooking, I was finding ways to have fun. For my care, there were three sets of nurses. The day nurses, then different ones at night. I felt cared for.

During the second evening, I began to feel excluded and ignored. It was taking a longer time for one nurse to come to my bed to help me get to the bathroom when I needed it. I would buzz and buzz for her to come and nothing happened. Later, I called out to any nurse walking around, and they would help me. As I spoke to this one nurse with brown hair and a kind smile, I started noting the differences between nurses. The late afternoon nurse I saw most often presented a strong, resentful silence. This nurse, a white woman with light brown hair, barely spoke or looked at me when she came to change my bed or check on me. When I tried to talk with her, she would ignore me. I started to feel a familiar feeling—as if I were in Japan.

That first night after my surgery, I rang for the nurse. I needed to pee. I squirmed my hips to keep from wetting the bed, but could barely move. I kept pressing the buzzer. The tape holding down the tubes and wires from my groin as well as the intravenous needle, began to hurt because I was moving more than allowed. No one was coming. The halls were silent.

I called out, "Nurse! Nurse!"

*Nothing. No one.*

I couldn't hold it. I began to pee. Because of the way the bandages were arranged, it shot up into the air. Just then, the one silent blonde nurse reached my bed. She looked at me in amazement, her eyes glaring at me.

"You!" She began running around to gather mops, towels, and pans, cleaning me up silently and hurriedly. She changed my hospital gown after changing all the sheets and wiping down the bed and floor. She did everything without looking at me or speaking a word. I felt that she was not here while she was here. But there was something else.

The next morning, as I finished my breakfast, that same nurse came in, took my empty food tray away, and returned. I had just laid my head back onto the pillow to rest when I suddenly heard her say, "You little nigger boy."

Startled, I turned my head and saw her huge face a few inches from mine, leaning into me. "You nigger. You'll wish you never peed again in your life when I'm through with you."

Now this proved what I had felt inside. She hated me for who I was.

Then, I felt a searing pain on my leg. She was pinching me. Hard.

"Ah!" I yelled.

"Quit being a baby, you nigger boy," she whispered, her hot breath against my cheek and her hair falling around my head—a haunting, dark, enclosed space where only her face and voice existed. I felt trapped. I shivered. Then she suddenly vanished. I continued to shiver. Then I began to cry. I knew I couldn't escape. I was disgusted at myself and the entire world. I had to figure out what to do. I wept and wept. I couldn't stop. In a few minutes which seemed like an hour, another nurse came.

"What's happening? Why are you crying?"

"The other nurse called me names," I said.

"It's okay. Don't worry."

She patted me on the head, smiled, and pulled the covers up over me. I didn't know what to think then. She didn't seem to care much. It seemed she was ignoring me too, but in a nicer way. Did she just not want to think about it? Was she the other nurse's friend? Was she part of a plan?

When Mom and Dad came to visit me the next day, I told Dad about the nurse. He immediately went to the front desk. I could hear him raising his voice at them. When that nurse came after being summoned by the supervisor, she said, "Oh, he's such a sweet boy. We love him here. What is he saying? Why is he upset?"

My father told her what I had said.

"I think you're mistaken. I'm a trained professional. I would never do such things."

Then Dad and the nurse walked quickly into another room, leaving Mama and I alone.

I don't know what happened after that. I wanted Dad to believe me, and not the nurse. I also thought that I was somehow a freak for always encountering these people and finding myself in these situations, but I couldn't help it.

I never saw that nurse again. I didn't ask about her. I wanted her far away from me. *Disappeared*. But now I was always afraid of the other nurses, and of the hospital. Were any of them her friend? I believe that Dad had protected me, and that was the reason I would never see that nurse again.

I don't trust people. At other times, I trust them without thinking. That nurse had the ability to smile and say I was a perfect child while hurting me as I laid in bed, recovering. I learned to be much more diligent, looking deeper at people and trusting my initial feelings. I acquired this skill at an early age, earlier than most children would, because I had to. It was this same skill that would not let it go. Certainly I did nothing to provoke this nurse's venom and her attacks, it was merely my existence that created this, in Japan and in the U.S. That link between wellness and terror was both my own and of historical conditions. The reality of identity and terror were now intimately joined in my body. 目

## CHAPTER NOTES

1. At the time of my operation, I didn't know I had a twin sibling.

# CHAPTER 47

# Woven Jungles

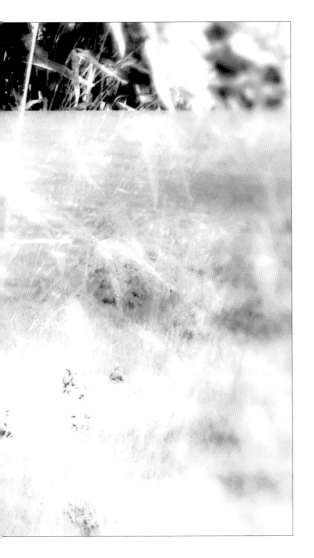

WE PERFORM, CONSTRUCT, and enact our "self," which may or may not be consciously linked to the community we come from. Creating self and self awareness is having a clear perception of your personality, including strengths, weaknesses, thoughts, beliefs, motivation, and emotions, which are often developed in response to or in alignment with certain benefits, privileges and the space we live in. How powerful we feel about self (in either a visible or invisible way) is part of the framework through which we see ourselves — a *self.* I used to hear some of my teachers in Albuquerque say that being mixed-race is special, and that mixed-race people were especially beautiful and exotic-looking. Other teachers would say that being mixed-race was a sad existence that brought enmity and violence upon them, or made the children confused.

I was never confused about who I was. I knew exactly who I was, and what my experiences were. I did not need to define them. Divisions and definitions were artificial and always positioned.[1] It was the world, and others, who were confused, trying to box me and my life into things they learned. What's there to like or not like or accept or not accept before they know you? I used to wonder: *Why can't they just live and be nice?* But the reality of the way people view difference cuts relations like a knife, segregating people on the basis of difference, herding people into groups, all before there is any contact, much less dialogue.

On the other hand, some people think that we are all the same, disavowing difference. This was just as bad. Color blindness is truly blindness. But the language of pain and retribution are impoverished when it comes to these divisions; this connects to things like loyalty and intimacy. *Always and Only Black. Always and Only American.*

*Always and Only Japanese. Always and Only Asian. Always and Only a woman, a non-heterosexual, an islander, someone indigenous, poor, or mixed.*

Differences, in this colonial-imperial framework, becomes internalized through national culture, and are then projected outward to separate the self from the other in a violent mapping. I have come a long way in handling my hybridity and in understanding my parents. This is one of the games we must learn: to negotiate our citizenship with being seen or risk being considered not a citizen, with or without the modern nation and its "communities."

"Black Japanese" or "black Asian" is just as artificial a label as "mixed-race." What is mixed? What is "pure and unmoving" through which a "mixed" can be identified? To do either, we rely on old constructions of race, and resulting categories of racism. This reliance racializes people and communities. But to say that we are not of these communities is also inaccurate. There is no place free from these labels, except in our own delusions, which parallels our alienation and dissociation. Intact. In place. *Made real.*

My Black Okinawan scholar-activist colleagues Eriko Ikehara and Mitzi Uehara-Carter[2] have both said that the mixed-space/place is not the sum of parts, nor apart from that. To acknowledge this in a world bent on easy definitions is a struggle. It needs to be said and seen. Off the radar the silences affirm ignorant and violent worldviews. This ignorance is the scaffolding for much of world suffering. To resist silence and remembrance, brings uneasy hierarchies and complex terrains of claiming ours and each other's lives into full view. I remember in 1966, a few months before our family was to move to Hawai'i, I was out in the yard on the rare day that Dad was home and we were all together. Mama was inside, getting snacks ready, while Dad and I were pulling weeds and mowing the lawn. The day before, I had a fight with my friend Anthony who lived across the street. His was the only black family I knew who lived in the neighborhood. I played with Anthony and his two sisters on occasion. After a recent argument, Anthony and I refused to talk to each other. This was the day when our friendship would be severed.

As I was out with Dad, quietly working, Anthony came out from his house. He saw Dad and me from across the street. I could feel his retreat. I felt indecisive. What should I do?

Should I acknowledge him with the hatred I felt for him at that moment? What would he do?

"You Jap!" Anthony yelled, retreating into his house.

"You nigger!" I responded.

Then there was quiet. Dad turned to me with a stern face, and said, "Don't you ever use that word again."

I said, "But he called me Jap."

"I don't care. Never ever use that word."

I was more confused than ever. I felt that Dad betrayed me. He didn't tell me that Anthony had spoken wrongly, that he shouldn't have used that J-word, but I was not allowed to use the N-word. I knew many Japanese American guys who would just stay quiet when they were called the "J-word." I remembered some of them talking back to the white or black kids who would call them that. There were fist fights and trouble too.

My own history as a black body in Japan, now carried into the U.S., became more complicated. What could I call Anthony when he called me the *dirty yellow* name? Was the N-word (nigger) worse than the J-word (Jap)?[3] At the time, I felt betrayed rather than protective of the N-word. None of these should be used. But should we remain quiet? What could Dad have said? What could I have thought and done?

It must have been hard for Dad. There were those fights when Mama would call one of his black woman-friends the N-word. I only used the word once. It was painful. It was painful for me to hear, and painful to say. But I thought it an equal weapon against African Americans who used the J-word against me. Now I understand that although we may use words as weapons, they cut deep, serving no purpose but to perpetuate pain and hatred. As we grow older, they must be transformed into weapons for understanding, rather than repetitions of violent subjugation. For a new community and new worlds, people must co-create new words with new meanings.

## Black, War, Father

WHAT DOES IT MEAN TO BE BLACK in the context of the Asia-Pacific wars? For those of us politically related to two or more cultures that were once oppressed for social and political reasons is one thing. However, I question writers and educators in the U.S. who never traveled to Asia, never married Asians, yet fought for their civil rights in the United States. It means different things. Different priorities. There were also those like my father. He invested his nineteen-year-old body into the U.S. military. His manhood, desperate to break free from American anti-black behaviors and laws, developed during the devastation of Asia. He participated. But not for dominance or evil. At home, my Dad expressed himself as human, as black, as a soldier. But what was his true self? He may have passed himself off as

This photo shows an aftermath after the Jeju Uprising (April 1948-May 1949) on Jeju island off the coast of South Korea, and is of one of many massacres perpetrated by the U.S.-ordered South Korean police. My Dad was stationed in Jeju. *Photo courtesy of U.S. National Archives.*

some anointed black, some kind of American man, some kind of father, but who was he, really?

When my father joined the military during the Korean War, he was sent to *Jeju-Do* (Jeju Island). Even today, those islands experience tensions with many anti-U.S.-military protests. The costs to the ecology, along with U.S. impunity it soldiers committing crimes, led to a continual reassertion of a longing for U.S. withdrawal. My father was there in the 1950s. According to him, his job was to keep the peace and establish relationships with the local villagers, a position eerily similar to his role in the U.S.-Southeast Asia war a decade later.[5]

He was stationed in Vietnam, and wanted to donate blood plasma at one time. Blood drives for American soldiers were constant. After all, being a G.I. wasn't just about uniforms and fighting. Cultures form. Friendships and bonds form.

*The need for blood is constant. The need for blood transfusions was everyday.*

*We gave our blood. Our filled tubes were put into these trays. I noticed the white woman with the Red Cross symbol on her hat had put a red sticker on the bottle me and my buddy had just finished giving. I was wondering what that red sticker was. My buddy tapped me on the arm and leaned over to me with a surprised expression, telling me to keep looking at her. We noticed that the red stickers meant they were from blacks. We both watched as the line continued to move and a few of the women took the full tray of the tubes of blood from all the GIs and took out the ones that they had put the red stickers on. We were pissed-off to see her pouring the blood from the tubes with red stickers down the drain. We can't even help save our own soldiers, our buddies. The divide between black and white remained the same for me, even where we were supposed to be fighting together against the communists.*

*When I was in Vietnam while you and your Mama were living in Albuquerque, some of my white friends, or those I thought were my friends, wound up dying in the hospital. They told the doctors and nurses that they'd rather die than to get blood from a negro. I couldn't believe it. Here I am sittin' in the hallway, waitin' to find out if they were going to die or not, prayin' and hopin' that they live. Shit. These things stay with you for life. I didn't know whether to cry or go in there and kill them myself.*

Protests on Jeju-Do in Korea, continue today. Christian nuns and civilians protest while South Korean police drag some protesters away, December 2012. *Photo courtesy of Carole Reckinger.*

In Vietnam, Dad's helicopter was shot down during an unofficial mission for one of his commanders. My father was the only one that survived. A special crew accidentally found the wreckage. With everyone seemingly dead, the mission was about to leave them there in the jungles where they had been shot down. He was told this story himself, as he could not remember what had happened. Apparently, when the mission troop was ready to leave, my Dad shook his leg. They pulled him out and got him to a hospital. He was given an honorable discharge.

Dad played important roles in Vietnam. They were positions that brought him pride and a sense of himself as a man. He was one of the few soldiers the local Vietnamese villagers trusted.

And this was because he used to do special things for them, like bring a barefoot villager a pair of boots. Dad said that, in the war, there was mutual fear of each other including the North Vietnamese, who were their assigned enemies. Many died from being bitten by poisonous snakes while sitting in the outhouse. Others were accidentally shot by terrified young soldiers who would shoot at anything that moved. Some were shot by their panicky friends.

The African American soldiers would remind some of the elders of the earlier French invasion of Indochina, and the presence of West African troops recruited for the French colonial military, loosely named the *Tirailleurs Senegalais*.[6] Southeast Asia was still seething and writhing from these complex configurations of color, invasion, displacement, and adjustment to contradictory ways of governance, subjugation, and the civilizing mission of globalization. There were many mixed-race babies born from the union between French colonial African soldiers and local women. Some things never change.[7] Or perhaps they change nations and its languages. The question of who has the right to conquer was imprinted onto the jungles around Phnom Penh, My Lai, Xiangkhouang, just as it had been in the steel blood dirt of Pyongyang, Papua, Tōkyō, Kakazu, and Manila. The French, Dutch, British, Americans, and Spaniards were all there looking for some advantage through destruction, murder, and benevolence. The U.S. continued where the earlier colonialists had left off.

This heritage of invasion, mixing and giving birth, abandonment, and control can be traced to the history and treatment of what the indigenous black tribes of the South Seas and Asia faced, including being rendered invisible. For example, the Aeta and other Negrito tribes of Southeast Asia and the Philippines, who may have once lived and thrived in China, Japan, Formosa (Taiwan), the Ryukyus, and other lands, are related most likely to the Aboriginals in the Aus-

Shown here are Vietnamese, as well as African Tirailleurs, being welcomed by commanders in Namh Dinh, Vietnam, 1951. *Photo courtesy of Félix Renard Family Photo Collection, used with permission from Pascal Renard.*

On July 14, 1951, on the streets of Namh Dinh, Vietnam, troops of the Senegalese Tirailleurs, a corps of colonial infantry in the French Army recruited from Senegal, French West Africa, line up while their French commander gives orders. *Photo courtesy of Félix Renard Family Photo Collection, used with permission from Pascal Renard.*

Cao Thi My Keiu (left) lives with her daughter, son and white Vietnamese Amerasian husband in Vietnam. Her African American father promised to return from the U.S. in 1970, but never returned. *Photo courtesy of Simon Lim.*

tralian and New Zealand territories. Today, they are ignored. The nations that existed before European and American colonization disappeared, including black tribal peoples from their homelands through massacre and genocide, imprisonment and sequestering. Today, they call for human rights, and ask the world to see and acknowledge them. The black body's treatment is already prefigured in the minds of most in the world, which lives peacefully with ignorance, exhaustion, and arrogance. But it is not "natural."

It's funny how over the years, my father never expressed any opposition to the war. I never really knew how he felt. For many years, I thought that he cared mostly about doing what was "right" in his eyes, not only for the nation that provided him privileges, but also within the Asian continent and islands where he spent his formative military years. But he did mention that while the Vietnamese people he worked with in Saigon or Bangkok viewed him as "a good man that cared," they also saw him through the veil of history. That veil was likely the result of scorched-earth policies that burned homes and families into smoldering ashes that took women's bodies at will, through the domination of the Americans, or the French, British, Dutch, or the Spanish before them. My father, as a black man, prided himself on having empathy, yet even he could not unpack that history through which the locals viewed him: the Spanish invasion and conquest with violent impositions of Christianity and Spanish culture; and the British following the French, who came to build their colonial empire and educate the Vietnamese about "bread." Even the Japanese had been there, brutalizing and controlling what they considered "darker and primitive races." Now my father stood as a symbol: *A good man.*

Intensifications of "black" and "enemy-baby" prejudices, brutalizations, and exclusions were guaranteed. The *bui doi* – the dust of life, the *Children of the Dust,* which mixed-race children born of foreigners were called — had a long history of being ignored by the world. The bodies of local women who slept with foreign soldiers, as well as the mixed-race children resulting from those unions, are realities recreated and kept secret in order to serve the local, European, or U.S. cultural elite's political and sexual "needs." Black men, in particular, whether colonial soldiers working for France, or African Americans in Southeast Asian wars, unwittingly brought specific prejudices and brutalities to the fore in Vietnamese society.

Dad played a role in this cultural-historical theater. Equally loved and hated by many locals, he represented the bombings, tortures and scorched-earth policies; the sexual use of village women and the emasculation of local men — an all-too-familiar theater my father entered.

Dad's presence in Asia empowered him as a soldier, teaching him many things as he participated in the Black-Orientalism required to assimilate into the ongoing, contentious, colonial globalist project. People like me, the offspring, are often ignored and expected to assimilate or disappear into history while oppressive exclusions are deployed by nations. We carry memories that governments and their military machines would rather do without. Nation states' global expansion and control requires its soldiers to fall in line. It is too late for a "secure" future to happen.

I include in this the precarious notion of "national security." This is the big sleep through which a "Dream," such as the one for "Water Children," can be conjured and told over and over again. Mixed-race children, like myself, or persons like my mother and father are not anything special per se. What is "special" is the repeated lack of accountability, and the violence maintained in a system that created these issues.

Dad fought for his dignity as a man and a soldier for a nation that despised his people. As desegregation dreams built a destabilizing U.S. military, race riots and the violence of democratization were already taking place, beginning in the Korean War.[7]

Japan's history of invisibility in the international arena made it desperate enough to turn its own chauvinistic violences into imperial strength in order to break from the yoke of global white supremacy. Both of my parents had battles to fight. I am a product of this bringing together of world colonialism, militarism, love, excruciating separations and loss, and necessary empowerment.

To write this, I had to figure out how to tell this. My concerns are regarding the empowerment of patriarchal, paternalistic militarism in patriotism, which creates poverty and racism that intervenes in women's bodies. There are an estimated 2,000,000 *plus* Amerasians living in the West Pacific today. This statistic includes only those living in the Pacific rim, or those abandoned or living on the streets, in orphanages, or born to single mothers in Asia. The American military continues to use bureaucratic methodologies to control the bodies of Pacific and Asian women, along with their mixed offspring, using discourses and realities of sexual and military forces in the global game of domination. 目

This photo, shows predominantly orphaned Amerasian children, being transported out during Operation Babylift—a United Statian airlift project transporting children out of Vietnam during the last days of America's participation in the war, circa 1975. This particular photo survived after this plane tragically crashed and killed almost all onboard. *Photo courtesy of Miami Valley Military History Museum.*

An Aeta family in The Philippines, December 2006, looks at events during a festival in Luzon. The Aeta are indigenous to the scattered isolated mountain parts of Luzon in the Philippines. Western scientific journals and textbooks often mistakenly categorize the Aeta as "negrito" or "Little Black People," because it is assumed based that they migrated to Luzon from Africa. *Photo courtesy of Rex Ramirez Deveraturda.*

Dad at his work desk at home, a sight I remember deeply. Nowadays when I think of him, I see the Geisha and the Mona Lisa over him as he works wearing his evening yukata. Black Orientalism circulates. *Fredrick Cloyd Family Archive.*

# CHAPTER NOTES

1. This is one way for me to place and examine cultural-political realities into the Buddhist concept of "Dependent Origination" which interlinks all reality with all reality — meaning nothing exists independently. Everything is dependent on its birth and existence and disappearance.

2. As of this writing, Eriko Ikehara is finishing her doctoral work in the Ethnic Studies Department at University of California, Berkeley. Mitzi Uehara-Carter is also working on her doctorate in the Anthropology Department at the University of California, Berkeley.

3. In American cultural politics, a "politically-correct" parlance has developed around words that express violent hatred and prejudice. For example, the hateful word for black people (nigger), is now commonly referred to as "The 'N'-word," which is a benign descriptor. The move to remove or change the use of this word does not change its historical context, nor does it go to the root of the race issues we continue to face in this country. I fear that if this type of thinking continues, the history of slavery and oppression will become erased, as if it never happened. Historical conditions and events can be erased through politically-correct language.

4. See *The Ghosts of Jeju*. Directed by Regis Tremblay, (U.S.: Pax Tibi Productions, 2013. Language: English.), a recently released documentary that features an interview with Oliver Stone, who provides a candid account of Jeju history, one that has been essentially barred by the U.S.

5. In its race for supremacy around the globe, French colonial troops formed almost as soon as France began colonizing Africa. French colonial troops in Indochina — The French Far East Expeditionary Corps (Corps Expéditionnaire Français en Extrême-Orient, CEFEO) were formed in 1945 to fight in the Korean War, and later in Vietnam, Cambodia, and Laos. The corps was disbanded in 1956.

6. There is not much information in English on the Tirailleurs Senegalais in Indochina. However, there are some good sections in Martin Windrow's, *The Last Valley: Dien Bien Phu and the French Defeat in Vietnam* (Boston: Da Capo Press, 2005).

7. See Santanu Das, ed., *Race, Empire and First World War Writing* (Massachusetts: Cambridge University Press, 2014), an excellent work.

8. *Indochina — Traces of a Mother*. Directed by Idrissou Mora-Kpai. (MKJ Films, Noble Films, 2011.) is a wonderful documentary. Its story is about the orphaned sons of West African soldiers and Vietnamese women, told primarily through interviews.

9. I do not use "democratization" to mean the making of a "democratic government" *à la America*, but rather I use it to describe an interpersonal democratic ideal, where differences are negotiated and hierarchies are minimized. I believe this definition is closer to the kind of democratic societies that existed in relation to the egalitarian societies that existed before colonization.

10. I received this 2,000,000 figure from a synopsis of a documentary on Vietnamese Afro-Am-erasian in which the author estimates the total number across the Pacific: http://blogs.bauer. uh.edu/vietDiaspora/feature-articles/a-vietnamese-afro-amerasian-testimony-in-search-of-the-%E2%80%9Cplace%E2%80%9D-in-displacement/. The reason I chose this is to logically do math. Most Amerasians are not recorded or counted (they are hidden, they hide themselves, choose other identities and names, don't understand the language, etc.) and the number of Fil-ipino-American Amerasians is estimated to be 250,000 or more. The number of Japanese Am-erasians alone is estimated at 200,000. A small percentage arriving from one country—Viet-nam to the United States only, according to an Ohio State University study, is about 77,000 while others quote to over 100,000. These statistics are from the article by Peter Kutschera, "Military Pan Amerasians and 21st Century Implications for Diasporic and Global Studies," *Asia Journal of Global Studies* 6, no. 1 (2014-15): 30-47. These numbers are close to other figures cited—with all of them stating that these numbers are almost always low because of the political conditions of our world and the status of Amerasians in it. Furthermore, most Asian countries do not include Amerasians in their statistics because they are non-people according to them. I choose the higher numbers to be more accurate than lower numbers.

# CHAPTER 48

# Brides Beautiful 美しいお嫁

> "Beauty finds language wanting because of beauty's profound inexhaustibility; pain finds language wanting in pain's excruciating particularity."
>
> – E. Valentine Daniel, Charred Lullabies[1]

JAPANESE WOMEN WORKING in the administrative offices of U.S. occupation buildings, military facilities or civilian establishments that catered exclusively to the U.S. military (like their counterparts in the Philippines and Korea), were largely controlled with the threat of the ever-present reality of forced sex. Most of these women became the breadwinners of their family, but it didn't matter. Romantic relations between Asian women and American servicemen were seen as extensions of internalized desire borne from colonialism, which, for many, justified the threat of rape. There is that same element in heteropatriarchal relations in general, because colonization and the construction of nations are linked.

*Comfort facilities created by the Tōkyō central government and the U.S. SCAP offices were made to provide U.S. and Allied servicemen with women. The districts where the prostitutes were licensed (Yoshiwara, Senju, and Shinagawa) were for white soldiers. The houses for unlicensed prostitutes (Mukojima, Kameido, and Suzaki) were for black servicemen. The splitting along the lines of clean/dirty and black/white were from Japanese thought and linked perfectly with the U.S. administration's dominant thinking on race at the time. The RAA brothels that served the black soldiers became well-known so that those prostitutes working there could never be licensed to work someday for the white servicemen.[2]*

345

Dad and his two MP friends at Yokosuka, Japan, 1969. *Fredrick Cloyd Family Archives*

The everyday resilience of transnational wife-mothers who emerged from the ruins of war can't be defined. Beauty often refers to things that we are not to alter, as if they were "natural." But they are already altered before we encounter them. History makes beauty and ugliness. There are acts of power relations, acts of empowerment and becoming that are the substance of histories coming together. Beauty and ugliness are inseparable.

こんな女に誰がした？ *Who made me into this kind of woman?*

These are the famous words of one of Japan's most enduring pop songs from the postwar era.

Who made me? What I did made me, but what the world was doing also made me. People do not make themselves alone. Time is past-in-the-now. We come from those historical and cultural places and spaces, and live through them. Places that are symbiotic to the traumas and joys of living. Places that challenge hierarchical arrangements that determine what actions we will or will not take. Places that engulf mothers and children, even when there is no physical separation or boundaries.

And in order to maintain real world power relations, these gulfs are created by using race, ethnicity, caste and socioeconomic classes, gender and sexuality so that the nation states can maintain their power. A patriarchal abuse of power. Military and civilian. The victor and the defeated. Occupier and occupied.

Many of the stories about the Asian war brides who immigrated to the U.S. were sanitized. Sometimes it needed to be sanitized so that the women themselves could believe in it in order to survive. Are they tortured enough? Rebellious enough? Exotic enough? Asian enough? Black enough? Woman enough? Confused enough?

Some women invest in these identities because they know nothing else, and do not care enough to find out more and why. It takes hard work to explore self and identity. It's easier to be engulfed, surrender and assimilate.

War brides in particular were eager to make themselves acceptable. The woman who marries the American military man shortly after World War II, is the sacrificial lamb *(aren't women supposed to sacrifice for their love of country and their men?).* These women crafted themselves into beings the world expected. They married the occupier, the former enemy, the "other." In the U.S., they were often reduced to perfect women who had "made it" whether it was in business, volunteer work or as the ideal housewife.

Japanese life, before the intensified sanitizing, westernizing, and modernizing process during the Tokugawa period, began its own erasures to synthesize a unified single-ethnic Japanese identity during the Asia-Pacific wars. Women's complex lives were rendered invisible, either through the dissemination of propaganda, from their own hands, or our ignorance. "Woman" becomes an effective tool in submerging her. Woman, as we remember and know through nation-making, are unmarked, except by other women. Palatable places that have been charred and bombed; penetrated, impregnated, and finished. Like human history, there has been dislocation and violence. Where does all that go?

In her later years, Mama stayed relatively secluded in Albuquerque. There was no choice. There was no Japanese community larger than her small group of friends and one Japanese grocery store. Struggling with memory, she moved around in her wheelchair or walker. We saw each other in the elder care facility in Albuquerque where she lived alone amongst others, living a foreign language, not able to fully understand the television or the conversations around her. Her seclusion, though, did not hide her power.

西をむいてもだめだから 東を向いていただけよ、
Did me no good to face west, so I just tried facing east, that's all

どうせ儚い涙花 夢に流れて行くだけね
After all we are ephemeral tear-flowers just flowing away in a dream

扇ひろ子さんの1967大ヒット：新宿ブルーズ
Ōgi Hiroko's hit song of 1967: *Shinjuku Blues*

When I finished high school and attended college in Long Beach, California in 1977, Mama was left to herself in Albuquerque. Dad had moved to Texas where the U.S. Air Force stationed him. For me to feel okay about leaving, a college friend of mine who was looking for a place to live, moved in and helped take care of Mama. They communicated between her broken half-English and his patience.

When we first moved to Albuquerque and before Dad left for Vietnam, he had been asking his friends and making careful inquiries about Japanese women who lived in Albuquerque so that Mama would not feel so lonely. Dad felt that if she knew other Japanese people, she would be better off. He also sought out Nisei and Sansei (first and second-generation Japanese Americans) that he knew, thinking Mama would have an abundant array of friends to keep her from feel-

Me and Mama circa 1956. Mama loved being a mother, but rebelled at being pigeon-holed into the requirements of Japanese womanhood. *Fredrick Cloyd Family Archive.*

ing isolated in the new country by maintaining cultural ties with her former one. But the Japanese Americans in Albuquerque ostracized her. During the 1950s and 1960s, war brides, which was what Mama was, represented the pain of Japanese Americans being forced into U.S. relocation camps. So the many Nisei and Sansei that Mama and I knew of didn't want to have anything to do with Japanese wives of American soldiers, even as many of them worked for legislation that would allow Japanese American men serving in the U.S. military to marry Japanese women in Japan.

Mama told me years later:

*After trying to be friends with some Nisei your father introduced me to, I gave up. I remember one Nisei woman poked her finger in my face and told me I betrayed Japan and was the enemy of the U.S. I almost slapped her. She said I betrayed my Japan and I could never be Japanese anymore. Only a whore to an American. I never wanted to talk to a Nisei after that. But now you tell me that they were interned in camps in the U.S.? I didn't know that.*

In Japan, Mama and her kind were considered traitors and whores up until the late 1980s and the 1990s, when books were being published about the courage and resilience of the Japanese war brides. For many Americans, at least in the early years, the Japanese brides of Americans were still "Japs": *insects and monsters who had tortured their uncles and brothers; who had killed their brothers and sisters in the jungles of Guam, the Philippines, Korea, Burma or China.* Many Japanese wives of white U.S. servicemen talked down to, and sometimes excluded those who were married to African American men. But not all of them. Most of the ones my father introduced to Mama did not practice those discriminations. In the end, Mama and many other Japanese women married to Americans in New Mexico had to find each other through mutual friendship links.

In the cactus-laden New Mexico desert, there was enough confusion, loneliness, and uncertainty for most of the war brides. Even as they recognized this hierarchy as painful, they continued to base their relationships on the mechanics of social status. Dominations and oppressions are parasitic, difficult to remove. These rules of clan hierarchies were judged alongside ancestral family histories (identified by name), as well as the military rank and levels of wealth associated with their American husbands. As an African American staff-sergeant, Dad was a middleman in the military.

What do cultural and familial displacement, the devastation of war killings, and raising children in the victor's land without knowledge of the local language bring for these mothers and wives who come from Japan?

One day, Mama and I put on some old 45s we loved. I put on the Ōgi Hiroko song called 新宿ブルーズ *Shinjuku Blues*. The singer's husky, emotional voice enveloped us, singing of falling in love with a man who from the beginning, was unable to keep his promises. Mama sometimes would shed tears *kono uta kiku to kanashiku naru.* This is why she didn't want to listen to any Japanese music or songs. It was too heartbreaking.

For Mama, as with many of her friends I knew who had come from Japan with American military husbands, the song, like others, exemplified the experience of loving an American serviceman.[3] The U.S. government prevented many African Americans and other families from bringing their adopted half-Black Japanese infants to the U.S.[4] Many military commanders didn't allow soldiers who returned to Japan from the Korean war front, to visit girlfriends. It was a multifaceted war for both soldiers and Japanese women.

Mama did not know, at first, if my Dad would ever return for us and take us out of Japan. Even though there were many relationships that worked and flourished, Mama's experience was mostly that of remembering the sadness of her friends whose American boyfriends never returned. There was constant movement, so there was difficulty finding allies and friends. Wondering who would call Mama a woman of the night, 夜の女 (whore) or make disgusting faces at the children beside them—children who were born either through love, one-night stands or violent rapes with the Westerners in uniform. In truth, people mostly ignored them.

There were those friends of Mama who left their newborns in trash bins, along with what they thought would be their shame. Others took a long train ride to leave their children with orphanages like the Elizabeth Saunders Home for Mixed-Race Children, or the Lourdes Home, or with one of the Christian churches. Others were not able to sleep soundly again after the trauma of knowingly strangling their newborns, or taking the stinging drinks that would kill them in their wombs before they came to term. Mama had endured to keep me. What and who was I? Was I only a child that she loved? For Mama, the moment my sister and I were taken from her slit-open belly, what dreams died while others were born?

Almost inseparable from the songs was the wandering fragrance of *miso shiru,* freshly steamed *gohan* and *gyōza* in the house. While having sips of me and Mama's favorite *genmai-cha,* I wanted to know more about the women that I had grown up with in America. Like Rie, who shared a love of volleyball with me and was quite the player.

"Her husband left her," Mama said.

Rie found a job as a barmaid. Her English was fluent, her beauty unquestioned. But she wasn't in her twenties anymore. The work pained her. One of her two children had to be continually bailed out of jail, draining her of any savings. She felt that since she had married a Latino-American soldier, things would be better and there would be an understanding. But no rank, nation, or ethnicity could save Rie from the pain of separation and single motherhood in her 50s, far from the dreams of her *kokoro*. *This was her American dream.*

One of Mama's other pals was Toshiko. Another beautiful Japanese woman with a seemingly ideal life, married to a high-ranked white American military man. I loved it when she used to visit. I sometimes joked with her that I wanted to marry her. She did not believe in the rigid rules of caste behavior so often enacted by the Japanese, and didn't engage in speaking ill of others like most of the other women, including Mama. There were always interesting conversations with her around. Mama told me that many of the other women were jealous of her. She was always struggling to bring equal relations between the small groups of friends, but it seemed that most of the other women didn't think of her as doing that. On one particular day, a group of the women gathered at a friend's home for the monthly food and gossip get together:

> *An argument started between two of the women. Toshiko attempted to be peacemaker. The argument later subsided and some thought it was over, with nothing more to be said. When the get-together wound down and the dishes had been done, Toshiko excused herself to go home. When she arrived home, there was a knock at the door. She opened the door and saw one of the women from the get-together who had been involved in the argument. Another one of the group was walking towards them from the car. As Toshiko opened the screen door to let her in, a large butcher knife appeared from behind this woman's back, and slashed Toshiko's face. She screamed. There was a loud struggle. The other woman screamed in horror but stood frozen. A passerby noticed and came to help. Toshiko was slumped on the porch, blood everywhere.*

When the police arrived, the woman who had slashed Toshiko was just standing there, dazed. She told the police that she just wanted to "maim Toshiko's face forever so she couldn't think that she was better than everyone else." Now her wish had been fulfilled. Toshiko was scarred for life.

I was dumbfounded, sad, and disgusted. Heartbroken. Even a bit confused. That woman is now in jail for attempted murder. My *kokoro* was heavy.

Toshiko was not seen for years afterwards by anyone.

Mama told me what she believed about the woman who had attacked Toshiko. This woman, "M," was the daughter of a struggling farmer in Japan. After the war, the family became destitute. She began selling her body to U.S. servicemen at the local bars where U.S. military men hung out. This helped feed her family. Earlier, when she was twelve, she had been raped by a family relative. At the bar, she met an American soldier, who she eventually married and moved to America with.

He soon left her. She barely spoke anything but the U.S. military/Japanese slang-English pidgin that she picked up from the bars. After that, she met another American man, but he sexually and physically abused her. She always spoke badly of everyone, and nobody liked her too much, but Mama also reminded me that she could relate to her more than anyone else in the group, even though they were not particularly close.

*In what ways do the women of war and devastation and cultural displacement find solace and empowerment?*

Life was complicated for these war brides living in the victor's desert, away from Japanese culture.

As Mama and I drove by Toshiko's house, the screen door still torn from that horrific moment of heightened violence, I thought of the community of women who struggled to heal. In our everyday greetings with them, they smile. They hold it together. *They sometimes survive.* 目

# CHAPTER NOTES

1. E. Valentine Daniel, *Charred Lullabies: Chapters in an Anthropography of Violence* (Princeton University Press, 1996), 138. Professor Daniel is a Sri Lankan Tamil academic, anthropologist and author.

2. Yasuhiro Okada, *"Gendering the 'Black Pacific'" Dower, Embracing Defeat; and Kovner, Occupying Power* (1980). See also Masayo Duus, *Makkāsā no futatsu no boshi: tokushu shisetsu* RAA *wo meguru senryō-shi no sokumen [Two Hats of MacArthur: One Facet of Occupation History Concerning the* RAA *Special Comfort Station]* (Tōkyō: Kodansha, 1985), 19, 192.

3. *Enka* (演歌 )is a song form that became the most popular genre of music in the postwar, up until the 1960s. It is a Japanese singing style that is informed by Portuguese fado and Spanish ballads, as well as Western jazz ballads that are often mixed with Japanese, Okinawan, and Ainu folk ballads and laments.

4. See for example, two articles by Ralph Matthews, "Future of Brown Baby in Japan Depends on An Act of Congress: Adopted Son Problem For Army Couple: Returning Sergeant And Wife May Not Be Allowed Baby," *Norfolk Journal and Guide,* September 22, 1951; and "Rankin Blocks Bill To Admit Japanese Child," *Norfolk Journal and Guide,* October 6, 1951.

# CHAPTER 49

# Ojī-chan 1973
## おじいちゃん1973年

I HAD SPECIAL AFFECTION FOR OJĪ-CHAN (grandfather), Mama's father. Amidst the terrible violence and prejudice I experienced, Ojī-chan was always kind to me, and gave Mama a break from taking care of me. He took me places, bought me *sekihan*, *okashi* and *oden* that I loved to eat, and *omocha no kisha* and *densha* (toy steam trains and electric trains) to play with, loving me in ways that very seldom came my way. Mama felt close to her father, despite her conflict with his second wife, who later died of cancer. Later, he married another woman who Mama was even more distanced from.

As a child, we had to visit her new stepmother out of respect. There were also the former concubines in China and Korea he was obligated to take care of financially, but who were kept secret, at least in the beginning of the Occupation.

With Mama and I in America, both Ojī-chan and Mama's brother Teruo were always sending us gifts and wrote often. My cousins Kazuko and Sachiko (Kō-chan) would also send gifts. One day, in my senior year at Highland High, Mama seemed especially quiet and upset after receiving a letter from Ojī-chan. Dad had been home for a week from his house in Texas.

The letter came in April, the date Dad celebrated Mama's birthday.

One day, after coming home from school, I found Mama and Dad arguing. Mama was in tears, talking in her broken English to Dad as he was climbing into his truck parked in the dirt driveway.

Mama, in tears, kept asking "Why? Why? Why no can do?"

Dad backed out of the driveway, and said, "That's all we can do, Amy." Then he sped away.

"Mama, *dō shita no?*" I asked.

Ojī-chan and I around early 1959 in Ōme, on the road across from the front of our house. *Fredrick Cloyd Family Archive.*

She kept crying and ran into the house. She couldn't talk. I didn't know what to do. As Lawrence Welk sang a tune with pretty blondes and redheads behind him, Mama wiped her tears with a handkerchief. She turned to me and told me that Ojī-chan had written her. He was asking Mama if he could come and live with us in America because life in Japan was unbearable. She told me that Dad said that he could, as long as he paid his own money to come as our family could not help financially.

Ojī-chan, as was the norm in Japan, lived with Uncle Teruo, my two cousins, and Uncle Teruo's wife. He was used to one of the family members running a hot bath for him everyday. But, he wrote to Mama, they would no longer do this for him. In those days, the baths required coal to build a fire to heat the water. This took quite a bit of time to sit in front of the coals to fan the flames. Ojī-chan was too old. But my younger cousins didn't want to do it either. He said that, for the past six months, he had to ride the train to the nearest public bath, which was costing money and time, and he questioned why he had to do this when they had a working bath in the house.

There were more arguments between Ojī-chan and the cousins. He was used to the old ways, ordering them around. The younger ones wouldn't go for it. He blamed them for being more and more westernized and disobedient, even going so far as to physically attack them when he would make his demands. Ojī-chan's nationalism, leftover from the war-period, was also isolating for him. Many of his generation experienced ostracization and humiliations after the war. There were always criticisms of the nationalist older generation (which would intensify to the present). For Ojī-chan, this added to the sting of being demoted and isolated, stacking itself on the already heavy burden of growing older. Ojī-chan had an argument with my younger cousin about her falling grades and her increasing unwillingness to do homework. He felt that she needed to be more disciplined, which my cousin didn't want to hear. She knocked Ojī-chan's glasses off of his head and didn't apologize or offer to replace them. Teruo's new wife wanted him gone because it was too much stress for them, even though Ojī-chan paid some of the household expenses through his part-time work. Teruo's wife forced him to tell his father that unless he paid his share, he shouldn't stay in the house because they wouldn't be able to take care of him financially. Ojī-chan resented that, and felt ashamed. After all, they had once been among the richest clans in Japan. It was through his lineage and work that they still had one property left after the war.

Ojī-chan said that he was being treated like he wasn't wanted, and was not respected. He felt useless and abused. In his late seventies, he didn't think that at his age, after surviving the war and working all his life to keep the clan safe, he should receive this kind of treatment.

Nationalism, war, and Occupation's bitter fruits now prevailed in nuclear family homes. Mama, my cousins, Teruo, and his wife lived with this tension. Mutual duties were something foreign to the younger generation, who pursued personal happiness; for Ojī-chan, personal happiness was selfish.

Mama felt obligated to her father, and understood through her own experience how he felt. That night, I watched Mama write a letter to Ojī-chan, sadly imparting to him what my Dad had said, and that she would do her best to come through for him. She sobbed as she wrote the letter. Her first try had to be crumpled and thrown out when her tears soaked the ink and made it illegible. She began again, finishing by licking and sealing the envelope, kissing it and putting it in a letter-sized bag colored with beautiful Japanese black and gold brocade, which she placed in her purse.

I think she mailed it. But I'm not sure. Perhaps she changed her mind. For a few days after, we passed our days in quiet communion, only together when she would prepare meals. These were TV dinners of salisbury steak with gravy and mashed potatoes with the rice Mama would make. At other times, she would make us simple things like ハムたまご焼き *hamu tamago-yaki* (fluffy scrambled-egg dish with thinly-sliced green onions and bits of ham), sprinkled in *shōyu* (soy sauce) and かつおぶし *katsuo bushi* (dried bonito fish flakes), おしたし *oshitashi* (broiled spinach and vinegar-lemon sauce), *miso shiru*, and *gohan* (rice). A month passed. It was a few weeks after my graduation from high school. Mama received a telegram about twenty minutes after I arrived home from the mall. Neither Mama nor I had ever received a telegram before. We hurriedly opened the envelope and found a Japanese-written letter with official type. Mama and I sat down beside each other as she carefully and quickly opened the envelope. She looked worried. She couldn't read the English so I translated the part that said that it was a special message from Japan. Inside, there was another letter on fragile paper which Japanese offices used for sending delicate news in those days. I handed that to Mama.

*Gilligan's Island* was just ending on the television, and I could hear the clanging pot of hot water brewing in the kitchen. The kettle whistled. When I stood up to get to the kettle, Mama screamed. I ran to Mama in the living room. Tears were flowing down her face. Catching her breath sharply between every two words, she quivered intensely. She said, "お父さん 。。。 死んだって. 自殺したって。 *(Granddad is dead. He committed suicide)*. Then Mama broke.

She stood up with the letter shaking in her hand, walked to her room, and closed the door.

*I sat stunned.*

Ojī-chan had committed ritual *seppuku* in the family shrine room with the ancestral sword. The head of the Kakinami clan, who led the clan's heritage, which had survived for generations, leaving behind a rich legacy of respected warriors and officials that was maintained with respect and dignity, had left this world. In losing almost the entire five hundred year legacy of the clan's wealth, property, and position, there was shame in being emasculated by Japanese women who married Americans, and the westernization of Japanese culture. He gave life and honor back to himself through the age-old tradition of ritual disembowelment.

Mama never quite forgave Dad, who she blamed for the death of her father. She also blamed her brother, Teruo, and his family for forcing Ojī-chan to kill himself. In her mind, Mama felt that Americans didn't understand obligation and that Dad was incapable of understanding what her request had meant and how serious it was, how spiritually obligated she felt. She blamed herself for not being there for him. She felt that she was a bad daughter.

This incident would play a large part in the divorce battle that Dad and Mama would go through later. For two months I became quiet and stayed in my room more than usual. I immersed myself in volleyball coaching and playing. I would never forget the complete kindness Ojī-chan showed me, or how respectful he was to my Dad. But we were now individuals, not a clan. I had already learned that family was a lonely thing in my own life, if not in others. 目

# CHAPTER 50

# Visitors 1999

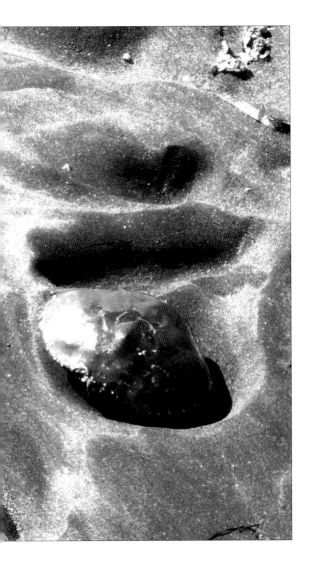

*To articulate what is past does not mean to recognize "how it really was." It means to take control of a memory, as it flashes in a moment of danger.*

— Walter Benjamin, *On the Concept of History*[1]

*There is an empty room. It is dark and a bright white light came through the large window on the right. I am flying slowly around the room. There is a large Japanese bath in the back of the room, resting on wooden-plank flooring. There are Japanese wooden pails and a wooden bench to rinse outside of the tub. There is a long old faucet. In the silence, the faucet slowly and patiently leaks drops of water every few minutes.*

*The tub is full of hot water. The furnace beneath it burns bright with fire. The room smells like burning coal. The steam rises from the hot bath water. Then, as if a volcano was erupting, the bath water changes shape. Something protrudes up from inside the tub. It rises. It is a woman. She is soaked, beautiful, elegant. She is slender, glowing in a white Chinese robe. Her hair is long, black, and straight, unendingly long, covering the entire floor behind her. She continues to ascend through the water as if she were coming from the center of the earth. The light in the room is glowing. I see her face. A Cherokee ancestor. She looks at me lovingly, powerfully. Her right arm rises from the sides of her body. She stands in the water, her body showing above her knees. A glowing white light emanates from all around her. Her arm extends out to me. "You shall," she says. "You shall."*

361

*She touches the top of my head.*

*I awaken.*

*One of your great-great-aunties was on the Trail of Tears.*[2] *She died there with her child, thin to the bone, one of her surviving babies in her arms, in the desert where the white man came to build cities and machines. Now they rode on horseback alongside her, guns pointed.*

*Her father was a great chief. You come from the great Cherokee warriors. You must remember.*

忘れないで *Don't forget me.*

## Families 家族

ACCORDING TO ONE STORY, Mama/Emiko was born on 昭和 年 4, or 1929 年 月11 or 霜月の 2 日 November 2, 1929, the Shōwa period Year 12, in the Month of *shimobuki*, or *shimotsuki* (Month of the Frost: the eleventh month, on the second day). Always the same day. But the years changed at various times whenever she brought it up or if I asked.

Sometimes she'd say she was born in 1931, or 1937. But the month and day remained unchanged. It's entirely possible that I could be as much as eight or ten years off the actual year of events in Mama's life. I think nowadays that she has her sisters' birthdays and her own mixed up. Perhaps even with other people she has known. In any case, each of these years are not random. They are important in her history, markers of sisters and a war that marred her otherwise lively and humorous way of living and relating to the world.

War, military occupation, displacement, and violence does this. The separation between people, especially in conditions of being subaltern, non-mainstream, other, enemy, traitor, whore, mixed, and/or inferior — all while assimilating into and within the former elite, now defeated and occupied dominant — makes remembering more difficult. Mama's memory carries so many deaths. What she remembers and what she forgets mixes with what she forgets and what was made to be forgotten.

Back in those days, most Japanese conceived the flow of time in multiple ways, a part of cultural memory that has been burned away, along with family and friends. During the 1950s, our family knew the Shōwa year, but also the Gregorian calendar which had been coming into wider use via the U.S. and Allied

Occupation. Nowadays, younger Japanese increasingly want to make everything English or French, and stick to the Gregorian calendar. It's singular. Easier than remembering two or three calendar times. But most still use both.

The use of a Western calendar in Japan is not seen as anything important to care about. But I have seen the disruption and violence this causes. Mama staying up nights to remember the calendar. Memorizing something from the country that defeated her own, making her own Japaneseness feel weaker, inferior, less important, and obedient. This mixed with her empowerment as an upper-caste woman and internationalist. This mixed with feelings of patriarchal domination, and what American culture imposed upon her to become a successful wife. What various positions and roles played in her strengths and skills?

I've met so many people who consider their ancestors' burdens in an individual life, as people to visit on holidays. As an alienated, isolated Black Japanese Amerasian, I have been accustomed to thinking of all those close to me as far away.

Emiko was given both the Austro-Hungarian/Chinese name Anna, and named *Emiko* a year later when war intensified between Russia, China, and Japan. Mama was born in *Szuchou* 蘇州 (or Soochow), a beautiful city which experienced its heyday during the Song dynasty (960-1279 A.D.) in, say, 1937 — the year she most often claims as the year of her birth. The year Japan's imperial army invaded China.

Japanese Imperial forces destroyed a large part of Szuchou when it became a key invasion point. In colonial invasions and occupations, the intellectuals, artists, and journalists who carry memory and truths, especially of rival regimes, must be confined or destroyed. Emiko's mother's family was aristocratic, and among the most educated in the world. After her missionary grandfather was assassinated in China, her mother met the Kakinami patriarch that would help care for the children.

Emiko's family escaped to *Manshū* 満州 (Manchuria) the following year to be closer to the father — my grandfather — who had been sent to work on the Japanese national railroad project in colonial Manchuria. Emiko's family, with Chinese, European and Japanese heritage, could be targeted by any or all three groups during this time.

*Danger everywhere, within and without.*

How does a person consider themselves and their family? What is performed out of constant danger?

*I am this, I am other.*

I am dangerous to them. Does this go away completely?

In 1939, Emiko was two years old (or ten), and her family escaped to Japan by horse-drawn cart, by car, by boat, leaving their mother behind. My Dad's family, meanwhile, was going through violent interactions with police and the Klu Klux Klan.

Emiko's mother and father thought it safer if her mother came later as she was not "pure" Japanese, and they did not want to risk her capture. The incarceration and killing of Chinese people in Japan became more intense as the war progressed. Emiko's family often had to hide their Western cultural practices from the Japanese when they were in Japan. All the while, Japanese military and government officials kept doing business with Chinese factions in order to ally for greater control, given the struggles between various nationalist, socialist, and Marxist groups in China, Japan, Russia, and Europe.

In China, resistance to Japanese occupation was made more complex due to nationalist and Marxist factions, and issues surrounding the Formosan Islands. Russian invasion was a constant threat. In Japan, this was constructed as a "Greater Asian" resistance to white colonization. This was nation-building. It was, first, internal.

In this tense and ambiguous climate leading to war, Emiko's mother needed to be transported secretly from China to rejoin the family in Japan. The loss of family and the shredding of family ties appear in different ways; the terrains linking racism, nation, and "other" are interrelated. They are not universal. The more these acts are allowed, the more it becomes clear that it is not some natural and prefigured truth or providence.

I came to study cultural anthropology at the California Institute of Integral Studies in San Francisco in 1999 because of the remarkable scholar-activists that ran the program there. I was forty-four years old. That particular anthropology department was a way for me to analyze history and rage, my sadness and trauma, without having to leave it at the door, which almost every institution expects from us in the modern world. It also need not be psychological, which is typically a response to pain in America (and the West, in general).

To educate myself, I moved from Seattle to California to enter graduate school. Because I was poor and alone, and didn't know anyone in San Francisco, I asked one of my estranged uncles to put me up for a while. He had been living in the Bay area for decades and was well-established, although I had not been in contact with him since I was a teenager.

Everyone seemed to like my uncle when I was growing up. I remembered him as charming, friendly, and very popular, with his good looks and cheerful manner. I was excited for the possibility of sharing with each other, and discovering who we were and where we were headed. After all, we were "family." And in some ways, given my nomadic existence, I was seeking some kind of solace by being with family, especially given how hard it had been for my Dad's family to come together in adulthood. The men had tried to connect and maintain themselves as African American men when so much had to be given up in order to live. So much negotiating with whiteness and blackness. I, being considered one of the men in this family, had a chance to begin anew.

I contacted my uncle, and he agreed to put me up. He insisted that our relationship as uncle and nephew was to be separate from our "business arrangement" as landlord and tenant, and that we stick to a financial agreement that was workable for both of us. I knew I could barely do it, but I would force myself to survive somehow in order to come to San Francisco to educate myself.

The second week I was there, my Uncle came to see me on the first floor, where my very large studio was. He lived in the three floors above me by himself, sometimes entertaining guests. While I was there, no one else was living there except for him. As he and I spoke, I became aware that he viewed me as a nomad without a life. He treated me in a condescending manner, much like how he treated his older brother, the middle brother of my Dad's family. That middle brother was an alcoholic who had lived in his car for most of his life, having fathered many children with different women. I began hearing that tone from the 1970s in that room in 1999. I became painfully aware that this man, my Uncle, had no clue who I was and was speaking through ghosts in his life.

When he came to my room, he knocked and I welcomed him in. At that instant, I was eating a Japanese breakfast I'd made for myself with rice and scrambled egg with *shōyu* (soy sauce) and *katsuo* flakes sprinkled over them with some ginger. Just the night before, my Uncle had told me that I was "living in the past" when I answered his question about what I had been doing all these years. He probably wanted to know about jobs, or money, marriages and divorces. Money, status, women. But being raised in Japan by Mama and her friends, and wanting my uncle to know me through some things I'd experienced, I began talking about many things that, to my uncle, were "not right."

When he saw what I was eating, he sniffed the air, grimaced and said, "Why are you still living in Japan? You're in America now. You're American. You'd better get your shit together and understand that you're an American."

I said, "Sorry, but you or no one else isn't going to tell me who I am! I'll tell you who I am."

My Uncle continued, as if he didn't hear anything. "What kind of food are you eating? See, this proves that you're living in the past!"

At that point, I interrupted, "Mama is Japanese. You know that. What are you talking about? I am Japanese too. Not just black. And what kind of black are you talking about anyway? What kind of American are you talking about?"

At this point, he turned red and shouted, "You're twisting my words! You're screwed up!"

I told him to get out.

"I told your father that there's something wrong with you!"

His intention was to injure me. I don't know why. I continued to tell him to leave. He did. To his credit, his relationship with me as far as my landlord remained professional and communicative. I told him I refused from then on (until I moved out the next month) to talk about any family members or myself with him.

Life is too short. Family. What's family? I understood then that hybridity was not something many people who identified as a single identity such as "black," or "white" or "Japanese," or whatever else, were comfortable with. I think that between my uncle and myself, in that relationship, his anger revealed his true feelings.

When would we take responsibility for our own perceptions? Perception is not just something that is. It is also constructed—as history, as life.

Two or three months after I moved out of his apartment and started living with roommates in the Mission District, I spoke with Mama on the phone. She almost always asked me about him. She knew that I now lived in the same city as him. He had always treated her nicely, making her feel welcome to the U.S. and the family. But I always told her that I didn't speak with him because he made me feel bad. I couldn't help but feel strange, struggling through the many instances she would ask about him.

I was his visitor. The ghost of my Cherokee ancestor visited me, admonishing me, blessing me. The ghost of history, the nodes of racialization and separation, and my uncle's need to assimilate and overcome insurmountable odds to exist included a need to make an invisible "other." Death visited that room, standing between my uncle and me. There are many visitors that we must contend with, and speak to.

Since then, the anthropology program, as I knew it, had been dismantled by the institution. The program and its professors, the good work that they did and what we represented is gone. This is dominance.

As usual, my dream had to be altered. 目

# CHAPTER NOTES

1.  Walter Benjamin, *On the Concept of History* (Createspace, 2009).

2.  See for example, Theda Perdue and Michael Green, *The Cherokee Nation and the Trail of Tears* (NY: Penguin Books, 2008); and Gloria Jahoda, *The Trail of Tears: The Story of the American Indian Removals 1813-1855* (Austin TX: Holt, Rinehart and Winston, 1975).

# CHAPTER 51

# Mother 母ちゃん

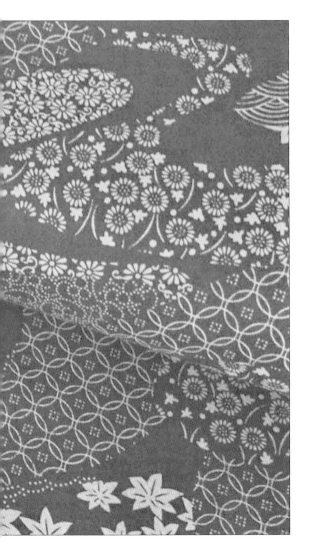

"Suffice more than that. SHE opposes Her. / SHE against her. / More than that. Refuses to become discard / decomposed oblivion. / Refuses to become discard / decomposed oblivion. / From its memory dust escapes the particles still material still respiration move. Dead air stagnant / water still exhales mist."

— Theresa Hak Kyung Cha, *Dictee*[1]

IN 1965, MY PARENTS BOUGHT THAT BROWN STUCCO HOUSE that stood across the street from the boundary fence separating the civilians from Air Force base military housing. We had moved into the off-base house after living on the base for a few years. We'd see Dad when he visited in the summers, though sometimes he wouldn't visit for a while. Mama spent some time with friends, but mostly alone. She had long given up thinking of Dad being by her side as she had once desired in her early years. Now, she began crafting another self, different from what she had created before.

She used to refer to her more individualistic, self-expressive side as her "Chinese personality." This, despite the fact that she'd only lived in China for the first three years of her life and had no recollection of it, save a few powerful memories. This was a way she enjoyed her individualism in those days, different from her more claustrophobic and subordinated experience growing up in Japan. Telling herself that she was exercising her Chinese womanhood was also a way to remember. Her solitude was not something she wanted, but it was how she empowered herself. It brought her certain freedoms, and helped her to exist as someone foreign living in a foreign land, crafting herself into someone she both could and could not recognize.

369

Her memories of her own birth mother were strong. She said she'd never forget her mother's fragrance, but remembering was painful for her. One of her strongest memories was when, in Manchuria, a neighborhood sage, an old man with a long beard, bound her feet, as was customary for many elite Chinese women. Since the clan was of that heritage, the elder was just following his duty. He did so for all the girls of her social status. But Emiko's mother had a conversation with the old man, and Emiko's feet were unwrapped. Even today, this is a painful yet, tender memory for Mama, as her feet are smaller than what she thinks they should be and are very weak and fragile. She would massage her feet everyday, soaking them in a bucket of warm water while we watched ズバリ当てましょう (Japanese rendition of *The Price Is Right*) or お笑い番組 (comedy), or other sitcoms. She sometimes said that whenever she massaged her feet, she would remember her mother's faint fragrance. For her, besides the one faded and torn photograph she had of her mother, she had little of her mother, who was so very missed.

In most of my conversations with Mama about her life before I was born, she was just as perplexed as I was, yet at other times, she seemed quite sure of her memories. As we spoke over the years of the same stories, there were contradictions, but I grew to understand memory as not as something we just remember or forget, but as something that connects intimately to society and what is allowed politically and culturally.

I remember that day in 1975. I was twenty years old. I had come home after spending the day visiting an old friend from high school. She had a great meal prepared. I ate it all with gusto while she ate, talking with a friend on our big pink dial telephone.

時には、母のない子のように、黙って、海を見つめていたい...
*Sometimes, like a motherless child, I want to silently remain looking out over the sea...* [2]
*What they call they used to call the blues*
*No need to talk it out, we know what it's all about...*
*Rainy days and Mondays always get me down.* [5]

It was about 8:00 p.m. when I heard Mama turn the bath water on. The familiar steam began wandering through the house. Mama would usually close the door when bathing, but the steam would escape anyway in these old homes.

About half an hour later, the house was quiet except for the sound of splashing water as she rinsed herself, when I heard a strange sound. I sprang upright in bed.

I listened again. A strange wailing and screaming. I bolted off the bed and went into the bathroom, toward the sound.

I found Mama leaning out over the edge of the white porcelain bathtub, hyperventilating. Her pale, glazy, bug-eyed face filled the entire room. I reached for her, helping her to stand. She began wailing and choking out, "*Okā-chan! Okā-chan! Okā-chan!*" (*Mommy, Mommy, Mommy*).

I did not stop her from wailing. I didn't know what was happening. I gently helped her out of the tub. She could barely move. She just crouched, screaming "*Okā-chan! Okā-chan!*" over and over and over. Tears streamed across her face. Breathing, crying, screaming, and gagging at the same time, she was heavy and awkward. I was afraid. I took her hands, guiding her slowly out of the tub. I covered her with a large bath towel, then a second one as she began to shiver. She just followed, leaning into me as I guided her slowly and carefully to her bedroom.

"*Mama! dōshita no? Mama...*"

I slowly and quietly tried to talk with her. *What's the matter, Mama?* She wept uncontrollably. I did not notice that almost an hour had passed before she was calm. I sat with her on the floor of the bathroom, her body covered with two towels. I guided her to her bed, helped her dress, and went to the telephone in the living room. My neighbors came over quickly, phoning for an ambulance. The men in white loaded her into the ambulance as I watched. Mrs. Lopez held me against her side as we both stood in the doorway watching the ambulance took Mama to the hospital.

I didn't know what happened. Even after Mama returned from the hospital the next day.

The following year, during another one of my visits home, I was just starting to fall asleep one night when I heard her calling me softly from the living room where she was watching television.

I headed to the living room and asked if she was okay. "*Daijobu?*"

"*Mm. Daijobu yo.*" Then she began telling me what happened.

*I suddenly remembered that time. I was scared about those times. Remember? I used to always tell you that my Mom died inside the bath? I always remembered that she died because of overheating. But I now remembered. (She began to cry.) Japanese soldiers came inside our home and held me, older sister, and Father down. And when they knew Mama was in the bathtub, they killed her there. The bath water became bloody. They stabbed*

*her again and again. They killed Mama for doing nothing wrong. Japanese*
*soldiers killed her…"*

A lump formed in my stomach and my throat. Tears welled up in my eyes. Mama was three or four years old at the time. That night, in the bath, she cut her finger, and when the blood moved through the water, it awakened the memory in her. I think that this was the first time in my young life that I became aware of the horrific history that Mama survived in China and Japan in World War II. And it links to my own existence as well. After this time, occasionally I would ask her about her childhood. She always found it painful to speak of, and would not elaborate too much. But she also seemed to appreciate my questions. I began to understand memory. That, more often than not, it was not a choice. Forgetting is a large part of our modern lives.

Over the years, I would ask her about her childhood, and she would diminish her own suffering. But she loved bathing. But the bath, for her, is not the same as it is for me. 目

## CHAPTER NOTES

1.  Theresa Hak Kyung Cha, *Dictee* (Berkeley: University of California Press, 2009). I love quoting her because her words are so appropriate to the text.

2.  From the song "Sometimes I feel like a Motherless Child" 時には母のない子のように by カルメン。マキ. based on the traditional Negro spiritual, "Motherless Child" by William E. Barton, D.D. (1899). Performed by the inimitable Carmen Maki in 1969, at the tender age of seventeen. It was one of the biggest hits in Japan during the 1960s.

3.  From the song "Rainy Days and Mondays" by Roger Nichols and Paul Williams (1971), performed by the Carpenters.

# CHAPTER 52

# Absence

Sometimes I am absent from myself.
Sometimes I feel there is a vacant place that cannot be filled.
Fulfilled. a pain vacancy.
Sometimes I don't feel. I know no-absence.
I long for something I cannot name.
Becoming memory before I am able to form Memory.
Bodies together in wombs.
Oh sister I long to see you.

*midnight shivers*
I swore I didn't want to be a father, continuing these things.

And as I became a lesser masculine
in the crucible of imperial masculinities
building chemical and hydrogen missiles and
killing dolphins wolves and polar bears ladybugs
African children rainforests mountains
salmon rivers and homeless poor

*wise men* on reservations
In glee, sorrow. Obedient nevertheless.

I look for the Ground they nurtured
others make that into malignant (dis)ease
My father mourns for his father       who
left him an endless sad.
Absences rip my eyes and make them blurred and colors faint.
and soon no longer     I long. I desire. I am absent from myself.

Mothers have tended to me and it becomes too much.
She must hurt me I think.

Residue of those longed for
in her life that she no longer can name.
In the end   Shiver. Lonely nights—perhaps
filled with someone's body that I think I love.

Yet I confess, I don't recognize this person.
I cannot name that absent Absent.
I grieve in the throes of passion. I know it is endless now.
How many fire bombings
from your bloated planes bodies?
did I cover you with

napalm
bodies in the A-bomb
Ukishima Maru       Trail of Tears     the
removal of my people from their lands and
into plantations and reservations jungles
corporations alcohol and crack
blankets of death,     my brothers hang
from trees,   make me predictably absent from
myself.
If you get rid of me. I will remain. There is no rid.
It lives in you.
Fragments displace the absence I feel. I long for absence.
I long for absence to end.
Shattered. Momentary moment.

Give me time to grieve the absence. Grieving. Cry the absence out?
give me time for grieving ancestors here,
longing. Eyes.
Fingernails. Toes. Belly buttons. Ears. Tongue Tastes. An Absence.

Is there time?

Is there time for me to cry. . . . . . for eons?
And when I do, and you do,  Can I live with you? 目

FREDRICK D. KAKINAMI CLOYD

In Memorium: Kiyoko Kakinami Cloyd, November 2, 1929 (?) to September 17, 2011. *Fredrick Cloyd Family Archive.*

# CHAPTER 53

# For Now

A BLACK JAPANESE MAN I MET at a literary reading in Seattle told me that for years, he told people he was Jamaican. It wasn't until he was twenty-eight years-old that he began telling people he was Black Japanese. He had not returned to Japan since he was an infant. He wanted to visit his mother's country, but he hadn't so far. He loved *tempura*, *sushi*, and *rāmen*, his only tangible connection with Japaneseness. He didn't speak Japanese. He always considered himself "black." For a while, his lack of interest in, or knowledge of, his Japanese heritage made me sick. Because he wasn't like me, a Black Japanese from Japan, my feelings toward him were a combination of mental colonization, and a lack of self acceptance and the diversity of Black Japanese lives. There's also the fact that men continually disconnect from their mothers' lives, a form of heterosexism and sexism, mixed with nationalism.

He was a nice guy, but for me he was just another person who doesn't know or really care about their heritage or history.

His mother was who, and what to him? His legacy was what, and for what? But this was arrogance and forgetting on my part. I had ignored my mother for so long, living my own life. I had also forgotten. When will this nightmare of an American self, its constant dislocation, and generations of resentment end?

### Going over my Notes

*The Japanese government "integrates" mixed-race babies into mainstream Japanese society after the war, but only if the father is "unknown" (unclaimed and not named). However, it's a double-edged sword. If American fathers are named, Japan rejects them as non-Japanese. If they are of single Japanese mothers, they are non-Japanese citizens. If they are claimed by a Japanese father, they are full Japanese citizens. Most Black Japanese babies, in this dynamic, are rejected by the Japanese, regardless of policies.*

*The McCarran-Walter Act of 1952 allows entry of biracial American-Japanese adopted children into the U.S., overriding the 1924 Racial Exclusion Act.*

*In Congressional hearings on the McCarran-Walter Act, Korean war babies, Japanese war orphans, and G.I babies were discussed.*

*The idea of "nationality," as Japanese, Korean, or American, was debated.*

*American Christian groups in the U.S., Korea and Japan become prominently involved in mixed American Asian baby issues.*

*James Finucane, Associate Secretary of the National Council for the Prevention of War during the 1950s, says, "American soldiers have fathered in almost every quarter of the globe an estimated 150,000 to 300,000 babies." He recommends the U.S. take responsibility and establish American paternity for these children.*

*From June 1953 to 2000, applications were received for the quota of "half-Japanese" children with 185 available slots allowed to immigrate to U.S. Average waiting period for eligibility screening was ten to twelve years. What happens to the others that don't make it?*

*The U.S. government does not want its racism and the proliferation of U.S. inattention to "war baby" issues to be a sore point in Cold War strategic discussions. Soviet criticism of American civil rights and racism could create "unstable" relations with Japan, Korea, and China. At the same time, the dominant U.S.. military and government view was that mixed-race babies were Japan's responsibility, or Korea's or the Philippines' or Okinawa's, not America's. Land replaces blood in these politics, while U.S. American laws contain nothing but the law in relation to discourses on "blood." Myself and Ritchie and the hundreds of thousands around the Pacific become convenient tools for the government's image in its march toward dominance.*

*In 2010, Brian Hjort, one of the most tireless workers reuniting American soldiers with their Vietnamese children, quits due to a lack of financial backing. He has said that between a near complete lack of financial support, hate mail, and threats, he couldn't keep it up anymore. However, as of this writing, the organization he founded (fatherfounded.org) continues to survive through the kind and tireless work of two or three others. Increasingly, requests by siblings of dead U.S. veterans seek the children their sibling fathered and orphaned.*

*The American Joint Committee was established as a smokescreen to research and publicize America's care for mixed-race children. It withheld publicity on its own existence until the "Japanese response" was established. The committee, however, arrogantly created policies that instructed the Japanese how to "deal properly" with mixed-race children.*

*Pearl S. Buck, famous for her work with mixed-race children from the 1930s through the 1990s, and credited with coining the term "Amerasian," is a strong proponent for U.S. responsibility for these children. She also states that in order to counteract anti-American attitudes in the Pacific during the Cold War, negative images of U.S. disinterest may be buffered by establishing certain protocols.*

*Many Japanese officials counteract American measures, citing America's racist legacy of refusing non-whites as reason the children would be better off in Japan. These officials were against the U.S. instructing the Japanese on how to handle mixed-race children, stating that they were intelligent enough to fashion their own policies. Kanzaki Kiyoshi warned that mixed-race children in Japan were becoming pawns in the political games between the U.S., Korea, Japan and Okinawa.[1] He warned that the issue of mixed-race children's population control was not an act of humanitarianism on America's part, but was part of their anti-Communist strategy. He warned that friendly gestures by the U.S. were not based on humanitarian global concern for Japanese, but on diplomatic calculation. Kanzaki further urged Japan to care for the mixed-race children as a way to truly become more cosmopolitan, generous, and open-minded beyond mere rhetoric. Editor Aoki Kei-Ichi in his editorial, "Konketsuji wa nihon-jin ka [Are Mixed bloods*

*Japanese?],"* states that Japanese should care for the mixed bloods themselves and to do so with pride so that Japan would "no longer have to listen to America's paternalistic instruction or slavishly wait for its aid to arrive." [2]

*Koga Yukiyoshi, a renowned sociopsychologist of the postwar period, criticized white societies for their emphasis on physiological and biological aspects of mixed bloods as a social problem. He called for more research on the development of prejudice (henken) and discrimination (sabetsu), and criticized pseudo-science in Japan where questionable links were made between genetics and misleading data, but are more about cultural construction. He resisted the predominant racial scientific notions and argued that blacks were not intellectually inferior, but were forced into lower socioeconomic realms that led to lower performances.*

*Americans were furious at some early films about Konketsuji. They were less concerned with how mixed-race children were portrayed, and were more furious at the negative portrayals of the U.S. military, even going so far as to call the films anti-American communist conspiracies.[3] Bertha and Harry Holt became famous in the United States in the post-Korean War period when they adopted mixed-race Korean children. They founded Holt International, which is still in operation today. The Holts believed that the Americans should be responsible for all of the babies in the world that U.S. military personnel abandon in Asia. Sometimes, the Holts are called the "founders of transnational adoption." Korea had the dubious distinction of being the country with the most outsourcing of mixed-race and orphaned Korean babies for decades. Even today, it is an issue. This is frequently discussed on the internet and in publications around Transnational and Cross-racial adoption.*

*Mixed-race issues become invisible and silent. The intensity of Japanese prejudice and discrimination against mixed bloods continued unabated. U.S. adoptions waned. Brazil became a hope for many Japanese officials while some believed mixed bloods should be sent to an island somewhere. Rumors of black market sales of mixed blood babies intensified in 1957.*

*The U.S. presence in the Pacific today is a massive, transnational apparatus that expands across five sovereign states and Micronesia. The U.S.-Pacific*

*Command is an integrated and covert organization, comprised of mobile forces on land, sea, and air, as well as through unseen and virtual technologies and physical bases. The states and nations within which this structure operate have nominal sovereignty and self-governance in relation to these systems, although, in most cases, U.S. personnel are not governed by any local laws.*

*In 2010, the International news group France24 offered a segment about mixed Katanga-Japanese babies that were taken away from their mothers at birth and killed by Japanese doctors who were then serving in the Congo. In the 1970s, Japan made a huge push to control some of the natural resources in Africa and sent many workers there. During this time, of course, relations were formed between Japanese men and the local women. In this France24 report, some of those mothers whose babies were killed, as well as surviving children, tell the world their stories.*

*Some sensational news reports and touching articles begin to proliferate in the 1970s on Amerasians. One movie, "キクとイサム Kiku and Isamu" (1959), wins a prestigious film award. It depicts a Black Japanese Amerasian brother and sister in their childhood village in the early 1950s. Other movies such as "人間の証明 Ningen no Shoumei (Proof of a Human Being)," which features Black Japanese themes, become large enough hits to warrant multiple remakes and long-running television series. Both of these movies were banned in the United States.*

*Some B-movie satires became huge successes. One very popular one featuring white-Japanese and Black Japanese were called "混血児リカ Konketsuji Rika," and another more serious movie named "合の子マリ Ainoko Mari," proving to be also a hit, with the part of the Black Japanese played by a Filipino girl.*

Although there was a virtual explosion of publications after the war, they were censored by SCAP. These magazines were checked for anything remotely oppositional to the U.S. Occupation and Americans. When reading became incredibly popular in Japan, Mama often read novels and short stories from different genres, hiding that she sometimes enjoyed writings by rebel women. She would read *Shōsetsu Shinchō* 小説新著 or *Josei Jishin* 女性自身, both publications that began shortly after the war and became leading magazines. Ideas of motherhood and family, and government and democracy, *à la America*, were often laid out in these pages. They were freeing for Mama, and many women like her. The confines of male social and interpersonal control under an ancient caste system and imperial forms of patriarchy became even more oppressive during the war years.

Yet the idea of women's subordination changed only slightly. Now it was democratic patriarchy she needed to resist in order to survive. Where could she belong?

One evening, while she laid in her bed reading, Mama called me over and read to me from her book, saying how much she admired these words: "In the beginning, women, in truth, were the sun. We were authentic human beings. Today, women are the moon. We live as dependents and simply reflect the light that emanates from another source. Our faces are pale blue, like the moon, like the sick." The passage was from *Seitō* (*Blue Stocking*) by *Hiratsuka Raichō* 平塚らいちょう, published in 1911.[5]

Up until then, I didn't know much about what she read. Sometimes, when she called me over, it was usually some funny pun or scene she came across that she would share with me. At other times, I didn't understand. The lines from Raichō surprised me. Both she and I admired those lines together. I felt those lines to be not just about women, but about all people who toil in this world who understand resistance against the norm has become more difficult, and how we often do not recognize ourselves or our violence under dominant forces. It was a statement about how we may not even recognize how slavish we have become in our self-definitions — as individuals, systems, cultural groups, and nations. The collisions of our lives in globalization create feelings of falsity because we may not understand how connected we are in history, connected through the lens of war, battles, division, and dominance.

Mama often felt she needed distance. I have felt that too. My twin sister's absence marks her presence. Mama's sisters, her mother, her daughter, her grandfather, her father — could all be considered premature deaths, and are my ancestral ghosts. Those on the Trail of Tears who died for justice for their communities, are my ghosts. As I consider our mortality, I can't help but think of how absences must be made apparent and spoken for, for those who are no longer here, for ideas that were banned, burned or sequestered. This condition isn't only lonely or longing. It is also honoring, forgiving, and acknowledging those which weren't permitted — then and now. More and more, we learn the impossible, and keep it alive. If it is held away, hidden, or killed, freedom is dead. There are also those things that masquerade as that freedom.

Mama is now in an elderly facility in Albuquerque. No Japanese people there, except for when I telephone her to talk, when I can afford it. She tells me she has forgotten. She tells me so much she wants to forget. She tells me it is too painful to remember anything, even the most cherished memories. She is lonely. She doesn't understand what she is doing in the world. I tell her that I must write about her to the world. It is something I must do so that her life becomes preserved in a world that would erase her.

*My mother and I crossed the Pacific on an unknown journey. My father had to come across it first in order for this to happen. The water is vast, and yet it comprises so much of our own bodies.*

## September 17, 2011

MAMA DIES IN HOSPICE after being sent from her Senior Care facility.

I was there, holding her hand.

I cried for hours with my head on her chest, which was no longer heaving from her slow breaths. Soon, the warmth would leave her.

She had died from neglect at the elder facility. I am now running an investigation to hold those responsible accountable.

I apologized to her before she died, over and over, for being such a terrible son, who could not do anything for her. She died in a world foreign to her.

*Her dreams died with her.*

## Today

MAMA APPEARS SOMETIMES. In dreams. In the fragrance of puffy steamed rice with *misoshiru* and *tempura* that the waitress brings. *Tears.*

Or when I glance at the stuffed koala bear and cub that I have in my room, sitting on top of a stack of books. The stuffed koala was one of the few things Mama had by her bedside in the elder care facility. Now it is Mama, by proxy.

I'm a bit sad today, and decide to eat some Vietnamese food at Tu Lan on 6th Street. The folks there are fantastic and the food is great. It has that old Asian feel that reminds me of old Japanese restaurants Mama and I frequented on the side streets in Ōme, my place of birth. I sometimes talk with two of the Vietnamese Amerasian cooks who work there, as well as the evening manager, a young Vietnamese man in his thirties. On this day, as I waited for my food, I could only glance at people's shoes as they sat at the counter by the door or squeezed past me in the narrow entryway.

I was a bit startled as the young manager came up to me and asked me what was wrong.

"My mother died recently. So I'm just getting by these days."

He said, kindly, "Today's meal is on me. Your mother's Asian, isn't she?" I told him that she was Japanese and Chinese mixed.

He winked at me and smiled, handing me my order. "I understand. We are immigrants and we understand our mothers. Take care and you don't pay today."

I walked out into the cool afternoon air and tears flowed, a mixture of gratitude and sadness. It gave me further inspiration to work on widening the possibilities of this book. 目

Mama and me in Albuquerque, 2010. *Fredrick Cloyd Family Archive.*

# CHAPTER NOTES

1.  See Kanzaki Kiyoshi, "Shiro to Kuro—Nichi-Bei Konketsuji no Chôsa Hôkoku," in *Fujin Kôron* (1953): 139. Kiyoshi (1904-1979) was a well-known and highly respected social activist, critic and reporter in the Shōwa period (1926-1989).

2.  See Yukiko Koshiro, *Trans-Pacific Racisms and the U.S. Occupation of Japan* (NY: Columbia University Press, 1999); and Walter Hamilton, *Children of the Occupation: Japan's Untold Story* (NJ: Rutgers University Press, 2013), for a look at some of the discussions on the issue of mixed-race children during the U.S. Occupation (1945-1952).

3.  Hiratsuka Raichō (平塚 らいてう)(1886-1971) was a writer, journalist, Marxist activist, feminist, anarchist, who established 青鞜 *Seitō (Blue Stocking)* in 1899 the first feminist magazine in Japan. After she graduated from Tōkyō Women's University in 1903, she began a women's movement that survives to this day. Constantly surveilled and attacked during her lifetime, she protested, wrote, and lectured until her death. My segment is from the first issue of *Blue Stocking* is quoted in the introduction of the emotionally moving English language collection edited by Mikiso Hane, *Reflections on the Way to the Gallows: Rebel Women in Prewar Japan* (Berkeley: University of California Press, 1993).

4.  This poem was previously published in a slightly shorter version in *Kartika Review,* Issue 12, Spring 2012. Note: In the Japanese Language: Vow, promise. Without Kanji characters and written in hiragana or katakana, this can have the meanings "near, close" as well as "attic." "Chikai" means: a promise, a vow, nearness, closeness, the attic (things put above and kept as a memento or hidden), historical and personal continuities, relics, secrets, baggage, preciousness.

5.  *Seitō (Blue Stocking)* by Hiratsuka Raichō 平塚らいちょう, published in *Kartika Review*, no. 12 (2012)

# CHAPTER 54

# For Kiyoko, Epitaph/Chikai

Mama's silent hand in mine
we remember
traverse
history's ten million wars.

Her last breath
passes through me
survival's constant fire.

I, her Occupier's baby

tremble in black yellow
through tombs
ancient colors
falling
bombs
Mama
persimmon blossoms.

Time after time
Kiyoko becomes
sword
desire
wounds
rain. 目

391

# Afterword

"The problem after a war is the victor. He thinks he has just proved that war and violence pay. Who will now teach him a lesson?"

A.J. Muste, Former Chair of Fellowship of Reconciliation (1926-29)[1]

THE QUESTION IS WHETHER THE VICTORIOUS—nation or citizen—will continue to commit violence upon people and communities in the name of good, with or without remorse. As someone who writes, presents, consults, and mediates, I have wrestled with these behaviors as they relate to self in society, especially the impact of words and actions that influence thinking and motivate social change. Always challenged, I prepared for this struggle, strategizing in a specific way. I grounded my book in stories about the domestic and mundane, in order to scrutinize the Pacific and how it decides who should live or die (the necropolitical),[2] as well as the internalized nationalisms that construct my identities.

Once I wrote the book, a different struggle unfolded. In some ways, it involved more important work for me to do, which operated within the liminal space between words, moments, and images I shared and the responses I received from people as they grappled with their own thoughts and ideas. These responses gave rise to possibilities that confronted, challenged, engaged, affirmed, questioned, and attacked me, as well as the subject matter as I traversed within a specific channel of memory few people are willing to access, much less attend to.

Although some of the stories and issues were specific, such as traditions like the honor killings of mothers of Amerasian babies in Korea, Japan, and Vietnam, and often linked with some of my family stories with wider stories that joined across the Pacific, it required me to prioritize and listen to the voices both within and outside of myself. Intervening within this ongoing phenomenon in the present-day, is the survival of identities around the world, which challenged me to write, to reveal, to break silences and open constructed realities.

For instance, in March 2015, a Black Japanese woman, Ariana Miyamoto, was voted Miss Universe Japan, and caused a national stir.[3] It caused some Japanese to further align themselves with deeply racist and nationalistic tendencies: *oh she's not Japanese, this year's Miss Universe Japan is not "truly" representative of the Japanese people.* They cried it was unfair. I have personally heard these things about *hāfu* (mixed Japanese) my entire life and in particular, about dark-skinned people like me. This deep-rooted insularity and racism has been a part of Japan's history dating back to at least 1639, when the ruling Tokugawa shogunate cut Japan off from the rest of the world. This nationalism continued when Commodore Matthew C. Perry forced open Japan's doors, granting his sailors access to interact with Japanese and Okinawan women, leaving mixed-race children in their wake, an interaction that heightened during World War II and the Korean War. This ideology about the purity of race has spread throughout Southeast Asia, which today, has become part of this unbroken thread of nationalism. Though centuries have passed, the ideas of racial superiority and separatism (which is ingrained both psychologically and socioculturally) remain deeply influential in Japan's mindset. The sympathy the dominant tries to attract as it bemoans Miyamoto's rise as a national Japanese figure by questioning her Japaneseness because she has brown skin, is the crux of this issue.

Of course I feel no sympathy for their tears since they come from a socially-acceptable and agreed-upon dominant position. However, I do feel sad that they have so totally immersed themselves in a singular Japanese identity that excludes diversity. If one cannot see how this developed, one cannot effectively bring change. For instance, some people, through social media, attack Japanese people for their "racism," which is laughable, when nations such as the United States, Britain, and the Netherlands can hardly be absolved for their racist actions and policies.

So it is not surprising that Miyamoto, along with others in China and Korea, are offering a kind of Pan-East Asian resistance to the oppression of people based on physiognomy, color, and race. South Korea, for example, has faced backlash for their continual presentations of blackface on national television, just as in Japan. In 2013, after repeated denials and claims of ignorance by the Korean broadcast industry, a petition circulated on the Internet that received broad attention, as if to say, "Hey, this matters!"[4] But again, even as American forms of blackness that allege an "urban African American" identity proliferate in Asia, it is still "black." It remains to be seen if any actions will be taken as a result of the visibility of South Korean or Japanese anti-black racism in entertainment circles. Let us bear in mind that this is not total. There are those Koreans and Japanese who still fight and struggle to change this idea of nationalism, as it pertains to culture and race in Japan and Asia.

Mixed-race-ness in a global mono-racializing system, is not only about legal state policies, personal prejudices and violence. It also speaks to ghosts over and over again, a silence we don't often know or see. In 1999, stories began to appear in Japanese and non-Japanese books and articles about the Negishi Foreign General Cemetery in Yokohama, Japan where over 800 mixed-race babies are buried in unmarked secret graves.[5] Most of them were aborted fetuses or murdered babies born to local women and the Occupation soldiers, as well as some who died of starvation and illness. The locals, who were aware of these forgotten unmarked graves, wanted to set up a memorial in the mothers' and children's memory, but the local government refused to do so. Facts about the cemetery were altered to cover-up the real story about these babies. Yet news of the memorial grew, along with the popularity of an urban legend centered around a ghostly woman's figure that visited the graves at night, which became the impetus behind a book and a movie called 天使はブルーズを歌う〜横浜アウトサイドストーリー (*Angels Sing the Blues: Yokohama Outside Story*).

[6] It was only recently, and at the insistence of the locals that the city approved the memorial, but with the stipulation it could reap a financial benefit through tourism. So while the silencing of the lives and histories of mixed-race babies and their mothers continue to produce ghosts, the refusal to allow such things to happen continues.

This is why Miyamoto's aim to promote diversity, which shifts the xenophobic and racist ideologies embedded in old nationalisms, is so important because it reveals transnational interactions of unspoken conditions and forces. Her determination to run for the title and work for a more inclusive Japan came after her close friend, who was biracial, committed suicide. Among the disconcerted Japanese, there were many who publicly called for Miyamoto to be heard, who believed it was time for Japan to reexamine its practices and concepts of identity and culture. What impact she has in the long-term remains to be seen.

≋ ≋ ≋

IN 2014, DAD CONTACTED ME to reconnect, to rekindle our relationship. Although he lived in Texas, twice a year he comes to San Francisco and we eat meals together and have small conversations—nothing too extended. The first meetings were cordial and friendly, except when he would talk about Mama. Whenever he did this, I felt he had no right to criticize her, especially when he talked about her years after he divorced her and no longer lived with her. He had ideas of what I thought or didn't think, which were all erroneous from my point of view. However, I was somewhat surprised at how quickly he divulged what might be from his own guilt at not being a good husband or dad.

When Dad and I talk and I reveal a thought or behavior he does not approve of or agree with that presents a distance between Japaneseness and blackness, he says such things like, "You're your mother's child." When he says this I am reminded of how gender, race and nation are intertwined in these statements. Don't get me wrong, I do not think our differences need to be reconciled. Only from a dominant assimilationist, hetero-monogamist, American position would someone expect a father and son to completely understand each other and have no differences between them. These fantasies have not been, nor will they ever become an aspect of my being. Our differences are but one to glide on, climb over, and rediscover, with an understanding that some of them will never be understood. My dad was not a Black Japanese child in postwar Japan. I was not a soldier in the segregated U.S. military. But there are similarities we share, like certain aspects about being a man, being black, being an outsider, being a citizen, and enacting justice. There is a sadness in our relationship, built from living in realities created by maintaining nations and hierarchies, and internalizing these ideas of dominant societies. I often ask why he says such things, and he would reflect on what he said and sometimes re-think it. Sometimes he would begin with "I guess I'm being macho." Very interesting indeed.

He has begun to catch himself on the spot, change his mind and even sometimes apologize. This has been one of his best traits. He listens. He re-thinks. But first, we had to agree for him to never talk negatively about Mama in any way. He agreed.

The crevices created by years lost are not considered a loss. Perhaps because there wasn't much to miss, since Dad was gone for most of my life. Mama and I were tight, difficult as it had been. Although he was my father, I had not established any strong bond with him. When Dad said to me at one point, "I should've never left you and Mama,"

I laughed. When he was around, it wasn't very pleasant. Sometimes yes, but rarely. Dad laughed too, and acknowledged I might be right. Compared to many families I've known, ours was pretty normal, but the historical conditions of the times, the different cultures from which we emerged and our positions within them had created a distance that we each lived out, separately.

Among so many Black Japanese people I've known, their lives and experiences are diverse. There is no Black Japaneseness to call upon when it comes to this experience, except when we communicate about certain intercultural issues such as food, language, and how we relate with one another. My mother, being sort of a rebel from the upper class, had completely different notions of reality and chose to live her life differently from many of the other mixed-Japanese mothers I have known. Many of them were more entrenched in the dominant Japanese mainstream identity and thought of life as such. Endless differences exist in all people's lives, but as Black Japanese, as *hapa*, as Mixed-Japanese, or *hāfu*, we are a politically-made anomaly—an identity within a hierarchy.

I asked him about his time in Japan and Korea during the 1950s and 1960s, Vietnam, and his feelings about women and racism. It has been an incredible time of listening, where I have found myself changing my mind about him by allowing him to become a fuller personality and influence in my life. His comparisons between Korean and Japanese women remained, as did his positive memories of his Vietnam days, like when his bosses looked kindly upon him because of his empathy toward the South Vietnamese villagers and their trust in him, earned after bringing them shoes after seeing their bloodied feet when they led American soldiers to safety in the jungles.

He knew nothing of the massacres ordered by the American occupiers on Jeju-do Island in Korea, but said, "I wouldn't doubt that one bit." By then, he said, he had grown weary of white commanders in the military. This, in many ways, continued his need to find humanity in all people everywhere, but at the same time, reaffirmed his dissatisfaction with white supremacy. His love of Japanese and African culture remains intact and he speaks fondly about different cultures. But he also knew of the many troubles his buddies in the military had who married Japanese or Korean women after the war. For me, these revelations connected many of the stories in my father's life with my own, and with strangers I began meeting at my public presentations on the Black Pacific.

≋ ≋ ≋

AT A RECENT READING, I noticed four white males about my age in a sea of mostly non-white bodies watching me as I stepped down from the stage. As I gathered my belongings, one approached me. I sensed a reticence and tension about him. After a few moments, he thanked me for a thought-provoking presentation and then asked me if I would lend an ear for something he had on his mind.

"My father died a few months ago. He served in the Occupation of Japan and Korea, and when he died, the last words he said to me, his only living son, was that he had a half-Japanese daughter somewhere in Japan and always wanted to know if she was all right."

I remained silent, trying to assess why he felt it necessary to share this with me. "What do you think of this?" I asked him. I wondered how he was feeling, what he was thinking, and what questions this news provoked in him.

In 2011, a group of Black Japanese and Black Okinawans from the U.S. and U.K. gathered around Jero (fourth from the right), who is an American popular Enka (traditional Japanese 'blues' genre) singer popular in Japan whose mother is Black Japanese Amerasian, for a photo together at a hāfu conference at University of California Berkeley. I am second from the left. *Fredrick Cloyd Family Archive.*

His father had died without any further explanation. I'm sure he would have rather heard that his father loved him instead of this confession: a family betrayal, a mystery, anger, emptiness, relief.

A jovial and husky black man, who looked about a decade older than me, came up to me at that moment, along with what looked to be his Japanese wife and two children—a boy and a girl. Before anyone could interrupt, I wanted to ask further about his "white man's burden."

"Do you want to look for her? Is there any emotion about it, or maybe you're feeling not-so-great because of what your father told you? I hope you are doing okay."

His eyes welled with tears. But his expression remained still, distant.

"No, I don't feel any need to go look for her. I wouldn't know where. I don't even know how to feel about it, much less what I feel about her." He trailed off and couldn't say more. Perhaps he was still in shock and couldn't really acknowledge any particular feeling. Or he didn't know how to articulate the desolation he felt at that moment. Perhaps he refuses to feel. The privilege of distance and normalized alienation along with the history with his father—how should one respond to such silences? Especially one generated by a secret his father placed within the web of their particular nuclear family. His father is one of perhaps millions of fathers who have already experienced this, or experience this now, throughout ages of conquest, takeover, governance, weaponization, loneliness, entitlement, and sex.

At this moment, I felt uncomfortable, wondering what happened to this mixed-Japanese baby girl who grew up in Japan. And what of her mother who gave birth to this man's baby and was abandoned? What, exactly, were the circumstances? I wished I could feel empathetic, given how much I understood his plight. I understood that listening could be the most powerful tool, and that solutions aren't always apparent. I am constantly reminded that so many stories join, link, and echo across time and space, across generations, cultures, nations, and intimacies, like ocean waves.

≈ ≈ ≈

IN A HEGEMONIC AND MILITARIZED PACIFIC, how do we create alliances and solidarities in our struggle for liberation? Memory results from encounters between an individual, larger forces, and time. Dreams persist. As I review my book now, I am reminded of how text operates in imparting this reality, as well as how it fails—as it often does. Personal ideas of how to live a life of social justice connects with larger cultural patterns and positions, oppressions and directed currents of so-called progress (whether from the center of power outward, or looking inward).

In 2011, then-U.S. Secretary of State Hillary Clinton evoked a dream (a political tool) of "The Pacific Century" that sought to continue the European trade wars which began in the sixteenth century. On February 4, 2016, in Auckland, New Zealand, President Barack Obama signed into law the Trans-Pacific Partnership (TPP),[7] which awaits ratification. In some way, these acts continue the work of the Bandung Conference, and the unaligned movements that followed. However, they diverge greatly from a "Partnership" on one main point: that, once again, the United States and Europe have made themselves and their privileged entitlements central to the future of the Pan-Pacific, Asian, and indigenous peoples by positioning themselves as the leaders. What "agreements" had been made? Who benefits? Who has a seat at the negotiator's table? Is there equal access, inclusion, or the freedom to adopt other forms and processes?

The *Pacific*—an American word—is nothing but an object of a neocolonial game. I wanted to share the events I and others have experienced in the ongoing struggle against disempowerment. Intergenerational time, whether we are aware of it or not, is where oppression and liberation are born. When I link processes of Black-Amerasian identity and life-making, this unacknowledged and untold Pacific history reveals itself, and it was my intention to engage readers in linking identity relations to social justice. The Black Pacific has become salient.

Social justice is not about balancing the scales or joining the ranks of the privileged and becoming "equal." It is about the acknowledgement of incommensurable differences and negotiating these conflicts in order to be able to live with dignity side-by-side on "unequal" terms. Nowadays, this is not normal thinking. It is not normal even though it has been made this way. We have placed everything on hierarchies, creating emotional and spiritual necessities, capturing, fracturing, exploiting, and cannibalizing systems and cultures, creating a need for militarism and defense. Being in this vacuum becomes a normal state. A dream state—a spectacle.[8]

But life does not happen in a vacuum.

There is no life without history and historical relations of power.

*So this book could not possibly present all of these links and actions.*

The need to homogenize, co-opt, assimilate, and annihilate is inserted into relationships among various people, groups, and institutions that interrupt those connections by inserting hierarchies of language and ideas. Can't we permit our differences to exist? Writing with scholars and artists, I became acutely aware of how people and their responses changed according to the sociopolitical climate or their relationship between communities and generations.

Mixed-race movements have also expanded in the United States. Being a person presumed to be "mixed" in nation, color, race, and other ways, people assume I have the same issues and concerns as other mixed-race people. The personal, cultural, and global have become linked. In my book, I worked carefully to show how racial formations of histories were grafted onto me to pre-form an assumed identity of either Japanese or black, or a confused integration of both. Because race and nation-states are fictions of territorial imperialism, themselves histories of invasion and cross-cultural integration between generations, everyone who identifies as an unmarked monoracial identity may not be monoracial. Everyone has multiple heritages and cultures and, as far as I am concerned, I do not fit the criteria of being mixed-race as far as dominant notions go. For example, many people who identify as mixed-race speak of national and cultural confusion about who they are. I never struggled with this existential question. So if we only attend to what is dominant in society and our lives, or what is appealing and "important," then won't we repeat these mistakes of perception and identity construction? It's like the exchange between the two main characters in *Hiroshima Mon Amour*: "You know nothing."

Liberatory possibilities open up when they are not placed in a morally superior position that assumes upward mobility is an escape, especially when dealing with issues of identity. Opening up is not about dislocating assumptions in a vacuum, or making bad or primitive language disappear. I wanted to use history to point out power relations of cultural and social change, and push at the dominant narratives we have internalized about people and communities; opening up a space of resistance to domination especially among the many marginalized communi-

Storefront in Japan promoting the release of the DVD for the popular cartoon characters in *Ufu and Mufu: The Cute Little Twins' Big Adventures*. Blackface was introduced by Commodore Perry to the Japanese in 1854 and continues today, appearing in the form of anime, dolls, pennants, and other assorted forms of marketing and with pop artists. *Photo courtesy of Robert Steven Moorehead, Copyright © 2011.*

ties who struggle for dominance among themselves (what diversity consultants often call Oppression Olympics, which looks at the ways communities claim "we suffer more than you do"). To combat disturbance, to make things "peaceful," nation-states engage in many strategies that prioritize their own demands instead of those of their communities. It is not that nation-states do not desire peace; they do not wish to confront the necessary priorities and contradictions arising from the multiplicity of unaligned binary and singular realities, which they seek to control.

≋ ≋ ≋

IN THE EARLY 1990S, Australian Prime Minister Paul Keating became the first high official in Australia to formally apologize to the Aborigine and Torres peoples for anti-Aboriginal policies in a moving speech at Redfern.[9] In 1997, a report entitled "Bringing Them Home: The 'Stolen Children'," was published.[10] These events pushed many to change structural practices in government, especially those Australians grappling with histories of identity-making. The 2000 Sydney Olympics made Australia's commitment to Aboriginal liberation and Australia's "black liberation" supposedly visible. Yet all of this could be seen as a smokescreen. As a failure. At the Sydney Olympics, for instance, there were numerous protests by more than 600 distinct Aboriginal groups, each unhappy with being used for Australia's public glory while violence and discrimination persisted, including ongoing displacement and the impoverishment of thousands of Aboriginal peoples in order to construct the Olympic facilities.[11] And yes, even the *National Sorry Day* celebrated in March every year, which became an indigenous holiday following Rudd's speech, couldn't hide those facts. In 2013, research revealed the rise in the killing of Aborigines, directly and indirectly, while they were in police custody; the issue intensified in 2015,[12] much like the United States' rising debate over the Black Lives Matter and Native American movements.

As West Papua in New Guinea continues to reel under the violent subjugation of Indonesian rule, Australian, U.S., Asian, and Dutch links to these events are mostly hidden from view or ignored by the public. Any Papuans resisting the nation-state are labeled "rebels" and "terrorists," and are imprisoned or killed. Even as a report published by the Asian Human Rights Commission reiterated the impact of scorched-earth policies and ethnic cleansing in the name of modernizing the economy on indigenous Papuans, such terror still goes relatively unnoticed by most people around the world.[13]

Additionally, Fiji is working to change its national flag as new leadership has voted to dislodge British colonial emblems from their national symbol. After decades of coups and betrayals, many of the smaller countries in the Pacific allied with greater powers, such as the United States, in order to survive, leashing themselves to the destiny of those nations and serving agendas of those larger nations. This movement to revise the flag proves to be another smokescreen within the already transformed nation, but is still at the same time, liberatory.

On Jeju Island in Korea, daily protests have continued since the Korean War. Okinawa too maintains intermittent protests since the end of the Asia-Pacific War. In both cases, the United States, Korean and Japanese governments are targets of critical engagement and protest. Okinawans struggle with both Japanese and U.S. governments that have suppressed Okinawan voices, have made decisions that do not take them into consideration, and remain unaccountable for their actions. There are ongoing joint protests as well among Okinawans and South Koreans against

U.S. military base actions. In one particular alliance, Okinawan and South Korean Amerasians abandoned by their American fathers met in 2002.[14]

These forms of national and cultural identity oppression play out across individual lives in similar ways. I have known Amerasians from Japan, Korea, Vietnam, Cambodia, and the Philippines who routinely cut themselves (usually on the wrists and forearms). Some wanted to know their fathers, but could not find them, or had discovered their fathers passed away. Others were rejected after crossing the ocean following years and years of saving money. Others were bound to subjugation by the traffickers that paid their passage to America or Europe. Still others hated their fathers and wanted to go out on their own in the United States to forge new lives. Others became quite successful after working hard at learning English. Still others were unable to improve their English, so they were forced to work menial jobs. One woman contacted me about coming to a presentation, but was unable to attend because her boss wouldn't let her off. That particular woman praised me for what I was doing, but felt what I proposed was impossible because people do not care about Amerasians.

It is assumed that hierarchies are in place and their operations are a fixed reality. Patriarchy is not about inferior morality. It is a term that defines a ubiquitous system, which is not exclusively masculine. Yet masculinity is one thread to explore how patriarchy assumes its privilege in our world, further shaped by culture and everyday meanings. [15]

≋ ≋ ≋

THE ESTRANGEMENT WITH MY FATHER began long before my parents' divorce in the 1980s. There was a distance between him and my mother and I, which had to do with his position as a Black-American military occupier in Japan, in relation to my mother and me, who lived there and had to contend with life in the climate of the postwar. My father's life was in a segregated military that was psychologically divorced from Japanese life. This does not include the various oppressions related to the black experience he experienced in different ways across two different countries. Martin Luther King Jr. meant something to him. Only my mother meant something to me, with no other obvious historical anchor with my own *mixedness*. Blackness in Japan was not the same as being "black" in America. In learning about Black-American history later in life, it remains outside of me, with trajectories of political positioning and baggage from that history having not much to do with me, just as much as *Anpō, Manshū, Senryō* and *yakeato*, have nothing to do with black history. But all of these things have formed me. What conditions ensue? Well, for one thing, both Americans and Japanese will refer to African American and Japanese stereotypes and general cultural definitions as a way to respond to me and those like me and Miss Miyamoto. Or else they try to "ignore" cultural difference by hollowing it out to create a sameness. Very invisiblizing. The distance carries and invents the dreams we create for ourselves. And the dream carries the distance.

≋ ≋ ≋

I SEEK TO TELL STORIES OF UNHEARD THOUGHTS AND HISTORIES, to archive as resistance to the forgetting encouraged by dominating nation-states. What is unseen and marginalized, violated and made violable, while militaries and nations flex their muscle in displays of masculinity? How do relations between nations go forward? Is it only a binary reaction that either supports or opposes the people? In our everyday interactions with each other, do we push this binary forward?

When the Chinese government opened its first foreign military installation in Djibouti, Africa, in November 2015,[16] with the world growing suspicious and fearful of the "Guam Killer" missile,[17] what happened to the people in Guam and the Pacific? Or Africa? The centrality of Guam and the Marshall Islands cannot be trivialized in the face of strategies seeking to displace U.S.-Asian hegemony in the Pacific. After all, these were the sites of the atomic and hydrogen bomb tests, which were conducted at the dismay of the locals, who were not consulted. But, for an uninformed public, Chinese weaponry threatens U.S.-Asian "democratic" dominance. (That is not to say that China does not also want to dominate.) Between the ignorance of history and education in nations, the naturalization of power struggle, and the need for change, cultures and people proceed to survive for different reasons, with oppression central yet invisible. How does this survival enact itself? How can these survivals be recorded and recognized without repeating the ghettoization that happens when writing about non-dominant people in history?

I grappled with this question during a conference in September 2015 at UC Berkeley: "Koreans and Camp-towns: Mixed-race Adoptees and Camptown Connections." It was a powerful, moving event attended by a mix of scholars of Korean history and ethnic studies, Korean camptown activists, orphanage organizers, Korean political leaders, and mixed-race Koreans, many of whom were adoptees out of Korea to the United States. Nearly 60 percent of the audience were adoptees from Korean orphanages, adopted during the post-Korean war period. Over half of those present were of Black Korean descent. Among the diverse group of scholars there, we discussed the possibilities of creating a Pan-Amerasian movement as a strategy to bring many of these issues to light.

There were many tears shed. Many had not seen each other in decades; adoption directors from Korea, now elderly, were present and searching for those they sent to America. Through interpreters, the directors gave passion-ate and tearful presentations, speaking directly to the adoptees they had not seen since they were children. While transnational adoption resulted in happy lives for many of them, they still understood their own displacement and shared intense stories about their lives.

Stories of patriarchal threats to "not speak with their mothers in Korea" or of having no connection to Korean-ness were plenty. For these histories, almost all the adoptees experienced dissonance and a longing to differentiate themselves from their adoptive parents. Some of the parents welcomed the change. Others threw them out of the house, while others came to understand their adoptive children's needs over the years after much struggle. The sto-ries were not mine, yet they were so familiar. What was this connection? I attempted to excavate this in my book, although problematically. Words are reality.

Of course there were a few awkward moments that, to be honest, I expected to happen more frequently. One Korean mixed person told me that he was not interested in Pan-Amerasianism because he hates the Japanese and they can't be trusted. I attempted to intervene by saying that not all people mimic what they learn from their parents, and while prejudice and hatred might be a bone of contention between children and their parents, it needs to be cut away, no matter how painful. I do not know what effect these words had on him. When I think of these kinds of estrangements, I think of my own, configured differently but living most expressively in our inter-relationships and worldviews. For everyone, this cannot be avoided. Lives are constructed in a world.

≋ ≋ ≋

ALL OF THIS FLOATS AND MOVES through the conditions of our times, whatever they are. Color and gender, flags and weapons, lullabies and runaways, all form the stories we tell ourselves. Dream of peace. Dream of power. Dream of what is not here. Dream of what is gone. The waters are life. They dream us. What do we do with dreams?

I take this all as the *Dream of the Water Children,* ongoing. ≋

Dreaming in my Uncle's garden, circa 1962 in Shakudō. *Fredrick Cloyd Family Archive.*

# CHAPTER NOTES

1.  "Statement of 1941," as quoted in Harold Zinn's books, *A People's History* (Harper Perennial, 1980), 416, and *The Twentieth Century : A People's History* (Harper Perennial, 2003), 159.

2.  An outgrowth from Michel Foucault's oft-discussed term "biopolitics," the term necropolitics was coined by Achille Mbembe, and it concerns the politics of the control of social killing and death. Achille Mbembe, "Necropolitics," *Public Culture* 15, no. 1 (2003): 11-40, accessed January 21, 2017, https://docs.google.com/file/d/0B2ImKVpIaKl2V0dMNDVJVFlha0k/edit

3.  There are several articles about Ariana Miyamoto in the U.S., Japanese, and international press. For an introduction, see, *The Japan Times,* accessed January 21, 2017, http://www.japantimes.co.jp/tag/ariana-miyamoto.

4.  For example, see the petition to the South Korean broadcasting companies (now closed) on this matter: https://www.change.org/p/south-korean-broadcasting-companies-to-end-the-use-of-blackface-on-korean-television, accessed January 21, 2017.

5.  Most articles on the Negishi Foreign General Cemetery (http://www.yfgc-japan.com/history_e.html ) are in Japanese. Here is one in English, *Japan Times,* acccessed August 29, 2017, http://www.japantimes.co.jp/news/1999/08/25/national/headstones-mark-yokohama-haunt-for-the-unknown/#.WMYFJ1BtkUF. Here is also an article on the KanaLoco Website about the G.I. Baby graves in Japanese: http://www.kanaloco.jp/article/114888, acccessed August 29, 2017.

6.  山崎洋子。 天使はブルーズを歌う〜横浜アウトサイドストーリー *Angels Sing the Blues: Yokohama Outside Story* by Yoko Yamazaki. Mainichi Shimbun. October 1999.

7.  "Text of the Trans-Pacific Partnership," New Zealand Department of Foreign Affairs and Trade. November 5, 2015, accessed January 21, 2017, http://tpp.mfat.govt.nz/text

8.  This word can be taken both as the dictionary definition, and how Guy Debord uses it in *The Society of the Spectacle (La société du spectacle)* (NY: Zone, 1994).

9.  Former prime minister's Paul Keating Speech: *The Redfern Address* (1992) ABC News Australia video accessed January 21, 2017, http://www.abc.net.au/archives/80days/stories/2012/01/19/3415316.htm and transcript, accessed January 21, 2017, http://media1.aso.gov.au/docs/Redfern_Speech10121992.pdf.

10. *Bringing them Home: the 'Stolen Children,'* prepared and published by the Australian Human Rights Commission, accessed January 21,2017, http://www.humanrights.gov.au/our-work/aboriginal-and-torres-strait-islander-social-justice/publications/bringing-them-home-stolen

11. See, for example, Patrick Barkham, "Divided we fall," *Guardian News*, September 13, 2000, accessed January 21, 2017, http://www.theguardian.com/sydney/story/0,7369,367879,00. html, while the whitewashed version reported in another British news source silences the issues while glorifying the single unitary state, Mike Corder, "Olympics gave indigenous Australians their biggest ever stage," *The Independent (U.K.),* October 1, 2000, accessed January 21, 2017, http://www.independent.co.uk/news/world/australasia/olympics-gave-indigenous-australians-their-biggest-ever-stage-634982.html.

12. See Martin Cuddihy, "Aboriginal deaths in custody numbers rise sharply over past five years," *The World Today,* May 24, 2013, accessed January 21, 2017, http://www.abc.net.au/news/2013-05-24/sharp-rise-in-number-of-aboriginal-deaths-in-custody/4711764. Also see Eddie Cubillo, "Aboriginal deaths in custody: NT's 'paperless arrest' police powers need urgent review" *The Age,* May 31, 2015, accessed January 21, 2017, http://www.theage.com.au/comment/aboriginal-deaths-in-custody-nts-paperless-arrest-police-powers-need-urgent-review-20150531-ghdf8u. html.

13. *The Neglected Genocide, Human rights abuses against Papuans in the Central Highlands, 1977–1978* by the Asian Human Rights Commission Human Rights and Peace for Papua (ICP), 2013, accessed January 21, 2017, http://freewestpapua.org/wp-content/uploads/2013/10/AHRC_TheNeglected_Genocide-lowR.pdf. See also Duncan Roden, "West Papua: Report details genocide by Australian-backed occupiers Indonesian forces breakup a protest by West Papuans in 2011," *Green Left Weekly,* October 28, 2013, accessed January 21, 2017, https://www.greenleft.org.au/node/55243.

14. "Amerasians of Japan, South Korea to meet in Okinawa," *The Japan Times,* accessed January 21, 2017, http://www.japantimes.co.jp/news/2002/08/15/national/amerasians-of-japan-south-korea-to-meet-in-okinawa/#.VojEYSfdz18

15. See Cynthia Enloe, "Masculinity As Foreign Policy Issue" in *Foreign Policy in Focus* 5, no. 36 (2000).

16. Jane Perlez and Chris Buckleynov, "China Retools Its Military With a First Overseas Outpost in Djibouti," in *The New York Times,* November 26, 2015, accessed January 21, 2017 http://www.nytimes.com/2015/11/27/world/asia/china-military-presence-djibouti-africa.html

17. See for example, Wendell Minnick, "China's Parade Puts US Navy on Notice," *Defense News,* September 3, 2015, accessed January 21, 2017 http://www.defensenews.com/story/defense/naval/2015/09/03/chinas-parade-puts-us-navy-notice/71632918/

# Bibliography

Abraham, Nicholas, Maria Torok, and Nicholas T. Rand. *The Shell and the Kernel: Renewals of Psychoanalysis.* IL: University of Chicago Press, 1994.

Agha, Shahid Ali. *The Country Without a Post Office: Poems.* NY: W.W. Norton, 1997.

Anderson, Wanni Wibulswasdi, and Robert G. Lee. *Displacements and Diasporas Asians in the Americas.* New Brunswick, NJ: Rutgers University Press, 2005.

Appadurai, Arjun. *Fear of Small Numbers: An Essay on the Geography of Anger.* Durham, NC: Duke Univ. Press, 2007.

Ballantyne, Tony, and Antoinette M. Burton. *Bodies in Contact: Rethinking Colonial Encounters in World History.* Durham, NC: Duke University Press, 2005.

Barrows, David P. *The Negrito and Allied Types in the Philippines.* Lancaster, PA: New Era Printing Co, 1910.

Berrigan, Darrell. "Japan's Occupation Babies." *Saturday Evening Post,* 24-25-117. June 19, 1948.

Bhabha, Homi K. "Dissemi Nation: Time, Narrative and the Margins of the Modern Nation." *Nation and Narration.* London: Routledge, 1990.

Bhabha, Homi K. *The Location of Culture.* London: Routledge, 2010.

Blount, James H. *The American Occupation of the Philippines, 1898-1912.* NY: London: G. P. Putnam's Sons, 1912.

Brantlinger, Patrick. *Dark Vanishings: Discourse on the Extinction of Primitive Races, 1800-1930*. Ithaca (NY): Cornell University, 2003.

Brocheux, Pierre, Daniel Hemery, Ly Lan Dill-Klein, Eric Jennings, Nora A. Taylor, and Noemi Tousignant. *Indochina: An Ambiguous Colonization, 1858-1954*. Berkeley: University of California Press, 2011.

Broome, Richard. *Aboriginal Victorians: A History Since 1800*. Crows Nest, N.S.W.: Allen & Unwin, 2006.

Buck, Pearl S. *For Spacious Skies; Journey in Dialogue*. NY John Day Co, 1966.

Burkhardt, William R. "Institutional Barriers, Marginality, and Adaptation Among the American-Japanese Mixed Bloods in Japan." *The Journal of Asian Studies* 42, no. 3 (1983): 519.

Butler, Judith. *Precarious Life: The Powers of Mourning and Violence*. London: Verso, 2006.

Calichman, Richard. *Overcoming Modernity Cultural Identity in Wartime Japan*. NY: Columbia University Press, 2008.

Caprio, Mark, and Yoneyuki Sugita. *Democracy in Occupied Japan: The U.S. Occupation and Japanese Politics and Society*. London: Routledge, 2007.

Carlton, Eric. *Occupation The Policies and Practices of Military Conquerors*. London: Taylor and Francis, 2013.

Caruth, Cathy. *Unclaimed Experience: Trauma, Narrative, and History*. Baltimore: Johns Hopkins University Press, 2016.

Césaire, Aimé, and Robin D. G. Kelley. *Discourse on Colonialism*. NY: Monthly Review Press, 2000.

Cha, Theresa Hak Kyung, and Constance M. Lewallen. *Exilée; Temps Morts: Selected Works*. Berkeley, CA: University of California Press, 2009.

Cha, Theresa Hak Kyung. *Dictee*. Berkeley, CA: Univ. of California Press, 2009.

Chatterjee, Partha. *The Nation and Its Fragments: Colonial and Postcolonial Histories*. NJ: Princeton University Press, 1993.

Cheng, Anne Anlin. *The Melancholy of Race: Psychoanalysis, Assimilation and Hidden Grief*. NY: Oxford University Press, 2001.

Chizuko, Ueno, "The Politics of Memory: Nation, Individual and Self." Jordan Sand, trans. *History & Memory* 11, no. 2 (1999): 129-152.

Cho, Grace M. *Haunting the Korean Diaspora: Shame, Secrecy, and the Forgotten War*. Minneapolis: University of Minnesota Press, 2008.

Cho, Grace M. "Voices from the Teum: Synesthetic Trauma and the Ghosts of the Korean Diaspora." In Patricia Ticineto Clough, and Jean Halley, *The Affective Turn*, Durham, NC: Duke University Press, 151-169. 2007.

Choi, Chungmoo. *The Comfort Women: Colonialism, War, and Sex.* Durham, NC: Duke University Press, 1997.

Christopher, Emma, Cassandra Pybus, and Marcus Rediker. *Many Middle Passages: Forced Migration and the Making of the Modern World.* Berkeley: University of California Press, 2007.

Chuong, Chung Hoang, and Le Van. *The Amerasians from Vietnam: A California Study.* Folsom, CA: Southeast Asia Community Research Center, 1994.

Clements, Nicholas. *Black War: Fear, Sex and Resistance in Tasmania.* University of Queensland Press, 2014.

Cloyd, Fredrick D. *War Brides and Homelands. In Your Ear: Selected Writings from Oakland Word,* 2010. Accessed September 12, 2017, https://issuu.com/liusan/docs/ow_in-your-ear

Cohen, Theodore, and Herbert Passin. *Remaking Japan: The American Occupation As New Deal.* NY: Free Press, 1987.

Conn, Peter. *Pearl S. Buck: A Cultural Biography.* Cambridge: Cambridge University Press, 1998.

Connor, John W. *A Study of the Marital Stability of Japanese War Brides.* San Francisco: R and E Research Associates, 1976.

Constantino, Renato, and Letizia R. Constantino. *A History of the Philippines: From the Spanish Colonization to the Second World War.* NY: Monthly Review Press, 2010.

Cook, Haruko Taya, and Theodore Failor Cook. *Japan at War: An Oral History.* NY: New Press, 1992.

Cortazzi, Hugh. *Japan Experiences: Fifty Years, One Hundred Views: Post-War Japan Through British Eyes 1945-2000.* Richmond, Surrey: Japan Library, 2001.

Creef, Elena T. "Discovering My Mother as the Other in the Saturday Evening Post." *Qualitative Inquiry* 6, No. 4 (2000): 443-455.

Cudd, Ann E. *Analyzing Oppression. Studies in Feminist Philosophy.* Oxford University Press, 2006.

Cumings, Bruce. *The Korean War: A History.* NY: Modern Library, 2013.

Daniel, E. Valentine. *Charred Lullabies: Chapters in an Anthropography of Violence.* NJ: Princeton University Press, 2001.

De Matos, Christine, and Rowena Ward. *Gender, Power, and Military Occupations: Asia Pacific and the Middle East Since 1945.* London: Routledge, 2012.

DeBonis, Steven. *Children of the Enemy: Oral Histories of Vietnamese Amerasians and Their Mothers.* Jefferson, NC: McFarland, 2013.

Debord, Guy. *Society of the Spectacle.* Eastbourne, East Sussex, UK: Soul Bay Press Limited, 2012.

Denoon, Donald, Gavan McCormack, Mark J. Hudson, and Tessa Morris-Suzuki. *Multicultural Japan: Palaeolithic to Postmodern*. Cambridge: Cambridge University Press, 2011.

Derrida, Jacques, Pascale-Anne Brault, and Michael Naas. *The Work of Mourning*. IL: University of Chicago Press, 2003.

Dikötter, Frank, and Barry Sautman. *The Construction of Racial Identities in China and Japan Historical and Contemporary Perspectives*. London: C. Hurst, 1997.

Dikötter, Frank. *The Discourse of the Race in Modern China*. London: Hurst, 1992.

Dōgen, Kazuaki Tanahashi. *Moon in a Dewdrop: Writings*. San Francisco: North Point Press, 1985.

Dommen, Arthur J. *The Indochinese Experience of the French and the Americans Nationalism and Communism in Cambodia, Laos, and Vietnam*. Bloomington: Indiana University Press, 2001.

Doolan, Yuri W. "Being Amerasian in South Korea: Purebloodness, Multiculturalism, and Living Alongside the U.S. Military Empire," Master's thesis, Ohio State University, 2012.

Dower, John W. "Black Ships and Samurai: Commodore Perry and the Opening of Japan 1853-1854" [Scholarly project 2008.]. In *MIT Visualizing Cultures*. Accessed January 15, 2014, http://ocw.mit.edu/ans7870/21f/21f.027/black_ships_and_samurai/pdf/bss_essay.pdf

Dower, John W. *Embracing Defeat: Japan in the Wake of World War II*. London: Penguin, 2000.

Dower, John W. *War Without Mercy: Race and Power in Pacific War*. NY: Pantheon Books, 2006.

Dudden, Arthur Power. *American Pacific: From the Old China Trade to the Present*. Oxford University Press, 1995.

Duras, Marguerite. *Hiroshima Mon Amour*. NY: Grove/Atlantic, Inc, 1994.

Duus, Masayo. *Makkāsā no futatsu no Boshi: Tokushu Shisetsu RAA wo Meguru Senryō-shi no Sokumen [Two Hats of MacArthur: One Facet of Occupation History Concerning the RAA Special Comfort Station]*. Tōkyō: Kōdansha, 1985.

Dyson, Freeman. "Part I: A Failure of Intelligence." *MIT Technology Review,* November 1, 2006. Accessed September 12, 2017, https://www.technologyreview.com/s/406789/a-failure-of-intelligence/.

*Ebony Magazine*. "The Loneliest Brides in America." *Ebony*. 8, no. 3 (January 1953): 19.

Echenberg, Myron J. *Colonial Conscripts: The Tirailleurs Sénégalais in French West Africa, 1857-1960*. Portsmouth, NH: Heinemann, 1990.

Efird, Robert. "Japan's 'War Orphans': Identification and State Responsibility." *The Journal of Japanese Studies* 34, no. 2 (2008): 363-388.

Eng, David L., and David Kazanjian. *Loss: The Politics of Mourning.* Berkeley: University of California Press, 2003.

Enloe, Cynthia H. Bananas, *Beaches & Bases: Making Feminist Sense of International Politics.* Berkeley: University of California Press, 2000.

Eperjesi, John R. *The Imperialist Imaginary: Visions of Asia and the Pacific in American Culture.* Hanover, NH: Dartmouth College Press, 2005.

Fabian, Johannes, and Matti Bunzl. *Time and the Other: How Anthropology Makes Its Object.* NY: Columbia University Press, 2002.

Fanon, Frantz. *The Wretched of the Earth.* NY: Grove Press, 2011.

Fenkl, Heinz Insu. *Memories of My Ghost Brother.* London: Anchor, 1998.

Field, Norma. *From My Grandmother's Bedside Sketches of Postwar Tōkyō.* Berkeley, CA: University of California Press, 1997.

Firpo, Christina. "Crises of Whiteness and Empire in Colonial Indochina: The Removal of Abandoned Eurasian Children From the Vietnamese Milieu, 1890–1956." *Journal of Social History,* 433, 587-613. 2010.

Fish, Robert A. "The Heiress and the Love Children: Sawada Miki and the Elizabeth Saunders Home for Mixed Blood Orphans in Post War Japan," Ph.D. dissertation, University of Hawaii at Manoa, 2002.

Foucault, Michel, and Donald F. Bouchard. *Language, Counter-Memory, Practice: Selected Essays and Interviews.* Donald F. Bouchard and Sherry Simon, trans. Oxford: Blackwell, 1977.

Foucault, Michel, and François Ewald. *Society Must Be Defended: Lectures at the Collége De France, 1975-76.* London: Penguin, 2008.

Foucault, Michel. *Security, Territory, and Population. Lectures at the Collège De France, 1977-1978.* Picador USA, 2009.

Fujitani, Takashi, G. M. White, and Lisa Yoneyama. *Perilous Memories The Asia-Pacific War(s).* Durham NC: Duke University Press, 2001.

Gage, Sue-Je Lee. "The Amerasian Problem: Blood, Duty, and Race." *International Relations* 21, no. 1 (2007): 86-102.

Gallicchio, Marc S. *The African American Encounter with Japan and China: Black Internationalism in Asia, 1895-1945.* Chapel Hill: University of North Carolina Press, 2000.

Gallicchio, Marc. *The Unpredictability of the Past: Memories of the Asia-Pacific War in U.S./East Asian relations.* Durham, NC: Duke University Press, 2007.

Gatewood, Willard B. *"Smoked Yankees" and the Struggle for Empire: Letters from Negro Soldiers, 1898-1902.* Urbana: University of Illinois Press, 1971.

Geiger, Andrea. *Subverting Exclusion: Transpacific Encounters with Race, Caste, and Borders, 1885-1928.* New Haven, CT: Yale University Press, 2015.

Goodman, Grant Kohn, and Barry D. Steben. *America's Japan the first year, 1945-1946.* NY: Fordham University Press, 2005.

Gordon, Andrew. *Postwar Japan As History.* Berkeley: University of California Press, 1993.

Gordon, Avery. *Ghostly Matters: Haunting and the Sociological Imagination.* Minneapolis: University of Minnesota Press, 2011.

Goto, Kenichi, and Paul H. Kratoska. *Tensions of Empire: Japan and Southeast Asia in the Colonial and Postcolonial World.* Athens: Ohio University Center for International Studies, 2003.

Goto, Miyabi. *Liberation or Exploitation: Representations of Pan-Pan Prostitutes in Japanese Women's Literature.* University of Massachusetts Amherst, 2007.

Graburn, Nelson H. H., John Ertl, and R. Kenji Tierney. *Multiculturalism in the New Japan: Crossing the Boundaries Within.* NY: Berghahn Books, 2008.

Green, Michael Cullen. Black Yanks in the Pacific: Race in the Making of American Military Empire After World War II. Ithaca, NY: Cornell University Press, 2010.

Grieg, Kai. *The War Children of the World.* War and Children Identity Project Rep. Bergen. 2001.

Griffiths, Owen. "Japanese Children and the Culture of Death, January – August 1945." In *Children and War: A Historical Anthology.* James Marten and Robert Coles, 160-171. NY: New York University Press, 2002.

Grossman, David. *On Killing: The Psychological Cost of Learning to Kill in War and Society.* Boston: Little, Brown, 1996.

Gruesser, John Cullen. *The Empire Abroad and the Empire at Home: African American Literature and Era of Overseas Expansion.* Athens: University of Georgia Press, 2012.

Gustafsson, Mai Lan. *War and Shadows: The Haunting of Vietnam.* Ithaca: Cornell University Press, 2009.

Haebich, Anna Elizabeth. *Broken Circles Fragmenting Indigenous Families.* WA: Fremantle Arts Centre Press, 2000.

Hall, Christine Catherine Iijima. "The Ethnic Identity of Racially Mixed People: A Study of Black Japanese," Ph.D. dissertation, University of California, Los Angeles, 1980.

Hamilton, Walter Stuart. *Children of the Occupation: Japan's Untold Story.* New Brunswick: Rutgers University Press, 2013.

Hane, Mikiso. *Peasants, Rebels, Women, and Outcastes: The Underside of Modern Japan.* Lanham, MD: Rowman & Littlefield, 2003.

Hane, Mikiso. *Reflections on the Way to the Gallows: Rebel Women in Prewar Japan.* Berkeley: University of California Press, 1998.

Hara, Kimie. *Cold War Frontiers in the Asia-Pacific: Divided Territories in the San Francisco System.* London: Routledge, 2006.

Hemphill, Elizabeth Anne. *The Least of These: Miki Sawada and Her Children.* NY: Weatherhill. 1980.

Hicks, James L. "Japanese or American Girls: Which? Why?" *Baltimore Afro-American,* October 7, 1950.

Hill, Robert A. *The FBI's RACON: Racial Conditions in the United States During War II.* Boston: Northeastern University Press, 1995.

Hiltz, Jackie, Steven I. Levine, and Philip West. *America's Wars in Asia: A Cultural Approach to History and Memory.* Armonk, NY: M. E. Sharpe Incorporated, 1997.

Hobgood, Mary E. *Dismantling Privilege: An Ethics of Accountability.* Cleveland, OH: Pilgrim Press, 2000.

Hogan, Michael J. *Hiroshima in History and Memory.* Cambridge, England: Cambridge University Press, 1997.

Höhn, Maria, and Seungsook Moon. *Over There: Living with the U.S. Military Empire from World War Two to the Present.* Durham, NC: Duke University Press, 2010.

Horne, Gerald. *Black and Red: W. E. B. Du Bois and the Afro-American Response to the Cold War: 1944-1963.* Albany: State University of New York Press, 1986.

Horne, Gerald. "The Revenge of the Black Pacific?" *Callaloo* 24, no. 1 (2001): 94-96.

Horne, Gerald. *White Pacific: U.S. Imperialism and Black Slavery in the South Seas After the Civil War.* Honolulu: University of Hawaii Press, 2007.

Houston, Velina Hasu. *But Still, Like Air, I'll Rise: New Asian American Plays.* Philadelphia: Temple University Press, 1997.

Hoyt, Edwin P. *Inferno: The Firebombing of Japan, March 9-August 15, 1945.* Lanham, MD: Madison Books, 2000.

Hunter, Edna J. and D. Stephen Nice. *Children of Military Families: A Part and Yet Apart.* Office of Naval Research Arlington VA, 1978.

Ifekwunigwe, Jayne O. *'Mixed-race' Studies: A Reader.* London: Routledge, 2004.

Iga, Mamoru. *The Thorn in the Chrysanthemum: Suicide and Economic Success in Modern Japan.* Berkeley: University of California Press, 1986.

Igarashi, Yoshikuni. *Bodies of Memory: Narratives of War in Postwar Japanese Culture, 1945-1970.* NJ: Princeton University Press, 2000.

Isaacs, Jennifer. *Australian Dreaming: 40,000 Years of Aboriginal History.* Sydney: New Holland Publishing, 2009.

Ivy, Marilyn. *Discourses of the Vanishing: Modernity, Phantasm, Japan.* IL: University of Chicago Press, 1995.

Jager, Sheila Miyoshi, and Rana Mitter. *Ruptured Histories: War, Memory, and the Post-Cold War in Asia.* Cambridge, MA: Harvard University Press, 2007.

Jahoda, Gloria. *The Trail of Tears: The Story of the American Indian Removals 1813-1838.* NY: Wings Books, 1995.

"Japanese-Filipinos Seek Citizenship." *The Japan Times,* August 7, 2013. Accessed September 12, 2017 https://www.japantimes.co.jp/news/2013/08/07/national/japanese-filipinos-seek-citizenship-2/#.WcF74MZryM8

Johnson, Carmen. *Wave-Rings in the Water: My Years with the Women of Postwar Japan.* Alexandria, VA: Charles River Press, 1996.

Johnson, M. Dujon. *Race and Racism in the Chinas: Chinese Racial Attitudes Toward Africans and African Americans.* Bloomington, IN: AuthorHouse, 2011.

Kato, Mariko. Occupation Orphan Traces Roots: 'Eureka' Visit Sets Emotional Bond. *The Japan Times,* June 6, 2009. Accessed September 12, 2017 https://www.japantimes.co.jp/news/2009/06/06/national/occupation-orphan-traces-roots/#.WcF82MZryM8

Kato, Naoko. "War Guilt and Postwar Japanese Education," Master's thesis,University of British Columbia, 2002.

Kauanui, J. Kēhaulani. *Hawaiian Blood: Colonialism and the Politics of Sovereignty and Indigeneity.* Durham, N.C: Duke University Press, 2008.

Kawai, Kazuo. *Japan's American Interlude: Kazuo Kawai.* IL: Chicago University Press, 1979.

Kawarasaki, Yasuko. *Negative Stereotypes of Japanese War Brides: An Outburst of Japanese Frustration.* Los Angeles: University of California, 1994.

Kawash, Samira. *Dislocating the Color Line: Identity, Hybridity, and Singularity in African American Narrative.* Stanford, CA: Stanford University Press, 1997.

Kearney, Reginald. *African American Views of the Japanese: Solidarity or Sedition?* Albany: State University of New York Press, 1998.

Kim, Eleana. *Adopted Territory: Transnational Korean Adoptees and the Politics of Belonging.* Durham, NC: Duke University Press, 2011.

Kim, Hyun Sun. *Lives in Kijich'on: U.S. Military Camptown in Korea.* Seoul: Saewoomtuh, 1999.

Kinnear, Penny Sue. "Setting Assumptions Aside: Exploring Identity Development in Interracial/Intercultural Individuals Growing Up in Japan," Ph.D. dissertation, University of Toronto. Ottawa: National Library of Canada Bibliothèque nationale du Canada, 2002.

Kirk, Robert W. *Paradise Past The Transformation of the South Pacific, 1520-1920.* Jefferson, NC: McFarland & Co, 2012.

Koikari, Mire. "Rethinking Gender and Power in the US Occupation of Japan, and 1945-1952." *Gender & History* 11, no. 2 (1999): 313–335.

Kondo, Dorinne. "The Narrative Production of 'Home,' Community, and Political Identity in Asian American Theater." In Smadar Lavie and Ted Swedenburg, *Displacement, Diaspora, and Geographies of Identity.* Durham, NC: Duke University Press, 1996.

Koshiro, Yukiko. *Trans-Pacific Racisms and the U.S. Occupation of Japan.* NY: Columbia University Press, 1999.

Kovner, Sarah. "Base Cultures: Sex Workers and Servicemen in Occupied Japan." *The Journal of Asian Studies* 68, no. 3 (2009): 777-804.

Kovner, Sarah. *Occupying Power: Sex Workers and Servicemen in Postwar Japan.* Stanford, CA: Stanford University Press, 2013.

Kramer, Paul A. *The Blood of Government: Race, Empire, the United States, & the Philippines.* Chapel Hill, NC: University of North Carolina Press, 2006.

Kutschera, Pete C. "Military Pan Amerasians and 21st Century Implications for Diasporic and Global Studies." *Asia Journal of Global Studies* 6, no. 1 (2014-15): 30-47.

Lavie, Smadar, and Ted Swedenburg. *Displacement, Diaspora, and Geographies of Identity.* Durham, NC: Duke University Press, 2001.

Lawler, Nancy Ellen. *Soldiers of Misfortune: Ivoirien Tirailleurs of World War Two.* Athens: Ohio University Press, 1992.

Lee, Christopher J. *Making a World After Empire: The Bandung Moment and Its Political Afterlives.* Athens: Ohio University Press, 2010.

Leenaars, Antoon A., and David Lester. *Suicide and the Unconscious.* Northvale, NJ: Aronson, 1996.

Lie, John. *Multiethnic Japan.* Cambridge, MA: Harvard University Press, 2004.

Lucious, B. S. *In the Black Pacific: Testimonials of Vietnamese Afro-Amerasian Displacements.* In W. W. Anderson and R. G. Lee eds., *Displacements and diasporas: Asians in the Americas,* 122-158. New Brunswick: Rutgers University Press, 2005.

Lutz, Catherine A. *The Bases of Empire: The Global Struggle against U.S. Military Posts*. London: Pluto Press, 2008.

Ma, L. Eve Armentrout. *Farms, Firms, and Runways: Perspectives on U.S. Military Bases in the Western Pacific*. Chicago: Imprint Publications, 2001.

Maclear, Kyo. "Drawing Dividing Lines: An Analysis of Discursive Representations of Amerasian 'Occupation Babies'." *Resources for Feminist Research* 23, no. 4 (1994).

Marable, Manning, and Vanessa Agard-Jones. *Transnational Blackness: Navigating the Global Color Line*. Basingstoke, UK: Palgrave Macmillan, 2009.

Marten, James Alan. *Children and War: A Historical Anthology*. NY: New York University Press, 2002.

Mathews, Ralph. "Wacs and Pom Poms Wage War in Yokohama." *Baltimore Afro-American*. September 22, 1951.

May, Elaine Tyler. *Homeward Bound: American Families in the Cold War Era*. NY: Basic Books, 2002.

McFerson, Hazel M. *Blacks and Asians: Crossings, Conflict, and Commonality*. Durham, N.C.: Carolina Academic Press, 2006.

McKelvey, Robert S. *The Dust of Life: America's Children Abandoned in Vietnam*. Seattle: University of Washington Press, 1999.

McNeill, David. "The Night Hell Fell From the Sky." *The Asia-Pacific Journal: Japan Focus* 3, no. 3 (2005).

Miller, Stuart Creighton. *Benevolent Assimilation: The American Conquest of the Philippines, 1899 - 1903*. New Haven, CT: Yale University Press, 1984.

Mirante, Edith. *The Wind in the Bamboo: A Journey in Search of Asia's "Negrito" Indigenous People*. Bangkok, Thailand: Orchid Press, 2014.

Moen, Sveinung J. *The Amerasians: A Study and Research on Interracial Children in Korea*. Seoul: Taewon Publishing 1974.

Molasky, Michael S. *The American Occupation of Japan and Okinawa: Literature and Memory*. London: Routledge, 2001.

Moon, Katherine. "International Relations and Women: A Case Study of US-Korea Camptown Prostitution, 1971-1976," Ph.D. dissertation. Princeton University, 1994.

Moon, Katharine. *Sex Among Allies: Military Prostitution in U.S.-Korea Relations*. NY: Columbia Univ. Press, 1997.

Moon, Seungsook. *Militarized Modernity and Gendered Citizenship in South Korea*. Durham, NC: Duke University Press, 2007.

Moore, Joe. "Development and Democracy in Postwar Japan." *Asian Studies Review*, 103, 11-17. 1987.

Moore, Joe. *The Other Japan: Conflict, Compromise, and Resistance Since 1945*. Abingdon, Oxon: Routledge, 2015.

Morikawa, Suzuko. "The Significance of Afrocentricity for Non-Africans: Examination of the Relationship Between African Americans and the Japanese." *Journal of Black Studies* 31, no. 4 (2001): 423-436.

Morris, Errol. Director. "The Fog of War: Eleven Lessons from the Life of Robert S. McNamara." [Motion picture on DVD]. 2004.

Moses, A. Dirk. *Empire, Colony, Genocide: Conquest, Occupation, and Subaltern Resistance in World History*. NY: Berghahn, 2010.

Moses, A. Dirk. *Genocide and Settler Society: Frontier Violence and Stolen Indigenous Children in Australian History*. NY: Berghahn Books, 2005.

Mullen, Bill V. *Afro-Orientalism*. Minneapolis: Univ. of Minnesota Press, 2004.

Mullen, Bill V., and Cathryn Watson. *W. E. B. Du Bois on Asia Crossing the World Color Line*. Jackson: University Press of Mississippi, 2005.

Murphy-Shigematsu, Stephen L. H. "The Voices of Amerasians: Ethnicity, Identity, and Empowerment in interracial Japanese Americans." Ph.D. dissertation, Harvard University, 1986. Disseration.com, 2000.

Nakamura, Masako. "Reconsidering Japanese War Brides in the 1940's US History," Ph.D. dissertation, University of California, Los Angeles, 2003.

Nishi, Toshio. *Unconditional Democracy: Education and Politics in Occupied Japan, 1945-1952*. Stanford, CA: Hoover Institution Press, Stanford University, 2004.

Oe, Kenzaburo. *Teach Us To Outgrow Our Madness: Four Short Novels*. NY: Grove/Atlantic, Inc, 2011.

Okada, Yasuhiro. "Race, Masculinity, and Military Occupation: African American Soldiers' Encounters with the Japanese at Camp Gifu, 1947-1951." *The Journal of African American History,* 962, 179-203. 2011.

Okada, Yasuhiro. "Gendering the 'Black Pacific': Race Consciousness, National Identity, and the Masculine/Feminine Empowerment Among African Americans in Japan Under US Military Occupation, 1945-1952," Ph.D. dissertation, Michigan State University, 2008.

Onishi, Yuichiro. *Transpacific Antiracism: Afro-Asian Solidarity in 20th-Century Black America, Japan, and Okinawa*. NY: New York University Press, 2014.

Osada, Kazuko. "Nationalism, Gender, and War Brides: Reeavluating Ariyoshi Sawako's HISHOKU," Master's thesis, University of Colorado, 2007.

Osur, Alan M. *Blacks in the Army Air Forces During World War II: The Problem of Race Relations*. Honolulu, HI: University Press of the Pacific, 2005.

Palmer, R.N. *Kidnapping in the South Seas: Correspondence Respecting a Book by Captain Palmer R.N.* Sydney: Government Printer, 1871.

Pascoe, Peggy. *What Comes Naturally: Miscegenation Law and the Making of Race in America*. NY: Oxford University Press, 2009.

Pearl S. Buck Foundation, *America's Forgotten Children, the Amerasians*. Perkasie, PA: Pearl S. Buck Foundation, 1981.

Perdue, Theda, Michael Green, Colin Calloway. *The Cherokee Nation and the Trail of Tears*. NY: Penguin Books, 2008.

Perry, John Curtis. *Beneath the Eagle's Wings: Americans in Occupied Japan*. NY: Dodd, Mead & Company, 1980.

Peyton, Boyd L. "Identification in Husbands of Japanese War Brides," Master's thesis, Sociology, University of Chicago, 1956.

Pinaroc, Joel D. "'G.I. Babies': Little Outcasts." *Manilla Times*. April 25, 2004

Rashidi, Runoko, and Ivan Van Sertima. *African Presence in Early Asia*. New Brunswick, N.J.: Transaction Publishers, 2009.

Rexroth, Kenneth, and Ikuko Atsumi. *Women Poets of Japan*. Archiwum Czesława Miłosza. NY: New Directions, 1982.

Rhodes, Richard. *The Making of the Atomic Bomb*. NY: Simon & Schuster, 2012.

Ricœur, Paul. *Memory, History, Forgetting*. IL: University of Chicago Press, 2004.

Rizzuto, Rahna R. *Hiroshima in the Morning*. NY: Feminist Press, 2010.

Rodriguez, Dylan. *Suspended Apocalypse: White Supremacy, Genocide, and the Filipino Condition*. Minneapolis: University of Minnesota Press, 2010.

Roehner, Bertrand M. "Relations Between Allied Forces and the Population of Japan 15 August 1945–31 December 1960 and Okinawa: 1945–1972" Working paper. Paris: Institute for Theoretical and High Energy Physics, University of Paris, 2009.

Root, Maria P. P. *Racially Mixed People in America*. Newbury Park: Sage Publications, 1998.

Root, Maria P. P. *The Multiracial Experience: Racial Borders as the New Frontier*. Thousand Oaks, CA: Sage, 1999.

Rosenbaum, Roman. 2006. "True Survivors: The 'Yakeato Sedai' in Contemporary Japanese Literature - Towards a Definition. 16th Biennial Conference of the Asian Studies Association of Australia (ASAA) 2006, Canberra: Asian Studies Association of Australia (ASAA).

Rosenbaum, Roman. *Legacies of the Asia-Pacific War: The Yakeato Generation*. NY: Routledge, 2010.

Roy, Denny. *The Pacific War and Its Political Legacies.* Westport, CT: Praeger Publishers, 2009.

Rubin, Arnold. *Black Nanban: Africans in Japan During the Sixteenth Century.* Bloomington: The Program, 1974.

Rublack, Ulinka. *A Concise Companion to History.* Oxford: Oxford University Press, 2012.

Rushdie, Salman. *Midnight's Children: A Novel.* NY: Random House Trade Paperbacks, 1991.

Russell, John G. 2008. "Excluded Presence: Shoguns, Minstrels, Bodyguards, and Japan's Encounters with the Black Other." Departmental Bulletin Paper. Jinbun kagaku Kenkyusho, Kyōto University. Zinbun, 40, 16-51.

Russell, John G. "Interracial Intimacy in Japan: Western Men and Japanese Women, 1543-1900." *The Journal of Japanese Studies* 31, no. 1 (2005): 209-214.

Ryan Lyndall. "List of multiple killings of Aborigines in Tasmania: 1804-1835," *Online Encyclopedia of Mass Violence.* March 5, 2008. Accessed September 19, 2017, http://www.sciencespo.fr/mass-violence-war-massacre-resistance/en/document/list-multiple-killings-aborigines-tasmania-1804-1835, ISSN 1961-9898

Saada, Emmanuelle. *Empire's Children: Race, Filiation, and Citizenship in the French Colonies.* IL: University of Chicago Press, 2012.

Saewoomtuh. *Lives in Kijich'on: U.S. Military Camptown in Korea.* [Tongduchon-City, Kyunggi-Do [i.e. Dongducheon, Gyeonggi-do], Korea]: [Kim, Hyun Sun], 1999.

Said, Edward W. *Orientalism.* NY: Vintage Books, 2003.

Sakai, Naoki, and Hyon Joo Yoo. *The Trans-Pacific Imagination: Rethinking Boundary, Culture and Society.* Singapore: World Scientific Publishing Company, 2012.

Sakamoto, Rumi. "Pan-pan Girls: Humiliating Liberation in Postwar Japanese Literature. *Journal of Multidisciplinary International Studies,* [S.l.], v. 7, n. 2. Accessed September 12, 2017 http://epress.lib.uts.edu.au/journals/index.php/portal/article/view/1515

Sato, Barbara Hamill. *The New Japanese Woman Modernity, Media, and Women in Interwar Japan.* Durham, NC: Duke University Press, 2003.

Sawada, Miki. *Sawada Miki: Kuroi hada to shiroi kokoro : Sandāsu Hōmu e no michi.* Tōkyō: Nihon Tosho Sentā, 2001.

Schaller, Michael. *The American Occupation of Japan: The Origins of the Cold War in Asia.* NY: Oxford University Press, 1987.

Schnepp, Gerald J. and Agnes Masako Yui. "Cultural and Marital Adjustment of Japanese War Brides." *American Journal of Sociology,* 611, 48. 1955.

Schrijvers, Peter. *The GI War against Japan: American Soldiers in Asia and the Pacific During World War II*. NY: New York University Press, 2002.

Sebald, William Joseph, and Russell Brines. *With MacArthur in Japan*. London: Cresset, 1965.

Selden, Mark. "A Forgotten Holocaust: US Bombing Strategy, the Destruction of Japanese Cities and the American Way of War from the Pacific War to Iraq." *Japan Focus* 5, no. 5 (2007).

Seraphim, Franziska. *War Memory and Social Politics in Japan, 1945-2005*. Cambridge, MA: Harvard University Press, 2008.

Shay, Jonathan. *Odysseus in America: Combat Trauma and the Trials of Homecoming*. NY: Scribner, 2002.

Shigehiro, Takahashi. "Child-Murder/Mother-Suicides in Japan." *PHP* 8/5, (1977): 61-76.

Shigematsu, Setsu, and Keith L. Camacho. *Militarized Currents: Toward a Decolonized Future in Asia and the Pacific*. Minneapolis: University of Minnesota Press, 2010.

Shimazu, Naoko. *Japan, Race, and Equality the Racial Equality Proposal of 1919*. London: Routledge, 1998.

Shukert, Elfrieda Berthiaume, and Barbara Smith Scibetta. *War Brides of World War II*. Novato, CA: Presidio Press, 1988.

Silva, Noenoe K. *Aloha Betrayed: Native Hawaiian Resistance to American Colonialism*. Durham, NC: Duke University Press, 2004.

Simpson, Caroline Chung. "Out of an Obscure Place: Japanese War Brides and Cultural Pluralism in the 1950s." *Journal of Feminist Cultural Studies* 10, no. 3 (1998): 47-81.

Smith, Bardwell. "Buddhism and Abortion in Contemporary Japan: 'Muzuko Kuyō' and the Confrontation with Death." *Japanese Journal of Religious Studies* 15, no. 1 (1988) 3-24.

Smith, Milton A. "GIs Spurn Korean Gals, Wait For Jap Lassies." *Chicago Defender*. December 16, 1950.

Soh, Chunghee Sarah. *The Comfort Women: Sexual Violence and Postcolonial Memory in Korea and Japan*. IL: University of Chicago Press, 2009.

Sontag, Susan. *Regarding the Pain of Others*. London: Penguin, 2004.

Sorensen, Lars-Martin. *Censorship of Japanese Films During the U.S. Occupation of Japan: The Cases of Yasujiro Ozu and Akira Kurosawa*. Lewiston, NY: Edwin Mellen Press, 2009.

Spickard, Paul R. *Mixed Blood: Intermarriage and Ethnic Identity in Twentieth-Century America*. Madison, WI: The University of Wisconsin Press, 1991.

Spurling, Hilary. *Pearl Buck in China: Journey to the Good Earth*. NY: Simon & Schuster, 2010.

Stoler, Ann Laura. *Carnal Knowledge and Imperial Power: Race and the Intimate in Colonial Rule.* Berkeley: University of California Press, 2010.

Stoler, Ann Laura. *Race and the Education of Desire: Foucault's "History of Sexuality" and the Colonial Order of Things.* Durham, NC: Duke University Press, 2004.

Stoler, Ann. "Sexual Affronts and Racial Frontiers: European Identities and the Cultural Politics of Exclusion in Colonial Southeast Asia." *Comparative Studies in Society and History* 34, no. 3 (1992): 514-551.

Stone, I. F. *The Hidden History of the Korean War, 1950-1951.* Boston: Little, Brown, 1988.

Sturdevant, Saundra Pollock, and Brenda Stotlzfus. *Let the Good Times Roll: Prostitution and the US Military in Asia.* NY: New Press, 1994.

Suenaga, Shizuko. "Goodbye to Sayonara: The Reverse Assimilation of Japanese War Brides," Ph.D. dissertation, Boston College, 1996.

Suh, Alexandra Chung. "'Movie in My Mind' American Culture and Military Prostitution in Asia," Ph.D. dissertation, Columbia University, 2001.

Svoboda, Terese. *Black Glasses Like Clark Kent: A Gi's Secret from Postwar Japan.* St. Paul, MN: Graywolf Press, 2012.

Takahashi, Yoshitomo and Douglas Berger. "Cultural Dynamics and Suicide in Japan." In David Lester, *Suicide and the Unconscious.* Lanham, MD: Rowman & Littlefield/Jason Aronson, Inc., 1977.

Takemae, Eiji, Robert Ricketts, and Sebastian Swann. *Inside GHQ: The Allied Occupation of Japan and Its Legacy.* NY: Continuum, 2002.

Taketani, Etsuko. "The Cartography of the Black Pacific: James Weldon Johnson's Along This Way." *American Quarterly,* 591, 79-106. 2007

Taketani, Etsuko. *The Black Pacific Narrative: Geographic Imaginings of Race and Empire Between the World Wars* (Re-Mapping the Transnational: A Dartmouth Series in American Studies). Dartmouth College Press, 2014.

Takeuchi, Michiko. "Pan-Pan Girls and GIs: The Japan-U.S. Military Prostitution System in Occupied Japan 1945-1952," Ph.D. dissertation, University of California, Los Angeles, 2009.

Takeuchi, Yoshimi, and Richard Calichman. *What is modernity? Writings of Takeuchi Yoshimi.* NY: Columbia University Press, 2005.

Takeyama, Michio, and Richard H. Minear. *The Scars of War: Tōkyō During World War II: Writings of Takeyama Michio.* Lanham, MD: Rowman & Littlefield Publishers, 2007.

Tamayama, Kazuo, and John Nunneley. *Tales by Japanese Soldiers of the Burma Campaign 1942-1945*. London: Cassell & Co, 2001.

Tanaka, Toshiyuki. *Japan's Comfort Women: Sexual Slavery and Prostitution During World War II and the US Occupation*. London: Routledge, 2003.

Tansman, Alan M. *The Culture of Japanese Fascism*. Durham, N.C.: Duke University Press, 2009.

Taussig, Michael T. *Shamanism, Colonialism, and the Wild Man: A Study in Terror and Healing*. Chicago: University Press, 1991.

Tierney, Robert Thomas. *Tropics of Savagery: The Culture of Japanese Empire in Comparative Frame*. Berkeley: University of California Press, 2010.

Trouillot, Michel-Rolph. *An Unthinkable History: The Haitian Revolution As a Non-Event*. Boston: Beacon Press, 1995.

Tsuchiya, Tomoko. "Interracial Marriages Between American Soldiers and Japanese Women at the Beginning of the Cold War." *Journal of American and Canadian Studies*, 29. 2011

Tsurumi, E. Patricia. *The Other Japan: Postwar Realities*. Armonk, NY: M.E. Sharpe, 1988.

Turse, Nick. *Kill Anything That Moves: The Real American War in Vietnam*. NY: Picador, 2013

Ueno, Chizuko, and Jordan Sand. "The Politics of Memory: Nation, Individual and Self." *History & Memory* 11, no. 2. (1999): 129-152.

Uno, Kathleen S. *Passages to Modernity Motherhood, Childhood, and Social Reform in Early Twentieth Century Japan*. Honolulu: University of Hawaii Press, 1999.

Uno, Kathleen. "The Death of 'Good Wife, Wise Mother'?" In Andrew Gordon, *Postwar Japan as History*. Berkeley: University of California Press, 1992. 293-322.

Van Staaveren, Jacob. *An American in Japan, 1945-1948: A Civilian View of the Occupation*. Seattle: University of Washington Press, 1994.

Ward Crawford, Miki, Katie Kaori Hayashi, and Shizuko Suenaga. *Japanese War Brides in America: An Oral History*. Santa Barbara, CA: Praeger, 2010.

Ward, Lorrayne Sachihi. "Bilingual, Bicultural, Biracial: The AmerAsian School in Okinawa and the Breakdown of Japan's Monoethnicity Myth," Ph.D. dissertation, Harvard University, 2003.

Wawn, William Twizell. *The South Sea Islanders and the Queensland Labour Trade*. 1973.

Weiner, Michael. Japan's Minorities: The Illusion of Homogeneity. London: Routledge, 2009.

Weiner, Tim. "C.I.A. Spent Millions to Support Japanese Right in 50's and 60's." The New York Times. October 9. 1994. Accessed September 12, 2017. http://www.nytimes.com/1994/10/09/world/cia-spent-millions-to-support-japanese-right-in-50-s-and-60-s.html

Weiner, Tim. Legacy of Ashes: The History of the Central Intelligence Agency. NY: Doubleday, 2007.

Weinstein, Jay. "Fu Manchu and the Third World. *Society* 21, no. 2 (1984).

West, Philip, Steven I. Levine, Jackie Hiltz West, America's Wars in Asia: A Cultural Approach to History and Memory. Armonk, NY: M. E. Sharpe, 1998.

Westheider, James E. *Fighting on Two Fronts: African Americans and the Vietnam War.* NY: New York University Press, 1997.

Williams, T. K., and Thornton, M. C. "Social Construction of Ethnicity Versus Personal Experience: The Case of Afro-Amerasians." *Journal of Comparative Family Studies* 292 (1998): 255

Williams, Teresa Kay and Michael C. Thornton. "Social Construction of Ethnicity Versus Personal Experience: The Case of Afro-Amerasians." J*ournal of Comparative Family Studies, "Comparative Perspectives on Black Family Life" Volume II* 29, no. 2 (1998): 255-267

Williams, William Appleman. *Empire as a Way of Life: An Essay on the Causes and Character of America's Present Predicament, Along With a Few Thoughts About an Alternative.* IG Publishing, 2006.

Willis, David Blake, and Stephen Murphy-Shigematsu. *Transcultural Japan: At the Borderlands of Race, Gender and Identity.* NY: Routledge, 2009.

Wolff, Leon, and Paul A. Kramer. *Little Brown Brother: How the United States Purchased and Pacified the Philippine Islands at the Century's Turn.* NY: History Book Club, 2006.

Woodard, William P. *The Allied Occupation of Japan 1945-1952 and Japanese Religions.* Leiden: E.J. Brill, 1972.

Wright, Richard, and Cornel Ronald West. *Black Power: Three Books from Exile: Black Power, the Color Curtain and White Man, Listen!* NY: Harper Perennial Modern Classics, 2008.

Wynn, Neil A. *The African American Experience During World War II.* Lanham, MD: Rowman and Littlefield, 2011.

Wynn, Neil A. *The Afro-American and the Second World War.* NJ: Holmes & Meier, 1993.

Yamaji, Gloria. "The Impact of Communication Difficulties in Family Relations Observed in Eight Japanese War Bride Marriages," Master thesis, School of Social Work, University of Southern California, 1961.

Yarborough, Trin. *Surviving Twice: Amerasian Children of the Vietnam War.* Washington, DC: Potomac Books, 2005.

Yoneyama, Lisa. *Hiroshima Traces: Time, Space, and the Dialectics of Memory.* Berkeley: University of California Press, 1999.

Yoshida, Takashi, 2008. "Historiography of the Asia-Pacific War in Japan" *History Faculty Publications.* Paper 4. Western Michigan University

Yoshimizu, Ayaka. "Performing Heteroglossia Contesting 'War Bride' Discourses, Exploring 'Histories of Kokoro' With Four Senryu Writers," Ph.D. dissertation, Simon Fraser University, 2008.

Young, Marilyn Blatt, and Toshiyuki Tanaka. *Bombing Civilians: A Twentieth-Century History.* NY: New Press, 2010.

Young, Robert J. C. *Colonial Desire: Hybridity in Theory, Culture and Race.* London: Routledge, 2002.

Yuh, Ji-Yeon. *Beyond the Shadow of Camptown: Korean Military Brides in America.* NY: NY University Press, 2004.

Zeiger, Susan. *Entangling Alliances: Foreign War Brides and American Soldiers in the Twentieth Century.* NY: New York University Press, 2010.

Zylstra, Henry, and Steve VanDerWeele. *Letters from Occupied Japan: September to December, 1945.* Orange City, IA: Middleburg Press, 1982. 目

# List of Photographs

# Index

culture, 169
  displacement of, 54
  family, 356, 357
  internalized, 279, 334, 393
  internationalism, 106, 167
  Japanese, 106, 225n29, 277, 394, 395
  racism, sexism, 124, 379
National Police Agency, 217
National Sorry Day, 401
Nation of Islam, 2
nation-states, 16, 32, 399, 401, 402
necropolitical, necropolitics, 393, 406n
Negro Propaganda Operations, 258,
  262n34
neocolonization, 123, 169
New Guinea, 7, 401
New Zealand, 15, 22, 147, 150n18,
  314, 338, 398, 406n
*Ningen no Shoumei* (Proof of a Human
  Being), 383
*nissei*, 165, 201
Northern Luzon Inquirer, 111
Nuremburg War, 79

## O

Obama, Barack, 398
Occupation, occupied, 6, 176
  by the U.S. xiv, xv
  cultural, 2, 26, 194, 271, 276, 294,
    325
  defeat, 173
  effects of, 48n5, 62, 91, 113n13, 189,
    260, 362, 363
  history, 314
  meaning of, 24, 41, 45, 71, 100n12,
    305n14, 327

mixed-race, xv
  of Japan, xiv, xv, 22, 25, 136, 206,
    257-260, 269, 273, 326, 345, 364
  soldiers, 13, 85
Ōgi, Hiroko, 347, 349
*ojī-chan. See* grandfather
*ojī-chan. See* Teruo
*okā-chan* (mommy), 137, 145, 229, 371
*Okairinasai!*, 231
*okā-san* (mother), 60, 61, 227-229
*oka-yu*, 249, 250
Okinawa, Okinawan, 62, 125, 173,
  200, 283, 380, 407n
  Black Okinawan, xi, 271, 334
  Japanese aggression, 249
  military, 138n16, 173, 290n38, 325
  mixed-race, 191n23, 394
  music, 352n48
  occupation, 103, 104, 274, 305, 325
  Perry, Commodore Matthew C., *see*
    Perry
  protest, 401, 402
  racism, 381
  rape, 100n12
  relationship to, 270
  suicide, 249, 266
  teasing, 289
  oriental, orientalism, 36, 41, 80, 177,
    182, 206, 207, 250, 277, 280n36,
    296n39, 339, 341
*onē-san* (older sister), 43, 228, 229
*Ōsaka-ben* (Ōsaka dialect), 227
*otō-san* (father), 228, 229

## P

P-17, 208

Pacific Century, The, 398
Pacific Movement of the Eastern World, 2
Pacific War, 2, 15, 83n10, 93, 114,
  271, 318n43, 347, 401
Pan-Amerasian, xi, 403
Pan-Asian, 276
pan-pan girls, 222, 223
Papua, 337, 401n, 407n. *See also under*
  New Guinea
patriarchy, 260, 384, 402
Peace Movement of Ethiopia, 2
Pearl Harbor, 1, 24, 25, 51, 52, 198,
  199, 217. 247, 248, 291
Perry, Commodore Matthew C., 94,
  95, 290n38, 394, 400
*Petticoat Junction,* 284
*Phil Donahue Show,* 221
Philippines, 15, 136, 139, 249
Popeye, 44
prejudice, 338
  against Koreans, 277, 278
  Amerasian, 123
  Cloyd, Fredrick, 136, 190, 197, 199,
    205, 279, 355
  China, 262n34
  in the U.S, 342n47
  Japan, Japanese, 200, 202, 382
  Mama, 215, 303
*Price is Right, The,* 72, 370

## R

race riots, 339
racism, 33, 79, 113n13, 169, 262n34
  Dad, 107
  in the U.S., xiv, 1, 47, 163, 211n26,
    272, 380

Tuskegee, 82-83

*Twelve-o-Clock High,* 238

twin sister. *See* sister.

## U

Uehara-Carter, Mitzi, 334, 342n47

Ukishima Maru, 279, 280n36, 376

Uncle Teruo. *See* Teruo

U.S.-Japan Securities Bureau, 136

U.S.-Japan Security Pacts, 200

U.S.-Pacific Command, 382

## V

Vietnam

Amerasian, orphans, 22, 57n6, 130n35, 191n23, 339, 342n47, 381, 393

Dad, 22, 165, 206, 276, 336-338, 347

devastation of Vietnam, 94, 161

French colonization of, 55, 57m6, 337, 342n47

Japanese aggression, 247, 249

racism, 23, 146, 165, 278-279, 396, 402

soldier relationships, 262n34

food, 277, 385

U.S. Occupation, 7, 22, 249

violence, 123, 128, 203n25, 218, 250, 384, 393

Cloyd, Fredrick, 202, 336, 275-279, 333, 339, 351

culture, 18n2, 25, 26, 231

Dad, 122

historical meaning, 135

Japanese, 190, 269

Korean War, 122

Mama, 108, 193, 194, 287-289

political, 56, 326, 327

racial prejudice, 107, 165, 176, 177, 215n27, 394, 401

sexual, gender, 15, 104, 124, 150n18

Tripler, 172

U.S. dispels notion, 52, 94

war, military, 25, 122, 173, 362, 393

women, 310

volleyball, 31, 65, 156, 201, 213, 214, 275, 301n40, 350, 358

## W

WAAC, 257, 258

war brides, 165, 345-351

War Brides Act, 316

Washington, Booker T, 1

Water

bath, *sencha,* 209, 248, 265, 266, 277, 356, 361, 370-372

beaten by the river, 155, 156

*benjo,* toilet, 34, 156, 227, 265, 266

cooking, eating, 277, 357

drown, drowning, 34, 35, 109, 190, 191n23, 288, 295

mizuko, 5, 13, 25-27

water child, water children, xvi, 27, 109, 339

washing clothes, 34, 94, 118

Wayne, John, 198

weaponization, 398

Du Bois, W. E. B., 1, 105

white supremacy, 2, 15, 16, 32, 35, 54, 92, 93, 105, 274, 339, 396

whore, 36, 221, 222, 283, 348, 349, 362

World Cup, 24

World Trade Center, 24

World War I, 124

World War II, 40, 83n10, 113n13, 114, 229, 318n43

African American, blacks, 15. 92, 121, 130n15, 258, 262n34

bombings, 208

Japan, xiv, xv, 230

Japanese identity, 25, 62

Mama, 7, 372

mixed-race, 53, 109, 394

postwar, 26, 72, 113n13, 188, 259, 346

prostitution, 225n29

Wright, Richard, 35, 37

## Y

*yaeyama,* 94

*yakeato,* 82, 83n10, 109, 303, 402

*yakimandu,* 277

Yamato, 197, 218, 270, 290n38

Yokohama, 81, 256, 262n34, 314, 394, 406n

Yokota, 73, 80, 206

*Young Rascals, The,* 329

*yukata,* 238, 341

## Z

*zen,* 322

center, 10n1, 79, 80, 275, 313, 323

teacher, teachings xi, 10n1, 56n6, 79, 300, 326

*zengakuren* (student resistance groups) 243

*Zubari Atemashou!,* 72

# About the Author

Fredrick D. Kakinami Cloyd was born in 1955 in Ōme, Japan to an African-American father in the U.S. military and Japanese mother. He received a Masters degree in Cultural Anthropology and Social Transformation. Cloyd has been a teacher and consultant in cross-cultural, intercultural, diversity and anti-oppression trainings for over 40 years, and is regularly involved in academic, arts, cross-cultural, interdisciplinary spirituality and social justice/anti-oppression programs in person, online, in print, and on radio and television. He has been published in *Oakland Word*, the *National Japanese American Historical Society Journal*, as well as on *Discover Nikkei*, an online journal. His poem "For Kiyoko, Epitaph/Chikai" was published in *Kartika Review*, Spring 2012 issue, and was exhibited in "Generation Nexus: Peace in the Postwar Era" exhibit for the grand opening of the Historical Learning Center for the National Japanese American Historical Society in San Francisco in 2013. His essay, "On Being a Black-Japanese Amerasian Being," appears in the anthology, *The Beiging of America: Personal Narratives About Being Mixed Race in the 21st Century* (2017). He was a chief organizer for the first-ever symposium on Japanese war brides at the University of Southern California in June 2018. *Dream of the Water Children* is first book. http://dreamwaterchildren.net 目

# About the Contributors

## About the Editor

**K**AREN CHAU works as a writer and editor, including fiction, nonfiction, short form, and screenplays. Before her work for 2Leaf Press, Chau served as assistant editor at *phati'tude Literary Magazine*. She has also analyzed and critiqued novel manuscripts as well as screenplays for production/publication. As a writer, she has covered television, sports, and food for publications such as Racialicious and the tempest. Her fiction has been featured in *sunstruck magazine* and *furious gazelle*. A graduate of Brandeis University, Karen currently lives and works in New York City. 目

## About the Artist

**K**ENJI C. LIU, an activist, educator, artist, and cultural worker, is a 1.5-generation immigrant from New Jersey, now in Southern California. A Pushcart Prize nominee and first runner-up finalist for the Poets & Writers 2013 California Writers Exchange Award, his has published in *Barrow Street Journal, CURA, The Baltimore Review, RHINO Poetry, Generations, Eye to the Telescope, Ozone Park Journal, Kweli Journal, Best American Poetry's* blog, *Lantern Review,* and others. His poetry chapbook, *You Left Without Your Shoes,* was nominated for a 2009 California Book Award. A three-time VONA alum and recipient of residencies at Djerassi and Blue Mountain Center, he is the poetry editor emeritus of Kartika Review. www.kenjiliu.com. 目

# Other Books by 2Leaf Press

2Leaf Press challenges the status quo by publishing alternative fiction, non-fiction, poetry and bilingual works by activists, academics, poets and authors dedicated to diversity and social justice with scholarship that is accessible to the general public. 2Leaf Press produces high quality and beautifully produced hardcover, paperback and ebook formats through our series: 2LP Explorations in Diversity, 2LP University Books, 2LP Classics, 2LP Translations, Nuyorican World Series, and 2LP Current Affairs, Culture & Politics. Below is a selection of 2Leaf Press' published titles.

## 2LP EXPLORATIONS IN DIVERSITY
*Substance of Fire: Gender and Race in the College Classroom*
by Claire Millikin
Foreword by R. Joseph Rodríguez, Afterword by Richard Delgado
Contributed material by Riley Blanks, Blake Calhoun and Rox Trujillo

*Black Lives Have Always Mattered*
*A Collection of Essays, Poems, and Personal Narratives*
Edited by Abiodun Oyewole

*The Beiging of America:*
*Personal Narratives about Being Mixed Race in the 21st Century*
Edited by Cathy J. Schlund-Vials, Sean Frederick Forbes, Tara Betts
with an Afterword by Heidi Durrow

*What Does it Mean to be White in America?*
*Breaking the White Code of Silence, A Collection of Personal Narratives*
Edited by Gabrielle David and Sean Frederick Forbes
Introduction by Debby Irving and Afterword by Tara Betts

## 2LP UNIVERSITY BOOKS
*Designs of Blackness, Mappings in the Literature and Culture of African Americans*
by A. Robert Lee
20TH ANNIVERSARY EXPANDED EDITION

## 2LP CLASSICS
*Adventures in Black and White*
by Philippa Schuyler
Edited and with a critical introduction by Tara Betts

*Monsters: Mary Shelley's Frankenstein and Mathilda*
by Mary Shelley, edited by Claire Millikin Raymond

## 2LP TRANSLATIONS
*Birds on the Kiswar Tree*
by Odi Gonzales, Translated by Lynn Levin
Bilingual: English/Spanish

*Incessant Beauty, A Bilingual Anthology*
by Ana Rossetti, Edited and Translated by Carmela Ferradáns
Bilingual: English/Spanish

## NUYORICAN WORLD SERIES
*Our Nuyorican Thing, The Birth of a Self-Made Identity*
by Samuel Carrion Diaz, with an Introduction by Urayoán Noel
Bilingual: English/Spanish

*Hey Yo! Yo Soy!, 40 Years of Nuyorican Street Poetry,*
*The Collected Works of Jesús Papoleto Meléndez*
Bilingual: English/Spanish

## LITERARY NONFICTION

*No Vacancy; Homeless Women in Paradise*
by Michael Reid

*The Beauty of Being, A Collection of Fables, Short Stories & Essays*
by Abiodun Oyewole

*WHEREABOUTS: Stepping Out of Place,*
*An Outside in Literary & Travel Magazine Anthology*
Edited by Brandi Dawn Henderson

## PLAYS

*Rivers of Women, The Play*
by Shirley Bradley LeFlore, with photographs by Michael J. Bracey

## AUTOBIOGRAPHIES/MEMOIRS/BIOGRAPHIES

*Trailblazers, Black Women Who Helped Make America Great*
*American Firsts/American Icons*
by Gabrielle David

*Mother of Orphans*
*The True and Curious Story of Irish Alice, A Colored Man's Widow*
by Dedria Humphries Barker

*Strength of Soul*
by Naomi Raquel Enright

*Dream of the Water Children: Memory and Mourning in the Black Pacific*
by Fredrick D. Kakinami Cloyd
Foreword by Velina Hasu Houston, Introduction by Gerald Horne
Edited by Karen Chau

*The Fourth Moment: Journeys from the Known to the Unknown, A Memoir*
by Carole J. Garrison, Introduction by Sarah Willis

## POETRY

*PAPOLíTICO, Poems of a Political Persuasion*
by Jesús Papoleto Meléndez,
with an Introduction by Joel Kovel and DeeDee Halleck

*Critics of Mystery Marvel, Collected Poems*
by Youssef Alaoui, with an Introduction by Laila Halaby

*shrimp*
by jason vasser-elong, with an Introduction by Michael Castro

*The Revlon Slough, New and Selected Poems*
by Ray DiZazzo, with an Introduction by Claire Millikin

*Written Eye: Visuals/Verse*
by A. Robert Lee

*A Country Without Borders: Poems and Stories of Kashmir*
by Lalita Pandit Hogan, with an Introduction by Frederick Luis Aldama

*Branches of the Tree of Life*
The Collected Poems of Abiodun Oyewole 1969-2013
by Abiodun Oyewole, edited by Gabrielle David
with an Introduction by Betty J. Dopson

2Leaf Press Inc. is a nonprofit organization that publishes and promotes multicultural literature.

FLORIDA ■ NEW YORK
www.2leafpress.org